# Observability in the AI-Native Era



Leveraging AIOps to build, observe, and operate resilient systems

**Hilliary Lipsig**
**Andreas Grabner**
**Robert Rati**

# Observability in the AI-Native Era



**Portfolio Director**: Kartikey Pandey
**Relationship Lead**: Preet Ahuja
**Project Manager**: Sonam Pandey
**Content Engineer**: Arun Nadar
**Technical Editor**: Simran Ali
**Copy Editor**: Safis Editing
**Indexer**: Manju Arasan
**Proofreader**: Arun Nadar
**Production Designer**: Jyoti Kadam
**Growth Lead**: Shreyans Singh

First published: March 2026

Production reference: 1110326

Published by Packt Publishing Ltd.
Grosvenor House
11 St Paul's Square
Birmingham
B3 1RB, UK.

ISBN 978-1-80638-959-9
`www.packtpub.com`

*To my husband, Scott, for literally writing what I dictated while I recovered from surgery. And also for being my rubber duck. You stayed up with me until 2 in the morning many times for this one, and I appreciate it. Also to our kids, who celebrate every achievement with me, and who made me many meals while I was writing and recovering.*

*- Hilliary Lipsig*

*To my parents, who allowed and supported me to follow a different career path than they initially had in mind. Thanks for being the best role models one could wish for.*

*- Andreas Grabner*

*To my parents, who have always loved and supported me through all of life's journeys.*

*- Robert Rati*

# Foreword

We are looking into an AI-native era. Between hype, billion-dollar deals, and the hunt for AGI, current GenAI has, in many ways, the potential to optimize processes and activities and support white-collar workers in their capabilities. And while many organizations are still looking for relevant business cases and problems to solve with GenAI, AI excels especially in areas where we have more data than humans can imagine—where simple queries don't do the job anymore, and continuously evolving system landscapes are hard to adopt operationally.

Observability is such a domain. The systems we create today are more distributed, dynamic, and complex than ever before and produce endless logs, metrics, and traces. Due to the cloud-native nature of most systems today, nothing happens without other parts of the system knowing it too, and often reacting to it. This can become visible and actionable in your observability data if you not only rely on simple queries to operate your system, but also are one step ahead, by including AI. A traditional observability, while foundational, is no longer enough. We need intelligence embedded into the fabric of our operations.

This is where *Observability in the AI-Native Era* arrives as a guide, providing you with the starting point to include AI in your operational landscape. As long as I have known them, the authors don't just like to theorize; they draw from decades of experience. They walk you through how to integrate AI into your existing workflows through real-world case studies. You'll see how AIOps moves beyond hype to deliver measurable improvements in reliability, efficiency, and developer experience. You'll learn how to build observability platforms that don't just alert teams to failures but prevent them, and how to democratize these capabilities so every engineer can access AI-driven insights without becoming a data scientist.

The shift to AI-native observability isn't just technical, it's organizational. It challenges us to redefine what "operational excellence" means in an era where systems can learn, adapt, and even anticipate problems. The authors tackle these challenges head-on, offering frameworks for governance, cost management, and ethical AI that ensure your observability practice scales responsibly.

For engineering leaders, this book is a roadmap to building more resilient, efficient, and autonomous systems. For practitioners, it's a playbook for turning raw telemetry into intelligence. And for anyone who's ever been woken up at 3 AM by a paging alert, it's a promise: the future of operations is one where machines do the heavy lifting, and humans focus on what they do best: **innovation**.

The AI-native era has come to stay, to evolve, and to revolutionize. Let this book be your guide.

*Max Körbächer*

*CEO of Liquid Reply, CNCF Governing Board Member*

# Contributors

## About the authors

**Hilliary Lipsig** is an autodidact and start-up veteran who has frequently learned and applied technologies to get a job done. She's had her hand in every part of the application delivery process, honing her skills originally as a quality engineer. Hilliary is an IT polyglot, able to talk the lingo of both the Operations and Development teams. She's currently a senior principal site reliability engineer at Red Hat Inc., working on Kubernetes-based platforms. She's passionate about GitOps, continuous integration, scalable processes, consistency in tooling, and good developer documentation. Her open source activities include contributions to the CNCF Glossary, and she's a member of the Code of Conduct Committee for the **Cloud Native Computing Foundation** (**CNCF**).

*A big thank you to my family, friends, and colleagues who supported me and even volunteered to proofread for me. To the industry experts who took their time to help us help others: you are exactly what makes our industry great. To Natan Yellin, especially for all the Holmes help and general best practices you supplied or confirmed along the way.*

**Andreas Grabner** is a technical advocate for making distributed systems observable and making automated data-driven decisions across the software development lifecycle. In his capacity as a CNCF ambassador and a DevRel at Dynatrace, he connects and educates global software engineering communities on building and continuously validating digital services for resiliency, high availability, and security. Since his early days, he has been passionate about software quality and performance engineering, as it results in building excellent digital products. Andi uses his advocacy platforms to share best practices on topics such as observability, progressive delivery, DevOps, site reliability engineering, platform engineering, and digital business operations!

*I want to thank my wife, Gabi, for being supportive throughout the whole process, especially while writing during our vacation. Also, a big thanks to my employer and all the global tech communities that supported me along the way!*

**Robert Rati** is a software and platform engineer veteran of small, medium, and large corporations in regulated industries ranging from wireless communications to the financial sector. He is passionate about reducing noise and enabling teams to focus on creating business value. He emphasizes maintainability, consistency, user friendliness, and productivity when planning and implementing projects. He is currently an engineering manager with Second Front.

*I want to thank my wife for her support with this project. She continually encouraged me and did what was necessary to give me the time to take this journey.*

# About the reviewers

**Panos Tsilopoulos** is an engineering executive and a frequent speaker at industry conferences with over a decade of experience spanning cloud infrastructure, SRE, and platform engineering. Currently serving as the Director of Observability Platform Engineering at Nike, he has a track record of turning observability data into operational outcomes that deliver business value. He holds an MS in computer science and artificial intelligence from Georgia Tech and is passionate about AI-driven observability practices in cloud-native, distributed systems.

**Mark Helotie** has worked in MIS/IT his entire adult life, with over half of that experience being in the banking and finance sectors. He started out in system/network admin and later migrated into systems engineering. For the last 9–10 years, he has focused on the observability/monitoring arena with a specific interest in cybersecurity. Mark has mentored many people over the years, and looks forward to continuing to share his technical experience and expertise. Mark continues to pour his efforts into the larger community to improve the tools and processes we all use every day in observability.

# Table of Contents

# Preface

Over the past several years, the way we design, build, and operate software has shifted dramatically. Modern systems are no longer monolithic, predictable, or even entirely human-driven. Cloud-native architectures, internal developer platforms, and increasingly autonomous AI components have reshaped the software lifecycle into something far more dynamic—and far more complex. Amid this transformation, observability has emerged as one of the most critical capabilities for engineering teams. Yet as telemetry grows and AI becomes a first-class citizen in our stacks, the strategies that once served us well are no longer enough.

This book was written for engineers and leaders navigating that reality.

Whether you are a platform engineer improving developer workflows, a site reliability engineer ensuring resilience, a DevOps engineer optimizing operations, or an engineering leader striving to elevate operational excellence across teams, this book meets you where you are. You do not need to be an expert in AI or observability to start. If you are working on or moving toward an internal developer platform, books such as *Platform Engineering for Architects* may offer useful groundwork, but they are not required to read. Our goal is to make the concepts here approachable, actionable, and grounded in real-world challenges.

We wrote this book because observability is changing—and because AI is changing what observability can be.

Thanks to standards such as **OpenTelemetry**, organizations today capture more telemetry than ever before. But the volume and complexity of that data can quickly overwhelm the very teams it aims to empower. At the same time, advances in AI give us powerful new tools to make sense of that data: correlating signals, detecting issues earlier, reducing cognitive load, and unlocking new levels of automation and insight. We believe the intersection of these two trends—modern observability and practical AI—is where the next decade of engineering efficiency will be won.

Our approach is rooted in experience. Over many years spent working alongside engineering teams across industries, we have seen what works, what fails, and what truly scales. This book distills those lessons into best practices, patterns, and architectures you can apply immediately. To make the journey concrete, we weave these principles through the story of a fictional yet reality-inspired company as it adopts *modern observability and AIOps practices.* Their challenges reflect the same ones we see in organizations worldwide; their wins and missteps illuminate what's possible.

The journey begins with how observability has evolved—from monitoring static systems to understanding deeply dynamic, cloud-native environments. From there, we guide you through implementing scalable, AI-enhanced observability in production, and, ultimately, expanding those principles left into development. Our goal is to help you bring observability to every engineer through self-service patterns within internal developer platforms, turning it into a catalyst for engineering velocity rather than an afterthought.

By the end of this book, our hope is that you will not only understand how observability fits into the AI-native future, but also how to make it a practical superpower for your teams and your organization. When observability and AI work hand in hand, they become far more than a toolset—they become a force multiplier for reliability, innovation, and resilience.

Thank you for joining us on this journey into the AI age of software operations. We are excited to share what we've learned—and even more excited to see what you will build with it.

## What this book covers

*Chapter 1, Observability: The Art of Turning Data into Insights*, introduces the evolution and value of observability—explaining how high-quality data, modern tooling, and emerging roles transform traditional monitoring into a strategic capability that drives operational efficiency, innovation, and business impact.

*Chapter 2, The Elephant in the Room: Artificial Intelligence*, provides a clear foundation for understanding how AI complements observability by exploring why AI matters, what it excels at, where it fails, and why some AI initiatives succeed while others fall short—setting the stage for achieving effective AIOps.

*Chapter 3, From Observability to AIOps and the Use Cases it Solves Today*, explains why traditional monitoring approaches no longer scale and shows how combining modern observability practices with AI enables automated, context-rich, and business-aligned operations that better support the speed and complexity of today's digital systems.

*Chapter 4, ACME Financial Services: Implementing AIOps*, illustrates how a complex, regulated enterprise confronts and overcomes cloud-era observability challenges by applying the concepts introduced earlier, uncovering root causes, implementing effective solutions, and realizing meaningful business improvements.

*Chapter 5, Democratizing Observability: A Primer to Self-Service Platforms*, explores how modern self-service platforms—whether Backstage, commercial, or home-built—can seamlessly embed observability best practices and data delivery, enabling engineers to access the right insights automatically while ensuring consistent, scalable, and AI-ready operations across the organization.

*Chapter 6, The Observability Agent: Real-Life Use Cases*, examines how observability-aware AI agents—powered by emerging standards like MCP—can integrate with development and operations workflows to deliver proactive insights, automate decision-making, and significantly enhance the effectiveness of engineers, SREs, IT Ops, and platform teams.

*Chapter 7, ACME Financial Services: How to Move from AIOps to Agentic Platforms*, continues ACME Financial Services' transformation journey by showing how the company built on its initial observability improvements, identified remaining pain points, and began leveraging an agentic AI platform through a structured, milestone-driven approach to address new challenges and sustain long-term progress.

*Chapter 8, Evolving Operations: Proactive > Preventive > Self-Driven Architecture*, explores how to design self-driving IT systems that use observability, AI, and automation to predict issues, make autonomous operational decisions, and minimize business-impacting incidents through event-driven architectures, intelligent scaling, AI-assisted rollouts, and proactive security responses.

*Chapter 9, No Future Without Challenges*, prepares you for the real-world challenges of implementing AI by exploring how to build trust, control hidden costs, ensure security, and maintain compliance while mitigating risks such as hallucinations and unreliable outputs.

*Chapter 10, ACME Financial Services: How Will the AI Future Shape Our Company?*, concludes ACME Financial Services' journey by reflecting on their transformation, demonstrating how AI was embedded at the core of their operations, measuring its impact, and offering guidance for how your organization can chart its own path based on its unique industry and technology landscape.

# To get the most out of this book

You should have a good base understanding of modern cloud-native architectures and the steps in the software development lifecycle that bring software from idea to production. It helps if you have a base understanding of platform engineering and the problems it solves. For that, we also recommend reading *Platform Engineering for Architects*. A basic understanding of observability and AI is helpful but not mandatory, as you will learn everything you need to know in this book.

## Download the example code files

The code bundle for the book is hosted on GitHub at `https://github.com/PacktPublishing/Observability-in-the-AI-Native-Era`. We also have other code bundles from our rich catalog of books and videos available at `https://github.com/PacktPublishing`. Check them out!

## Download the color images

We also provide a PDF file that has color images of the screenshots/diagrams used in this book. You can download it here: `https://packt.link/gbp/9781806389599`.

## Conventions used

There are a number of text conventions used throughout this book.

`CodeInText`: Indicates code words in text, database table names, folder names, filenames, file extensions, pathnames, dummy URLs, user input, and Twitter/X handles. Here is an example: "If you have ever developed any type of code, you have probably used a `print` or `console.log` statement."

A block of code is set as follows:

```
"__inputs": [
    {
      "name": "DS_PROMETHEUS",
      "label": "Prometheus",
      "description": "",
      "type": "datasource",
      "pluginId": "prometheus",
      "pluginName": "Prometheus"
    },
```

Any command-line input or output is written as follows:

```
$ python rouge_score_example.py
```

**Bold**: Indicates a new term, an important word, or words that you see on the screen. For instance, words in menus or dialog boxes appear in the text like this. For example: "**PII**, which stands for **personally identifiable information**, is a protected class of information that may be collected during normal operations for a software system."

Note

Warnings or important notes appear like this.

Tip

Tips and tricks appear like this.

# Get in touch

Feedback from our readers is always welcome.

**General feedback**: If you have questions about any aspect of this book or have any general feedback, please email us at `customercare@packt.com` and mention the book's title in the subject of your message.

**Errata**: Although we have taken every care to ensure the accuracy of our content, mistakes do happen. If you have found a mistake in this book, we would be grateful if you reported this to us. Please visit `packt.com/submit-errata`, click **Submit Errata**, and fill in the form.

**Piracy**: If you come across any illegal copies of our works in any form on the internet, we would be grateful if you would provide us with the location address or website name. Please contact us at `copyright@packt.com` with a link to the material.

**If you are interested in becoming an author**: If there is a topic that you have expertise in and you are interested in either writing or contributing to a book, please visit `authors.packt.com/`.

# Free benefits with your book

This book comes with free benefits to support your learning. Activate them now for instant access (see the "*How to Unlock*" section for instructions).

Here's a quick overview of what you can instantly unlock with your purchase:

EPUB PDF

### DRM-Free PDF Version

Download DRM-free PDF and ePub copies of this book.

### 7-Day Packt Library Access

Get 7-day unlimited access to 8,000+ books and videos. No credit card required.

Available for first-time Packt+ trial users only.

### Next-Gen Reader Access

Read this book on Packt Reader with progress sync, dark mode and note-taking.

## How to Unlock

Scan the QR code (or go to `packtpub.com/unlock`). Search for this book by name, confirm the edition, and then follow the steps on the page.

UNLOCK NOW

*Note: Keep your invoice handy. Purchases made directly from Packt don't require one*

# Stay Sharp in Cloud and DevOps – Join 44,000+ Subscribers of CloudPro

**CloudPro** is a weekly newsletter for cloud professionals who want to stay current on the fast-evolving world of cloud computing, DevOps, and infrastructure engineering.

Every issue delivers focused, high-signal content on topics like:

- AWS, GCP & multi-cloud architecture
- Containers, Kubernetes & orchestration
- Infrastructure as Code (IaC) with Terraform, Pulumi, etc.
- Platform engineering & automation workflows
- Observability, performance tuning, and reliability best practices

Whether you're a cloud engineer, SRE, DevOps practitioner, or platform lead, CloudPro helps you stay on top of what matters, without the noise.

Scan the QR code to join for free and get weekly insights straight to your inbox:

`https://packt.link/cloudpro`

## Share your thoughts

Now you've finished *Observability in the AI-Native Era*, we'd love to hear your thoughts! Scan the QR code below to go straight to the Amazon review page for this book and share your feedback or leave a review on the site that you purchased it from.

`https://packt.link/r/1-806-38959-2`

Your review is important to us and the tech community and will help us make sure we're delivering excellent quality content.

# Part 1

# From Monitoring via Observability to AIOps

*Part 1* lays the foundation for understanding how organizations evolve from traditional monitoring toward true, insight-driven observability and, ultimately, AI-powered operations. Through core concepts, an exploration of AI's transformative role, and real-world use cases, you will learn how to turn data into action at scale. The part concludes with a concrete end-to-end implementation at ACME Financial Services, illustrating how AIOps delivers measurable value in practice.

This part of the book includes the following chapters:

# 1

# Observability: The Art of Turning Data into Insights

*How can you prove the value of observability?* It's not about capturing more data; it's about turning this data into information that allows your organization to make better-informed decisions about running your business more efficiently!

In this first chapter, we will give you an overview of everything we think you need to know about observability, including its history and how it has evolved from monitoring. We will discuss how to prove the value of observability and justify any investment into a modern observability strategy. We will also explain the importance of high-quality observability data as this is needed to successfully implement AIOps!

Be prepared to go on a journey through monitoring, learning how it has always helped IT operations to keep the lights on. You will learn how observability emerged from monitoring as we started to build more dynamic hybrid cloud-native distributed systems. Today, it's not just about keeping the lights on; it's about using observability to run systems more cost-effectively, enabling your software to become a competitive differentiator—and, with that, increasing business output. We will also discuss the new roles within an organization that have emerged over the years that benefit from observability and **Artificial Intelligence** (**AI**). This includes business leaders, developers, **Site Reliability Engineers** (**SREs**), observability experts, and platform engineers.

In this chapter, we are going to cover the following main topics:

- What is observability?
- Observability and distributed systems
- VMs, containers, and databases—oh my!

- Full stack: from networking to cloud to application observability
- Defining the focus of this book

Note

**Your purchase includes a free PDF copy + exclusive extras**

Your purchase includes a DRM-free PDF copy of this book, 7-day trial to the Packt+ library (no credit card required), and additional exclusive extras. See the *Free benefits with your book* section in the *Preface* to unlock them instantly and maximize your learning.

# What is observability?

"*Who needs observability anyway? I heard it's very expensive for the value it delivers, and we can probably live without it!*" This is a very common opinion that you'll encounter if you read through online forums such as Reddit, Stack Overflow, or LinkedIn.

Indeed, proving the value of a project—whether it's around observability, AI, or **Machine Learning** (**ML**) is a challenge.

Back in 2016, Gartner defined the term AIOps as referring "*to the application of machine learning and big data analytics to automate and enhance IT operations.*"

Initially, AIOps was about fixing the observability tool sprawl problem seen in many large enterprises. AIOps was about leveraging AI and ML to correlate all signals from various observability data sources to reduce alert noise. The value proposition of AIOps was to support IT operations by identifying the root cause of IT problems faster in very complex hybrid-cloud enterprise environments. While the promise of AIOps was great, the challenge for the initial solutions was operating on disconnected, not standardized, observability datasets from various tools. The early days of AIOps required a lot of configuration and data normalization across tools used on-premises versus for cloud observability. The lack of observability standards also made it harder to connect logs, metrics, traces, and events. Proving the **Return on Investment** (**ROI**) to all involved stakeholders across IT and business leaders was, therefore, a challenge for many teams that implemented AIOps!

In short, AIOps 1.0 mostly did not deliver on the initial promise!

But times have changed since the days when the term AIOps was initially coined. We—the authors—have worked with many organizations where IT operations successfully transformed! This is also due to the advances in observability solutions, the emergence of new open industry standards, and the improvements and availability of observability-optimized AI/ML solutions.

In 2026, 10 years after AIOps became a named practice, it is now possible to fulfill its original promise. We can move from reacting to problems like firefighters toward preventing problems through modern observability supported by AI. Throughout this book, we will give you plenty of insights from people we have interviewed—their stories, best practices, challenges, ways to prove the value of AIOps, and opinions on AIOps!

You may have already formed your own opinion on this topic—at least we hope so!

If you or your team is already responsible, or are asked to take responsibility, for the following, then we assume you understand the value that observability brings:

- Availability of a single server, a server farm, or multiple data centers
- Ensuring high-throughput networks between your office locations
- Maintaining stable connections between on-premises infrastructure and public cloud vendor(s)
- Keeping your business-critical databases up and running
- Ensuring a certain response time for your critical stored procedures
- Resilience of your Kubernetes clusters
- Right-sizing microservices to handle spike load
- Auditing system security and compliance
- Reporting on software-related business impact
- Ensuring healthy operations of business-critical software

Wherever you are on your organization's *observability journey*, in the constantly changing world we live in, this book is aimed to give you guidance on how observability can make your life easier, including how it can provide more accurate and faster insights into how your systems are operating and how observability can be used to drive better automation around remediation, cost optimization, and business reporting.

The goal of modern AIOps is to transform how we operate systems, that is, to shift from reacting to incidents and restoring services to proactively preventing problems before they occur. The advancements in observability and AI can give AIOps the necessary intelligence to move from the initial denoising of individual alerts to really connecting the dots of all observability signals to identify anomalies before they become problems.

However, let's take a step back for those who are not familiar with monitoring and see why and how it evolved into observability, as well as the role that AI plays in this.

# What is observability and how does it differ from monitoring?

If you ask, "*What is observability, what does it do, and how is it different from monitoring?*" you will likely get different answers depending on people's backgrounds and experiences.

## Let's ask ChatGPT!

As this book is about both observability and how AI can help organizations advance their observability practice to improve software delivery and operations, let's put AI to the test. If we ask the previous question to any of the available **Large Language Models** (**LLMs**) of the major search engines, we will get an answer similar to this:

> *"Observability is a characteristic of a system that allows you to understand its internal state by examining its external outputs, like logs, metrics, and traces. Monitoring, on the other hand, is the process of collecting predefined metrics and thresholds to track system health. Observability is more proactive and investigative, enabling you to understand why issues occur, while monitoring is more reactive, alerting you to issues after they happen."*
>
> *Google Search Lab – July 22, 2025*

## The early days: monitoring static systems

Not a bad definition at all that we received from our AI bot. The definition also highlights how observability has emerged from monitoring. When looking back to the late 1990s and early 2000s—the early days of monitoring for some of us authors—monitoring was typically done on predefined, well-known metrics, such as CPU, memory, garbage collection, disk utilization, network bandwidth, package drop rate, service response times, and database connection pool utilization. The next step was to specify meaningful thresholds to get alerted on when a metric was reaching a known (or sometimes made-up) critical threshold value; for example, CPU utilization greater than 90%, free disk space less than 5%, or TCP package loss greater than 1%.

Monitoring solutions were able to pull in metrics from the OS (using Linux system commands or Windows performance counters) or via standards such as **Simple Network Management Protocol** (**SNMP**). To monitor business applications, it was possible to either pull process metrics from the OS or leverage interfaces such as the popular **Java Management Extension** (**JMX**) that allowed querying Java runtime and application-specific metrics, such as garbage collection, thread count, and memory utilization.

As systems were more static in nature, it was easy to maintain **Configuration Management Databases** (**CMDBs**) with all of the details about your hosts, processes, and services.

Monitoring solutions could also provide a quick health overview of the critical server, process, and application metrics, as shown in the following screenshot:

| Host | Service | Status | Timestamp | Duration | Entities | Description |
|---|---|---|---|---|---|---|
| webprod03 | Check Users | OK | 01-26-2007 14:58:5 | 0d 0h 53m 23s | 1/4 | USERS OK - 1 users currently logged in |
| | Current Load | OK | 01-26-2007 14:59:5 | 0d 0h 53m 23s | 1/4 | OK - load average: 0.21, 0.08, 0.05 |
| | Memory Usage | OK | 01-26-2007 14:55:2 | 0d 0h 50m 29s | 1/4 | OK: Memory Usage 56% - Total: 511 MB, Used: 287 MB, Free: 224 MB |
| | PING | OK | 01-26-2007 14:56:1 | 0d 0h 50m 23s | 1/4 | PING OK - Packet loss = 0%, RTA = 0.16 ms |
| | Root Partition | OK | 01-26-2007 14:57:0 | 0d 0h 50m 33s | 1/4 | DISK OK [2433618 kB (5%) free on /dev/sda2] |
| | SWAP Usage | OK | 01-26-2007 14:57:4 | 0d 0h 50m 34s | 1/4 | Swap ok - (null)% (0 out of 16386) |
| | Total Processes | OK | 01-26-2007 14:58:2 | 0d 0h 50m 33s | 1/4 | OK - 95 processes running |
| | Xen Virtual Machine Monitor | CRITICAL | 01-26-2007 14:59:0 | 0d 0h 44m 34s | 4/4 | Critical Xen VMs Usage - Total NB: 0 - detected VMs: |
| webprod04 | Check Users | OK | 01-26-2007 14:59:5 | 0d 0h 15m 33s | 1/4 | USERS OK - 2 users currently logged in |
| | Current Load | OK | 01-26-2007 14:57:5 | 0d 0h 14m 53s | 1/4 | OK - load average: 0.30, 0.60, 0.44 |
| | Memory Usage | OK | 01-26-2007 14:56:1 | 0d 0h 14m 33s | 1/4 | OK: Memory Usage 37% - Total: 511 MB, Used: 190 MB, Free: 321 MB |
| | PING | OK | 01-26-2007 14:57:1 | 0d 0h 13m 23s | 1/4 | PING OK - Packet loss = 0%, RTA = 0.27 ms |
| | Root Partition | OK | 01-26-2007 14:57:4 | 0d 0h 12m 43s | 1/4 | DISK OK [3948940 kB (94%) free on /dev/sda2] |
| | SWAP Usage | OK | 01-26-2007 14:57:3 | 0d 0h 11m 53s | 1/4 | Swap ok - (null)% (0 out of 16386) |
| | Total Processes | OK | 01-26-2007 14:59:0 | 0d 0h 16m 22s | 1/4 | OK - 250 processes running |
| | Xen Virtual Machine Monitor | WARNING | 01-26-2007 14:58:5 | 0d 0h 1m 33s | 4/4 | Warning Xen VMs Usage - Total NB: 1 - detected VMs: migrating-xen-vm4 |

*Figure 1.1: Classical monitoring of hosts and critical processes based on static thresholds*

For those of you who remember those days, you will also know what came next...

## The dawn of more complex and dynamic systems

This traditional approach to monitoring worked really well for the rather static systems with a manageable, well-defined set of health indicators. The limitations became apparent as IT systems became more dynamic and complex in nature. Over the past years, many IT experts in the industry have done the following:

- *Moved* from a handful of physical servers to an x-fold of **Virtual Machines** (**VMs**)
- *Refactored* their old monolithic apps into many new microservices
- *Deployed* multiple pods per service across availability zones or regions
- *Implemented* business features using serverless or **Web Assembly** (**WASM**) technology
- *Migrated* workloads from on-premises to the cloud or hybrid cloud
- *Released* features dynamically using feature flagging
- *Integrated* with a broad range of SaaS-based API offerings

The new variety of technologies also required new ways to monitor those systems and runtimes. For some, it was no longer possible to simply install monitoring software or query OS stats directly. Hypervisors (VMware), cloud vendors (AWS, Azure, and Google), and **Software as a Service** (**SaaS**) vendors (Salesforce, Atlassian, SAP, and Workday) often provided their own built-in monitoring solutions with basic dashboards and alerts. An alternative approach was providing a proprietary interface to extract some of the metrics or logs into your own monitoring solution, for example, the AWS CloudWatch API or Atlassian's Monitoring API!

The challenges with those proprietary APIs were often around the lack of granularity of data, the lack of standards that resulted in a lot of effort to query and parse the data, as well as the additional costs that were charged by those vendors for using those APIs, including the network traffic it took to get the data back to the in-house monitoring solution.

## Cloud-native monitoring doesn't scale the way we need it to

When Google donated Kubernetes to the Linux Foundation, we not only saw the birth of the **Cloud Native Computing Foundation** (**CNCF**) but also a boost in what we call **cloud-native architectures**. Cloud native is not limited to running software on public cloud infrastructure; it's a set of architectural principles that has led to hundreds, if not thousands, more components that get developed dynamically rather than statically across public, private, or sovereign clouds.

We also deal with many new types and layers of systems that all provide lots of additional telemetry data in various formats and with various degrees of cardinality and accuracy. Gone are the days when a single metric could be combined with a static threshold to alert on a healthy or unhealthy state. To visualize the new complexity of modern cloud-native systems, see the following screenshot of a *rather small* environment hosting 9 applications that rely on 3,304 microservices distributed across over 10k pods/processes across 142 hosts in 7 different global data centers.

*Figure 1.2: Cloud-native systems became much more complex very fast*

With the ever-growing complexity of the systems and the explosion of observability data, we need a new way to turn this data into actionable information that doesn't require us to hire and train hundreds of new experts!

## AIOps 2.0: observability ready for the cloud-native AI era

Monitoring was great for static systems with static thresholds that one could maintain in a spreadsheet with clearly defined calls to action to remediate an isolated problem. Because our systems have become so complex and dynamic, monitoring has to evolve into observability, and we need automation and AI to cope with all this data to allow operators to make faster, automated decisions.

**AIOps 2.0** (for lack of a better term) has the chance to fulfill the initial promise of AIOps from 2016. To cope with the complexity and explosion of data, a cloud-native AI era observability implementation requires the following:

- **Automated discovery** of system components and their relationship, instead of manually tracking hosts, processes, or services in a CMDB
- **Automatic baselining** instead of manually setting thresholds on hundreds of thousands of metrics
- **Automated anomaly detection** that factors in seasonality, **Service-Level Objectives (SLOs)**, and dependencies between system components
- **Automated root cause analysis** that correlates abnormal signals based on end-to-end system dependencies
- **Automated remediation** that triggers and validates actions to keep a system in a healthy state

As the complexity of our systems keeps growing exponentially, we also see the amount of data growing at the same rapid pace. To make sense of all this data, observability needs smarter algorithms and not to only look at data points in isolation. We need to look to ML and AI to detect anomalies faster, understand the impact across highly dynamic and connected system components, and use this data to speed up the remediation of the root cause to keep business impact low. We must also leverage generative AI and LLMs to explain a situation and a detected problem in a human-understandable way. The power of those systems is that they have been trained on the global knowledge base created by experts over the years and shared on the internet, for example, Stack Overflow and Reddit. That allows generative AI and LLMs to help IT system operators to become more efficient while systems get more complex. Industry vendors as well as analysts have coined the term AIOps, which talks about applying ML and AI to support IT operations by making better decisions based on a large amount of observability data.

Throughout the book, we will cover use cases and provide details on which algorithms to apply to which data, which models to use for which use cases, and how this can be used to trigger actions like what we see in the current discussion around agentic AIs, which not only provide responses to questions but also act upon data.

The following screenshot shows a modern AIOps implementation. We can see the power of automated discovery (full dependency map of involved components), baselining and anomaly detection (service failure rate), and root cause analysis (Argo CD deployment of a specific Git commit as a potential root cause).

*Figure 1.3: AIOps – observability with the power of AI to detect root cause and impact*

Today's AIOps solutions can also integrate with your incident response systems, send notifications to the responsible teams, and even trigger remediation actions such as restarting services, rolling back a deployment, or opening up pull requests to right-size your environment through **Infrastructure as Code** (**IaC**).

By now, you should have a good understanding of monitoring and how it was focused on understanding and alerting on the health status of static systems that we operated in the late 90s and early 2000s. With the move toward more dynamic, complex, and cloud-native architectures, we needed a new approach to determine the health of our systems and identify and fix the root cause quickly to limit any potential business impact. This is where modern observability comes into play.

So far, we have only talked and given examples about metrics. However, metrics are just one of the three well-known observability pillars. In the following section, we will explore all signals that are relevant to modern observability. We will talk about emerging standards that make it easier to collect this data and discuss some best practices for extracting information from each signal to improve the quality of our observability implementation.

## Three pillars and beyond: use cases for logs, metrics, and traces

In our brief introduction, we only glanced at some observability data examples around metrics, such as CPU usage, memory consumption, garbage collection, service response time, and network packet loss rate.

Observability, however, is more than metrics. The observability community typically talks about the three pillars of observability: logs, metrics, and traces.

Thanks to innovation in the observability space, especially driven by open standards, development framework and runtime developers, as well as observability platform vendors, we see additional useful signals as telemetry data emerging that enable a lot of new use cases. Here are some examples:

- **Events**: Kubernetes events, continuous integration builds, or GitOps Deployment events
- **Real user behavior**: Opening a mobile app, reloading a frame, or changing screen orientation
- **Code profiling**: Detailed Java or .NET stack traces
- **Security and compliance**: Detecting vulnerable code functions or libraries, or detecting misconfiguration that leads to noncompliance with regulatory frameworks

Throughout the book, we will touch on best practices around the following:

- How to best capture signals and which metadata to enrich
- What information to extract and what information to remove
- What information to store, how long to retain it, and who should access it
- How to optimize the different cost aspects of each signal
- How to analyze those signals in isolation
- How to connect signals (for example, logs and traces) to get better answers
- What needs to be done to make data more understandable for AI to truly achieve a high standard of AI-driven observability

While you might already be familiar with individual signals, let's start with a quick introduction to the pillars.

## What are metrics?

Metrics are numerical data that we can capture from well-known entities such as network devices, servers, processes, databases, or applications. Metrics typically present the current state of the monitored entities, such as CPU usage, memory consumption, service response time, and service failure rates. When continuously capturing those metrics, it helps us understand system behavior over time. Metrics are typically used to set up alerting, for example, to warn about a high failure rate of an application. Performance engineers and SREs use metrics to optimize a system for better throughput, performance, or cost efficiency. For example, they might increase the number of worker threads in a **Java Virtual Machine (JVM)** to handle more concurrent requests.

The key challenges with metrics include high cardinality of metric dimensions, potential privacy concerns with dimension names, large data volume and noise, as well as the overhead of collecting, transporting, and analyzing metrics in real time.

### Challenge: being careful with high cardinality and privacy in dimensional data

Avoid the following common mistake: to identify suspicious activities from particular users or IP addresses of an application, a developer can easily create a request count metric with the dimensions *username* and *IP address*. While creating this metric is easy, analyzing it presents challenges:

- The backend data store needs to deal with potentially billions of unique IP addresses, which makes it hard to calculate or alert on abnormal behavior for each unique IP address
- It allows everyone in your organization to view all usernames through access to a technical metric, such as request count, which often poses a privacy concern

There is much more to learn about the proper creation and handling of metrics that we will cover throughout the book, but there are also many online resources that provide information on different types of metrics, metric value aggregation, dimensions, and more.

## What are logs?

Logs are structured or unstructured data that are created from similar entities that we can capture metrics from, such as network devices, OSs, databases, or applications. Logs are probably the oldest observability signal. If you have ever developed any type of code, you have probably used a `print` or `console.log` statement. Initially, logs were used for troubleshooting, allowing developers to better understand how their code executed on a remote system and what transactions/requests were executed to understand where things failed. When analyzing logs, developers often look for errors or exception stack traces, or for additional debug information that was added to their code to make troubleshooting easier.

Logs have evolved a lot since the early days of software engineering. Today, most logging frameworks used by developers produce structured log output with a set of standard fields, such as timestamp (when the log was created), log level (`ERROR`, `WARNING`, `INFO`, or `DEBUG`), context (request ID, application ID, etc.), and the content (the actual log message). Logs, typically captured and enriched through agents such as Fluentd, Logstash, or **OpenTelemetry** (**OpenTel**), are also typically sent through a log pipeline, which enriches the log with even more context, such as log source, server, or Kubernetes cluster, namespace, or Pod.

### Challenge: tackling high-volume, excessive, and unstructured logs

While there are several challenges with logs, the top challenge is that systems tend to produce high volumes of logs, and not every log line is relevant for daily operations. As many organizations operate a lot of software that has been around for a while, chances are also very high that many logs are unstructured and therefore hard to analyze. Because it's easy to create logs, we often see excessive logging by applications that can't be controlled easily. A common mistake is adding but never removing debug logs that were needed for a quick troubleshooting session.

Because of the high volume of logs across most software systems, logs are often considered very expensive. While this is true, one must not blame the observability backend as a first response. Logs are important, but it requires a good logging culture and automated checks to keep logs under control.

There is much more we will learn about proper log management throughout this book, such as extracting metrics out of logs and storing only those logs that are relevant for critical use cases, for example, compliance and security. As with metrics, please also consult the many online resources available on structured logging and log pipelines.

## What are traces?

Distributed traces are the *youngest* of the pillars. A distributed trace tracks a single request as it flows through multiple services in a distributed system, providing insights into the request's journey and performance across different components.

They were introduced in the early 2000s by **Application Performance Management** (**APM**) vendors such as Wily (now part of Broadcom), Dynatrace, AppDynamics (now part of Cisco), and New Relic. Initially focusing on Java and .NET, the agents of those vendors were able to instrument byte code when it was loaded by the JVM/.NET runtime. With this approach, no manual code changes were necessary. The automated distributed trace output gave developers an end-to-end view, starting from a web request entering the web or application server, moving through queues or middleware, and continuing to the backend services and finally the database.

The distributed trace was not only a great debugging tool for developers to understand dynamic code execution in distributed systems, but was also often integrated into performance testing and later production environments to understand the performance and load behavior of individual components.

The big challenge that distributed tracing had to solve was the propagation of the unique trace ID from the first service to the last. This was typically done via HTTP headers, message properties, or by passing it through thread-local storage in multi-threaded code.

What used to require proprietary instrumentation and data formats has recently been standardized through the CNCF project OpenTel. The following visualization shows the anatomy of an end-to-end trace captured through OpenTel. Each trace has a unique ID. Every piece of information captured, such as a web request, database calls, or method invocation, is represented as a so-called span. Spans have a relation to a parent span and to the trace they belong to.

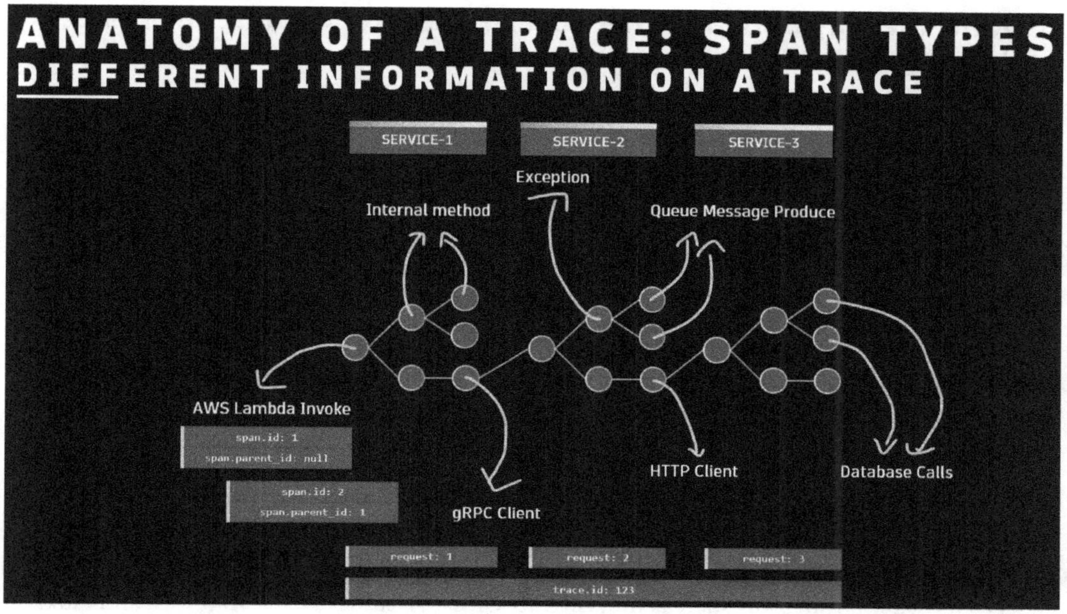


*Figure 1.4: From "Unleash the Power of Distributed Traces" – explaining the anatomy of a distributed trace when captured with OpenTel*

To learn more about the internals of distributed traces, spans, and requests, feel free to watch the *Unleash the Power of Distributed Traces* YouTube video [1]. We also cover more aspects of OpenTel throughout this book.

## Challenge: over-instrumentation, duplicated data, and sampling as challenges

Over the past 20 years, vendors have optimized their agents to avoid over-instrumentation (capturing too many calls or too much information), reduce the collection of duplicated data (same data as part of a trace and part of a log), and optimize their sampling strategies (deciding what data to store and what to filter out).

As many organizations try to reduce their dependencies on vendor agents, they are shifting the responsibility of instrumenting code to their developers. While OpenTel is maturing and more developer tools exist that support engineers with their instrumentation, the challenges of over-instrumentation, duplicated data, and proper sampling decisions need to be taken into consideration for every observability project looking into distributed tracing.

## Beyond the three pillars: use cases based on events, profiling, and real users

Besides logs, metrics, and traces, we have additional observability signals that enable additional use cases and benefits for roles such as DevOps engineers, platform engineers, line-of-business leaders, security teams, architects, and developers. The following are some real-life examples and use cases based on runtime or life cycle events, real user monitoring, code profiling, and security insights.

### Use case: track your software development life cycle through events

"*Where is my build? How long does it take to get a code fix into production? Which Git commit just broke production?*" These and similar questions can be answered by using observability to track the life cycle of your code and build artifacts from the first Git commit through your continuous integration, testing, continuous delivery, and finally release into production.

The OpenTel community has started to standardize semantic conventions for observability data from CI/CD systems to make this easier. Vendors such as Dynatrace have started to define **Software Development Life Cycle** (**SDLC**) events to track an artifact by ingesting observability data from tools such as Jira, GitHub, GitLab, Azure DevOps, Argo CD, and Flux.

Tracking artifacts through observability not only gives you the chance to report on efficiency metrics such as **DevOps Research and Assessment** (**DORA**) but also allows you to provide more context to your AIOps system for better root cause detection of a problem. When implemented, it allows you to automatically pinpoint the problematic pull request, Git commit, or pipeline run that caused a production issue.

### Use case: provide real-time business insights by extracting business events

"*What is the business impact of our latest feature rollout? Has the revenue increased since we enabled our new AI chatbots for our premium users? Why does it take a week to get the updated business impact report?*" These are common questions that we hear from business leaders. The biggest challenge is getting real-time business insights and understanding how technical changes impact business outcomes, either positively or negatively. By using observability to monitor logs, metrics, and traces from those business IT systems, we can typically extract business events and use that to provide real-time business reporting and insights connected with the technical data.

To give you an example, in an e-commerce platform, we can capture the shopping cart volume either from logs or traces or by asking our developers to export a custom metric. Combined with the additional context we have about the end user (such as their IP address range) and whether they completed a purchase (successful execution of the purchase API endpoint), we can provide real-time reporting about realized versus unrealized value by geographical region.

### More use cases on existing observability signals

Throughout *Chapter 3*, we will provide more detailed use cases covering areas such as optimizing user experience through real user behavior analytics, increasing developer efficiency through code profiling and live debugging, assessing security attack and vulnerability risks, and managing compliance by automatically validating mandatory compliance requirements. These are all use cases that can be implemented today with our existing observability signals!

### Use cases: more to come as observability is evolving

What started decades ago with monitoring metrics and then expanded to logs and distributed traces has now expanded into many more signals that have opened up new use cases, as explained earlier. As the observability space keeps evolving, thanks to the emerging standards and constant innovation in the space, there will be new use cases based on those existing signals. It's also likely that new signals will emerge. Throughout this book, we will dive deeper into more use cases, best practices, and how organizations go about implementing them as part of a modern observability strategy!

The next question we need to answer is: where does all this data come from? Are there any standards or is this all done by proprietary implementations of a small handful of observability vendors?

## Emerging standards over the years

Early monitoring of distributed systems focused on standard protocols such as SNMP or the OS's built-in basic monitoring tools and interfaces to understand the health of the OS, the running processes, and the utilization of the hardware it ran on.

Starting in the early 2000s, **Application Performance Monitoring** (**APM**) elevated basic system monitoring to sophisticated, real-time, end-to-end observability into performance, resiliency and execution behavior of distributed systems. APM vendors (Dynatrace, AppDynamics, New Relic, Datadog, Instana, etc.) provided custom-built proprietary agents that automatically captured metrics, logs, and traces on the systems (Linux or Windows) that they were installed on. Moving from one vendor to another wasn't an easy task as there were no real standards on both data collection and analysis that made switching easy.

This probably also resulted in **vendor lock-in** as one of the top arguments that organizations bring up when advocating for new open standards for modern observability. With the dawn of cloud-native architectures, especially around Kubernetes, we have seen several emerging standards driven by the open source community to standardize the way to collect, transform, and analyze observability data in modern cloud-native distributed systems.

Let's provide a quick overview of the most important standards and open source projects.

## OpenTelemetry

The most prominent of these standards is the CNCF project OpenTel [2]: an open source observability framework and toolkit designed to facilitate the generation, export, and collection of traces, metrics, and logs. In 2019, OpenTel emerged from the merger of OpenCensus and OpenTracing and has recently started to expand into more signals, such as code profiling and real user monitoring.

While OTel is *not* an observability backend for storing and analyzing data, this standard has opened up a lot of innovation across the full spectrum of observability:

- **Instrumentation**: The community, as well as vendors, contribute to auto-instrumentation agents for various runtimes and languages.
- **Collection**: The OpenTel Collector provides a vendor-agnostic way to receive, process, and export telemetry data. The community and vendors provide a huge range of extensions, making the OTel Collector a great observability data pipeline.
- **Analysis**: By commoditizing the collection of observability data, many new open source tools and vendors emerged, providing analysis capabilities on pure OpenTel data.

A key component in an OpenTel implementation is the OpenTel Collector [3]. The following screenshot is taken from the OpenTel website, highlighting its extensible architecture around receivers (pulling in data from various data sources), processors (normalizing, sampling, extracting, or enriching data), and exporters (sending it to the storage and analysis observability backends).

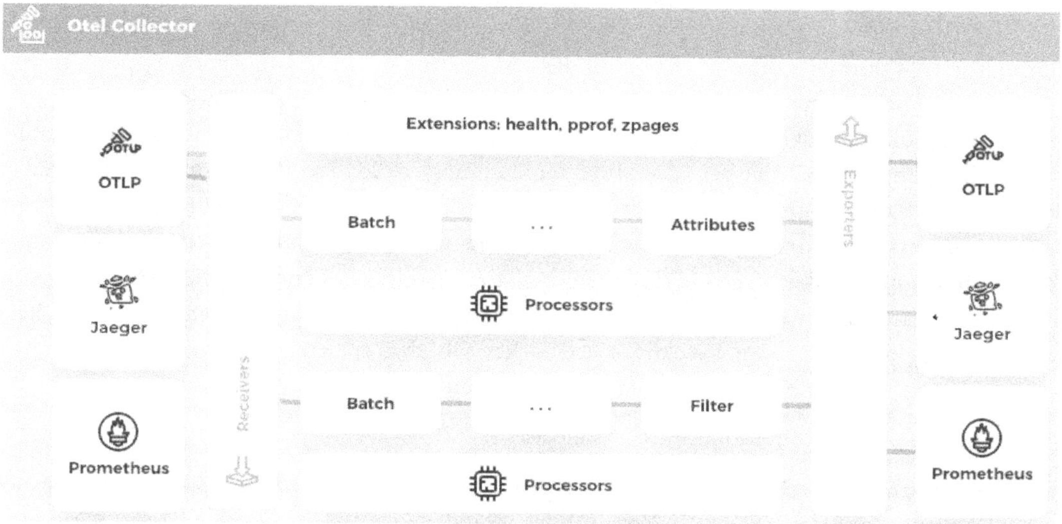


*Figure 1.5: OpenTel Collector architecture: a vendor-neutral way of collecting, processing, and exporting telemetry data*

The OpenTel Collector also plays a crucial role in solving some of the key challenges in observability we discussed earlier: over-instrumentation, duplicated data, and sampling. When implementing OpenTel as a data receiver and pipeline, please be aware of the constantly changing ecosystem. Make sure to educate yourself on the support for your technology stack and the proper configuration and sizing of your collectors.

Most commercial observability platforms support OpenTel, either by supporting the **OpenTelemetry Protocol** (**OTLP**) and ingesting the data directly from the source (the instrumented application) or through an OpenTel Collector exporter. Some vendors also provide custom-built OpenTel Collector distributions that are pre-configured, tested, and officially supported by the vendors.

Depending on what your observability backend is, make sure to understand the level of support for OpenTel and consult the best practices for deploying and configuring either the backend open source tool or commercial observability platform.

## Prometheus

Prometheus [4], initially developed at SoundCloud starting in 2012, is another very popular open source monitoring and alerting system. It was created to address limitations of existing monitoring solutions at the time, particularly around multi-dimensional data models, scalable data collection, and a simple yet powerful query language called PromQL. Prometheus joined the CNCF in 2016 and graduated as a project in 2018. Compared to OpenTel, Prometheus focuses on gathering metrics that get stored in a time-series database optimized for high-cardinality, which makes it a good choice for real-time monitoring and historical trend analysis. Metrics can be enriched with additional context in the form of key-value pairs, which address some of the challenges we discussed earlier, which is enriching metrics with information about their origin, as well as additional business data dimensions.

The key architectural components are as follows:

- **Exporting metrics**: Services need to export metrics via an HTTP endpoint that gets scraped by Prometheus. The community provides many existing exporters for various systems, frameworks, or APIs (for example, Apache, Nginx, Kafka, or BIG-IP). Developers can also export their own metrics using the available client libraries for the various programming languages.
- **Ingesting metrics**: The Prometheus server scrapes a set of configured endpoints (applications, servers, etc.) on a periodic interval by sending HTTP requests to those targets. It expects the endpoint to return the requested metrics, their metric type, and their values.
- **Storing metrics**: The Prometheus server provides a local on-disk time-series database for storing ingested metrics, but can also optionally integrate with remote storage systems.
- **Alerting**: Alerting rules in Prometheus servers send alerts to the Alertmanager. The Alertmanager then manages those alerts, including silencing, inhibition, aggregation, and sending out notifications via methods such as email, on-call notification systems, and chat platforms.
- **Visualization**: Prometheus is commonly used with Grafana, an open source analytics and visualization platform, to visualize and analyze Prometheus metrics and alerts on dashboards. As most observability platforms (open source and commercial) integrate with Prometheus, you are not limited to Grafana.

Prometheus is widely adopted, and thanks to the wide array of available exporters, most modern software components provide automatic Prometheus metrics that can be scraped by a Prometheus server or an OpenTel Collector, or directly from your commercial observability platform.

In a modern observability strategy, Prometheus will most likely play a key role in observing metrics. Make sure to look into all the best practices that the community suggests around setup, scale, and integrations. We will also provide more examples and guidance throughout this book on how to integrate Prometheus into your enterprise observability strategy.

### Visualization standards: Grafana and Perses

Grafana is a very popular open source platform used to visualize and analyze various types of observability data from various sources. Grafana is the default visualization tool for Prometheus metrics, and you will find lots of pre-configured dashboards for various system components (for example, Kubernetes, MongoDB, Kafka, and AWS) that the community has created and maintained. Grafana is created by Grafana Labs, which also provides commercial products on top of their various open source projects.

While there is no shortage of available Grafana dashboards, the dashboard file format is not standardized, which makes it hard to leverage Grafana dashboards with other observability visualization solutions. The open source project Perses is set to address this problem by providing an open specification for dashboards for Prometheus and other data sources. Perses is currently a CNCF sandbox project but has already been adopted by several observability vendors, as well as end user companies, based on information the Perses website [5].

Standardizing the way data gets displayed, analyzed, and alerted on is the next step toward providing a vendor-neutral definition for observability. While OpenTel and Prometheus have done a good job of reducing the vendor lock-in argument on the data collection side, Perses aims to do the same for visualizing the data.

By now, you have a good understanding of how observability has emerged out of monitoring. We have discussed the different signals of observability that go beyond logs, metrics, and traces. We have touched upon emerging standards to collect and visualize data and have discussed the need to leverage automation, AI, and ML to fully harness the growing amount of data to better support all the teams that require observability data to make better and faster decisions. But we are just at the start of our journey. Next, we will look into one of the biggest challenges that modern observability solves: understanding distributed systems.

## Observability and distributed systems

In this section, we want to dive into distributed systems and the critical role observability plays as our systems become more complex.

For starters, it feels odd to call out "a distributed system" because any system that is not exclusively running on a single host or server is, by definition, a distributed system. That has been true for many decades since we *escaped* the monolithic systems of the early days of the mainframe. One could also argue that even then, we had a distributed system because code execution and data storage were decoupled; hence, we could also talk about a distributed system that was able to execute business functions.

## Highly distributed systems and the increased complexity

What has drastically changed in recent years is the number of components involved in a distributed system, the distribution of those components across different platforms and locations, the additional layers of abstraction between the hardware and the code that executes business logic, as well as the dynamic elasticity when we look at the deployment models. All of this makes the management of those highly distributed systems more complex.

What used to be a handful of physical servers became an X-fold of VMs running on physical servers. What used to be many VMs running on a handful of physical machines turned into an X-fold of **elastic cloud compute instances** (for example, AWS **Elastic Compute Cloud** (**EC2**) instances in various sizes). If we look into cloud-native architectures, we see another X-fold in the number of pods or serverless functions deployed on-premises or in the cloud, orchestrated through platforms such as Kubernetes, OpenShift, or any of the hyperscaler-provided workflow services. The advances in deployment orchestration and auto-scaling have also increased the frequency of changes. Deployments that used to be done monthly or weekly are now fully automated and can happen multiple times a minute. These changes can range from deploying a new workload or right-sizing existing ones to cope with increased demand to moving workloads to different data center regions to optimize performance or cost, or switching feature flags to control the behavior of applications and services.

## Understanding distributed systems through observability

As somebody responsible for a distributed system, you need to be able to answer a handful of key questions around inventory, dependencies, APIs, health, SLAs, and root cause.

Observability can help you answer all these questions, allowing you to better understand, better manage, and, with that, better operate your distributed systems.

In the next sections, we walk through these questions with examples and give you some guidance on how you should go about answering those questions to validate how mature your observability strategy already is.

## Inventory: which components are part of the system we are responsible for?

We need a list of hosts, network devices, Kubernetes nodes, cloud infrastructure, processes, pods, serverless functions, and databases. With observability, we get insights into the systems we actively monitor (for example, through Prometheus or an observability agent). It also allows us to discover components that we are not actively monitoring, for instance, by analyzing network connections from a monitored host to other IP addresses or by querying a discovery API from the cloud provider or the orchestration platform.

Later in the book, we will walk through best practices on how to roll out observability, discover blind spots, and increase observability coverage.

## Dependencies: how are components connected and dependent on each other?

We need to know the vertical dependencies (which components connect to each other via a network) and horizontal dependencies (which components run on other components, for example, processes running on hosts). This helps us to understand, for instance, which processes share the same CPU or connect to the same database.

Metrics, logs, and traces that are enriched with metadata about the system where they are captured automatically tell us the vertical dependencies. For example, the CPU usage of a process includes information about the host it is running on. Monitoring network connections as well as distributed tracing additionally tells us the horizontal dependencies, since it contains the information of which system communicates with which other system.

## Interfaces/APIs: what are the boundaries of our distributed system to the consumers?

We need to know critical endpoints (HTTP, messaging, and so on) that need to be available and accessible by our users or third-party consumers. These endpoints can additionally be monitored through synthetic checks to ensure availability.

Observability can help us automatically detect endpoints by extracting this information from our network traffic logs or distributed traces, or by querying the information from exposed endpoints on load balancers and ingress definitions.

## Health: are all components working as expected or is there abnormal behavior?

We need to know how to determine the health status of any component to understand whether a component is a potential root cause of an incident.

Observability helps us ingest logs, metrics, traces, and events from our components. We can then set up health alerts such as high CPU usage, database connection timeouts, service failure rate, critical error logs, or slower-than-usual service response time. The latter is an example of automated baselining, whereas the former is often done through static thresholds.

A key consideration must be not managing hundreds or thousands of alert thresholds manually but using defaults for known health indicators, along with automated baselines and machine learning, to keep the management overhead to a minimum.

We will cover many examples later in the book about how to best set up health monitoring and alerting on abnormal behavior.

## SLA and root cause: are end-to-end critical transactions experiencing issues, and why?

We need to get alerted in case our critical transactions are unavailable, not returning accurate results, or not performing as expected to avoid potential impacts on our **Service-Level Agreements** (**SLAs**).

Observability doesn't just help us with being alerted when a problem is already occurring. The goal with a modern observability implementation is to get alerted before we breach our SLAs. This can be done by leveraging AI on all the observability signals, including the contextual information about which components are involved in the critical end-to-end transactions. If one of these components starts acting abnormally, a remediation action can be triggered to mitigate the situation before it impacts the whole of the system.

Later in this book, we will cover lots of examples and best practices on how to leverage AI and observability to move from reactive to proactive to preventative operations.

The following visualization shows a simple distributed system but allows us to answer all the questions mentioned earlier:

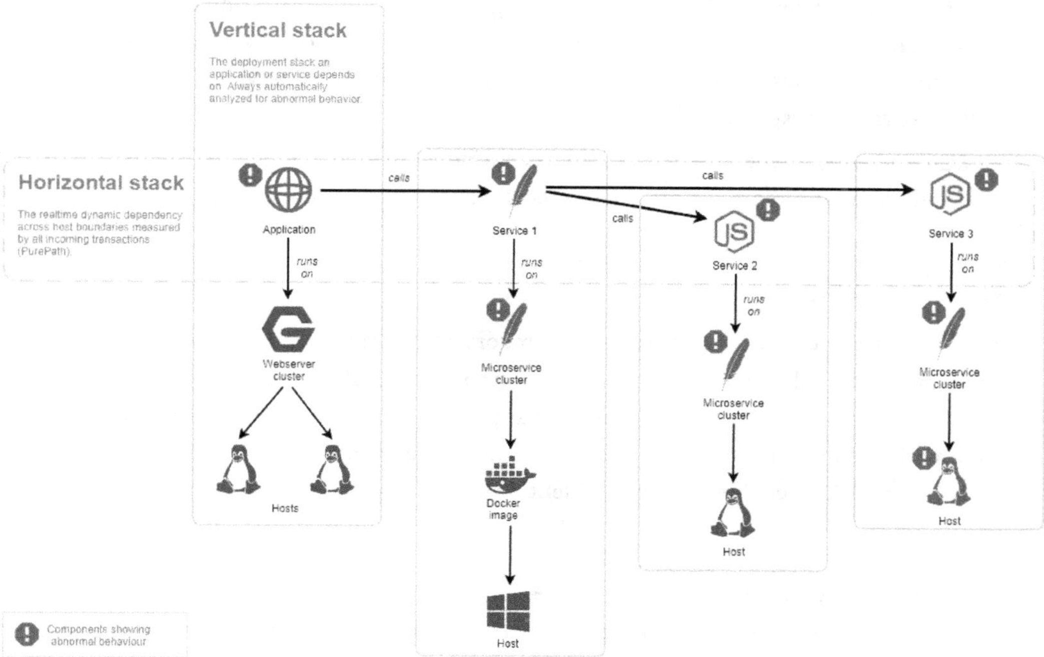


*Figure 1.6: Observability gives insights into distributed systems, including all components, and highlights normal and abnormal behavior*

Being able to answer these questions for your IT landscape and critical applications is critical. Depending on the current maturity of your observability implementation, you may already have this information out of the box, or it may take you a while to collect it from various sources.

You don't need to produce a visualization like in *Figure 1.6*. The example visualization, however, helps to explain a distributed system, its components, dependencies, and potential problems. Use whatever tool or visualization makes most sense to you. In our example here, let's quickly answer our five questions based on what we see in the figure:

- **Inventory**: Several Linux and Windows servers, web servers, app servers, and microservices.
- **Dependencies**: We know which service runs on which hardware and how those services depend on each other by analyzing distributed traces.
- **Interfaces/APIs**: Endpoints on each service and web server that we can extract from logs or distributed traces.

- **Component health**: A Linux host is having issues that are impacting the services that are running on it. We can get this information by setting up alerts on key OS metrics such as CPU, memory, disk, and network, as well as alerts on service metrics such as failure rate or response time.
- **SLA and root cause**: The application is experiencing an SLA violation because of a downstream unhealthy service (**Service 3**) caused by an unhealthy Linux host.

Tip

**Observability best practice**

When ingesting logs, metrics, or traces, it's important that those signals get *enriched* with information about the infrastructure it runs on. Observability agents or pipelines such as OpenTel can enrich the data as close as possible to the source. Make sure that information about the underlying host, data center, cloud vendor, namespace, and so on is captured. This enables the proper identification of dependencies.

What was already apparent in this section was that distributed systems have a lot of interdependencies, whether it is a failing service that impacts an upstream service or a host that impacts its services because it runs low on resources. The latter example is what we will now explore in depth, since shared infrastructure needs to be well understood when observing and analyzing distributed systems and their components!

## Shared infrastructure and how it impacts components

In a distributed system, we have a lot of shared infrastructure—whether that is the shared CPU and memory across all Pods on a Kubernetes node, the VMs that fight for the same hardware of the underlying physical server, or the individual processes on a Linux OS that share the same disks they want to read/write to.

From an observability perspective, it's important that we understand what infrastructure is available and who is using that infrastructure. This allows us to answer a lot of important questions, such as "*Do we have a noisy neighbor that impacts other services?*" and opens up a lot of interesting use cases, such as "*Can we optimize resource utilization to save costs?*" Besides ITOps and SREs, we see FinOps teams leveraging observability to optimize costs while keeping an eye on not negatively impacting critical components that are needed to ensure business objectives are met.

## Use case: identifying a noisy neighbor

If you've ever lived in an apartment with roommates where you also had to share a bathroom, and maybe had thin walls where you could hear every word spoken on the other side, you understand the *noisy neighbor problem*.

The same problem exists with shared infrastructure. Classic examples are VMs, processes, or pods that use excessive CPU, memory, network, or disk on a shared host or node. This behavior will impact all other processes. It will slow them down or even cause them to crash or not start at all. The problem typically happens if there are no **guardrails** specified around how much memory or CPU a pod can use, for example, by specifying request and resource limits.

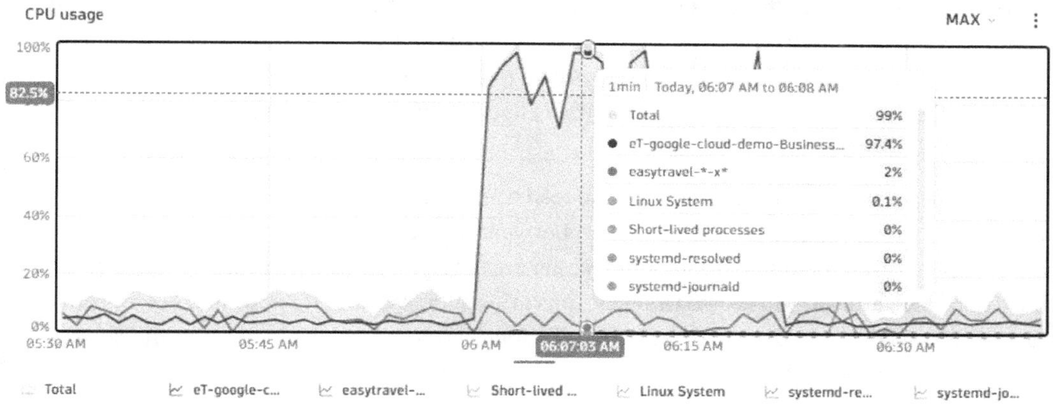


*Figure 1.7: Identifying noisy neighbors requires detailed observability of all key metrics (CPU, memory, disk, etc.) per consumer (VM, process, pod, etc.)*

It's a good practice to keep an eye on noisy neighbors not only when trying to identify root causes but also to identify missing guardrails on certain deployments. One alert to set up would be if individual processes constantly use more than 10 times the resources (CPU, memory, disk, etc.) than their neighbors. This is a good indicator to take action.

## Use case: right-sizing infrastructure based on real needs

Let's stay with our roommate analogy. Imagine you have an apartment with five bedrooms, yet you only use one room. That's a very large and probably costly apartment to maintain. The same is true for shared infrastructure. If you constantly have idle resources, it's a sign to reduce the size of the underlying shared infrastructure. This is more efficient and also saves costs. Talk with your FinOps department; they would be happy to get automated reports from observability with a list of resources that are not well utilized and can be downsized.

The opposite scenario is also possible: constant high utilization. You can use observability to analyze whether this increase in demand for the services that run on this shared infrastructure is constant or just seasonal. If there is a constant increase in service utilization (for example, an increased number of requests to that service over the past months), then either increase the size of the underlying shared infrastructure or consider moving this workload to a better-sized home.

From shared infrastructure, it's only a small step to shared communication. Distributed systems only work because components communicate via different means. Let's dive into the role of observability for synchronous and asynchronous communication!

## Synchronous and asynchronous communication

We discussed that distributed tracing is a great way to identify how services communicate with each other, as trace technology can follow a transaction from the end user (browser or mobile device) through all the middleware and microservices to the backend databases. This works by propagating the so-called **trace context** via the communication protocol (HTTP, messaging, etc.) from the service caller to the callee. We covered this topic in more detail earlier in this chapter.

From an observability perspective, a distributed trace is not always enough to fully understand whether there is a communication problem between two components. The trace will contain timestamps from the outgoing call on the caller and the incoming call on the callee. But what if the difference between those two timestamps varies a lot? What if it is 10 milliseconds on one trace and 10 seconds on the next? And what if some traces show a timeout error and the call never reaches the callee? What might be the reason for this slowdown or failure?

Observability also has a solution to answer these questions as we need to expand observability into the layers of the architecture that make synchronous and asynchronous communication possible. We are talking about the network, connections, and queues. All those layers also need to be observed to get the full picture of what is happening in distributed communication.

### Network: metrics or eBPF

Most communication happens via the network, whether this is on the same host or across continents. Observability can give us insights into the network layer around **traffic** (bytes and packets sent and received), **quality** (packet errors or dropped packets), and **connectivity** (number of sessions and timed-out sessions). These metrics are typically readily available from the OS as well as network devices.

A *new* player on the field is the **extended Berkeley Packet Filter** (**eBPF**), with **Cilium** being the prominent open source project that uses eBPF to provide insights into network connectivity between workloads. The online communities provide a lot to learn about eBPF, and we will also cover it in other use cases later in this book. What is important to know is that eBPF provides an additional way to answer the question: *Is it the network or not?*

Tip

**Observability tip**

If there are errors or slowdowns in communication, then it's advisable to analyze the health of the network. It could be another noisy neighbor that is consuming all network bandwidth or a faulty network component that drops packets. The answer lies in the observability insights we get from the network layer.

## Connections: pools on each side of the call

When two services communicate with each other, each side (also referred to as the client and server) typically opens a connection to then send messages. To better manage those connections and avoid the need to open a new connection every time, we have the concept of **connection pools**. Connection pools manage open connections that can then be requested when needed, used to make a call, and finally, returned to the pool for other requests to use. Those connection pools exist in most frameworks to open connections to an HTTP or database endpoint. Improperly sized connection pools and connection leaks are the most common issues when a client and a server can't efficiently communicate. One is about having too many concurrent requests for a connection, while the other one is about keeping a connection out of the pool for longer than actually needed. Both scenarios mean that the next request that needs a connection has to wait for one to become available in the pool.

Tip

**Observability tip**

Consult the documentation of the application runtimes and frameworks that your developers use for cross-service communication. Those typically provide metrics around pool size and pool usage. Pools that are constantly underutilized or fully utilized are a sign of improper sizing or bad connection handling. Also, when adjusting pool sizes, remember to adjust them appropriately on both sides where you have pools: the client and the server.

## Queues: the distributors of messages

RabbitMQ, Apache Kafka, Amazon SQS, Azure Service Bus, and Google Pub/Sub are some of the prominent message queues used in distributed architectures. The concept is rather simple: you have a *sender* pushing a message into the queue and a *receiver* pulling a message out to process it. Queues allow decoupling of components as they become the intermediary between the client and the server. Queues can also hold on to messages for a while until they are pulled, which makes them perfect for smoothing out spike loads of new messages until the receivers can process them.

Like the network and connection pools, queues provide good observability to understand whether the queue is healthy and doing its job or whether it is the problem of a slow or failed asynchronous communication.

Tip

**Observability tip**

Consult the documentation of the queue system you are using. Chances are there is an existing Prometheus exporter, or it already provides OpenTel metrics or traces. Key metrics that indicate health are queue length, message throughput, failed message delivery rates, and the time messages spend in the queue. If queues are not properly sized, or when too many messages are sent and not received, you will see an increase in queue length, leading to an increase in the time messages spend in the queue. You can also judge how stable a system performs by looking at message throughput and delivery rates.

Remember that queues will be present in almost every distributed architecture. They enable most of the communication, and you want to make sure you have proper observability and alerting set up.

With OpenTel becoming more widely adopted, end-to-end synchronous and asynchronous communication will be traceable through OTel. This is great news for everyone. Just remember that there is always a component between the two ends of a communication, whether it's a network, a connection pool, or a queue. These have to be observed as they are the backbone of any communication in a distributed system.

Networks, connections, and queues enable easier communication between an ever-growing number of components. Easier communication typically results in more components that take part across those communication channels. Those are all components and infrastructure that need to be managed. If you have managed dynamic infrastructure, you have probably heard about the *pets versus cattle* analogy. To learn more about what this means for observability, we have a dedicated section in *Chapter 3*, titled *Context is king: the quality of observability data*, where we focus on how to enrich observability data (such as logs, metrics, traces, and events) with additional context (such as infrastructure, services, and deployment) to make analysis and troubleshooting easier!

We will round off this chapter with some additional best practices on monitoring VMs, containers, and databases before we conclude by defining the focus of the rest of the book.

# VMs, containers, and databases – oh my!

In modern IT systems, we find all sorts of technical components and services. In our *Observability and distributed systems* section, we already covered how the evolution from VMs to containers and beyond is impacting the way we approach observability.

Many organizations that operate IT systems today have a wide variety of existing web servers, application servers, and databases, with some of those running on VMs, as containers, or even as serverless functions. It's important to cover best practices and ways to observe those critical components that operate the core system components of many enterprise organizations.

## Observing hypervisors and VMs

When using VMs, it's important to observe both the VMs and the underlying hypervisor. Whether that is VMware, Microsoft's Hyper-V, Citrix Hypervisor, VirtualBox, or KVM, these platforms typically provide their own observability tooling along with metrics that can be ingested into a central observability platform. Key metrics to focus on here are the same as what we discussed around shared infrastructure: CPU, memory, storage, and network. On top of that, those hypervisors typically also provide some basic monitoring of the VMs that they are orchestrating.

Tip

**Observability best practice**

While hypervisor monitoring gives you a good basic coverage of VMs, it's advisable to get insights into what is happening on the VM itself. You want to know which processes and services run on those VMs and who is consuming how many resources. Consult the documentation from your observability platform. There typically exists an option either by installing an agent or by querying those VM metrics through an extension, which might pull the data through Prometheus, **Windows Management Interface** (**WMI**), or other data sources provided by the OS running in the VM.

## Observing web and application servers

The landscape of web and application servers has drastically changed over the past decades. In the early days of APM, most applications ran on IBM WebSphere, Oracle WebLogic, or Microsoft's **Internet Information Server** (**IIS**). In modern cloud-native architectures, we typically see more lightweight servers such as Apache Tomcat, JBoss, or Wildfly, or containers using frameworks such as Spring Boot to run the business logic. Then we have ingress controllers or load balancers such as Nginx or Traefik taking a lot of the request handling and routing work that used to be done by the former web and application servers.

Regardless of what era of components you operate, it's important to observe the key metrics, logs, and ideally also traces that go through those servers.

> Tip
>
> **Observability best practice**
>
> Consult the documentation of your web and app servers. Java-based components typically expose a lot of metrics through JMX. Chances are that there is also a Prometheus exporter or support for OpenTel. If you use a commercial observability agent, validate the out-of-the-box support for your version and target platform (Linux, Windows, AIX, Solaris, etc.) of your servers! In all cases, you want to observe metrics around throughput (number of requests), duration (response time of requests), service failure rate, thread and request pool utilization, session counts, and CPU and memory utilization.

## Observing databases

"*It must be the database!*" Just like blaming everything on the network, it's very common to blame any type of problem on the database. Based on our experience, the database itself is hardly ever the real problem. It's more common that the way an application accesses the database is the root cause of bad performance or failures. Common examples include executing too many individual database queries instead of leveraging the power of the database query language (for example, SQL) to get data in bulk, or by executing inefficient queries that return too much data that is not needed.

> Tip
>
> **Observability best practice**
>
> When it comes to database observability, it's important to focus on both sides: the database server and the application that executes database queries. The database server typically provides some built-in observability; for example, Oracle and SQL

> Server provide great tools. However, to make analysis and root cause diagnostics more efficient, you want to ingest metrics from your database server around query performance, connections, I/O performance, storage, and session details. From the application side, you could either look at application logs or, even better, distributed traces that contain information about which database query is executed by which transaction. This gives direct insights into how efficiently your developers execute database queries.

The following screenshot is taken from the video *CSI Observability: Identifying Bad Patterns in Traces and Logs* (Kubernetes Community Day Slovakia 2025), where you can learn how to analyze bad database access patterns:

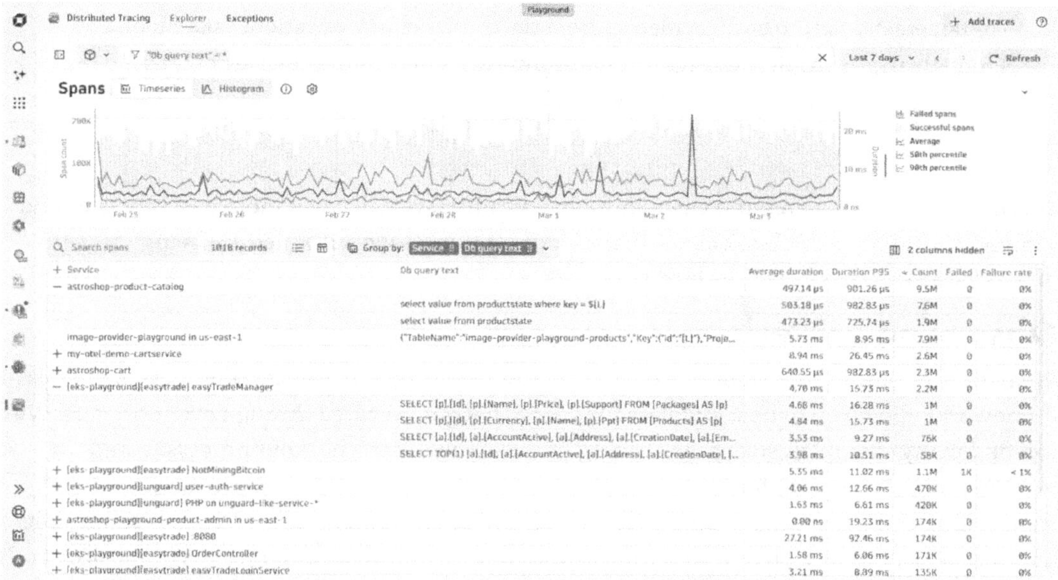


*Figure 1.8: Using OpenTel traces to detect database query access patterns from individual services*

To learn more about database patterns, see the video on the KCD Slovak YouTube channel (the relevant talk starts at minute 43).

## Observing containers

In fact, a container is not that different from a regular process that runs on an OS. The key difference is the container orchestration used, which defines how to access logs or metrics about the container. Essentially, it's about monitoring what runs within the container (for example, Java, Go, Python, or .NET applications) and monitoring the orchestration layer for the container (for example, Docker, Kubernetes, OpenShift, Apache Mesos, Rancher, or other hosted container orchestration services).

> Tip
>
> **Observability best practice**
>
> Consult the documentation of your observability solution on best practices to observe what's running within the container, how to ingest the logs that are produced by the container, and how to best get metrics from the container orchestration. Take a look at Prometheus, OpenTel, and logging frameworks such as Fluentd, which are the most common ways to ingest observability signals from your containers.

Specifically for Kubernetes and OpenShift observability, we will cover more best practices and samples throughout this book as the majority of containers we have seen are being orchestrated through those platforms!

## Observing serverless

Breaking monolithic apps didn't stop with microservices that are run as containers. Serverless frameworks allow you to host stateless functions that get executed through event triggers. We can find many examples, such as managing inventory updates, checkout processes, and recommendation engines for e-commerce solutions. For media, classical use cases are transcoding and generating thumbnails for user-uploaded content. The serverless community has provided a full GitHub repository [6] with examples for common serverless frameworks such as AWS Lambda, Microsoft Azure, and Google Cloud Run Functions.

> Tip
>
> **Observability best practice**
>
> As serverless functions are typically hosted in a runtime that you don't control, you cannot observe every single aspect; for example, when hosting it on AWS Lambda, AWS manages the runtime. However, there are typically metrics and logs that any serverless

framework and runtime exposes. Key metrics for serverless that everyone should monitor are as follows:

- **Invocations**: How often does the function get executed?
- **Duration and errors**: How long do serverless functions take to execute and how many abort with an error?
- **Init time**: Also called a **cold start**. The time it takes to initialize the runtime.
- **Concurrent executions**: How many functions execute in parallel.
- **Throttling**: The number of requests aborted because of concurrent execution limits.
- **Timeouts**: How many functions run into the maximum execution time limit.
- **Memory utilization**: An indicator of proper sizing of the serverless configuration.

While the metrics listed in the preceding tip box give great insights into general runtime behavior and errors, they do not give any insights into what the function is doing, where it spends its time, whether it potentially runs into timeouts, or why it errors out. Besides metrics, serverless frameworks allow developers to emit logs. With the emergence of OpenTel, we also see more serverless runtimes providing OpenTel support, such as **AWS Distro for OpenTelemetry** (**ADOT**), or by leveraging the OpenTel libraries to instrument any type of serverless function.

This gives you distributed traces within your serverless function and provides engineers with enough details for troubleshooting slow-running or failing executions.

As serverless functions are typically just one piece of execution in an event-driven architecture, it is recommended to capture distributed traces from all involved software components in an end-to-end request. This typically involves an API gateway that handles the initial request and triggers the serverless function, as well as any type of queues or message buses that are used in event-driven systems. To enable full end-to-end tracing, it's important to transport the trace context we discussed earlier in this chapter. That means that the API gateway either produces spans or correctly forwards the trace context from the initial request and passes it on to the serverless function. It also means that the trace context needs to be attached to any message being put into a queue so that the receiver of the message can leverage the trace context as its parent context.

The following screenshot shows a distributed trace that expands across multiple event-driven Lambda functions that are connected through an AWS SQS queue and that make updates to a DynamoDB database service:

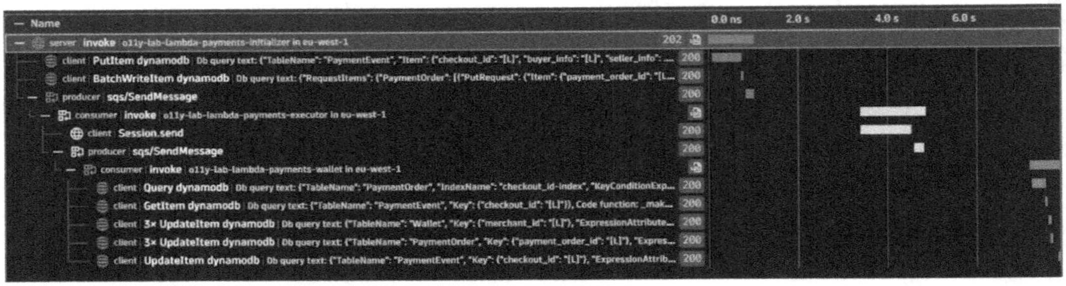


*Figure 1.9: OpenTel distributed trace for an event-driven serverless architecture*

To learn more about serverless observability, you can also follow the GitHub tutorial called *Serverless Unified Observability Done Right* by Damian Jankowski [7].

Up until now, we have covered a lot of best practices relating to observing relevant components in enterprise IT architectures. We have learned how to observe all components individually, as well as how all those signals connect, by enriching logs, metrics, traces, and events with additional metadata that allows us to do a better analysis of cross-component and end-to-end transactional impact.

While we discussed all components *across the stacks* (from network to application), it's important to recap what is meant by a *holistic and full stack observability approach*, as this is the goal for mature observability implementation.

# Full stack: from networking to cloud to application observability

This final section is a bit of a recap of what we have learned so far, but it puts everything into the context of carrying out **full stack observability**. Full stack observability is the foundation of good AIOps. It means providing high-quality observability data from network to business code (bottom up) and from the end user to the database (left to right). This high-quality and context-enriched data is what will decide whether any automation, smart algorithms, AI, or ML that you unleash on the observability data will result in more efficient and secure software development, delivery, and operations!

## What is full stack observability?

When asking a smart AI chatbot, we get a good answer to this question:

*"Full stack observability refers to a comprehensive approach to monitoring and understanding the performance and health of an entire technology stack, from the end-user experience down to the underlying infrastructure. It involves gathering and analyzing telemetry data (logs, metrics, traces) across all layers of the stack to gain deep insights into system behavior and identify potential issues. Essentially, it's about having a holistic view of your system, rather than relying on siloed monitoring."* (From Google's AI Bot on August 3, 2025, after providing the prompt "What is Full Stack Observability?")

In the *Observability and distributed systems* section, we talked about using full stack observability to answer key questions around the following:

- **Inventory**: Which components are part of the system we are responsible for?
- **Dependencies**: How are components connected and dependent on each other?
- **Interfaces/APIs**: What are the boundaries of our distributed system to the consumers?
- **Health**: Are all components working as expected or is there abnormal behavior?
- **SLA and root cause**: Are end-to-end critical transactions experiencing issues, and why?

Only when we have a holistic view of our systems, with high-quality and context-enriched data from our end users all the way to the network or backend database systems, can we truly claim that we have implemented observability the right way: the full stack way.

## The observability goal is 100% coverage: start with production infrastructure, then expand up and left

While it's not easy, it's important to aim for 100% coverage of observability. This doesn't mean 100% coverage of end-to-end distributed traces of every transaction, or capturing 100% of all logs, events, or metrics of all your components. There is a lot of observability data that is duplicated or too verbose. As an observability expert, it's about getting the correct 100% coverage to answer the questions outlined earlier.

Many observability teams start by rolling out basic infrastructure observability (hosts, network, and processes) on the most critical parts of the system, which run the most critical business applications. From there, you can expand up, left, and right in the stack:

- **Expanding up the stack**: Move from network and infrastructure into application-level observability. Once you know which applications and services are running on your hosts, VMs, or pods, you can start capturing logs, metrics, and traces from those components. Either enable your observability agent with deep insights or start collecting Prometheus or OpenTel data.
- **Expanding into other systems**: Move from your critical systems into adjacent systems that they connect to. Your observability will tell you which network connections are

made to other systems that are currently *unmonitored*. These could be systems that belong to you or third-party external systems. Either expand your observability by installing agents or configure Prometheus or OpenTel to ingest data from those systems as well. For third-party systems, you can also set up synthetic tests or ask them whether they provide any APIs to pull in more data via open standards.

- **Expand left toward development**: Observability must not stay siloed in your most critical systems in production. Your SDLC starts in development. So, expand your observability *left* and give your engineers the same level of insights as they will later have in production. The term *expand left* (in comparison to shift left) indicates that we are not pushing more responsibility to our developers but rather enabling them with new capabilities as we give them self-service access to the relevant data that they need in their day-to-day tasks.

"*Observability is expensive, that's why we only use it on our most critical systems!*" If this is an argument you are facing when trying to roll out full stack observability and into development, then you have not yet managed to show the value of modern observability.

In *Chapter 3*, we go into more detail about how to enable engineering teams to get value out of observability data without having to become an expert in analyzing observability data. In the *Observability-driven development* section of *Chapter 3*, we discuss how to turn observability data into actionable insights through practical self-service use cases, providing proactive answers to questions such as "*Which code should be optimized for performance?*" or "*What is the recommended container size to save on costs yet meet your availability requirements?*"

The same section also covers more details about how to use observability to track your software delivery process to answer questions such as "*Where is my build? How long does it take to get a code fix into production? Which Git commit just broke production?*"

So, stay tuned—you will learn more about use cases that you can use to prove the value and then expand.

Now it's time to make this more concrete. This was just the first chapter. Let's finish this chapter with a guide on how to leverage the rest of the book to help you on your path to AIOps and modern observability.

# Defining the focus of this book

"*Who needs observability anyway? I heard it's very expensive for the value it delivers, and we can probably live without it!*" is a very common argument many observability team leads hear from their upper management!

## You will be able to prove the value of observability and AI!

Proving the value of observability and AI is going to be one of the biggest technical and organizational challenges you will face. Why do we say that? Because it's what we have learned over the years of working in this space, and it has been reconfirmed in many of the interviews we have conducted in preparation for writing this book.

By the end of this chapter, we hope it will be clear that, when done right, observability is not just an expensive cost center; it is the enabler of modern, cost- and carbon-efficient software development, delivery, and IT operations that support your business objectives.

Throughout the book, you will learn about which KPIs other organizations have used to prove to their leadership the success and value of observability.

## You will use exponential data growth as an opportunity!

As we build more complex distributed systems, we will see observability data growing exponentially. As humans, we can no longer analyze and manage all this data by ourselves. We need the help of automation, ML, and AI to support us in making better and faster decisions. These decisions need to be based on high-quality and context-enriched data, as we have discussed numerous times already in this chapter. If we do this well, the growing amount of data can be seen as an opportunity, a true data gold mine. Correctly leveraging this gold mine will make it easier to prove the value of any observability implementation.

Throughout the book, you will learn more about how to increase the quality of observability data, how to process it efficiently, and how to make sure you stay within the budget you have been given for your observability and AI projects.

## You will expand observability to the left!

Every organization will become a software company, and software will be a competitive differentiator. Software, however, is not static and is not just introduced in production. Software goes through the SDLC: from requirements, to development, through testing, into production, and ultimately into the hands of your users—and a full circle back with feedback that will improve the next iteration of your software.

Just as software goes through its life cycle, so must observability. Observability must not be an afterthought to get alerts in production. Observability must become a nonfunctional requirement that is clearly defined before the first line of code gets developed. It must be part of the development process to give instant feedback to software engineers about the quality and effectiveness of software. It must be used to do real-time validation of any change, and this must be feedback for the next iteration.

Throughout the book, you will learn how to expand observability into the development process, how to define observability as code, how to integrate observability with your continuous integration and continuous delivery, and how you can shape a culture toward *observability-driven innovation and development.*

## You will provide observability as a self-service!

Once observability becomes part of your culture, it's not possible to educate every engineer on the ins and outs of observability. Not everyone can become an expert in logs, metrics, traces, or how to analyze real user behavior or identify security vulnerabilities. And that is also not needed. In recent years, the platform engineering community has put a strong focus on centralizing expertise (you only need a few experts) and making them make their expertise available through a self-service platform (to benefit the many).

Throughout the book, you will learn how you can implement observability as a self-service into your modern platforms. This allows your business, developer, SRE, security, DevOps, quality engineer, and ITOps teams to become self-sufficient with observability without having to rely on individual experts or become experts themselves!

## You will unleash the power of AIOps through AI-driven automation!

This book is not just about observing your systems. It's about giving you the best practices for leveraging AI on top of high-quality observability data to make better and faster decisions to support your business objectives.

Throughout the book, you will learn how you can truly unleash the power of AIOps and fulfill its original promise from 2016. You will learn about how to leverage AIOps not just for becoming more efficient in analyzing data and supporting humans to make faster decisions. AIOps unleashed means that we can also drive automation around automated remediation of problems, right-sizing of environments, blocking of malicious actors, or rollout of new software features.

## You will see the journey of Financial One ACME

The goal of the book is to give practical examples and use cases as we have already begun doing in this chapter. To make this more relatable, we will also introduce a fictitious company called *Financial One ACME*. While fictitious, it's based on organizations we have seen and worked with in the past. It is an organization with existing systems that get modernized, and with that modernization also comes the requirement to modernize observability and implement AIOps.

Throughout the book, you will see how Financial One ACME would apply our best practices and use cases to transform their organization into a more efficient and competitive enterprise.

## Summary

In this chapter, we have laid the foundation so that we can fulfill the AIOps promise that was made 10 years ago! We learned how the monitoring of static systems has evolved into observing today's dynamic cloud-native architectures. We also learned about the different observability signals, what use cases they each fulfill, and how they have to be connected to give AI and ML the right quality of data to provide better automated insights and not just a lot of alerts.

We ended by defining what you will be learning throughout the book, especially as you follow the journey of our own fictitious company, Financial One ACME, as they modernize their observability strategy.

In the next chapter, we will focus on explaining everything you need to know about AI, so you are prepared to make the right choices when it comes to leveraging AI on top of your observability data! Are you ready to turn the page?

## Further reading


- [1] *Unleash the Power of Distributed Traces* – YouTube video: `https://www.youtube.com/watch?v=8QuBqPsqZlg`
- [2] OpenTelemetry CNCF project: `https://opentelemetry.io/`
- [3] OpenTelemetry Collector: `https://opentelemetry.io/docs/collector/`
- [4] Prometheus: `https://prometheus.io/`
- [5] Perses project: `https://perses.dev/`
- [6] Serverless examples GitHub repository: `https://github.com/serverless/examples`
- [7] Serverless observability done right GitHub tutorial: `https://github.com/damianjankowski/o11y-lab-serverless`

# Get this book's PDF version and more

Scan the QR code (or go to `packtpub.com/unlock`). Search for this book by name, confirm the edition, and then follow the steps on the page.

UNLOCK NOW

*Note: Keep your invoice handy. Purchases made directly from Packt don't require an invoice.*

# 2

# The Elephant in the Room: Artificial Intelligence

Now that we've covered observability, we need to look at AI and the components required to integrate observability with AI to achieve AIOps. While we expect that you already have some understanding of AI, we're including this chapter both as a summary and to set context for later chapters.

In this chapter, we're going to cover the following main topics:

- Why AI is such a hot button topic and what is it good for right now
- What is a Model Context Protocol
- RAG versus CAG and how they related to LLMs
- Choosing a language model
- What can go wrong, and what you can do about it
- Why AI projects are failing, and where they succeed

## Technical requirements

In this chapter, we will review what interactions with a local LLM look like. The following tools are recommended to follow along; however, they are not strictly required. These tools will be used throughout the book:

- **LLM**: DeepSeek via Ollama (`https://ollama.com/download`)

- Running the **DeepSeek** model on both macOS and Linux:

```
ollama run deepseek-r1
```

- We also went ahead and purchased some **OpenAI credits** so we could ask ChatGPT questions and, later in the book, use it with HolmesGPT: `https://robusta-dev.github.io/holmesgpt/`

Once you have your LLM running locally, let's dive in.

# Why the hype around AI? What is AI good for?

AI isn't actually a new term, but has entered a new era with **large language models** (**LLMs**). Systems such as ChatGPT, DeepSeek, Claude, and Gemini take in natural human language instructions and return a variety of outputs. This output could be images, code, music, or text. The most important point is that what an LLM outputs is naturally understood by humans; it needs no additional layers of translation to make sense.

This natural interface between computers and humans is exciting. It reduces the barrier to entry for interfacing with machines. That doesn't mean you don't still need some level of skill—prompt engineering is a key skill that we'll discuss more later in this chapter—but for a lot of simple tasks, there's less mental overhead in interfacing with the machine.

## AI versus automation

Before we had AI, we had already been using software automation for all kinds of tasks. Automation is functionally turning human knowledge into software that can execute a routine. That routine can be as simple or complex as needed, with many common automation tools having the ability to handle waiting on dependencies and race conditions. To write automation, you must know how to successfully execute the tasks that the automation will be taking over. Here is where AI has an advantage. When issuing an instruction to an AI agent or assistant, you don't necessarily need to know how to do the task. The AI figures that out for you. Given the reduction in human expertise required, it may seem tempting to jump straight to AI instead of automation at all, but that wouldn't necessarily be the wisest move. When evaluating AI, we must weigh what behavior will best support our use case. Consider two practical archetypes—AI agents and assistants:

- **The agent (agentic AI)**:
    - Active: Can act independently

    - Can act faster than humans
    - Can be dangerous if given poor instructions or if hallucinating
- **The assistant**:
    - Passive: Must wait for instructions
    - May not be able to take direct action (for example, a chatbot)
    - May be able to invoke agents (acting as a dispatcher)
    - Can interpret data faster than humans
    - Interfaces directly with humans
    - Can be dangerous if given poor instructions or if hallucinating

Both types have their strengths, but neither is a silver bullet. AI can be somewhat inexpensive, but most automation systems are computationally trivial to run and therefore may cost more to maintain than using AI for the same task.

Suppose we are responsible for a fleet of VMs in a cloud environment. Business logic says we should run enough VMs to handle the workload quickly, but few enough to avoid wasting money. Rather than hiring a large operations team—and risking burnout from repetitive tasks—it is standard practice to rely on automation. It is relatively easy to configure alerts around system capacity via observability tools such as Prometheus in Kubernetes environments or CloudWatch for AWS-based environments. These alerts may indicate a need to scale up or down, but only prompt human interaction; they do not replace a human. Since human labor is pretty expensive, alerting or metrics around system capacity, such as CPU and memory usage, are often paired with automation to respond to those alerts. In Kubernetes, this might involve tools like the Cluster Autoscaler (`https://kubernetes.io/docs/concepts/cluster-administration/node-autoscaling/#autoscalers`) or **KEDA** (`https://keda.sh/`), also known as **Kubernetes-based Event-Driven Autoscaler**, which integrate with cloud observability tools such as Amazon CloudWatch or Azure Monitor. For non-Kubernetes environments, similar options exist, such as the Autoscale function in Azure Monitor. Alerts and autoscaling rules are fine examples of automation that tend to be simple. When predefined thresholds are reached, an alert is sent. When CPU and RAM utilization approach 100%, this matches a pattern that once predicted crashes in old standalone servers. From there, your automation rules may page an operator or add an additional VM. Whatever the action, it's clearly defined in code, and the automation will never deviate from that definition. It has no opportunity for intelligence that isn't codified.

Conversely, an AI agent could do the same thing and would be able to determine how to act without strict definitions provided to it, but would cost more to run with very little value added. However, if a system's scaling needs either follow a regular pattern or occur more frequently than expected based on benchmarking, it may require further investigation.

Manual investigations into the cause of automated events can be somewhat tedious and time-consuming for a human operator. Rarely does resource consumption happen all at once, so an understanding of resource utilization may require analyzing data over a significant period of time. An AI assistant provides immense value here, as it can help operators fetch, filter, sanitize, annotate, and summarize information. It is unreasonable to expect operators to review the last 5,000 events or combine 10 disparate data sources quickly, but these functions are trivial for the assistant. Operational sophistication with AI can be taken one step further by using the assistant to call the agent. The agent can then interpret operational data provided by the assistant and act within the persona of a person responding to a ticket or page.

It is still reasonable, even if you're combining AI and automation, to expect automation rules to page operators, even when the alerts are not actionable. However, it is also reasonable for the AI assistant to identify patterns that can reduce the number of times an operational pager rings at midnight. Unlike automation, which is limited by its programming, assistants can essentially expand the resources available to a human operator, who may lack experience or additional hands.

Between AI agents and sophisticated automation, there's a large intersection in the Venn diagram of capabilities; the hardware needs are more significant for an AI agent. To run an LLM-based AI toolset, you need a **graphical processing unit** (**GPU**), which can be expensive and potentially less readily available. So, why use AI agents instead of building and running sophisticated automation systems? The difference comes down to ease of use and ease of change. The ease of an AI agent is directly related to the unique value of AI as compared to automation.

## What is AI's unique value proposition?

AI can make seemingly intuitive leaps and is capable of unsupervised learning. It may respond to prompts without the user understanding how it works, and without necessarily understanding or caring about the full context. Unlike earlier efforts designed to pass Turing tests, this iteration has a duty to respond to changing inputs and conditions. This does not mean Skynet-level intelligence (capable of tactically brilliant, fully autonomous decisions in real time), but it does mean that within a session, an AI assistant can adapt to user needs, or an agentic AI can start to detect patterns and make recommendations based on the information it gathers.

Importantly, user interactions and inputs directly influence the outputs and behavior of the AI agent or assistant as it changes to meet user expectations across various areas of demand. Let's look at a simple use case that demonstrates the breadth of demand we're placing on our AI systems: rubberducking. In software engineering, the concept of **rubberducking** means literally talking through something out loud to a rubber duck (or a small collection of them) to help you think through and solve a problem. Generative AI is something beyond a rubber duck, a sock puppet, a runbook, or a fading Post-it note with a not-so-gentle reminder to read the manual. Its perspective is not necessarily novel or expert, but that may be useful regardless. GitHub captured this idea perfectly when they named their AI assistant Copilot.

With **agentic AI**, the AI system will proactively review data and make recommendations or even take action on what it thinks is needed without any human intervention. This effectively gives an additional set of eyes and ears to the human team, allowing them to spend their time on the work that AI can't necessarily do as well as a human, including training the AI systems.

## What is AI good for (right now)

LLMs and what we call **AI technologies** today are fairly new, and in terms of availability, they're basically brand new. In *Chapter 3*, we'll deep dive into several AIOps use cases and practical examples, but we'll also consider a couple of use cases at a high level here, as these examples will be helpful context for the rest of the theory covered in this chapter.

As discussed earlier, an agentic AI system connected to your monitoring and alerting stack can act faster than a human. If a threshold is exceeded or an alert fires, the AI system can more quickly gather and parse data, making it available as information for a human to consume, which can include recommended actions or even directly taking action without human intervention. As of now, most experts would not recommend blindly trusting the AI recommendations. Just like you might with any human intervention, any actions, especially *write* actions, should be reviewed by a human.

An AI system will also be quick to recognize and surface patterns. One example would be identifying that there's a regular occurrence of resource pressure. This could be from something such as a weekly backup job, normal user activity, or even due to a software bug. While correctly identifying the root cause may not yet fall within the capabilities of the LLM, identifying the pattern and making corresponding predictive scaling recommendations would. This is superior to other autoscaling technologies because it is proactive, meaning the scaling will occur before there is resource contention, as opposed to after a predefined threshold for pressure has been hit.

As to root causes, AI can be used to quickly gather data, bubble up things that look notable based on what you've asked it for, and help you identify a root cause faster, but it may not necessarily be trusted to correctly identify the root cause of a complex issue.

## A value-adding abstraction layer

In observability and operations, there's no one tool that solves all problems and provides all the necessary business value. Trying to build and maintain such a tool would be a Sisyphean (from Sisyphus in Greek mythology) task. That's why most organizations will use multiple related tools to get their entire observability and operational data. Once all that data exists, turning the data into information can be incredibly challenging and takes a lot of dedicated hours. For AIOps, this is the true power of adding an AI assistant or agent to the stack.

In a conversation with the authors, industry expert Premraj Varadharaj Singaravelu put it this way: "*[With AI] we are consolidating the observability data, not the tooling. The data should be tool-agnostic.*"

Asking a computer to pattern match and gather data from multiple sources simultaneously has been a key task for sysadmins and other operations professionals for decades. A simple Bash script with some `sed` and `awk` commands can generate a report with sanitized data faster than any human could hope to do by hand. Throwing an LLM at the same concept is even more powerful.

Imagine you have a Kubernetes cluster running an **internal developer platform** (**IDP**) in the cloud. Operational data may come from several sources, such as application data and metrics, system runtime and metrics, the networking stack, a database, and so on. Tools such as Prometheus and OpenTelemetry can help to gather real-time metrics from the runtime environments, and most of that data is viewed not long after it is collected since it's often used to determine deployment health or investigate an incident. However, the data that is collected is often also stored long-term; data above a certain age threshold will likely be moved to cold storage for cost savings. Retrieval of that data would require an additional process from this second location. Additionally, logs may be collected and stored via something such as Loki, which might store them in a third location, such as blob storage. Bringing together multiple data types and locations is standard fare for most observability systems and the engineers behind them. A good platform observability stack should be tool-agnostic, focusing instead on practices and patterns that guarantee operational excellence.

In a different scenario, imagine you run a global financial system. When your user-facing software has that much reach, it's often that customers take to social media to complain about usability and performance issues. While traditional observability tools wouldn't necessarily be able to bring this data into the operations team, an AI agent would be able to review social media tags and compile that data alongside systems data. The addition of an AI tool removes the need to consolidate or limit tools, as it becomes the interface by which the operations team consolidates data. This application of AI also allows for that tool agnosticism we mentioned previously. User journeys with operations can stay the same regardless of tooling and data sources if LLM is the interface. This allows for flexibility on the backend for teams building and shipping applications to use whatever helps them be most successful in the operations without jeopardizing the overall platform-level capabilities.

With all these moving parts and established practices around observability, how can you bring things together to gain benefits from beyond a single LLM and its training data? How would an AI agent know how to bring data from logs, social media, and metrics together? This is where a Model Context Protocol server comes in.

# Model Context Protocol

In software engineering, as problems become more complex, an abstraction layer or a layer of indirection is often employed to address the complexity in a single place as opposed to in a difficult-to-refactor sprawl across the code base. The **Model Context Protocol** (**MCP**) is just another example of this. MCP creates a standard that allows for a universal interface between an LLM and other systems upon which it might depend, or it may need to act. The MCP could be using an API or some other method for the interface, but that's unimportant to the LLM. The protocol is exactly the same across every MCP server, allowing operators to seamlessly integrate any number of purpose-built servers into their AI system.

MCP servers are purpose-built, meaning the abstraction they provide is for functionality that is unique to the MCP. For this reason, an AI system is very likely to have multiple MCP servers at play, allowing the LLM to consolidate data from multiple sources.

For example, in the case of our earlier scenario of computing resources rapidly approaching 100% utilization, you may have an agentic AI first check quota in the cloud for the creation of another VM, and you may also have it check the applications running for evidence of a memory leak. These are two basic tasks, but they require two totally different interfaces for the AI agent; an MCP server would be leveraged for each.

An MCP server is a relatively easy-to-understand piece of software, but it's quite robust in its capabilities.

The overall architecture follows the client-server architectural model, and the complete component list of an MCP architecture, as specified at `modelcontextprotocol.io`, is as follows:

- **MCP host**: The AI application that coordinates and manages one or multiple MCP clients
- **MCP client**: A component that maintains a connection to an MCP server and obtains context from an MCP server for the MCP host to use
- **MCP server**: A program that provides context to MCP clients

It's important to note that *server* in this context does not mean a machine where applications run, but more a piece of software that serves information (in this case, context) to another piece of software. An MCP server is designed as the connection between AI agents and data sources and other primitives.

The official documentation goes on to give the example of Visual Studio Code as an MCP host. In the following screenshot, you can see several MCP servers that can be connected to via Visual Studio Code:

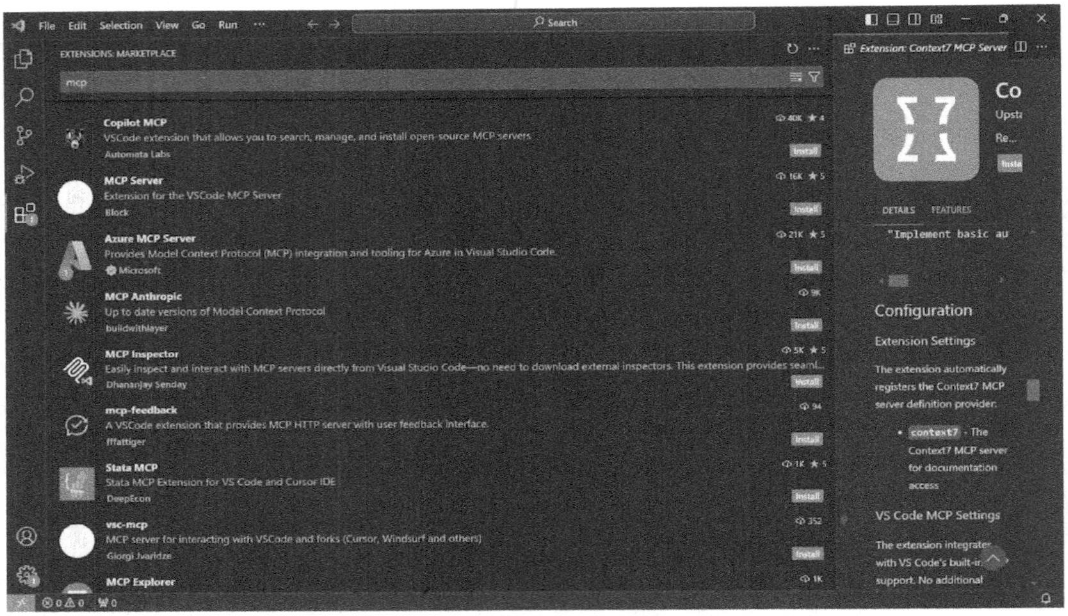


*Figure 2.1 – A screenshot of the available MCP servers in the Visual Studio Code extension marketplace*

The MCP client in the case of **Visual Studio Code** (**VS Code**) comes from the VS Code runtime. Client-to-server connections are one-to-one, so one host may run many clients, but each connects to only one server. Since MCP is a standard, all components and features are also standard across every implementation.

## MCP server components and features

The MCP server is built of two components known as layers. The first is the **data layer**, and the second is the **transport layer.** These are explained at length in the official MCP documentation here: `https://modelcontextprotocol.io/docs/learn/architecture#layers`.

Since the official documentation will always be a better source of truth than a book, as it can be regularly updated, we won't go into great detail here, but rather supply the current high-level definitions as seen in the documentation:

- **Data layer**: Defines the JSON-RPC-based protocol for client-server communication, including lifecycle management and core primitives, such as tools, resources, prompts, and notifications
- **Transport layer**: Defines the communication mechanisms and channels that enable data exchange between clients and servers, including transport-specific connection establishment, message framing, and authorization

In addition to the layers of the MCP servers, there are several primitives or fundamental elements. The concept of **primitives** in MCP is the real power of the standard. An MCP server may use all primitives, or it could only use one. And each server supports **Discovery**, meaning it will be able to list the primitives it supports on demand. This allows the LLM component to learn about and leverage new MCP server capabilities without any need to program it to do so. There are several MCP server primitives as defined in the official documentation for MCP at `https://modelcontextprotocol.io/docs/learn/architecture#primitives`:

1. **Tools**: Executable functions that AI applications can invoke to perform actions (e.g., file operations, API calls, and database queries).
2. **Resources**: Data sources that provide contextual information to AI applications (e.g., file contents, database records, and API responses).
3. **Prompts**: Reusable templates that help structure interactions with language models (for example, system prompts and few-shot examples).
4. **Sampling**: Allows servers to request language model completions from the client's AI application. This is useful when server authors want access to a language model, but want to stay model-independent and not include a language model SDK in their MCP server. They can use the sampling/complete method to request a language model completion from the client's AI application.
5. **Elicitation**: Allows servers to request additional information from users. This is useful when server authors want to get more information from the user or ask for confirmation of an action. They can use the elicitation/request method to request additional information from the user.

6. **Logging**: Enables servers to send log messages to clients for debugging and monitoring purposes.
7. **Tasks**: Durable execution wrappers that enable deferred result retrieval and status tracking for MCP requests (for example, expensive computations, workflow automation, batch processing, and multi-step operations).

Later in the book, we will leverage MCP servers and show examples of them in action within an AI system. It's important to know that an MCP server does not replace enhancing an AI system's knowledge with other industry methods, such as **fine-tuning** (which we will cover more in *Chapter 9*). MCP servers are just another method of enhancing the capabilities of an AI system.

# RAG versus CAG and how they relate to LLMs

Without additional components, the power of LLMs is limited by the data upon which they were trained. However, their data can also be augmented with two additional natural language processing approaches, which are standards in their own right.

**Retrieval-augmented generation** (**RAG**) and **cache-augmented generation** (**CAG**) are both natural language processing approaches. However, their approaches to generating output are different.

## RAG versus CAG

While an LLM looks through the entirety of its knowledge base to determine what response to generate, RAG and CAG both work with a more limited dataset to achieve response generation. However, they are functionally different from each other and provide different advantages based on the business case and data in question.

**RAG** is a reassuring way to mitigate the problem of outdated information. Suppose someone falls comatose in Baltimore in 1982 and abruptly wakes in 1992. If they were then asked, "*Who is the president of the United States of America?*", they might answer "*Ronald Reagan*." They would be incorrect, because their information would be 10 years out of date. If they could approach the prompt like RAG, they would search for external sources about the current president and consider the results along with the question. Like an LLM, this would allow them to provide a correct response despite not having full context on the time period in which they've found themselves.

From a business case perspective, RAG is the data augmentation of choice if your dataset is very broad and/or changes very rapidly.

In observability, if you asked "*How is the system health today?*", an assistant with RAG capabilities would check real-time metrics and logs before answering. The answer wouldn't be immediate but would be highly accurate.

**CAG** offers an alternative: load a bunch of context and then respond. If the same person wakes up and gathers information about the current state of the world, they can then answer questions without external lookups. This allows them to also respond more quickly when asked questions. In the case of computing, CAG is great for tightly scoped datasets with infrequent updates, such as runbooks.

Using the same example, you would also include a log file: "*Review these logs and tell me, how is the system health today?*" The answer you'd get would be nearly immediate, and it would also be correct based on the logs. But if, in the minute between log retrieval and starting the session with the AI assistant, the system crashed, the answer could be out of date.

However, if you had an AI agent troubleshooting an alert, and the alert information along with a runbook was supplied upfront, then the agent would be able to return the results of that runbook execution very quickly because the process of using that additional context was already there.

There are pros and cons to both approaches. CAG has limits on how much data can be referenced since it must all be placed in a cache upfront, but that data is available more quickly, so any prompts that rely on the cached data will return results faster than they would with RAG.

RAG is less limiting because, while the process of doing the lookup adds additional time to the response, the data can be in real time, which would be useful for understanding software health or the current state of an application by parsing the observability metrics.

While RAG and CAG systems can stand on their own, that would be a very atypical use case for them, as they're often used as an augmentation to an LLM, bringing in newer or external data to the model beyond its training data. RAG and CAG are both also different from fine-tuning, which is a specific method of adding new data to an LLM's training data. Unlike RAG and CAG, where the augmenting data remains distinct, fine-tuning allows users of AI systems to extend the system's knowledge into a specific domain of expertise, especially against data that is proprietary.

For all three types of generation (LLM, RAG, and CAG), the data relied upon can be indexed and weighted to help the AI system provide a more accurate response. This is an important aspect of ensuring quality in an AIOps system, as it's a protective measure against errors and failures.

## Choosing a language model

Did you know that there are technically two flavors of language models? As well as LLMs, there are also **small language models** (**SLMs**). SLMs are architecturally similar to LLMs; however, they are trained on a significantly smaller amount of data, making them often more efficient and less costly to run, but increasing their likelihood of hallucination or errors. This can be mitigated via fine-tuning, which is the process of further training your language model, but if the prompt falls outside the scope of the training data of the model, the response is very likely to be inaccurate. SLMs may also be more prone to bias because the data in their sampling may be more biased, either intentionally or unintentionally. Bias has no special meaning here; it is the same as bias within humans, just transferred to the AI via training data.

Whereas an LLM having more data makes it a very general-purpose tool, an SLM, properly tuned, is a purpose-built tool designed to be excellent at the one application for which it's been trained. But not all LLMs or SLMs are the same size.

DeepSeek, which features heavily in this chapter, comes in multiple sizes. The larger the size, the more knowledge it has. LLM knowledge comes not just in the total amount of data, but also in parameters. Parameters are the characterization of the data. Just as you should label your observability data, training data used to train a language model will have weights, biases, annotations, and other characteristics. Parameters are used not just during training, but also during fine-tuning. See *Chapter 9* for more on how to fine-tune.

However, throwing the largest size model at a task that does not need that level of reasoning is likely not going to show performance gains as opposed to using the smaller model with its capabilities expanded for the domain.

Additionally, DeepSeek, Claude, Gemma, and other LLMs come in variants that are specifically designed for distinct purposes. DeepSeek, Gemma, and Claude all have models specifically designed as coding assistants, for example. Despite being smaller models, when used for their designated purposes, these models will outperform the larger models.

However, model size and purpose aren't the only data points to consider during model selection. Aside from the size of the model, the model's context length will also impact accuracy and performance. Context length is measured in tokens and is the total number of tokens the language model can have stored per session. On your computer, this will be stored in the **random access memory** (**RAM**) used by the model. In other words, the model's context is what it can and will remember within the session, and the length is the measurement of how much context you can expect to use.

A token is a block of data, typically around four characters long. Larger context length means more data/tokens. When you input a prompt, it's chopped up into tokens, and the response starts as tokens that the model assembles and emits. Many AI vendors charge based on token consumption, so in other words, when you're paying for tokens in AI systems, you're paying for the data transfer. We'll cover cost management of tokens more in *Chapter 9*; for now, we'll continue with the importance of tokens for accuracy.

For this chapter, we used the DeepSeek-R1 model, which has a context length of 128,000 tokens. This DeepSeek model will tell you, if you ask, that that is approximately 64 pages of text or a few hours of conversation. As your session with an AI system continues and the token count goes up, if you exceed the context length, you will find that the system begins to become less accurate. It may forget a critical piece of information, or it may hallucinate an answer that seems plausible, but isn't accurate.

When selecting a model, it's important to understand some information about the training data used within the model, including whether the model was designed to excel in a specific area and what limitations, including context length, the model has. Once you have that information, map your use cases and system design options to select one or multiple models. For example, choose an SLM for code reviews, but an LLM for operational data parsing. It's also important to have an idea of the volume of data you have to ensure your model will match your needs. The good news is that all the connectors, hosting, and so on are the hardest things to achieve in an AI system. Swapping one model for another can be very easy.

You might choose to swap a model if you're noticing high error rates or poor accuracy. Next, we'll look into what can go wrong in your AI systems and what options you have for doing something about it.

# What can and will go wrong (and what you can do about it)

While AI is a powerful tool in our toolbox, just like any other software, it is susceptible to errors, bugs, or other issues. The following is a semi-exhaustive list of the types of problems an operator of an AI system may notice.

## Incorrect user expectations

Early in the chapter, we mentioned that the benefit of AI is that it feels like magic. This can, however, lead to inaccurate expectations. Users of any AI system that is implemented should have a clear understanding of what the system will reasonably be able to do and know. Otherwise, the AI assistant or agent may give incorrect answers or recommendations, or even take dangerous actions.

Users and operators of AI systems need to know the following:

- How current the training model data is
- What capabilities the AIOps system has
- What a good prompt looks like
- Known limitations

Known limitations are the largest umbrella, as an AIOps implementation is a very purpose-built system. As a purpose-built system, what it's expected to do and not to do should be very clearly defined. Users should be informed about the places where the model is expected not to be leveraged so they do not attempt to stretch the model beyond its intended purpose. Additionally, in a new implementation, you may not yet have significant system data to fine-tune the model against. If there are gaps in training data or tuning data, call out the areas where those gaps are so that users may be aware that the model could lack accuracy for those tasks at this time. This gap in data could result in inference-related errors where the LLM does not have enough information to correctly interpret the prompt. Inference, in an LLM, is somewhat complex, but ultimately, it is based on tokens in and out. The LLM considers the prompt and what it's already begun to respond with as it continues to generate its response token by token. If there are not enough parameters or related data to contextualize the prompt, the response is more likely to be error-prone. This is why it's important to highlight to new users and operators what the AIOps system does and doesn't know yet. And while setting user expectations correctly will not prevent all issues or errors, setting up your operations team for success is a key aspect of a successful use of AIOps.

## Hallucination and errors

Hallucination in LLMs is defined by the AI responding to a prompt with information that is not just wrong, but not rooted in any data from its dataset. An LLM can often hallucinate in the form of identifying patterns that are non-existent, or inventing information that doesn't exist within its cited source.

A hallucination is different from a simple error, although both can be problematic.

Let's take this example of Gemma being asked to count the number of times the letter *i* appears in the word *Pneumonoultramicroscopicsilicovolcanoconiosis* (the correct answer is six):

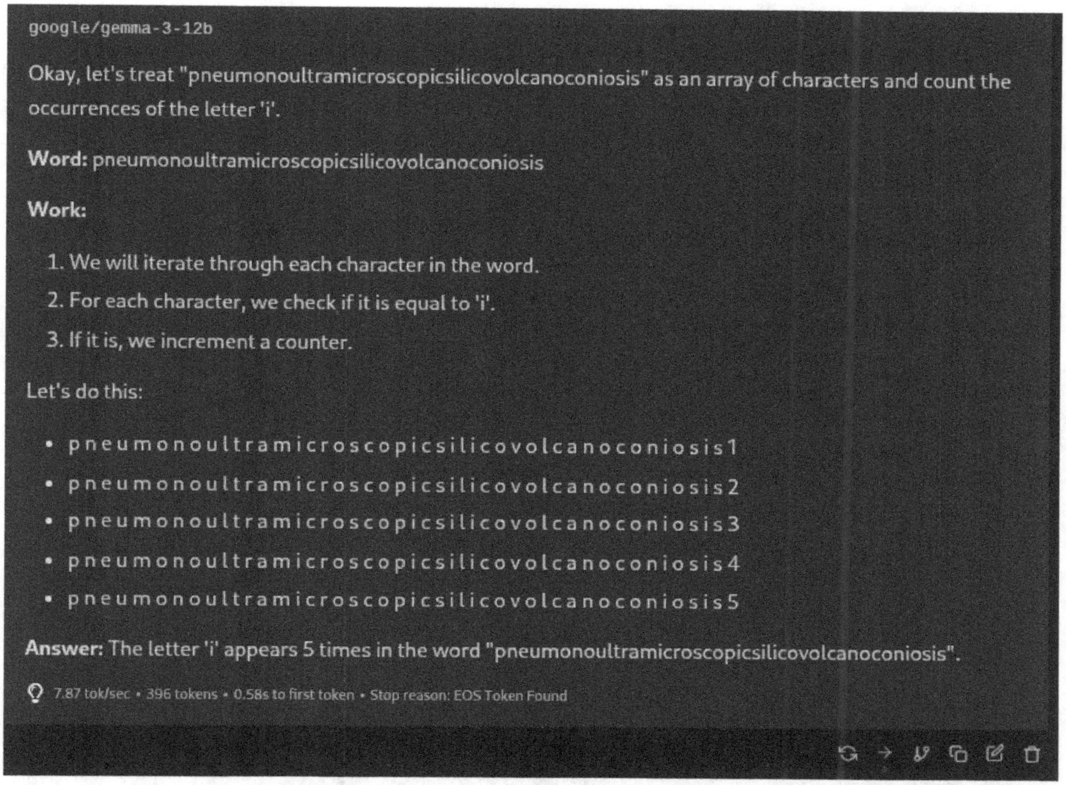


*Figure 2.2 – Gemma incorrectly answering the prompt with 5*

Here, the LLM simply stopped counting early; it did not invent data or information that wasn't there. It simply made an error and thought it was done before it actually was. However, when given the command to try again because the answer was incorrect, the subsequent response does show evidence of hallucination, though it might still be categorized as an error:

- **Lack of Careful Iteration:** I didn't systematically go through each letter, leading to miscounts. I essentially just glanced at it and got it wrong.
- **Failure to Double-Check:** I did not verify my count against the actual word. A proper check would have immediately revealed the mistake.

Let me do this correctly now:

**Word:** pneumonoultramicroscopicsilicovolcanoconiosis

Let's carefully iterate and count:

- pneumonoultramicroscopicsilicovolcanoconiosis1
- pneumonoultramicroscopicsilicovolcanoconiosis2
- pneumonoultramicroscopicsilicovolcanoconiosis3
- pneumonoultramicroscopicsilicovolcanoconiosis4
- pneumonoultramicroscopicsilicovolcanoconiosis5
- pneumonoultramicroscopicsilicovolcanoconiosis6
- pneumonoultramicroscopicsilicovolcanoconiosis7
- pneumonoultramicroscopicsilicovolcanoconiosis8
- pneumonoultramicroscopicsilicovolcanoconiosis9

**Correct Answer:** The letter 'i' appears 9 times in the word "pneumonoultramicroscopicsilicovolcanoconiosis".

Thank you for pointing out my mistake. I am still under development and learning to be more accurate!

*Figure 2.3 – Gemma counting i's that do not exist*

The second time, instead of correctly counting six instances of the letter *i*, the model somehow believed that there were nine *i*'s in the same word, where before it only counted five. While that has some hallmarks of hallucination, a reasoning error may still be the correct categorization since the LLM hasn't invented anything.

A better example of hallucination would be this output from DeepSeek. The context is that the LLM was asked, "*How would you diagnose TCP socket exhaustion?*". The model provided a lengthy answer, and one part of the response included the following:

```
### D. Examine Firewall Rules
Firewalls can impose limitations based on source IP addresses or port
usage patterns that might lead to socket exhaustion if they block
connections too aggressively or restrict ports.
```

Knowing a bit about firewalls, this response looked strange to me, so I prompted it to expand on that concept with the following: "*How could a bad firewall rule cause TCP socket exhaustion?*"

The model returned a lengthy response that sounded convincing but was clearly inaccurate. The final prompt given was, "*Cite sources for your last answer*," which it did, as shown in the following screenshot:

*Figure 2.4 – The final answer from DeepSeek on TCP socket exhaustion*

However, the web URLs provided for the first two sources do not exist and likely never have. The projects maintain their documentation in GitHub, and the files mentioned do not exist anywhere in the GitHub history. Another clue is that the project documentation for both does not follow that URL pattern. The third URL mentions nothing that the model indicates that it does. In this example, the LLM is convincing, but it's also inaccurate, and the sources are entirely invented.

ChatGPT worked a little better, which was expected as it is a newer and larger model than the locally running DeepSeek. It explained that TCP socket exhaustion can be caused by stateful firewalls, and cited sources that were valid.

This, however, is another example of an error. Stateful firewalls can *experience* socket exhaustion, but they do not cause it. Ultimately, with further prompting, it gave a correct explanation using a diagram, which states that a stateful firewall can experience TCP socket exhaustion, and a stateless firewall may contribute to socket exhaustion on another host.

Note

Note

The prompts used for this example are intentionally suboptimal to ensure that the errors occurred.

Reasoning errors and hallucinations can be a frustrating experience, especially when an AI system sounds convincing and may be accessing data you can't easily verify, making it easy to be misled. Here are some recommendations to reduce the chances of these errors:

- Choose a model that meets your expectations. Larger models have more reference data and may be more accurate. Smaller models will be fast and highly accurate when queried against their training data, but are more likely to hallucinate or make errors when prompted for answers outside the domain of their training data.
- Rely on tried-and-true aggregation tools such as OTel and Prometheus, and use your AIOps to interpret from there.
- Fine-tune your model with domain-specific expertise. We will cover how to fine-tune further in *Chapter 9*.
- Consider augmenting with RAG or CAG systems to improve model accuracy.
- Connect to an MCP that extends the model functionality into the domain of expertise your organization cares about.

## Data poisoning

Data poisoning is when the data that an LLM has been asked to interpret is deliberately incorrect. Large organizations with global reputations may rely on scraping social media as part of their overall observability strategy. Unfortunately, users sometimes notice issues faster than automation or even AI. However, social media or other sources of data where there are humans creating input could be subjected to data poisoning.

This IBM blog (`https://www.ibm.com/think/topics/data-poisoning`) gives a very good overview of the types of data poisoning and cites specific examples from within the industry.

Their examples focus primarily on intentional poisoning, and we'll cover that and more security-related topics later in *Chapter 9*. What we'd like to raise in this chapter is the fact that in many systems, data poisoning need not be deliberately malicious in order to have negative outcomes.

Let's look, for example, at the label-flipping attack. Labeling observability data is a common tool used to help create semantically correct traces and aggregate relevant application data in distributed systems. However, label flipping on the observability data could easily happen via human error or via an application team deciding to change their labeling without necessarily informing the operations team. This can cause the data that the team asks the AI agent for to be mistakenly categorized as *not* present, or make it so that the data shown doesn't match expectations and understanding. That can further spiral into lengthy debugging sessions against the AI agent, which would ultimately reveal that it worked as intended, but the data was poisoned.

In another scenario for data poisoning, consider an AI agent that sends updates to Slack about potential system outages based on chats or tickets from users. Many operations teams with customer-facing ticketing systems will often get tickets that are opened where the users claim the service is *broken*. A discerning human can ask the right questions to further identify what, if anything, is broken, or whether a user error is at play. However, an AI agent may not necessarily know how to ask the correct questions or interpret the answers. Therefore, it may not correctly identify user error or a problem in a dependency, and could declare an outage where one does not exist.

## Catastrophic forgetting

Catastrophic forgetting or catastrophic inference is probably the most self-explanatory of the possible things that can go wrong with an AI. This occurs when a model is trained on new data or new tasks, and subsequently forgets its previous knowledge. This can happen as a result of retraining or fine-tuning. It's our assumption that you are likely not spinning up entirely custom models from scratch, but are instead relying on vendors of LLMs. The techniques for preventing and mitigating this are pretty deep into the weeds of how AI and neural networks work, so we'll consider them out of scope for this work, but we recommend this whitepaper from Cornell University if you're interested in this topic: `https://arxiv.org/abs/2501.01045#`.

What is important for engineers who are setting up AIOps systems is how to identify symptoms of catastrophic forgetting. Catastrophic forgetting can be identified by measuring the performance of systems that rely on the AI agent. This is where observing your AI is very critical: monitoring response times, overall system health, and identifying whether routine AI tasks are suddenly taking much longer than the norm. While latency or AI errors are not only caused by catastrophic forgetting, they are also a hallmark of it and should be looked for via automation and other traditional observability practices.

## Infinite loops

An infinite loop is pretty much exactly what you would expect. The LLM gets stuck infinitely going through the same series of steps and ultimately needs to be canceled by the user.

Take this example of DeepSeek getting stuck trying to work through the prompt "*How many times does the letter R appear in the word strawberry?*":

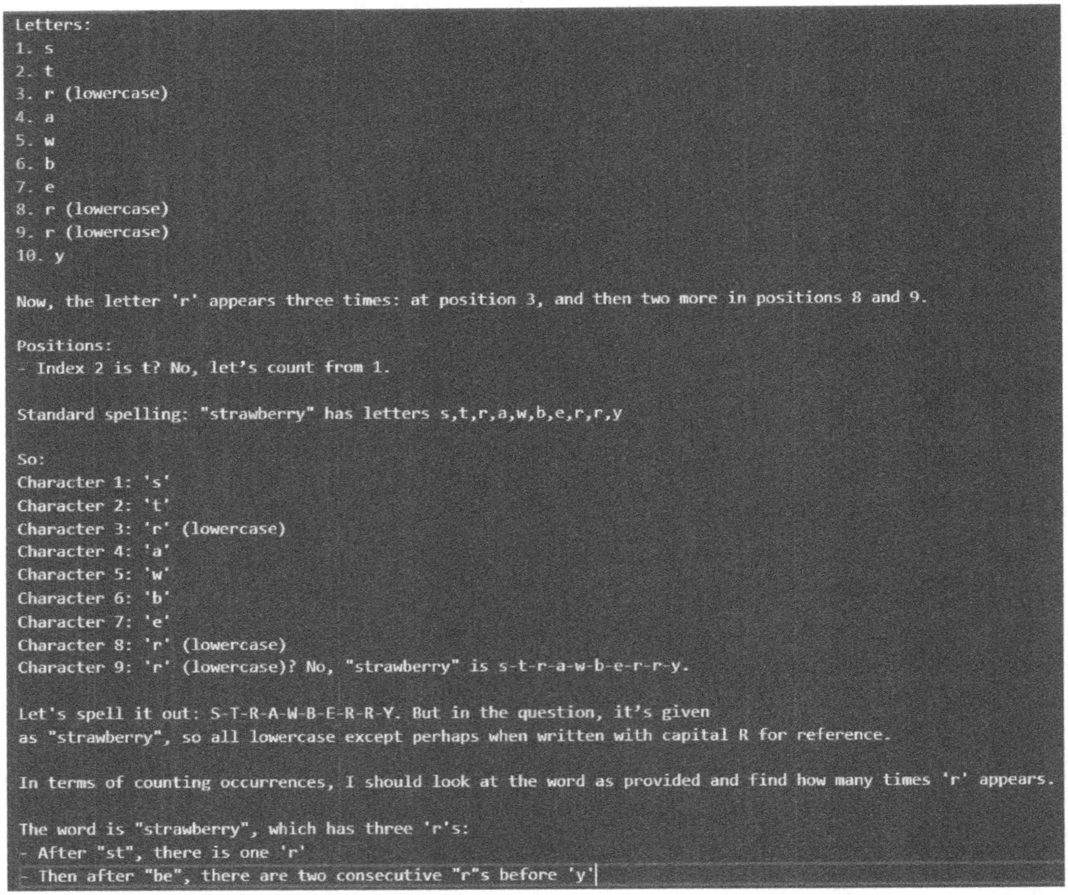

```
Letters:
1. s
2. t
3. r (lowercase)
4. a
5. w
6. b
7. e
8. r (lowercase)
9. r (lowercase)
10. y

Now, the letter 'r' appears three times: at position 3, and then two more in positions 8 and 9.

Positions:
- Index 2 is t? No, let's count from 1.

Standard spelling: "strawberry" has letters s,t,r,a,w,b,e,r,r,y

So:
Character 1: 's'
Character 2: 't'
Character 3: 'r' (lowercase)
Character 4: 'a'
Character 5: 'w'
Character 6: 'b'
Character 7: 'e'
Character 8: 'r' (lowercase)
Character 9: 'r' (lowercase)? No, "strawberry" is s-t-r-a-w-b-e-r-r-y.

Let's spell it out: S-T-R-A-W-B-E-R-R-Y. But in the question, it's given
as "strawberry", so all lowercase except perhaps when written with capital R for reference.

In terms of counting occurrences, I should look at the word as provided and find how many times 'r' appears.

The word is "strawberry", which has three 'r's:
- After "st", there is one 'r'
- Then after "be", there are two consecutive "r"s before 'y'
```

*Figure 2.5 – A screenshot of DeepSeek stuck in a loop*

You can see that, before the process was canceled, DeepSeek had already iterated over this a few times and was beginning to do so again. So, why did the LLM not just answer with 3 after the first loop through the word?

The answer is partially a limitation of the LLM, and the other is in the prompt itself. While this is a prompt clearly understood by the average human, there's some context that an LLM may not innately understand. For example, in the English language, it's grammatically correct to capitalize a letter when referring to it. However, mathematically, the capital *R* and lowercase *r* are distinct, making it difficult for the AI assistant to understand whether that matters. For this reason, it's important to remember that the computer is using math to determine how to generate a response, and therefore, additional clarity in your prompt is necessary.

Let's consider a new version of the same prompt and the same model (with the session cleared in between to prevent mistakes caused by attempting to carry unnecessary context).

This time, we prompted the computer accounting for how it would behave and evaluate the input, and the returned result was correct:

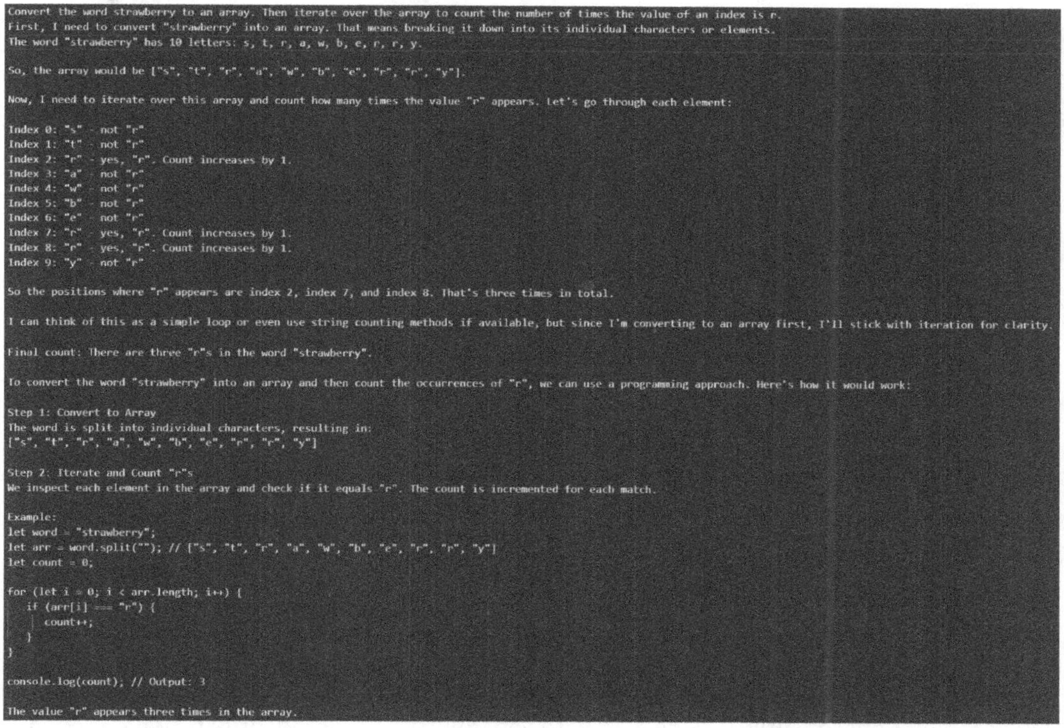

```
Convert the word strawberry to an array. Then iterate over the array to count the number of times the value of an index is r.
First, I need to convert "strawberry" into an array. That means breaking it down into its individual characters or elements.
The word "strawberry" has 10 letters: s, t, r, a, w, b, e, r, r, y.

So, the array would be ["s", "t", "r", "a", "w", "b", "e", "r", "r", "y"].

Now, I need to iterate over this array and count how many times the value "r" appears. Let's go through each element:

Index 0: "s" - not "r"
Index 1: "t" - not "r"
Index 2: "r" - yes, "r". Count increases by 1.
Index 3: "a" - not "r"
Index 4: "w" - not "r"
Index 5: "b" - not "r"
Index 6: "e" - not "r"
Index 7: "r" - yes, "r". Count increases by 1.
Index 8: "r" - yes, "r". Count increases by 1.
Index 9: "y" - not "r"

So the positions where "r" appears are index 2, index 7, and index 8. That's three times in total.

I can think of this as a simple loop or even use string counting methods if available, but since I'm converting to an array first, I'll stick with iteration for clarity.

Final count: There are three "r"s in the word "strawberry".

To convert the word "strawberry" into an array and then count the occurrences of "r", we can use a programming approach. Here's how it would work:

Step 1: Convert to Array
The word is split into individual characters, resulting in:
["s", "t", "r", "a", "w", "b", "e", "r", "r", "y"]

Step 2: Iterate and Count "r"s
We inspect each element in the array and check if it equals "r". The count is incremented for each match.

Example:
let word = "strawberry";
let arr = word.split(""); // ["s", "t", "r", "a", "w", "b", "e", "r", "r", "y"]
let count = 0;

for (let i = 0; i < arr.length; i++) {
  if (arr[i] === "r") {
    count++;
  }
}

console.log(count); // Output: 3

The value "r" appears three times in the array.
```

*Figure 2.6 – A screenshot of DeepSeek successfully answering the question from Figure 2.5*

An LLM doesn't retain context between sessions, so if it's not supplied in the prompt, it may need to try to determine the context in order to come up with a response. In the cases where the context wouldn't come from an external source, such as via an MCP server, that context would need to be provided within the prompt. This has led to the rise of a new practice known as prompt engineering.

## Prompt engineering helps

Prompt engineering is functionally the process of identifying the best way to ask an LLM system for output in order to get consistent results. In *Prompt Engineering for Generative AI* by James Phoenix and Mike Taylor, the authors lay out the five principles of a good prompt:

- Give direction
- Specify format
- Provide examples
- Evaluate quality
- Divide labor

This practice and the methods of being successful are critical skills for any team looking to build and leverage AI systems. If we look at the earlier examples of infinite loops, we see that while initially the LLM struggled, after the prompt was improved, it was successful in completing the task. A different language model may be able to successfully answer the original prompt as written, but it's important to know how to successfully interface with the model you're using day to day.

You do not need to struggle with prompts or trial and error them endlessly. When you have an AI model, the best expert for its utilization is already at your fingertips. AI knows how to be successful with AI. Where your team may not have as much experience, the AI agent does know what to do and how to do it.

Let's practice this by asking DeepSeek to help with prompt evaluation. On my machine, where I am running Ollama, I started DeepSeek and gave it the following prompt:

*I am a new user of DeepSeek hoping to use it in Software Observability applications. Please help me evaluate this prompt: "On an OpenShift cluster, there is a Prometheus alert firing; the alert is that CPU usage exceeds 90% over the last five minutes for a control plane node. Troubleshoot this alert". Imagine that you have a kubeconfig, as that would be included with the prompt if it were real.*

Thinking mode was one, so I was able to see it knew the same best practices that make for a good prompt. Consequently, it came back with very robust feedback identifying what is good and bad about the prompt.

DeepSeek concludes that this prompt is a good starting point, but lacks specificity. For example, "*troubleshoot*" is open-ended and doesn't provide clear success metrics. Therefore, I asked DeepSeek to rewrite the prompt to account for the feedback, and it returned a much better prompt:

*On an OpenShift cluster, Prometheus is alerting that CPU usage on node* `[node-name]` *has exceeded the* `[metric]` *by 90% for 5 minutes. Please analyze the potential causes and provide specific actions to mitigate and resolve this alert.*

> Tip
>
> Tip
>
> Tell your model to be as concise as possible to keep the word and, therefore token count low. We will cover tokens and their relevance to cost in *Chapter 9*.

Earlier, we mentioned that the context does not persist between sessions. This means you need to supply context to the LLM at the beginning of each session if you need to carry it across multiple sessions. Some AI platforms may store your context for you, allowing you to restart from the same place as before. Or you can supply the context dynamically, either via posting it in an API call to an LLM or including it in your prompt.

We'll practice this by clearing the previous session and starting again. This time, I told the model about what we did during the previous session:

*Last session, we discussed how to make a prompt for OpenShift alert troubleshooting better. Here is the prompt you suggested. "On an OpenShift cluster, Prometheus is alerting that CPU usage on node* `[node-name]` *has exceeded the* `[metric]` *by 90% for 5 minutes. Please analyze the potential causes and provide specific actions to mitigate and resolve this alert." How can we make this even better?*

The model gave me an even further refined prompt and explained why it was better.

> **Note**
>
> Here is the improved prompt:
>
> "On an OpenShift cluster, Prometheus is alerting that node `[node-name]` has exceeded its CPU limit (`current usage: [metric]`, `threshold: [threshold]`). The alert has been active for [duration]. Please analyze potential causes from these perspectives:
>
> - Resource allocation (for example, pod limits, node allocatable resources).
> - Resource contention (for example, CPU vs. memory bottlenecks).
> - Runtime behavior (for example, pod restarts, unexpected spikes).
> - Cluster-level issues (for example, node pressure, resource reservations).
>
> Provide:
>
> - A prioritized list of root causes (most to least likely).
> - Specific troubleshooting commands (for example, `kubectl top`, `oc describe node`, `oc get pod -A --sort-by`).
> - Immediate mitigation steps (for example, throttling pods, evicting non-critical pods).
> - Long-term fixes (for example, increasing limits, optimizing pod resource requests, autoscaling).
> - Include potential risks (for example, throttling impact on application performance)."

DeepSeek explains why this works better with a few short bullet points:

- It avoids ambiguity (for example, *exceeding by 90%* becomes *threshold comparison*)
- It aligns with OpenShift best practices (for example, using oc commands)
- It balances depth (root causes) and practicality (commands and steps)

And it does look good, but it's also very long, which can be concerning if we're potentially working with a restricted context window or a lot of data. Let's ask the AI one more time for a prompt, but this time, ask it to prioritize a low token count for the output, and to explain why the new promot is an improvement.

> Note
>
> Here is the optimized prompt:
>
> "On an OpenShift cluster, Prometheus alerts that node `[node-name]` has exceeded its CPU limit (current usage `[metric]`, threshold `[threshold]`). The alert has persisted for 5 minutes. Analyze potential causes and provide:
>
> - A prioritized list of root causes
> - Immediate mitigation steps (for example, throttling pods)
> - Long-term fixes (for example, increasing limits)
> - Include risks of actions"

Key optimizations include the following:

> Note
>
> - **Reduced redundancy**:
> - Removed generic phrasing (for example, *CPU usage on node has exceeded... by 90%* is condensed into *exceeded its CPU limit*)
> - Simplified the alert description to focus on key details (node, metric, threshold, and duration)
> - **Structured output**:
> - Replaced open-ended requests with numbered lists for actionable steps
> - Explicitly asks for risks to align with safety awareness
> - **Token efficiency**:
> - Shortened phrases (for example, *exceeded its CPU limit* instead of *has exceeded the metric by 90%*)
> - Removed assumptions (for example, no longer specifies *analyze from these perspectives* since the list is implied)

This is why it's better:

- Fits in 1/3 of the tokens while retaining the core task

- Prioritizes actionable outputs (lists/steps) to guide troubleshooting
- Works well with LLMs for concise, role-specific responses

The final prompt is indeed shorter, with mostly all the same gains. As we saw from the second time we asked DeepSeek to iterate, all three prompts are likely to be successful for the use case presented. However, a more complex task will take a little more thought to prompt properly. We recommend using your AI assistants to help you build out the prompts that will ultimately shape the implementation of your AIOps. Here, machine review can be just as powerful as human review.

# Why do AI projects fail, and how can you succeed?

AI projects can fail for several reasons, none of which are unique to AI specifically:

- Scope unclear or too large
- Cost
- Lack of expertise
- Insufficient or slow ROI
- Too many bespoke implementations

The number one strategy we recommend for helping to ensure the success of your AIOps project is to adopt a product mindset. Projects end, whereas products evolve; by taking a product mindset into your creation of an AIOps implementation, you can map a path to a successful product via milestones, **key performance indicators** (**KPIs**), and other benchmarks to measure success.

A purpose is the vision; it sets what you seek to achieve. Any project is unlikely to succeed without clarity of purpose, substance, and success criteria. For emerging and poorly understood technologies, doubly so. A quick, if not painless, litmus test of your purpose is to find the nearest person and explain it to them:

- Can you explain what the project is in 30 seconds?
- Can you explain how you'll know if it succeeded?

"*With AI*" is not a silver bullet. If the answer to either question is *No*, or lacks clarity, consider whether the project is too loosely defined or tries to do too much. This does not mean the project is too ambitious, just that the scope needs refinement. The risk of being on the bleeding edge of technical advancements is that it's easy to fall into the trap of a solution looking for a problem or trying to tackle all the world's problems at once. Those are the projects that will fail, so identify the problems you have early, and how you will know whether they are solved.

A good product has a clearly defined purpose, a set of principles to guide it, and starts as a **minimal viable product** (**MVP**). Principles are the guardrails against which you weigh decisions as you pursue your purpose, and an MVP is the small version you can implement of the product while still having something that works end to end.

Your principles may be technical limitations, business ethics, security and compliance requirements, or business goals. These should function as the laws you cannot violate in order for your product to be successful.

In project management, principles can be represented as requirements, but also as KPIs. KPIs are not one-and-done metrics of success, but rather are continuously evaluated. As you add features and functionality to a project, your KPI metrics must continue to reflect success, or the KPI may need to be re-evaluated. An example KPI would be *Our database backups are restorable within 15 minutes,* which would need to be validated every so often (quarterly, monthly, etc.) to determine whether it's being met or not. If it's not being met, say, because database size and complexity have grown, then the KPI could be adjusted, or the process improved to match.

These can seem similar to **objectives and key results** (**OKRs**), and they can be used with or independently of each other. However, an OKR is different because it is a time-bound objective. Like KPIs, OKRs should be measurable; the *objective* may not be as measurable, but the *key results* should be easily quantified with data. The key results are how you will seek to achieve the objective you've set.

Note

An example OKR is as follows:

- **Objective**: Users are delighted by the system's reliability
- **Key result**: System availability reaches 99.99%
- **Key result**: Releases can be observed and the success measured via the DORA framework
- **Key result**: Releases that are causing instability are rolled back
- **Key result**: User satisfaction surveys are within `{Parameters}`

It's okay for an OKR to be very big picture and a KPI to be more focused. These tools are intended for different aspects of business and product management. As long as your OKRs and KPIs can be measured objectively, you're doing it right.

In addition to being helpful for shaping the technical roadmap, OKRs and KPIs are useful communication tools. How does the CEO know that the AI project is doing great things? Especially for AIOps projects, which will largely be internal-facing and not as obviously revenue-impacting, it's important to set and communicate the business value of what you're doing. KPI successes and OKRs are an easy way to demonstrate progress and define what the product you're building is about in a way that executive leadership expects. They can also help you demonstrate **return on investment** (**ROI**), where the return is not as easily translated into dollars. Remember, human time saved is ROI and can be quantified if you're measuring along the way.

Other project killers, such as cost, will be covered in *Chapter 9*, as cost management is a very important challenge to overcome, and AI has some unique aspects to cost that are not present in your more traditional software projects. However, overall, to manage cost, you must track and observe your spending. The observability tools you're already familiar with are equipped to help you do this.

Lack of expertise will be a challenge as these technologies are new and rapidly evolving. Reading texts such as this one is a great start, and you will find a *Further reading* section at the end of most chapters to help you know where to go next.

By approaching your AIOps implementation as a product, you can keep track of costs and benefits. Organize work into user stories and centralize efforts if multiple teams are working on different projects around AI and observability. A centralized effort can also help to keep ahead of spiraling costs and unmaintainable technical debt.

For more information on how to approach an initiative like this with a product mindset, we recommend *Platform Engineering for Architects*, another Packt title, written by Max Körbächer, Andreas Grabner, and Hilliary Lipsig.

# Summary

In summary, AI as we define it today is an evolving space where the technology is still seeking a level of stability that we find in older machine learning technologies. It has some strengths and weaknesses, and requires human input and data tuning to be successful at tasks. However, with engineers guiding and defining the use of AI within an organization and applying a product mindset to its governance, AI projects for operations can be a powerful tool for the modern organization. In the next chapter, we'll dive further into the use cases AIOps can solve today.

# Further reading

For more information, explore these resources:

- AI overview: `https://www.ibm.com/think/artificial-intelligence`
- Small Language Models: `https://www.ibm.com/think/topics/small-language-models`

- Catastrophic forgetting: `https://spectrum.ieee.org/catastrophic-forgetting-deep-learning`
- Recovering from catastrophic forgetting from Cornell University arXivLabs: `https://arxiv.org/abs/2501.01045`
- *Prompt Engineering for Generative AI* by James Phoenix and Mike Taylor
- Prompt engineering: `https://platform.openai.com/docs/guides/prompt-engineering`

# Join us on Discord

For discussions around the book and to connect with your peers, join us on Discord at `packt.link/discordcloud` or scan the QR code below:

# 3

# From Observability to AIOps and the Use Cases it Solves Today

"*How do we set up 10,000 custom Service-Level Objective (SLO) alerts for our critical Tier 1 API endpoints? How do I create dashboards for my top 100 applications?*" Those are common questions that we hear from engineers and application owners. Those questions come up when they try to apply the same monitoring mindset, they used 10–20 years ago: handcrafting dashboards and custom alerts for a small number of critical systems. But the world has changed. This approach is not scalable in today's ever-growing dynamic hybrid cloud infrastructure, with new applications, services, and features being developed, deployed, and released daily.

In this chapter, you will learn why we, the authors, would respond to these questions with: "*I understand where this requirement comes from! You are responsible for ensuring the health, availability, and resiliency of your digital services as they are business-critical. As your architecture has evolved over time, so must your approach to monitoring. Let us show you an easier, scalable way to achieve your requirement by leveraging cloud-native approaches to observability and AI!*"

We are building on the foundation we covered in the previous two chapters: how observability has evolved from monitoring and how the recent advancements in AI can help us better manage and understand the explosion of observability data. We will discuss how these two technologies combined can improve the day-to-day challenges faced by IT operations, SREs, application owners, and business owners in ensuring that the digital services they are responsible for are running as expected.

In this chapter, we are going to cover the following:

- When data on glass and static alerts fail
- Observability-driven development
- Context is king: the quality of observability data
- AIOps: reducing the noise with anomaly and root cause detection
- From ops to business: SLO-based impact analysis

# When data on glass and static alerts fail

"*We used to have 1,000 dashboards. Now we are down to 50!*" is how a successful observability transformation story ends. It's a transformation where data was previously placed on many dashboards, but it was not actionable. If the same can be achieved with a more focused approach to data visualization and analytics, we are moving away from "*just putting data on glass*" towards making data visualization actionable. But it often starts very differently.

"*Can our monitoring tool set 10,000 custom thresholds?*" is a question we have heard more than once. The answer is, "*Yes! But why do you have this requirement? Where does it come from?*"

Static thresholds were great on static infrastructure. When having three database production servers, five applications, and two web servers, it made sense to set static thresholds on CPU, memory, **Garbage Collection** (**GC**), worker threads, and connection pool utilization. IT operators knew those machines well. They probably gave them easy-to-remember names, such as *sql-prod-1*, *app-frontend-4*, or *ws-lb-2*. Traffic to those applications hosted on those servers was *predictable* and stable. Therefore, setting static thresholds was a good solution to get alerted if one of those servers wasn't as *healthy* as it was supposed to be.

The following dashboard is a good representation of classic infrastructure observability, with static thresholds highlighting whether individual components are healthy (green), unhealthy (red), or on the path to becoming unhealthy (orange).

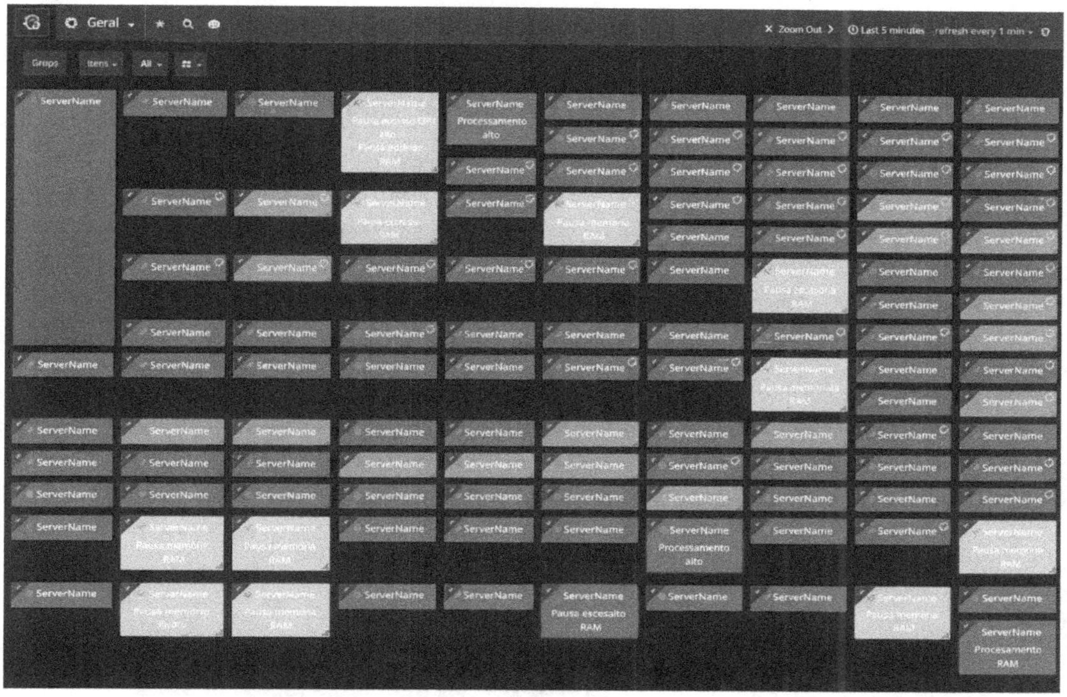


*Figure 3.1 – A static approach to visualization of health indicators doesn't scale in our cloud elastic world! (Source: https://community.grafana.com/t/status-panel-for-more-than-200-servers/2710)*

Fast forward to 2026: instead of three database production servers, we have several different database cloud services—some used for storing records, some acting as caches, and others just as a data lake. Instead of application servers that run monolithic Java applications, we have something between 100 and 500 Pods running across various Kubernetes clusters. The number of running Pods changes depending on event-driven and load-driven scaling, which is why it's hard to pinpoint a specific number at any given moment. And the web servers? Most of them have been replaced with load-balancing services, Ingress controllers, or API gateways. The architecture has changed quite a bit! But when it comes to monitoring, we often see the old mindset and approach simply being applied to modern architecture. This is where the requirement of "*Can our monitoring tool set 10,000 custom thresholds?*" comes from. Instead of a handful of neatly named servers, we now have thousands of components. If you still want to get alerted to every CPU spike or GC activity, that's when you really need to set 10,000 custom thresholds. But that's neither practical nor necessary.

## Alternatives to static alerts on infrastructure metrics

The curious mind will probably have the following questions: "*Why do you say we do not need those alerts anymore? Don't we have CPU, memory, or GC that we need to keep healthy?*"

The answer is "*Yes, we still rely on CPU, memory, disk, network, and more! But orchestration layers such as Kubernetes or cloud service providers take care of providing the right amount of CPU, memory, and disk based on the current required load. This eliminates a lot of the need for static thresholds as we leverage elastic infrastructure and automated orchestration to provide exactly the right amount of compute, memory, and storage that is needed to ensure we can deliver on our SLO.*"

You may now think: "*Wait a minute, that seems like really bad advice! We could quickly end up in a situation where our systems just keep scaling up, potentially endlessly, without any governance and cost control!*" You are spot on again! Hence, we need to clarify where we still need static thresholds, where we don't, and where we have new ways to get alerted or scale.

### Static thresholds: where they make sense

Static thresholds are still very relevant and efficient for the following:

- Well-defined critical system boundaries, such as **API rate limits**
- Known limits in runtimes or design, such as **worker threads** or **queue lengths**
- Contractual obligations such as **Service-Level Agreements** (**SLAs**) or **SLOs**
- Easily predictable metrics such as **latency**, **retries**, or **wait time**

The following figure shows how tools typically allow defining and visualizing static thresholds:

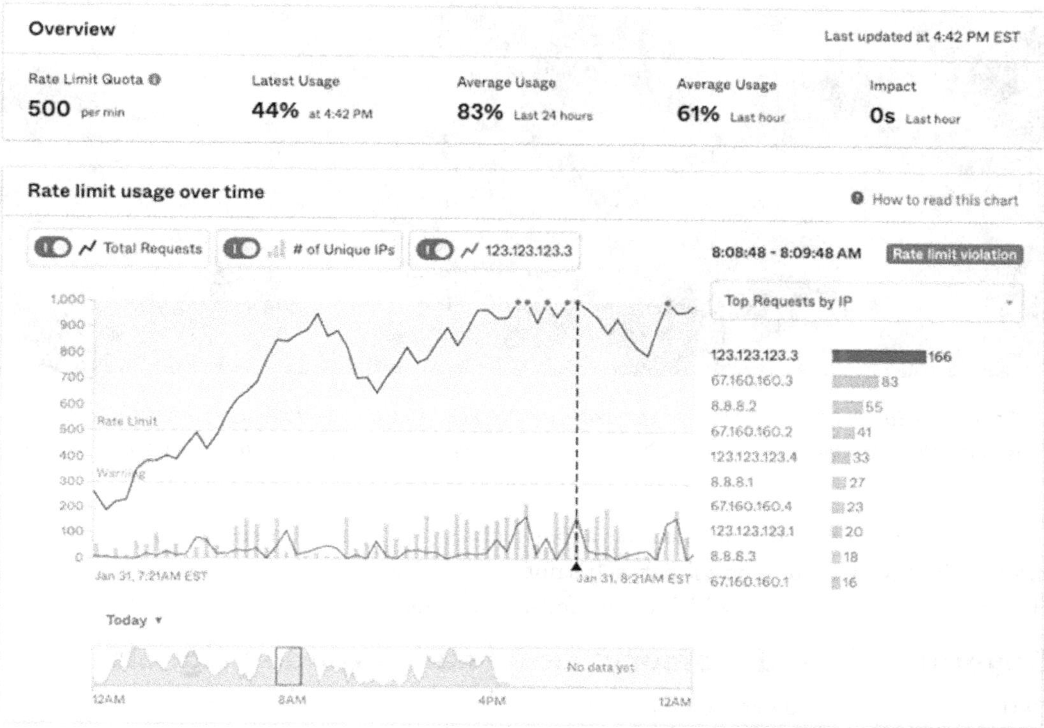


*Figure 3.2 – API rate limits are a good example of static thresholds as these are well-known system boundaries*

## Baselining: where static thresholds are impractical

In highly dynamic systems that also leverage dynamic scaling techniques, such as **Kubernetes Event Driven Autoscaling** (**KEDA**) and Karpenter (open source cluster autoscaler), we need to think about alternatives to static thresholds. Various baseline approaches exist that allow us to adapt to the dynamic nature of our workloads and environments, such as the following:

- **Auto-adaptive baselining**: Automatically adapts the threshold based on a rolling window of historical data, for example, the last seven days
- **Multi-dimensional baselining**: Calculate baselines on various data dimensions, such as service endpoints or geographics
- **Seasonal baselining**: A baseline that understands distinct seasonal behavior, such as business hours or holidays

The following figure shows that dynamic baselines are typically visualized with confidence bands, and most tools also allow adjusting the baselining methodology depending on the use case:

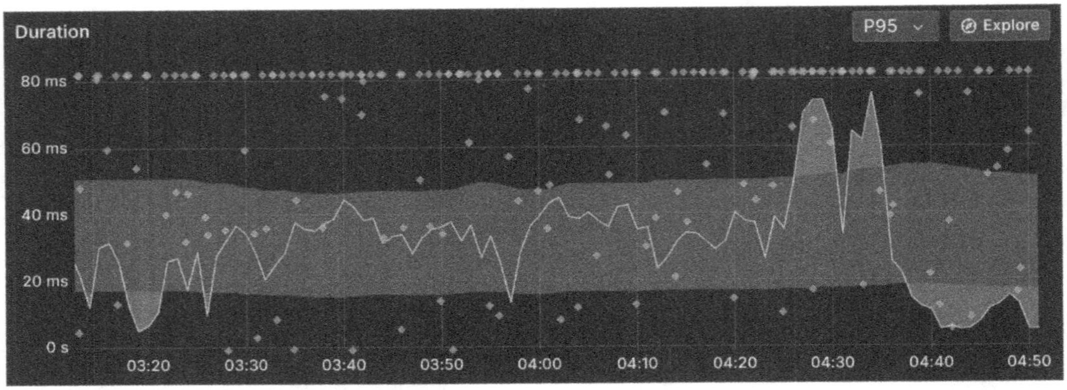


*Figure 3.3 – Baselining on certain data eliminates the need to define and manage static thresholds at scale (source: https://grafana.com/docs/grafana-cloud/monitor-applications/application-observability/manual/automatic-baseline/)*

While static thresholds will always have a role in observability, we need alternatives in our modern, highly dynamic environments. It's not only the way we set thresholds that needs to change, but also the data on which we are setting thresholds.

# Beyond CPU and memory: cloud-native golden signals

CPU, memory, disk, and network have always been great metrics to get alerted on, or as a trigger for infrastructure scaling. Expanding on that, many site reliability teams follow the Google SRE handbook's definition of the "*four golden signals*" (latency, traffic, errors, and saturation). SRE and ITOps teams, therefore, typically know the limits of their system very well and can take corrective actions to remediate the situation, for example, resizing a virtual machine to meet current memory and CPU demand, restarting a rogue or hanging process that stopped handling requests, or distributing incoming load across multiple virtual machines behind a load balancer to ensure faster individual response times.

Modern cloud-native architectures, especially container orchestrators such as Kubernetes, introduced new components, layers, and built-in automation that automate or simplify those tasks. The Kubernetes operator pattern, for instance, with its built-in control loop, automates some of those tasks that ITOps teams had to implement themselves, changing the focus for the ITOps teams:

- **Automated restarts of hung processes**: Kubernetes takes care of restarting unhealthy Pods for us. Alerting, therefore, shouldn't necessarily be on unresponsive Pods, but more when certain Pods get restarted very frequently, when restarts start having issues, or if they impact other components.

- **Automated resizing and scaling of Pods**: Kubernetes can resize (vertical scaling) or deploy more instances of (horizontal scaling) Pods based on changed resource requirements or a change in workloads. Alerting, therefore, must focus on detecting when those resizing and scaling tasks are running into issues or cause service disruptions.
- **Automated scaling of clusters**: Like any system, Kubernetes is limited to the amount of CPU, memory, and disk of all its nodes. Cluster autoscaling, however, can provision new nodes from the underlying infrastructure virtualization. Alerting, therefore, must focus on whether scaling of the cluster itself works as expected, and whether it finishes in a timely manner to avoid any disruption of the Pods that are deployed.

With some of the automation moving into the various layers of our cloud-native platform (Kubernetes, OpenShift, or managed cloud services), we need to focus on the new health indicators and then decide how to best alert on them and which ones to use for scaling decisions.

When it comes to cloud native, we—the authors—feel it's time to redefine the *golden signals* that help us monitor health and get alerted on and scale every layer of our dynamic stack. The following figure depicts a modern platform, including the indicators for each layer:

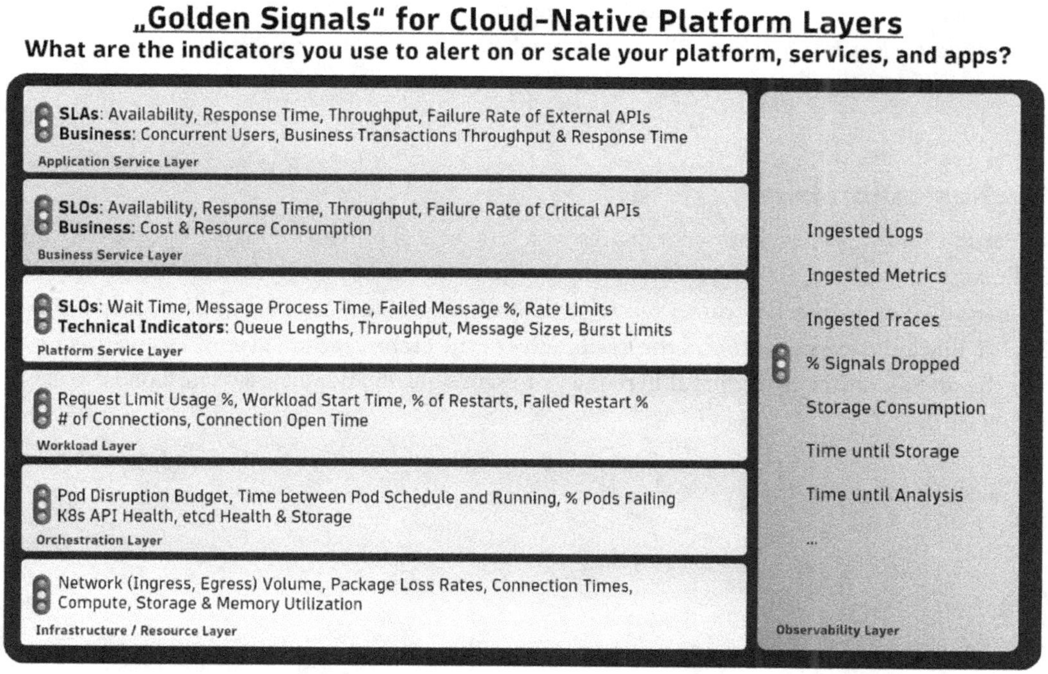


*Figure 3.4 – Golden signals redefined for cloud-native platform layers*

Let's look at some of those metrics across the cloud-native stack, starting from the infrastructure layer (bottom) to the application layer (top), as well as the observability layer (across).

## Resource layer

Without a doubt, we need sufficient resources to handle all workload requests. Doing proper testing and capacity planning and then setting up alerting and scaling based on compute, storage, and memory doesn't change all that much.

In cloud-native architectures, we see more components that communicate via various channels. More than ever, network latency, throughput, and quality of service play a critical role in overall stability and performance.

Tip

**Cloud-native observability tip for infrastructure**

We recommend baselining Ingress and Egress traffic volume. A significant spike or drop could indicate a misconfiguration, for example, a developer accidentally turning on debug logs in production or the SRE team enabling a 100% sampling rate for distributed traces. As all this data needs to be sent over the network, any change in expected behavior has the potential to impact network health for your business-critical services. The same baseline will also detect whether a misconfiguration on DNS or firewalls blocks traffic from reaching the desired destination.

## Orchestration layer

Kubernetes is the leading container orchestration layer and provides a lot of important health indicators. If you are not using Kubernetes, then your orchestration layer of choice (homegrown or an offering from a vendor) will have similar indicators that allow measuring health. Key indicators are around the availability of the orchestration layer API as well as how fast the orchestration layer can fulfill requests to schedule and deploy new workloads.

Tip

**Cloud-native observability tip for Kubernetes**

We recommend baselining the scheduling latency and deployment latency of new workloads. That's the time it takes from `kubectl apply` until Kubernetes finds the proper node to deploy it, and how long it then takes until the Pod is deployed. An increase in *pending Pods* will ultimately lead to slower deployments and is an indicator that your clusters are not healthy or don't have enough resources to fulfill all those incoming schedule and deployment requests.

## Workload layer

A workload is a set of Pods and containers that run an application or a service on a Kubernetes cluster. It defines the Pods and containers, how they should be deployed, how they are sized, and how they communicate.

The most important thing is that workloads can be started in a timely manner, keep running, or restart successfully when needed. Keeping an eye on Pod failure rates, the reasons why they fail (for example, running into limits), and the number of failed restart attempts is essential.

Tip

**Cloud-native observability tip for container workloads**

On top of that, we recommend baselining the time it takes to start a workload and how long workloads are running. The startup time depends greatly on the type of workload. A database-like workload will most likely take much longer to start and run much longer than a small microservice that is only needed for certain use cases and otherwise spun down. Init containers or dependencies, on the other hand, can also impact small workloads. We therefore recommend baselining the workload start time and workload lifetime by the type of workload. Any change in timing behavior deserves to be looked at more closely!

## Platform service layer

Platform services are typically shared services that are used by business services and applications. Examples of those are **message queues**, **service meshes**, **databases**, and other **storage services**, as well as critical shared business services such as an **authentication service** or **Single Sign-On** (**SSO**). All of these services provide some type of API to their consumers and, therefore, we see that the four golden signals (latency, throughput, errors, and saturation) are used to monitor and alert on health.

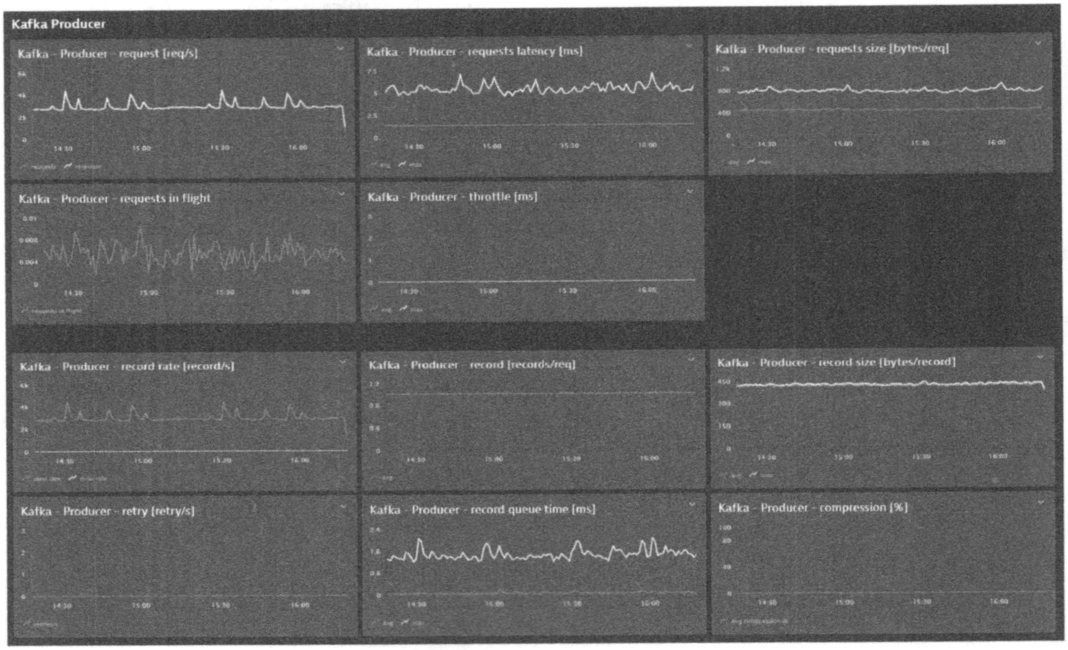


*Figure 3.5 – Key technical indicators for ensuring Kafka health*

> Tip
>
> **Cloud-native observability tip for queues and critical services**
>
> We recommend baselining key health indicators of queues, such as wait time, queue length, message sizes, compression, and processing time. A queue that keeps growing or where wait time increases over a period of time is a warning signal that needs to be addressed to avoid impacting dependent services. As most critical services also have API rate limits, it's good practice to monitor and alert on rate limit usage or burst usage. Those can indicate a misconfiguration on the caller side or a need to adjust the limits for certain callers in case of overall increased volumes of transactions.

## Service layer

With *services*, we mean all business services that power the applications that run on your platform. For a financial services organization, those might be services such as `account-service`, `trading-service`, `transfer-service`, or `currency-service`.

SLOs around availability, performance, and failure rate for those services are a good idea as they give a good indication of whether the services are delivering on their promise. While SLOs and their error budgets and burndown rate are great tools, they also come with management and operational costs when not done right, hence the following tip!

> Tip
>
> **Cloud-native observability tip on SLOs**
>
> Too often, we have seen organizations define SLOs for every single internal and external API endpoint of every service. That results in thousands of SLOs without any consistent thresholds across the organization. A better approach is to define SLOs only for end consumer APIs along the critical path of your business transactions. Even then, it's best practice to provide templates for gold, silver, and bronze or tier 1, tier 2, and tier 3 APIs with predefined company-wide standards on thresholds and alerts. For all other APIs, we suggest using anomaly detection and then seeing whether the anomaly of an internal API is really impacting the upstream SLO. More on that topic later in this chapter, in the *From ops to business: SLO-based impact analysis* section.

## Application layer

Most services provide critical APIs for business applications and their critical business transactions. Examples are the number of users that are logged in to their online banking system, creating a new bank account, or transferring money between accounts.

For any organization, this is the most critical layer, as this is where your business generates revenue or where you enable your employees to do their job!

At a high level, you want to make sure that those systems and critical transactions are available. At a minimum, we suggest using synthetic tests to validate that those key transactions work from end to end and then alert on any availability or performance degradations.

Tip

**Cloud-native observability tip on business**

We also suggest baselining key indicators on whether your business is healthy. That includes the number of concurrent active users on your system, the throughput of business processes and transactions, how long critical transactions take, and the number of transactions per user or session. If those numbers start to deviate from normal behavior during a regular day or work week, then you should act. Focusing on the business impact has become key in modern observability, which is why we cover this in more detail later in this chapter in the *From ops to business: SLO-based impact analysis* section.

## Observability layer

There is a saying: *the best comes last*. No alerting or scaling would be possible if we didn't have any observability data. Therefore, it's important that we also apply the same health principles to the observability stack. This includes the health of the instrumentation, collection, storage, and analysis. When using OpenTelemetry, for example, we need to make sure that all collectors are properly sized, all receivers are healthy, no data is dropped, and all observability signals are forwarded to the backend analytics platform.

Tip

**Cloud-native observability tip for your observability stack**

Besides following the best practices around self-monitoring of your observability tooling, we suggest baselining the received, processed, and ingested volume of all your observability signals. The baseline will show you whether you have a sudden spike or drop in observability data. Root causes could be misconfiguration or an unexpected change in manual or automated instrumentation. We have seen examples where the number of spans increased 100x because of a coding mistake using manual instrumentation.

A key indicator where a static threshold can be used is the percentage of dropped signals, as ideally, you don't have any dropped signals unless it's intentional.

The time until analysis indicator defines how long it takes from data collection until that data point is available to be charted in a dashboard or available for alerting. The longer this time, the more reactive rather than proactive your responses to issues will be.

These discussed indicators and metrics should give you a good starting point when it comes to understanding the health of your cloud-native platform. As not everyone runs on Kubernetes, OpenShift, or other container orchestration platforms, it's important to understand the layers of your specific environment. Make sure to consult the best practices documentation of the vendors you use. A great additional and recommended way to choose the right metrics is by conducting some load and performance tests.

# Choosing the right metrics through proper load testing

Every application and distributed system is unique. Therefore, it's not possible to provide a golden rule template that includes all metrics one should keep an eye on. While the metrics we discussed previously will be important for most systems, it's important to understand the characteristics and dynamic behavior of your system under different conditions.

Load and performance testing is a key practice that helps you understand the dynamic behavior of your application. It allows you to identify the critical components in your architecture, for example, which queues or shared services are causing ripple effects when they start slowing down or failing, or what the expected maximum throughput a critical component can handle is before it starts breaking.

Going into all of the relevant details about setting up proper load testing is beyond the scope of this book. We do, however, want to give you some guidance on what the key steps are and give you pointers on where to find more information.

## Step 1: setting up a test environment

We could stop right here if you can *test in production*. For very *bold* people, that means you don't do any upfront testing at all and just deploy and react to whatever happens. For those who are less adventurous, it may mean using the failover production environment for load testing. Some organizations also use the live production system during *low traffic times*. Both scenarios depend heavily on how your production environment is set up and whether it's possible to deploy a different version of your software in those environments. For those who can't do that, please keep reading.

Ideally, test environments reflect production environments as closely as possible. This, however, is not always possible due to the costs of running those large systems and the time it takes to set up and operate such a system. While standing up the required infrastructure for a short period of time has gotten easier, thanks to automation and on-demand available cloud resources, it's most often very challenging to replicate *production-like* datasets of your **systems of records**.

There is plenty of material available online about how to overcome some of these challenges, such as generating representative production data without running into any compliance issues or even considering mocking or simulating those data layers.

If a production-like system is not achievable, we suggest setting up a scaled-down version that you can stand up and operate within acceptable costs, because it helps you understand which indicators across your layers are leading indicators for problems at scale. And remember, that's really what this exercise is all about.

## Step 2: defining realistic scenarios

When testing a sports car, you would not just test it by driving in first gear at 20 miles per hour. That would not reflect how the car will be used by a real driver. The same is true for software testing. Before creating any test scenarios, you need to understand what the top real end user scenarios are. Ideally, you would get this information from the owners of the applications and services you are testing. Also, ideally, you would simply look into your observability stack and extract this information from there; for example, what are the top hit APIs, or what are the most common click sequences in your web UI or API call chains? Also, you can get a sense of how this load is distributed across those scenarios and in the course of a regular 24-hour day. These are all insights that allow you to best model your load test to be *as close as possible* to production.

Once you have this, you can pick your load-testing tool of choice and create your test scenarios.

There is no shortage of available tools, including lots of open source options, such as JMeter, Gatling, k6, and Locust. Pick the one that works best for you and allows you to easily create and maintain your test scenarios.

## Step 3: expand-left observability

The term *shift left* has been used quite a bit over the past years. Typically, this means that we shift tasks and responsibilities earlier in the **Software Development Life Cycle** (**SDLC**). A better term for our case is *expand left* because what we really want to do is expand the usage of tools and practices from production earlier into the life cycle. For testing, this means we simply use the same observability tools and practices for our load-testing environment. This not only allows us to capture relevant data to identify our critical indicators for production monitoring but also allows us to validate that our observability setup works as expected. For example, are you capturing all your logs, metrics, and traces? Can you access them in the way you expect to in production? Does your observability setup alert you on bottlenecks during your load testing automatically because you have set up some dynamic baselines or use machine learning to identify anomalies?

We hope you can see how powerful the concept of "expand left" is.

## Step 4: running tests

Ideally, you would run your tests continuously, kind of like simulating production load all the time. This allows you to continuously validate that your test system can be run. It also allows you to identify how the system behaves under continuous load. For example, this approach is great to identify any memory or connection leaks that only materialize after a certain time. If you have such a setup, you can also validate how a running system behaves under load when you deploy a new version of a component while it's still under load. That's a great test as this is what will happen in production when you have to roll out a new change.

Now, if such a continuous test is not possible, then we suggest running shorter tests at a regular cadence, maybe once a day or a couple of times per week. This provides continuous feedback to your engineers and gives you continuous insights into how changes affect the internal behavior of the system.

There are also different types of tests with different load behaviors, such as increased load, steady load, spike tests, and stress testing. You can find more information about different simulated behaviors and their goal in many online resources. You can also apply chaos testing, where you simulate failures throughout the load test to bring the system into a critical situation, for example, artificially slowing down a network connection, killing Pods, or turning off a critical service such as your database.

All of these tests and the simulated chaos should give you plenty of observability data to analyze and identify new technical indicators that you can apply to your production monitoring and alerting. This brings us to the next step.

## Step 5: identifying critical indicators

Load tests fulfill several purposes. On one side, they tell us whether the system behaves as expected under the simulated load. On the other side, they allow us to optimize system parameters and configuration to optimize the system's output under load, for example, tweaking our connection pool sizes or adapting resource and request limits on our containers for optimal resource usage. It also allows us to validate that our observability captures all the data we need to identify problems, performance bottlenecks, and their root causes. This gives us more confidence that, once we deploy in production, we can also find those root causes if there is an issue in production that we need to fix. If we didn't find any indication of an issue when we should have, then it means we need to think about what additional metrics, logs, or traces we need our developers to put into their system for better insights!

The other benefit is that we can look at all the data collected after the test is finished and see whether there are certain metrics, logs, or traces that contain information that serves as early warning indicators of a performance or availability problem that was uncovered during the test.

Once you have those indicators, make sure to monitor them in production as well. Use them as early warning health indicators, as we discussed earlier in this chapter. Also remember that as systems constantly change with every release, you want to continuously validate and update those critical indicators as they may change over time.

Now you should understand that modern observability is about looking beyond CPU, memory, and disk. While those metrics still play an important role, we have new indicators of system health, for example, how fast a Kubernetes cluster can deploy Pods. We also discussed that setting and maintaining static thresholds for alerting doesn't scale when we have to deal with thousands of cloud-native components compared to traditional architectures. There are simple and sophisticated baselining algorithms that modern observability platforms provide as an alternative that automatically adjust their alerting based on historic behavior.

To conclude this section, let's look at a specific implementation scenario from one of the organizations we have worked with.

## Use case: baseline alerting on Kubernetes health

There are various ways to define the health of a system, and the same is true for Kubernetes. One method to observe health is to look into how well and successfully Kubernetes provisions the requested resources. The nature of Kubernetes is that it retries failed attempts, thanks to its implementation of the controller and operator pattern. Therefore, just alerting on a failure is not a good thing because the system will retry upon failure. A better way is to analyze trends and alert on abnormal behavior. This is where a baseline is a perfect fit. The following screenshot shows using a baseline on the number of **Kubernetes Provisioning Failed** events. When we ingest these events, we can baseline what "normal" looks like and then alert on "abnormal" or "out of baseline" situations, as shown in the following graph:

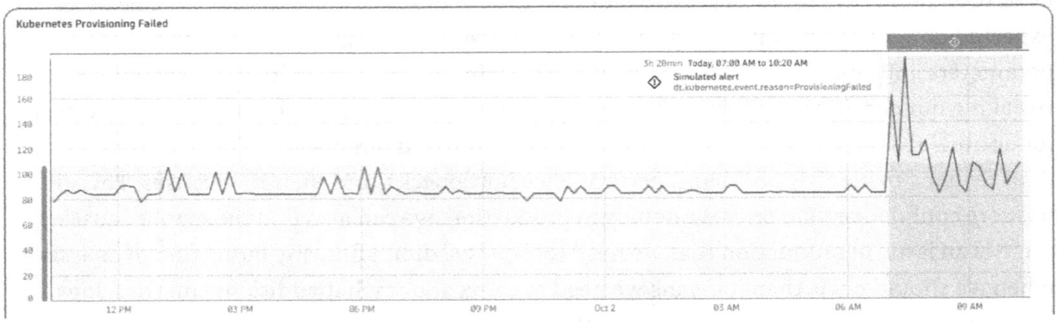


*Figure 3.6 – Baseline-based alerting on the number of Kubernetes Provisioning Failed events is better than using static thresholds*

The preceding graph shows that at 7:00 a.m., there was an unusually high number of provisioning failed events. Using a static threshold would potentially lead to too many false positives, as we can see that there are constant failed events happening. Using a baseline here also means our alerting will automatically adjust if the "base error events" decrease or increase over time. What we are really after is abnormal, out-of-baseline behavior.

Now that we have seen practical cases of how to elevate monitoring from static threshold alerting on well-known infrastructure metrics to leveraging baselining across the different layers of a modern platform, it's time to think about how we can fundamentally change the approach to observability.

We need to move from trying to understand a system once it's running in production toward having software engineering teams including observability as a key software requirement before even starting to write a line of code.

# Observability-driven development

"*Here is the new software package from development. Now, you in operations take it and figure out how to run it in a stable way.*" This is the classical "*throw it over the DevOps wall*" mentality that many organizations applied in the past.

We can debate whether the term *shift left* or *expand left* is a better description for embedding observability as a requirement earlier in the software development process. We, the authors, prefer the term **observability-driven development** because it describes the mental shift that needs to happen within an organization to treat observability as a software requirement. Similar to **test-driven development**, which focuses on creating tests before writing the business code, observability-driven development focuses on defining *what* and *how* to observe software before it gets deployed for the first time in a testing or production environment.

Transformations such as this don't happen overnight or because somebody mandates it. As with many other transformations, it has proven successful to start with a **lighthouse project** that executes on the new way of embedding observability in the development process. If that project succeeds, others will follow. Let us walk you through the key ideas and steps for such a lighthouse project's implementation.

## Step 1: defining internal and external system health indicators

When you look at your mobile phone and see the battery charge turning from green to yellow and eventually red, you know that you must act quickly, otherwise your phone will die. The same is true when driving a car and the dashboard shows the engine's heat moving toward the red zone. This means the engine is moving to an unhealthy state that could result in unrepairable damage. The root cause can be bad driving, such as putting the motor in constant high RPMs, or it could be a leakage of cooling water.

Just like those simple health indicators, we need to define how to measure the health of our software systems and components. We typically start with measuring health from how the system is perceived by the caller or consumer of the system. When the system is called through an API, we can follow the best practices around the four golden signals:

- **Throughput**: Can our system process the number of requests per time interval that we designed it for?
- **Latency**: Can our system finish processing the request in a time acceptable to our end users?
- **Errors**: Is our system returning valid responses for valid inputs most of the time?
- **Saturation**: Is our system using the expected resources based on our capacity planning?

But as with our example of the car engine overheating, we must define additional technical leading indicators to get alerted before the system becomes unhealthy for the user. We need to define metrics that give us an early warning signal and can also be used for root cause analysis. Here are examples:

- **Cache hit ratio**: For systems that have internal caches, this metric is a great indicator of whether the cache works as expected or needs an update before it impacts overall performance and stability.
- **GC**: For memory churn-intensive systems, GC runs and GC time are good internal health indicators. A change in behavior suggests that there might be some memory leak, or that the memory behavior has changed, which may require adjustment to heap sizes or GC strategies.
- **Incorrect request format**: For any request/response systems, it's important not to waste too much time on incoming messages that have an incorrect format. It's typically a sign of wrong usage by the caller or could also indicate some type of denial-of-service attack. Knowing the percentage of incoming request messages that are invalid by nature can be a good health indicator as it allows us to react to the problem before it impacts the processing of correct messages.

Once we know what good external and internal health indicators are, we need to make sure these indicators can be measured.

## Step 2: defining how to measure health indicators

For most health indicators, there might already be an existing way to extract them from logs, metrics, or traces. The response time of an API, for example, is something we can measure by enabling a Prometheus exporter on the Ingress controller or extracting it from the HTTP request logs. If none is available, developers can export additional data using Prometheus or OpenTelemetry, or write it as a log that can then be converted into a metric in the data pipeline, for example, through the OpenTelemetry Collector. When using an agent-based observability approach, chances are high that you get those metrics out of the box without any additional development involvement.

For system-specific internal indicators, such as *incorrect request format* or *roundtrips to the database*, or any business indicators, such as *number of opened bank accounts*, it will be necessary to define how to measure them and how to expose this information to the observability tool (Prometheus, OpenTelemetry, logs, and so on). You also need to specify what value ranges of those metrics indicate healthy or unhealthy; otherwise, nobody would take action if those indicators fall outside the expected value range.

## Step 3: providing easy access to this data for engineering

*Capture everything, everywhere, and make it easily accessible!* This is the only way observability-driven development has a chance to become adopted as it avoids an additional step for engineers to find the data they are looking for.

For this to work, we need to answer two critical questions.

### Where was the data captured, and who needs it?

Later in this chapter, in the *Context is king: the quality of observability data* section, we will dive deeper into how we can enrich observability when it gets captured with all this additional metadata. This metadata is needed to answer the following question.

### Where and when does this data need to be made available, and to whom?

First, we need to learn which tools our engineers use on a day-to-day basis and where they spend most of their time for certain tasks:

- Which IDP is used for self-service, for example, Backstage, Kratix, or Confluence?
- Which IDE is used for coding, for example, Visual Studio Code or IntelliJ?
- Which Git platform is used for commits, for example, GitHub, GitLab, or Bitbucket?

- Which chat platform is used for communication, for example, Slack, MSTeams, or Discord?
- Which ticketing system is used for task management, for example, Jira or ServiceNow?

Next, we need to analyze what decisions engineers need to make in these tools for which tasks and how observability data can help. For example, when troubleshooting problems, would engineers benefit more from viewing the latest critical logs of their components in their service catalog, or would it be more efficient if they got this information presented in a new Jira bug ticket?

A good example of how these thoughts materialize is explained in the following self-service use case that was implemented by an airline to improve software quality and performance based on observability data without having engineers identify hotspots themselves.

### Self-service use case 1: providing the top three database queries for team standup

Most development teams have daily standups to discuss their daily tasks and get advice from their colleagues on things they are blocked on right now. This is a perfect opportunity for observability as a self-service.

By leveraging distributed traces that include calls to database queries, the team can build automation that identifies the top three database queries per service in the last 24 hours running in production, similar to what we discussed in *Chapter 1*, in the *Observing databases* section. With the additional context-enriched information about which teams own that service and in which version that service is currently deployed, they can also send this information directly to the team's internal chat channel just in time for their 8 a.m. standup.

This is an immediate value moment for engineers as they get actionable insights provided in the tools where they spend their time discussing issues, such as Slack or MSTeams.

## Step 4: refining, enriching, and automating toward production

*"Is this data really useful? Can you take action on it? Would this help you to troubleshoot a problem if it happens in production?"*

If the answer to these questions is no, then it is time to refine the definition of health indicators and update what data you are capturing and what you do with this data.

As software moves closer to production, you also want to ask these questions: "*Is there a health indicator that you want to get alerted on? One that should trigger scaling? Or one you need to access when troubleshooting a problem?*"

The answers to these questions will allow you to set up alerts—using either custom thresholds or baselines, as discussed earlier in this chapter. Those alerts can then either create a problem ticket for troubleshooting or trigger a self-service GitOps process by opening up a pull request, as explained in the next self-service use case.

## Self-service use case 2: right-sizing container recommendations as a Git pull request

Specifying good requests and resource limits is a very challenging thing. That is why most workload definitions on Kubernetes do not have any limits at all or just rely on defaults.

Having metrics for the actual CPU and memory consumption of containers and comparing that with the current set limits allows us to build automation that automatically opens up a pull request with suggested limits that are aligned with actual resource requirements from a production system.

This is an immediate value moment for engineers as they get actionable insights provided in the development process they are following, for example, a pull request with suggestions on how to modify the workloads.

We will cover this use case in more detail in the *AIOps: reducing the noise with anomaly and root cause detection* section, as it requires both automation and some GenAI to correctly open a pull request with proper formatting of those Kubernetes workload definitions.

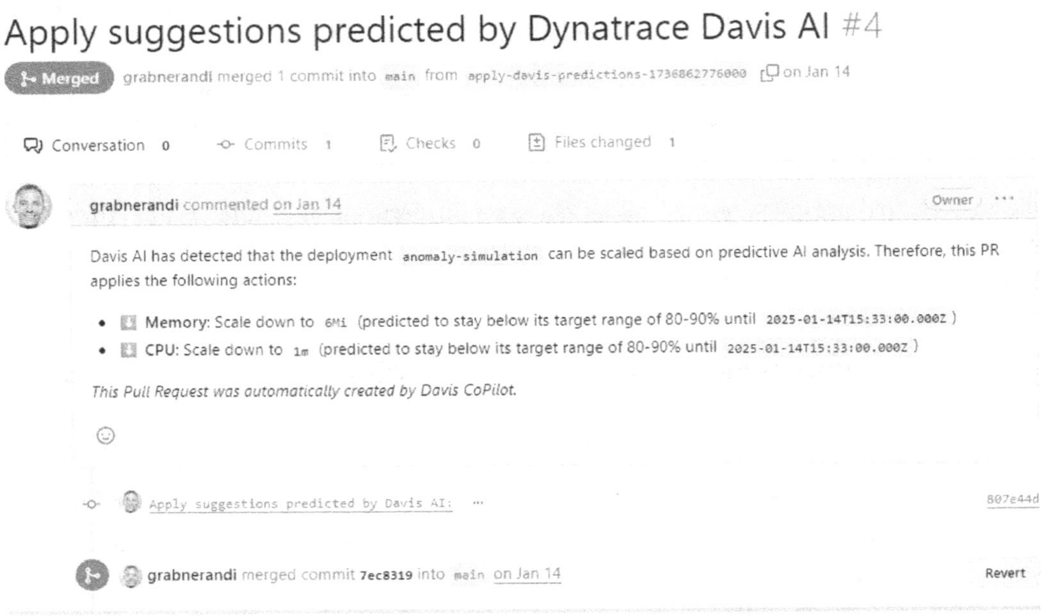


*Figure 3.7 – Automated pull request with suggested request limits based on observability data*

These two simple yet powerful self-service use cases highlight how important ingesting context-enriched observability data across the full stack is. We will cover more use cases throughout the book, especially when we talk about how those use cases align with self-service platforms.

When following these steps, there is a high chance that both operations and development will see the benefit of this approach; operations gains insight into what observability data is important for a new software component, eliminating the need for their own research or identifying it during an outage as part of a triage session. Development, on the other hand, defines what information is important for them and gains access to this data whenever they need it, making the troubleshooting and fixing issues process faster and easier.

The more software teams that adopt this new approach, the more observability data will be captured. But more is not always better, especially when data is captured without the right context about the software component, version, and team. To scale modern observability that starts in development, we must therefore define a good strategy for enriching our data with more context. This enables many new use cases, such as those already discussed earlier, for example, sending the top database queries to the responsible team. It also ensures that the IT operations team is not drowning in data and potential alerts without knowing who is responsible for this and who the data should be sent to.

Let's dive into the details!

# Context is king: the quality of observability data

We've said it before and we'll say it again: *observability data is growing and will continue to do so!*

The challenge is how to deal with that growth and ensure that it provides valuable insights, rather than just letting it sit in a big lake of data that accumulates costs for storage.

We know that we need the help of AI to manage this data, but AI can only help us if the data is of the right quality and is enriched with enough context about where it comes from, how it relates to other data, and which part of the data is needed for decision-making.

We will walk through best practices around how and where to enrich data and the use cases where this enriched data enables us to get more value out of our observability implementation.

Let's start with the challenge of scale and the need for semantic conventions.

## From pets to cattle: semantics for observability

If you have managed infrastructure before, you have probably heard about the *pets versus cattle* analogy. Instead of treating every server like a unique, cared-for pet with a lovely name and even a remembered birthday, we need to think about infrastructure more like cattle. **Cattle thinking** means that we have a potentially unlimited number of components that we treat as disposable and replaceable when problems occur. For that to scale, we also need to think about automating tasks versus manually taking care of every individual component.

In cloud-native architectures, there are no pet names by default. But there are certain semantic conventions when naming entities. Objects in Kubernetes, for instance, get a new **Unique Identifier** (**UID**) when the resource gets created and a **generated name** that will be different for every new object instance even though the object may have been created before. Take a Pod as an example. If you create a workload with the name `my-critical-svc`, then every Pod for that workload (can be a single replica or multiple) will have a unique name, such as `my-critical-svc-1694` and `my-critical-svc-4352`, whenever the Pod gets restarted or scaled up.

This also means that in observability, we need to adjust the way we think about monitored entities: a host, cluster, node, workload, Pod, service, serverless function, or database. All of these entities might no longer just have a unique name throughout their lifetime, especially when they are restarted, scaled up, or scaled down. Gone are the days of creating a dashboard for servers named Joe, Sally, and Hugo. Instead, we now create dashboards that are specific to certain use cases and tech stacks, which can then be filtered based on agreed-upon metadata with standardized semantics. This metadata can be extracted from labels, annotations, or tags applied to the cattle infrastructure we are observing.

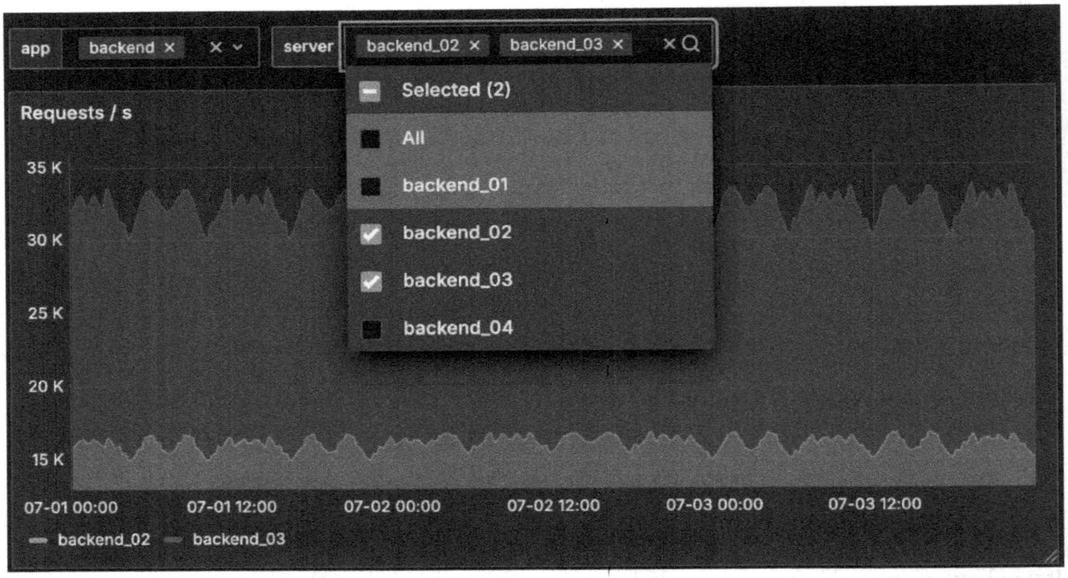


*Figure 3.8 – Observability dashboard that can be filtered by metadata such as service name, server, cluster, or cloud region (source: https://grafana.com/docs/grafana/latest/dashboards/variables/)*

Let's dive into modern best practices around organizing observability data that scales with our organizational and operational needs.

# Enriching observability data across the stack

When it comes to organizing our observability data and enriching it with context, we need to look at all metadata across the full stack (from host to namespace, to container, to service, to endpoint). A log line, for example, must not just be enriched with the information from which API call it was generated from. It should also contain information about the Pod, workload, namespace, Kubernetes node, and cloud region. This is essential for troubleshooting and root cause analysis, as we can answer critical questions:

- Does this error happen across all our cloud regions?
- Does it happen across all of the various versions of our Kubernetes clusters?
- Is it limited to a specific deployment with a very specific configuration?

Let's discuss the best practices for context enrichment from the top to the bottom of the stack.

## Enriching with tags from your infrastructure

Most infrastructure teams have worked out a good way to tag their infrastructure. When creating new virtual machines through IaC tools such as Terraform, Ansible, Chef, or AWS CloudFormation, the individual server instance typically follows a naming scheme but is enriched with tags that indicate why this infrastructure exists, what its purpose is, and who owns it. Here's an example:

- **Name**: `foneacme_p_w_csp_web3`
- **Environment**: `Production`, `Dev`, `Staging`
- **Group**: `Web`, `DevTools`, `BusinessApps`, `Backoffice`
- **Application**: `CustomerServicePortal`, `OnlineBanking`, `TimeManagement`, `Salary`, `SalesPortal`
- **Project**: `Project-A`, `Project-B`, `Project-C`
- **Owner**: `CustomerService`, `Engineering-TeamA`, `LOB-OnlineBanking`, `SalesUSEast`, `CFO`
- **CostCenter**: `Dev`, `Sales`, `Finance`, `LOB`

To learn more about good tagging strategies, please consult the available white papers and best practices documentation of your cloud partner, such as the *Best Practice for Tagging AWS Resources[1]*.

When ingesting logs, metrics, traces, or any type of events (deployment, configuration, security, and so on), the best practice is to enrich those signals with the same tags. This ensures proper filtering, alerting, and access control, which is all managed through all the already-available tags and doesn't need to be configured on top of the metadata that already exists. To continue the previous example, let's discuss two scenarios.

### Use case: logs only accessible for sales

If logs from the sales portal backend are ingested with the `Owner:SalesUSEast` tag, then these logs are most likely only for the eyes of the sales organization of that region, as well as for the global sales team. The backend observability storage can be set up so that all logs with that tag can only be seen by those team members by specifying what some observability vendors refer to as the *security context*.

### Use case: traces from development only kept for two sprints

When ingesting traces in the lower-level development environments, and those traces are enriched with the `Environment:Dev` tag, they may only be stored for two sprints. Why? Because traces captured during a development cycle are typically only relevant for the time when active development is done. Most developers don't need traces from their development environment at a later time. So, retention of those traces can be set to a shorter timeframe, and with this, the organization can save on observability storage and retention costs.

Think about your own current tagging strategy for your infrastructure and make sure that those tags can be used to enrich any ingested observability signal, including logs, metrics, traces, events, real user data, and profiling.

After looking at these use cases, let's move a level up the stack: from infrastructure to your application deployments!

## Enriching with tags, labels, and annotations from your deployment

Infrastructure allows us to deploy applications and services. When deploying workloads on Kubernetes, serverless functions, or any other cloud SaaS services, such as load balancers or database services, we can specify additional metadata about those deployments in the form of more tags, labels, or annotations.

Here is a snapshot of a Kubernetes Deployment definition template with additional metadata around the version, environment, service dependencies, and environment:

```
template:
  metadata:
    labels:
      dt.owner: "engineering-team1"
      app.kubernetes.io/name: authentication-svc
      app.kubernetes.io/part-of: customer-service-portal
      app.kubernetes.io/version: 4.0.2
      dynatrace-release-stage: "preprod"
      backstage.io/component: "default.authentication-svc"
```

Similar to the tags on your infrastructure, these labels can be used to enrich any ingested log, metric, trace, or event from the Kubernetes Pods that run based on this deployment. This will then enable use cases such as the following.

### Use case: is version 4.0.3 good enough to keep, or do we need to roll it back?

When analyzing metrics, logs, or traces, we can now compare the difference in response time, execution behavior, memory consumption, or error logs between different versions of a service. If the team decides to push a new version to a group of customers, they can now selectively analyze and compare those signals. Additionally, we can leverage AI and automatic anomaly detection between data on different metadata. This allows the development team to get an automated alert if a newly released version sees a higher failure rate than the previous one. This allows the team to quickly roll back to the more stable version.

### Use case: is the quality of customer-service-portal in preproduction good enough for production?

Ingesting deployment signals enriched with metadata from all environments (development, quality assurance, preproduction, and production) also makes it easy to compare versions. Too often, the question comes up: "*Will the new version we have in preproduction be better than what we have in production?*" By having the metadata on logs, metrics, and traces, you can actively compare performance, errors, and runtime behavior to make a more informed decision about promoting a new version from preproduction to production.

## Enriching observability data across the SDLC

We talked about enriching our observability data with information across the stack so that we know that a log, metric, or trace comes from a specific data center region, cluster, namespace, workload, pod, or service. We can even enrich it with information about our release version or deployment stage.

The enriched observability data is already the basis for what we call SDLC observability. Let's dive deeper and explain what problems it solves.

## Tracking the SDLC

"*Where is my build? How long does it take to get a code fix into production? Which Git commit just broke production?*" These are some of the questions we briefly discussed in *Chapter 1* in the *Three pillars and beyond – use cases for logs, metrics, and traces* section. It was about ingesting events from any tool that is involved in the SDLC when creating, building, testing, or deploying software artifacts. This might include tools such as Backstage, Jira, GitHub, SonarQube, Jenkins, Harbor, Argo, or any other tool you have in your DevOps toolchain.

The following figure gives an overview of such representative SDLC events and from which tools they can be ingested (typically through webhooks, notifications, event logs, or traces):

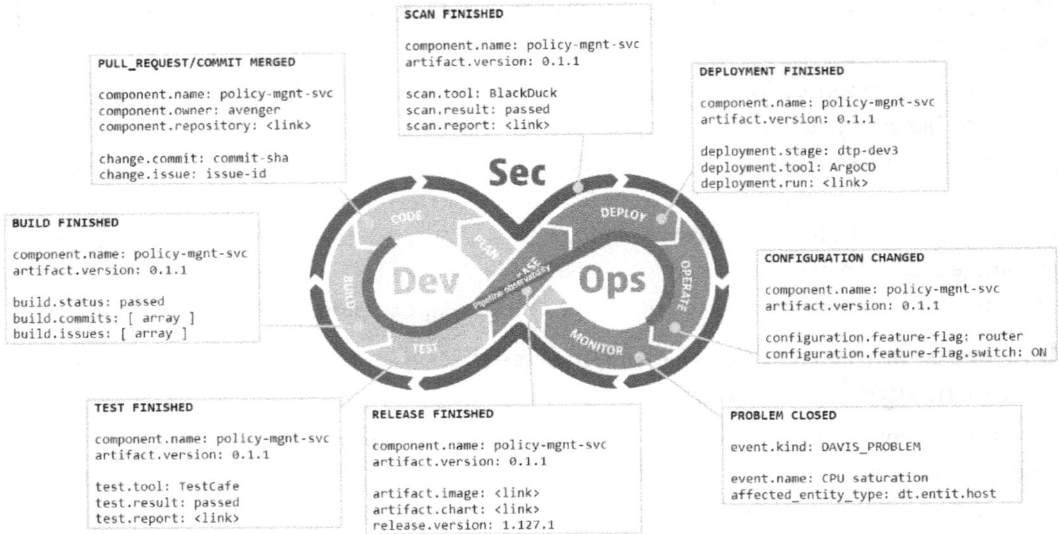


*Figure 3.9 – SDLC as a standard to track the life cycle of artifacts*

Ingesting these events into the observability backend and connecting them with the logs, metrics, and traces from the running processes or Pods of those artifacts enables the following use cases.

## Use case: automated real-time artifact inventory and software catalog

By ingesting events from every delivery pipeline run (GitHub Actions, GitLab pipeline, Azure DevOps, Jenkins, Argo, Flux, and so on), including information about which artifact was deployed in which environment, we can provide an automated real-time overview that answers questions such as: *Which service in which version was deployed where, and by whom?*

In most organizations, answering this question is very hard. Observability across the life cycle provides these insights out of the box.

## Use case: tracking DORA and other DevEx efficiency metrics

By ingesting events from Git commits, pull requests, pipeline runs, and deployments that contain the same metadata about the artifact (for example, which image version was built), we can provide automated real-time information such as **lead time for change** (time from commit to deploy) or **deployment frequency** (how often a component gets deployed).

Most engineering leads try to capture these metrics in a consistent way across the organization to provide engineering efficiency insights. Using SDLC events allows you to provide those KPIs and more to your engineering leads.

## Use case: automated correlation of deployment changes with problems

When ingesting deployment or configuration change events into the same observability backend that monitors the health of the deployed components, we can automatically correlate those changes to detected problems. This allows us to automatically answer the question: "*Did my Git commit break production?*"

Besides automatically correlating the event to a problem and identifying it as the potential root cause, we can also set up automation that can immediately open up a new pull request that suggests rolling back the change that is currently causing an issue. Mature organizations often adopt this as a standard approach to automated remediation.

A side benefit of integrating our DevOps tools into observability by having them send events on critical life cycle stages is that we can expand on this and also observe these tools in terms of health and activity. After all, nothing is worse for a development team than having the supporting tools fail when they are most needed.

# Observing your DevOps tools

"*Why is Jira so slow today? Why is my latest code change still not running through our build pipeline? Why do I keep getting errors when using our Visual Studio Code AI agent for code reviews?*"

Sometimes the answers to these questions are straightforward. It could be that Jenkins pipelines are taking longer to execute because of a shared infrastructure issue. Jira might be unavailable because of a misconfigured network route, or a misconfigured MCP server might have executed too many GitHub API calls, causing your other users to run into rate limiting.

While those answers sound simple, they are typically not identified automatically, but only when people have been impacted and started to complain.

Thanks to the broader adoption of open standards such as OpenTelemetry, we see better observability support built into all those tools. This allows us to apply the same observability practices on those tools as we apply to our business-critical apps.

Ideally, you should also set up observability with proper alerting for your Jira, GitHub, GitLab, Argo, Harbor, and similar tools. This gives you the chance to fix problems before they impact the majority of your engineers.

The following is a dashboard based on OpenTelemetry traces out of GitHub and GitHub Actions, giving insights into activities across all repositories of a GitHub organization, with indications on problematic repositories or workflows. Having this insight helps you keep your tools running healthily.

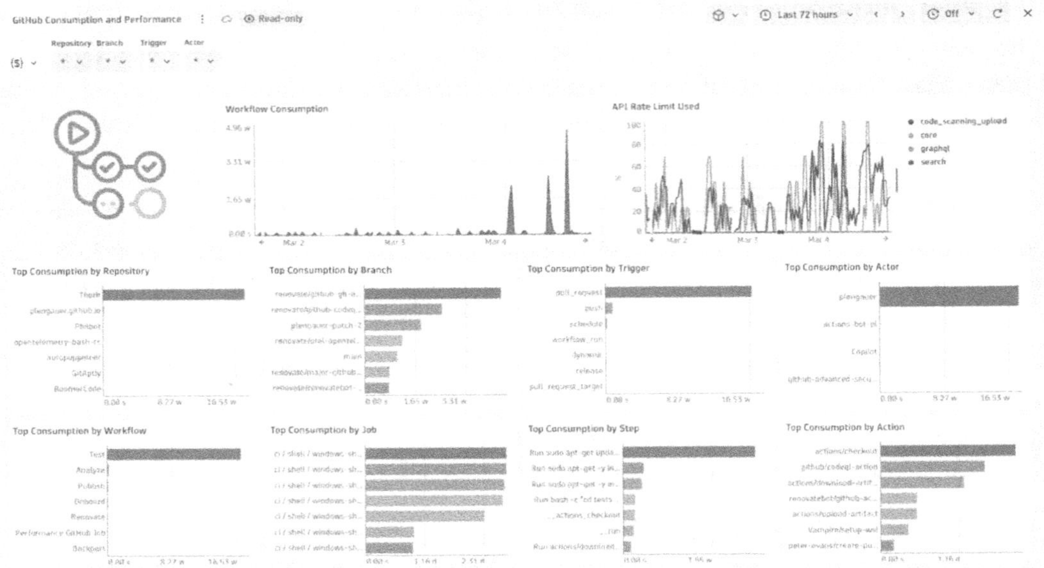


*Figure 3.10 – Open standards such as OpenTelemetry provide observability into new use cases, such as observing your DevOps tools*

As a thought experiment, think about all the tools that you have in your engineering organization. How many of them have proper observability and alerting set up? Which ones don't? And how many engineering hours could you have saved by having a proper alerting setup to fix problems before they impact the majority of your engineering teams?

We hope that by now you have a good basic understanding of modern observability and how high-quality context-enriched observability data enables automation and AI to produce better actionable insights as you are developing, deploying, and operating your IT software systems. In the *AIOps: reducing the noise with anomaly and root cause detection* section, we will see how all of this fits together to make the day-to-day life of those engineers who need to keep systems up and running easier.

To conclude this section, we need to address one question that has probably already occurred to you: "*This seems like a lot of data that also needs to be enriched with even more data points. How do we ensure its quality and manage the quantity?*"

# Quality of data: where to enrich it and what to sample

We have talked a lot about how we need to enrich observability data by providing more context across the stack and the SDLC. The remaining questions are about where to enrich our logs, metrics, traces, and events, and how to strike the right balance between capturing everything and capturing what we need, to control costs and make data analysis more efficient.

## How and where to enrich observability data with context

Enriching observability data close to the source, where it gets generated, is the best and most efficient way to increase the quality of your observability data. Quality is what matters once we start discussing how the observability data can be analyzed using machine learning or AI. As the saying goes: *garbage in, garbage out.*

The same is true for observability data. *Only* if the observability data is of good quality and enriched with additional context will we be able to leverage the full potential of AI. Why? Because, like humans, AI will produce better outcomes on better observability data.

In other words: *high-quality observability in, high-quality insights out.*

Depending on the tooling used for collecting observability data, there are different options for when and where to enrich it. Observability agents from vendors typically enrich the logs, metrics, traces, and events right where the agent picks up those signals. For example, Dynatrace's OneAgent has the option to enrich the data right at the cluster, host, or process level. Dynatrace also has a public semantic dictionary that defines what metadata it looks for and what it will do with the observability data once it gets analyzed[2]. A common alternative is to use a data pipeline such as the OpenTelemetry Collector. The Collector provides so-called processors that allow defining rules of what additional metadata should be used to enrich logs, metrics, or traces before they are sent to the observability backend. For best practices on OpenTelemetry enrichment, check out the many available tutorials and best practices, such as the GitHub tutorials from *isItObservable [3].*

## Do we need all the data? Sampling strategies

While context-enriched data is higher in quality and easier to analyze, we also need to bring up an important question: "*Do we really need all observability data all the time?*"

Think about a bank that wants to observe every single banking transaction from end to end with logs, metrics, and traces. With potentially thousands of transactions per second, we are talking about a lot of data. That's a lot of data that needs to be captured, enriched with context, transmitted to the backend, stored, and later analyzed if a transaction fails. But what if only 0.1% of transactions ever fail? Do we still need the successful 99.9% in all of that detail? Or is it enough to capture a representative sample of that data in detail and just create metrics for the total number of transactions and the response time for reporting and alerting?

These are very critical questions that we need to answer that will have a major impact on the size and cost of the observability backend where all this data gets stored.

If we decide that we do not need all the data in all its detail, we can apply **sampling strategies**. As the name implies, sampling is about making a decision on which observability data should be part of the sample that we look at and store, and which is ignored because it doesn't give us any additional value.

The topic of observability data sampling is too big to cover as part of this book. There is plenty of literature and best practices available from the OpenTelemetry community. Observability vendors also provide good documentation about the sampling strategies that their agents or data pipelines provide. Some of them provide basic percentage-based sampling, while others provide highly sophisticated sampling by dynamically adjusting sampling rates based on observed behavior in logs and traces of individual service endpoints, workloads, or infrastructure components.

If you go down the route of implementing your data pipeline yourself and decide not to use agents with built-in automated sampling strategies, be aware that you have to take care of sampling yourself! For that, you need to become familiar with the available strategies in the tools you are using.

As a reference, please review the following key sampling strategies and their approaches:

- **Probabilistic sampling**: You define a certain percentage (e.g., 5%) of traces you want to sample, meaning that you want to store them. It's efficient, and with a large volume of data, there is a good chance that that 5% includes important traces such as those that commonly fail or take long. If you have a small number of failed or slow requests, chances are high that you don't capture the details for those outliers!
- **Adaptive sampling**: The sampling rate automatically adjusts based on incoming traffic. This avoids collecting too much additional information during peak loads and, with that, causing any type of issues, either where the data gets captured, on the network where the data gets transported, or in the observability backend where the data needs to be stored and analyzed.
- **Rule-based sampling**: You can configure what is important and what is not based on attributes such as specific URLs, requests that tend to take longer than a certain time or fail, or requests from specific IP address ranges. The challenge here is configuring and maintaining the rules that also need to be evaluated on every single trace.

The next question is which component decides on whether a certain data point gets sampled or not. Head-based sampling decides at the root span (beginning), while tail-based sampling decides when all spans of a trace are received. Tail-based sampling can make better decisions because it sees the full trace and can analyze whether this trace is interesting, for example, showing a problem or error or taking very long. The drawback, however, is that tail-based sampling requires a lot of memory as first, all the spans need to be captured and analyzed before a decision is made to sample or not. This can become very resource-intensive in large-scale, highly distributed, and high-volume environments. Head-based sampling, on the other hand, makes the decision at the start of a trace. This is low effort but is limited to making decisions only based on information that is known at the beginning of a trace.

A good rule of thumb is to start with head-based sampling and then maybe combine it with tail-based sampling for critical transactions where you need all the details for failed transactions or where you need specific details for regulatory or compliance reasons.

To learn more, we highly recommend another tutorial from *isItObservable*: *Sampling Best Practices in OpenTelemetry [4]*.

The systems we need to manage will continue to get bigger. We need to apply the same practice of treating our monitored entities as cattle and no longer pets, just like we did with classical infrastructure. We need to leverage the existing metadata and enrich our observability signals to provide a unified experience based on a well-understood semantic dictionary. Also, we must go beyond just observing our applications; we must also observe the tools that make changes to our software—ideally, from the first requirements definition, when the first code gets written, tested, and deployed, until the software gets retired. This highly enriched data will allow us to better leverage observability data for AI and machine learning. It will give us better and faster insights into ever more complex distributed systems, especially when they don't operate as expected.

So, let's see how this can look in action.

# AIOps: reducing the noise with anomaly and root cause detection

What would it look like to live in a world where, without any human interaction, incident analysis and remediation recommendations are fully automated? You've been focused on other tasks when your AI agent says in Slack:

"*The latest Argo CD sync triggered by pull request PR-342 has caused a higher-than-usual failure rate in our payment service. We also see new logs containing java.lang.abcdException in the frontend service as a result causing HTTP 500 errors for end user requests. The recommended action is to roll back this pull request to mitigate the issue.*"

What sounds like science fiction can be a reality today. How? By building on the foundation of context-enriched observability data, leveraging automated baselines and machine learning to detect anomalies, and using trained models that can traverse connected observability data to detect root causes. The following screenshot illustrates such an implementation.

*Figure 3.11 – A problem card showing the impact (1,070 users) and root cause (high failure rate + Argo CD sync)*

The last step is using an LLM to generate a human-readable description of the following:

- **The finding**: What is the impact?
- **The root cause**: What is the reason behind that impact?
- **The recommendation**: What can we do about it?

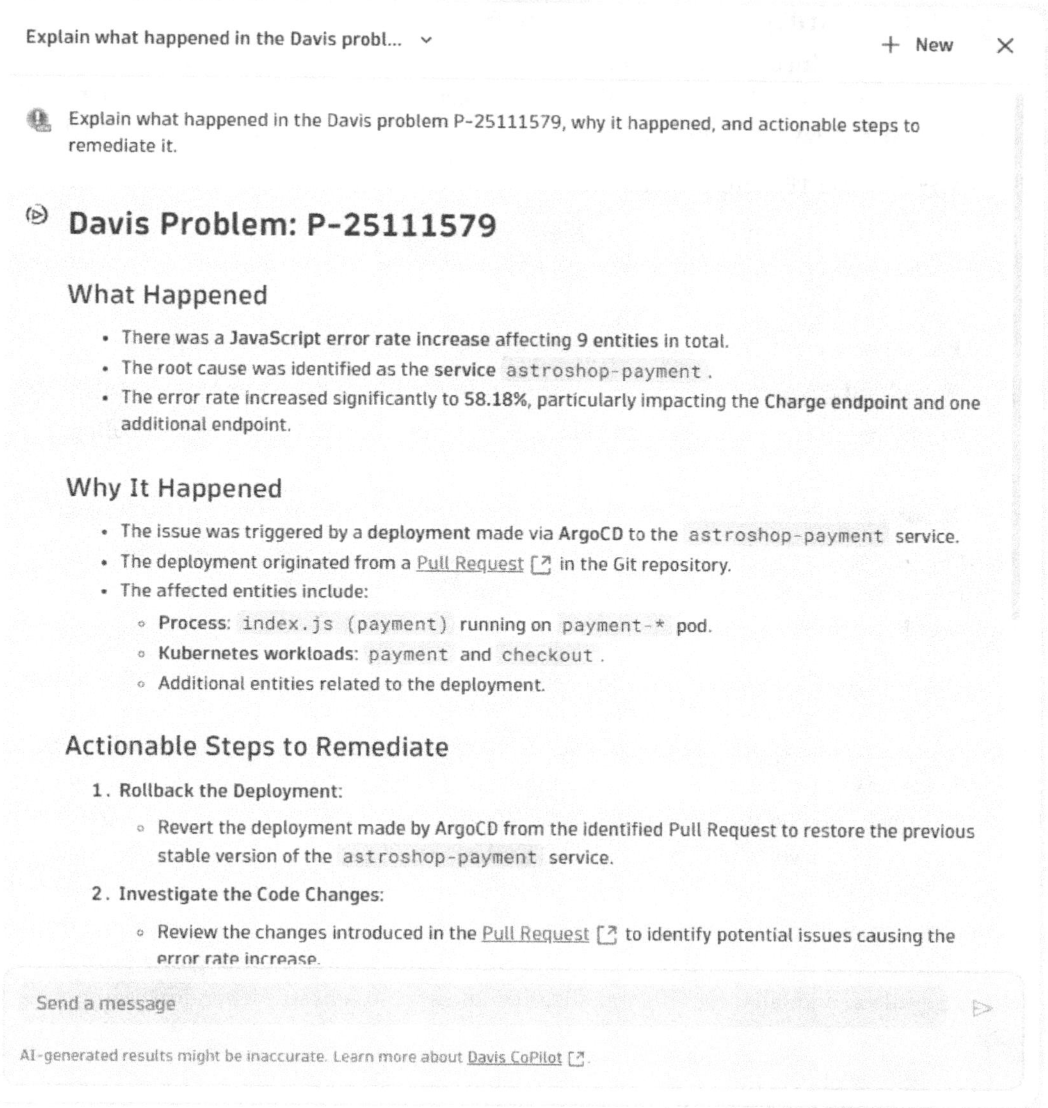


*Figure 3.12 – An LLM explaining a detected problem and the root cause and giving remediation actions*

Let's dissect all the details here so that you can identify what it takes to implement such an AIOps approach given your choice of signals and tools.

## Step 1: detecting abnormal events

Our journey starts with detecting abnormal behavior across all relevant indicators. In the *Beyond CPU and memory: cloud-native golden signals* section, we discussed that we need to look at metrics across all layers (from top to bottom):

- **Application**: The four golden signals of external APIs, concurrent users, and user behavior
- **Business service**: The four golden signals of internal APIs, resource consumption, and costs
- **Platform service**: Wait times, queue lengths, throughput, and rate limits
- **Workload**: Request limit usage, percentage of Pods failing, and connection timeouts
- **Orchestration**: Kubernetes API health, number of pending Pods, and scheduling latency
- **Resource**: Network Ingress/Egress and compute, storage, and memory utilization

Whenever we detect an anomaly on any of those indicators because a static threshold or dynamic baseline was breached, we can consider this as an *abnormal event* for a specific component in a specific layer of our stack.

Let's visualize this with a simple example. Let's say that we have a customer-facing web app that needs an external-facing business API for user login. This business API is slower than usual and impacts the application's end user performance. That API is implemented by one of our business services running on a specific Kubernetes cluster. The API depends on a queuing platform service and communicates with a database as well. All of these services share resources such as network, memory, and CPU as they are all deployed on the same shared hardware. The following figure shows how we could visualize this in a heatmap dashboard. We have all our key indicators across our stack on the *y* axis. On the *x* axis, we visualize the state of each indicator in one-minute intervals. The state is represented with good=green, degraded=yellow, and fail=red. This visualization allows us to observe a handful of patterns easily:

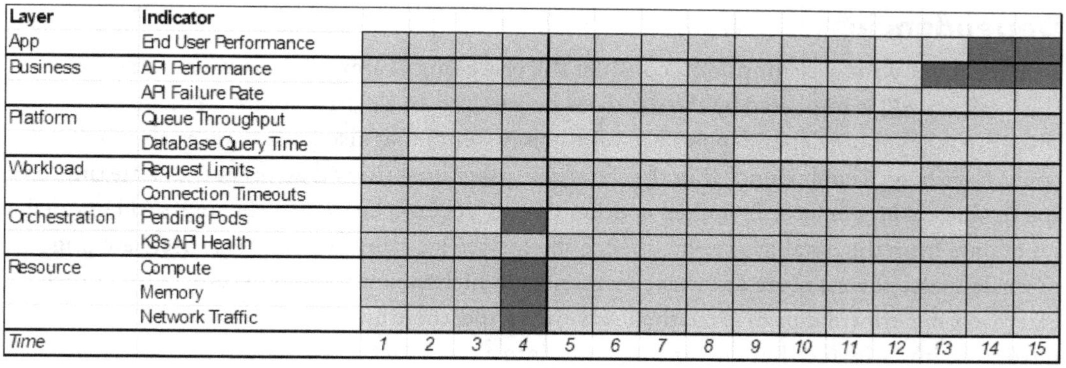


*Figure 3.13 – Simplified observability heatmap across all layers of the stack for a specific app and API endpoint*

Here are some observations when looking at the heatmap:

- There is a problem at time interval 4 that impacts pending Pods, but it has no impact on the business or application layer.
- The business API performance always degrades one minute after the database query time degrades.
- The business API performance recovers when the database impact is short. However, in timeframe 13, we see it fails after being in a degraded state for a while. It also correlates to the database query time being degraded for a longer period.
- The application layer also starts failing in timeslot 14 after the business API starts failing.

Visualizing abnormal behavior is most effective when done on key indicators over time. Putting this information on a dashboard based on our architecture makes it possible for the human eye to detect patterns rather easily. In the preceding example, it looks like the problem is related to a database query time issue, which impacts the business API and subsequently the application's performance for the end user. However, there are a few limitations to this approach, which we will review next.

## Scope

This is an extremely minimalistic example, as we are only looking at a small number of indicators for a very specific API endpoint. In a real-world scenario, we may have hundreds of applications and thousands of API endpoints, each using many shared platform services. Modern observability, therefore, needs to be able to analyze potentially millions of different data points. The challenge is not generating a lot of noise by alerting on false positives, false assumptions, or anomalies that do not have a business impact.

### Dependencies

Talking about wrong assumptions, consider the preceding example where we assumed that the business API is impacted by the database query time. In a distributed system, however, there are many more dependencies between components that also need to be analyzed. It could have been a coincidence that the database query time slowed down at the same time as the business API. We haven't looked at other factors. It could be that the business API queried a lot of data from the database service, hence the service was slower in its response. Fetching more data also means more data kept in memory, which means more pressure on GC, which can result in performance degradation. As you can see, there are too many data points that need to be investigated that we can't easily fit into a table such as the one in *Figure 3.13*.

### Shared resources

The business API shares resources with other services on the same cluster. We haven't looked at any *noisy neighbors* that may impact the performance of our business API. Network traffic is shared between all components running on shared infrastructure. We haven't investigated how network latency has impacted our service, the database service, or any other dependent component. Dependencies and shared services can both be extracted from the context-enriched metadata we discussed earlier. Additionally, we can use information from distributed tracing to see the transactional dependencies from one service to other services. All of this data needs to be considered to improve the accuracy of alerting. It also allows reducing the noise as we can aggregate anomalies that we know result from dependent systems.

### External events

So far, we have only looked at indicators from within the layers of our stack. In the *Enriching observability data across the SDLC* section, we discussed the importance of ingesting events from our delivery or configuration change tools. We could have missed a configuration change of the request and resource limits for the business API to give another API more CPU and memory. Such a change could result in CPU throttling of the business API and, therefore, result in performance degradation.

The point of all of this is that we need to detect anomalies across the stack. Yet, anomalies alone that are not enriched with information about dependencies, shared resources, and external events will only allow us to carry out *guesswork*. We need all this context-enriched data, as discussed in the previous section, to have all of the evidence available. Only then can we scale our observability and feed it to machine learning or various AI systems to connect all those dots and find the real root cause of abnormal behavior.

## Step 2: connecting the dots to find the root cause

In this step, we explain how to walk through the observability dependency model.

In *Chapter 1*, in the *Observability and distributed systems* section, we discussed how knowing the dependencies across the vertical and horizontal stacks will allow us to quickly point to the technical root cause of a problem that impacts our end users, our API consumers, or our SLAs.

Borrowing that same visualization from *Chapter 1* but applying it to our use case from the previous section makes it easier for us to see dependencies, cross-impacts from shared resources, and external events.

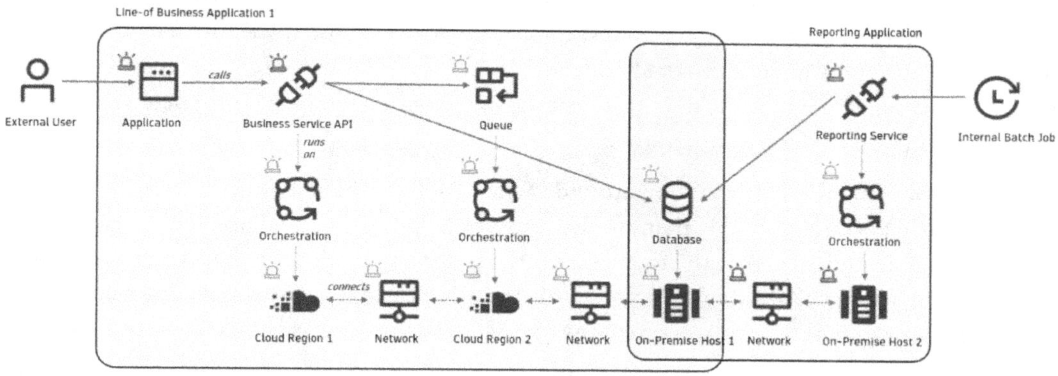


*Figure 3.14 – Finding the root cause requires connecting all abnormal events across the full stack, considering dependencies and shared services*

The preceding figure highlights how modern observability becomes more effective with context-enriched observability data. Thanks to metadata on logs, metrics, traces, and events, we can better analyze the cause and effect across the vertical and horizontal stacks. Since we are able to ingest and analyze lots of data at scale, we are no longer limited to just one application. Instead, we can, and have, to go across all applications and services to detect any type of cross-dependencies. Let's break this down.

## Horizontal stack, or call chain

Which service calls which other services, and how does the response of the callee (latency, failure rate, and throughput) impact the caller? For example, we can learn how database query time or the number of database rows returned impacts the performance of the business API call.

## Vertical stack, or runs on another component

Which component runs on or within another component, and how does this impact the component itself? For example, we can learn how the GC of the Java runtime impacts the performance behavior of the business API, and how the GC itself is impacted by the resource and request limits enforced by the orchestration layer.

## Network connectivity

How is the distribution of components across local, remote, and cloud networks impacted? We can learn how the quality of a network impacts point-to-point connections made between business and platform services.

## Cross-application or cross-stack

*Figure 3.14* also brings in a new player: another application or another stack that relates to the part of the system that the line-of-business application cares about. If we only focus on the information we know about but not about the systems around it, we might never find the real root cause. We may point to the database, but the database itself might be impacted by other services that put it under too much stress.

With the new contextual information around vertical, horizontal, network, and cross-stack dependency, we would probably point to the problem as being the database, but we can also say, with high confidence, that the root cause is the reporting service that gets triggered on a schedule by an internal batch job. This job is also causing the database to slow down for our business API, which in turn causes problems for the end user.

For our final and last point, we can collect all this information with observability, but how can we make this more explainable?

# Step 3: explaining all the evidence

Not everyone can constantly draw diagrams about how components are related and how the *evidence trail* of abnormal events leads to identifying the root cause of a known problem.

This is where automation can help us. Everything that was explained in the *Step 2: connecting the dots to find the root cause* section can be automated. Many observability platforms already do this today by connecting all the observability data, thanks to the metadata, and then following the dependency trees as we did. Some do it more efficiently than others, as the speed heavily depends on data quality, as well as how efficiently observability data is stored, can be accessed, can be connected, and can be analyzed.

In whatever way you decide to implement your anomaly and root cause detection, a key step toward making this data more actionable and ensuring our users see the value is being able to take all this data and make it explainable in a way that humans can easily understand without having to be an expert. What can this look like?

Look at *Figure 3.15*. It shows the evidence trail of a JavaScript error rate increase problem, including information about the dependencies, a list of detected anomalies, and external events that have a high possibility of being relevant to the root cause analysis. When putting an LLM on top of this data, we get a good explanation of the problem, its root cause, and recommended actions:

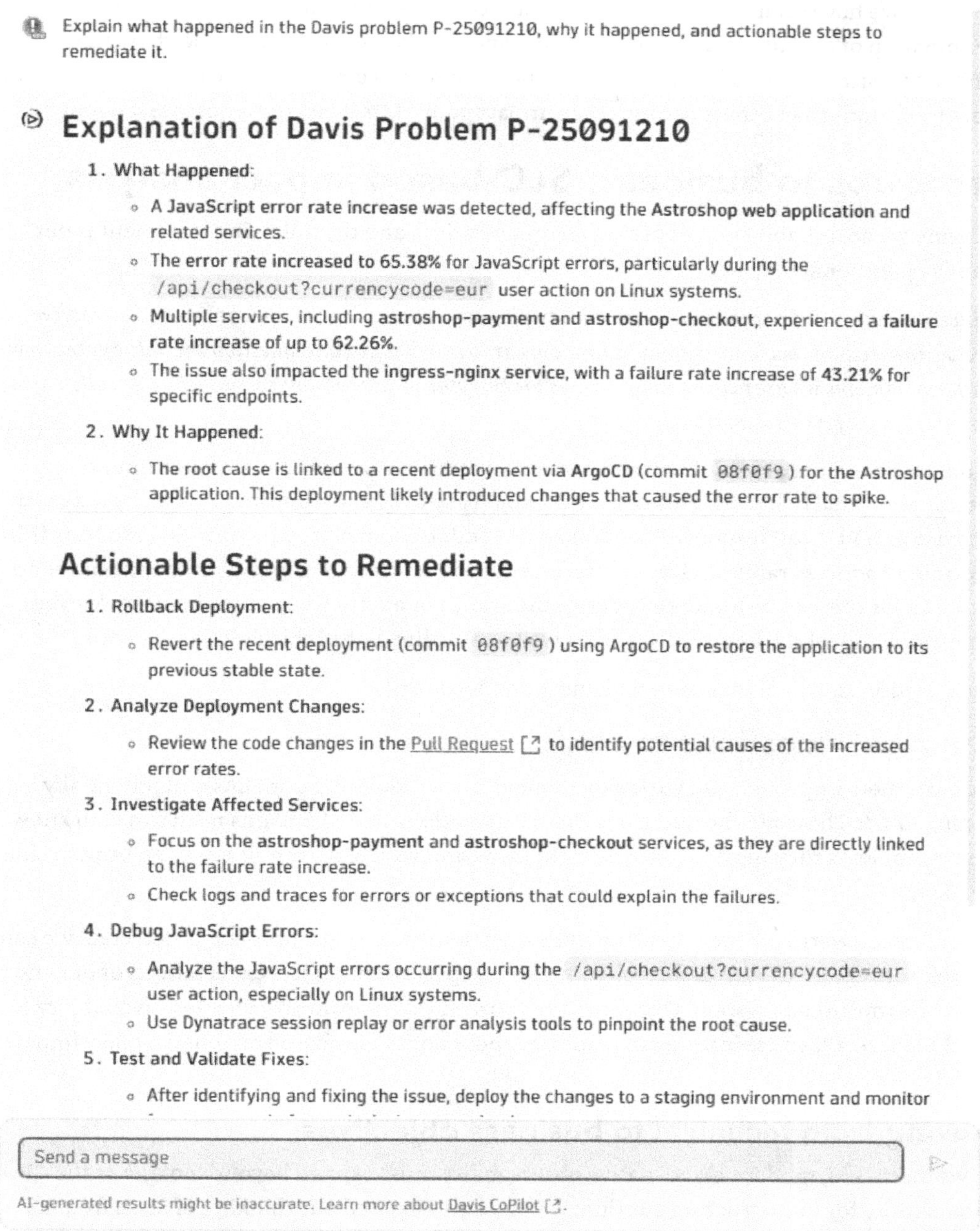


*Figure 3.15 – Using an LLM to explain the details of the detected problem and even receiving recommendations*

Now that we have seen how modern observability can be put to use by leveraging a combination of baselining, machine learning, and AI, it's time to address one challenge that AI can't solve without our help: providing business context to better assess which anomalies are more important than others because they impact your SLOs if you don't react fast enough.

# From ops to business: SLO-based impact analysis

Imagine we are reliability engineers in an organization, and the following statement is our team's operational reality:

"*Since we have rolled out the new observability platform across all our applications and stacks, we receive hundreds of incidents per day. Our teams are overwhelmed and question the value of the new platform. It seems we are getting notifications for everything, but we don't know what is really business relevant. Please fix this situation.*"

Anomaly detection, as explained in the previous section, does what the name implies: it detects abnormal behavior. This could be an increase in queue wait time in Apache Kafka, an increase in HTTP 500 response codes on an API endpoint, or a drop in incoming requests from a certain IP address range. In large enterprises with hundreds or thousands of applications, it's common for there to be hundreds or even thousands of anomalies detected per week, even when applying all the best practices that we have outlined until this point in the book.

The question is: which of those problems do we focus on?

## The right questions to ask!

Are customers impacted? Are we losing money? Are we violating our SLAs and potentially getting fined? These are the questions that IT operations and SRE teams need to ask to know which problems they need to jump on right away and which other problems can be put aside for now.

Instead of answering those impact analysis questions when each problem is detected, we can use the concept of SLOs to define what our own expectations, or the expectations of our end users, are toward our system. Once we have those SLOs, for example, 99.999% availability of a core business API endpoint, we can prioritize those anomalies based on whether they impact an SLO.

## Moving from technical to business objectives

As we discussed, modern cloud-native observability must expand beyond looking at the CPU and memory for infrastructure alerting; we must also expand our thinking of SLOs from its original definition to looking at the four golden signals: availability, throughput, latency, and resource consumption. Modern observability must look at business signals such as the number of active users, number of orders placed, time to process claims, or revenue at risk.

In this final section, we will go a bit deeper into the reasons why you may drown in incidents at the beginning. You will then learn the basic concepts of SLOs, how to expand from technical to business objectives, and how they can be used in incident response to focus on anomalies that have a potential business impact.

## Why we still drown in incidents

If you need to defend why your observability implementation produces more incidents than you'd hope, the following sections will give you enough explanation for why that is, as we have seen this in many projects that we have worked with.

### Expanded scope

Many organizations that move to a new observability platform often use this as an opportunity to expand to more layers of their stack and expand to more applications. That's why more data is suddenly available. More data also means more anomalies detected and, therefore, results in more initial incident noise.

### Tool consolidation

Moving to a new observability platform typically means replacing one or several existing point solutions that were used for specific applications or specific layers of the stack. Those tools often didn't automatically alert but were just used for troubleshooting in case of a wider issue. All of this additional data now feeds into the anomaly detection and can increase the initial incident noise.

### Gaps in end-to-end observability

In the previous section, we showed the importance of having end-to-end observability. Remember the database that was overloaded by a backend batch job and impacted a business application? If we didn't have the insight that the database is used by those two applications, we would have ended up with three incidents instead of one, as our anomaly detection would see a problem in the business app, the batch job, and the database itself. But it would be able to connect it all together and treat it as a single anomaly.

When organizations start to roll out modern observability, the same problem often happens. They have some blind spots or observability gaps until the system is fully rolled out. This gap is what can result in initial incident noise.

## Missing ownership

Ideally, incidents are automatically assigned to the right team that has to take action to fix the problem. But who is responsible for a component? In the *Context is king: the quality of observability data* section, we discussed the importance of enriching our data with ownership so that we know which teams own an application, services, or a cluster. In many organizations, this information is initially not available, or at least not easily available for the observability platform. In that case, all new detected incidents get assigned to a *fallback team*, which is typically the IT operations or SRE team. You can imagine that those teams feel overwhelmed when all of a sudden they get a lot more incidents than before. Defining ownership is therefore key to reducing incident noise.

## Lack of criticality and business impact

Not every anomaly is equal, but most often, every detected anomaly is treated the same if we don't have the information on whether the impacted system has high or low criticality and whether there is a potential business impact. Having this information allows automatic filtering and routing of detected problems. Those with low criticality, for example, a slowdown on an internal reporting service, can be assigned a lower-priority incident response process. Those that impact our business, for example, when our users can no longer log in, should be elevated as they need immediate attention, as this could have a very negative impact on our reputation and revenue.

Context is again king. One best practice is to assign a criticality tag to each component, for example, high, medium, or low. Once we detect a new anomaly, we can analyze the criticality of the components impacted, and with that, steer the incident response process; for example, use the highest criticality as the default value for the incident ticket that gets created.

But what about business impact? Is there a way to better quantify this than just low, medium, and high? Is there a way to factor in the risk or potential lost revenue for every minute our systems are suffering from a problem?

The answer is yes! This is where SLOs and SLAs come in. SLOs allow us to specify the expected system behavior over time, and we can use this to measure how far off we are from expected behavior, for example, 99% uptime over 30 days, or 95% of critical API response time must be faster than 500 ms. What are SLAs then? Well, they are like SLOs but are typically written down in contracts as they define what happens if we do not meet our objectives. A good example would be having to pay a penalty if we fail to deliver the uptime we promised. If you think about banks, they need to guarantee a certain level of availability. If they don't meet it, they need to pay penalties or they will potentially lose their banking license.

There is a lot of literature around SLAs and SLOs. We highly recommend reading the Google SRE handbook, which does a great job of explaining the core principles behind SLIs, SLOs, SLAs, error budgets, and burndown rates[5].

In the following sections, we will only cover SLO basics, but we will explain how SLOs allow us to elevate our impact analysis from purely technical (is it available? Is it fast?) to answer questions such as *is it highly critical because we are negatively impacting our business objectives?*

# A primer on SLOs: learnings from Google's SRE handbook

We don't need yet another book about SLOs as there is plenty of material available. There are also many different tool vendors and even open standard initiatives around how to define and calculate SLOs. We therefore suggest you read up on this information.

The most important guideline we want you to take away is: *You do not need an SLO for everything!* Sounds harsh, but we have seen organizations that have tried to define 10,000+ different SLOs across their applications. They followed some of the information they read too literally and defined the four golden signals with custom thresholds and alerts on every service endpoint in their organization.

Let's quickly recap the basics of SLOs so we understand what we are talking about when we use terms such as SLI, SLO, SLA, error budget, and burndown rate.

We will use the example of defining the SLO for the *request success rate* of a particular API endpoint.

## Service-level indicator

The SLI is the metric for understanding the health of our objective. The SLI is typically a rate metric that delivers a value between 0 (fail) and 100 (pass). In most scenarios, we calculate this ratio by dividing the "good events" (for example, successful API calls) across all valid requests (for example, all measured API calls). The following is a full example of defining an SLI for the request success rate, where we divide the total number of HTTP requests that return a status code of 200 by the total number of requests:

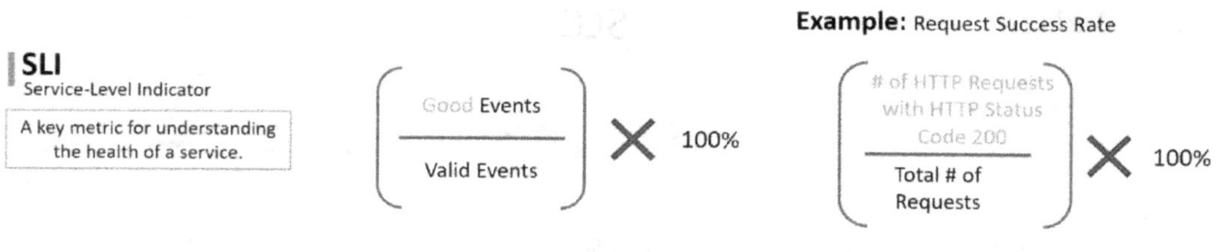


*Figure 3.16 – The SLI is a metric to understand the health of a component*

We ideally normalize the SLI to a value between 0 and 100 as this will make it easier to define our objective, the SLO.

## Service-level objective

Building on top of the SLI, we can define what the objective of that metric is over a specific time period. In our example, we could specify that the request success rate should be 99.98% over a certain observed time period. This means we want to ensure that 99.98% of requests are returning an HTTP 200 status code and that we only allow 0.02% of requests to return a value other than HTTP 200.

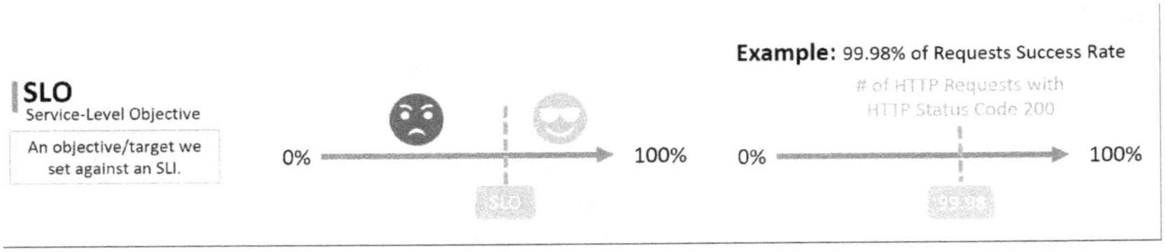


*Figure 3.17– The SLO defines our objective for a metric over a period of time*

The SLO is really defining the threshold—or the expected value—for the SLI. Besides a single threshold, we often also see a warning and an error threshold to differentiate more granularly, not just success or failure.

## Error budget and burndown rate

Once we have our SLI and the threshold for the SLO, we can calculate how much room we have for error without violating our defined objective. This is what we call an **error budget**. It's also often referred to as *100 – SLO*. In other words, it's the percentage of time that we allow the system to not work before we violate our SLO. The following figure depicts a simple calculation of what that means if our SLO has a threshold of 99.9%. It means that for 0.1% of the time, we are allowed to not be available or not be as fast as we should be (depending on what the SLI measures).

*Figure 3.18 – Error budget is the time we allow the system to not meet our objective*

Looking at those numbers often shows us how stringent a 99.9% availability target is. It really only allows us 43.2 minutes of not meeting our SLO over the period of a year. You can easily do the math on how that time shortens if you add more nines, for example, 99.999%.

What do we use the error budget for? Well, we can use it to make decisions on whether we can take some risk, such as deploying a change that will have a short-term impact on our SLO. By looking at the remaining error budget, we can weigh the desire to make a change against the potential risk of violating our SLO.

While the error budget is a great indicator and reporting tool, it's the error budget burndown rate that's more useful. It's a good tool for getting alerts in case we are burning through our remaining error budget too fast.

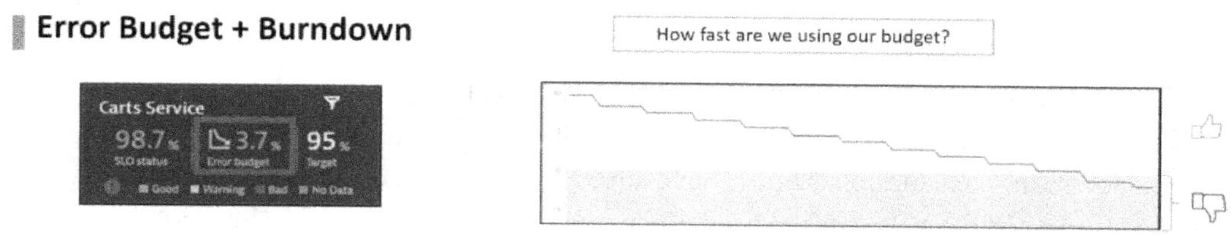


*Figure 3.19 – Error budget burndown rate tells us whether we are on the trajectory to violate our SLO at the end of the reporting period*

The idea behind the burndown rate is that you can trigger alerts not only when you fail to meet your objective by the end of the reporting period but also when you are consuming your error budget too quickly. For example, if the burn rate is too steep, it allows you to react fast to a critical problem that eats up your error budget.

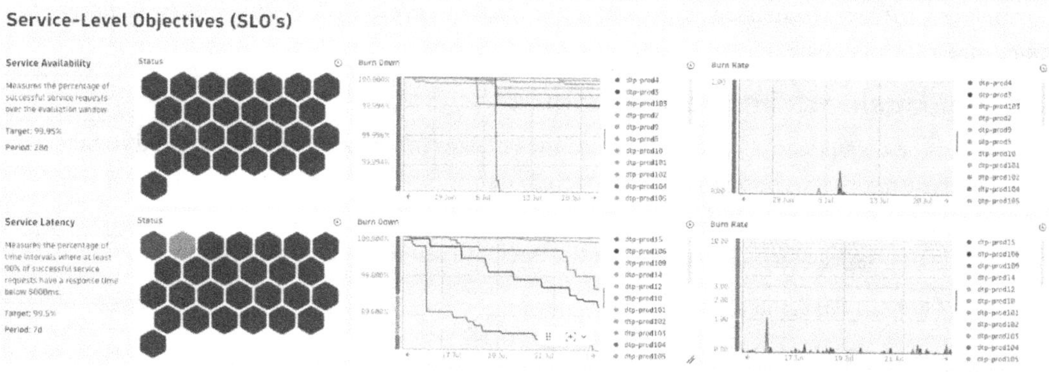


*Figure 3.20 – Burndown and burn rate as good indicators of when to react to a problem*

If you have investigated this area in the past, you may think: *this sounds very similar to an SLA*. You are right. So, what is the difference?

## Service-level agreement

Technically, an SLA is similar to an SLO because both are used to measure the health of our system over a period of time. A classic example is maintaining 99.999% availability of your system to the end consumer. We can measure it in the same way as an SLI if we analyze the ratio between when a system is available and is not available.

So, what's the difference? SLAs are typically used in contracts. When you sign up for any SaaS service, they typically put in an SLA for availability and maybe even for performance. We also see SLAs defined for how fast the response to problems or incidents is; for example, as a premium customer of our SaaS service, we guarantee that in 95% of the cases, we will respond within one hour to critical issues.

SLOs, on the other hand, are typically used internally for additional indicators. These are typically leading indicators that, when violated, will most likely also result in an SLA violation if we are not acting fast enough. Think about our availability SLA example. We can define several SLOs on critical APIs that are used when users access our services. These APIs need to be available in order for the system to be perceived as available. This is why we would typically specify more technical and more stringent SLOs to act as an early warning signal.

# From SLOs to business objectives

Availability, response time, and error rate are very common SLOs for technical services such as login, purchase, and recommendation services. Wait time, message process time, and message delivery success rate are typical SLOs for queuing systems that we typically find in distributed architectures. While all those SLOs are great for technical service owners, they do not allow us to answer a key question: is our slow service or backed-up queue impacting our end users and, therefore, our business?

## Asking business impact questions

To elevate the discussion around indicators that matter for your business, we need to take a top-down rather than a bottom-up approach to defining SLOs. Consider a use case of a new mobile app for a financial services company. The most important metric for the business is not how many messages can be processed by the backend queue, but the following:

- How many users are using the new app?
- How many users are logging in?
- How many users can make money transfers or purchase other financial products through the app?

As we get to the more technical side, the questions would be the following:

- What's the rating on the mobile app store?
- What's the crash rate of the app that prevents users from doing business with the company?

These are all the right questions to define. Use observability to capture the indicators and then apply the concept of SLOs to report and alert when we are not meeting our business objectives.

## Connecting business objectives with technical objectives

The following figure is taken from the talk *Tips for running successful SLO workshops in under one hour* from SLOconf 2022[6]. In the talk, a top-to-bottom approach to defining SLOs is explained, starting with the topmost business objective and then breaking it down into leading indicator objectives:

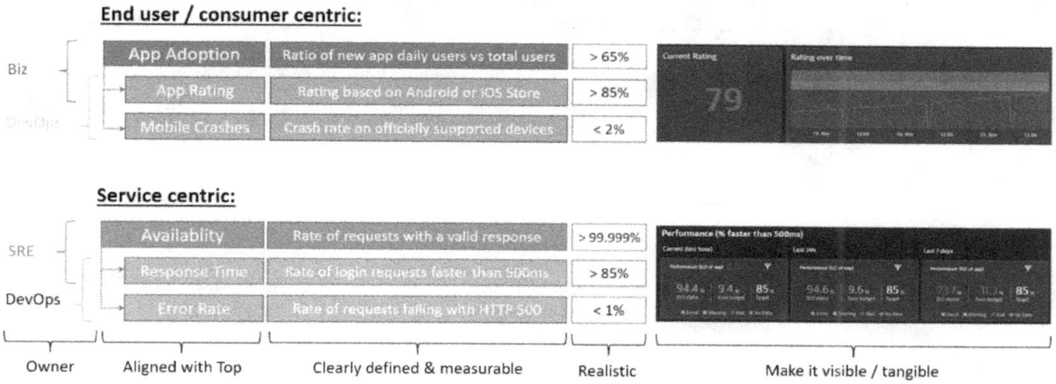


*Figure 3.21 – Good SLOs start with business objectives that are linked to leading indicators toward the technical implementation*

From that talk from SLOconf, there are a couple of clear takeaways and best practices regarding setting SLOs:

- **Clearly defined**: Have a clear definition of the objective and why it matters.
- **Measurable**: How do you measure that objective—through metrics, logs, and so on?
- **Realistic objective**: What is a realistic threshold that everyone agrees is achievable?
- **Ownership**: Who owns the objective? Who acts on it when it's violated?
- **Aligned with business**: How do all bottom technical SLOs map to top business objectives?

For more information about this topic, also read the blog post *How to start with SLOs to align Business, DevOps, and SREs [7]*.

## Business impact analysis as part of incident response

Once we have our SLOs, we can expand our AIOps implementation to include business impact analysis. For each problem detected, we can factor in which of the impacted components have an SLO assigned to them and which don't. Assuming that components with an SLO are more critical, we can prioritize which anomalies should get a higher priority for incident response.

### Incident analysis without SLO context

When looking at a real-life system, we often end up with a lot of different problems. The following dashboard shows how to get an overview of all these problems, grouped by problem area.

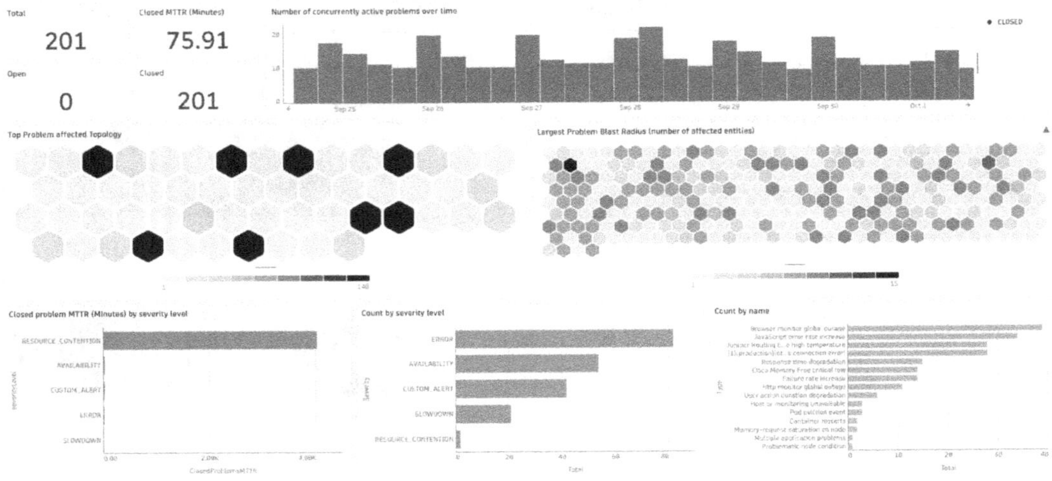


*Figure 3.22 – Getting an overview of problem areas highlights hotspots and provides a baseline to optimize problem prioritization through SLOs*

That is a lot of alert noise, and it seems that most of those problems are around resource contention issues, and only very few are around availability, performance, or errors. That's already a good indication that there are a lot of detected anomalies that might not have an impact on our business-level objectives.

### Connecting the SLO with the incident

Now, if we have a chance to connect those detected anomalies with SLOs, we can easily filter those problems based on whether they *impact* the SLO and *do not impact* the SLO. The following examples show two detected problems with clear indicators on which one should have higher priority and which one should have lower priority.

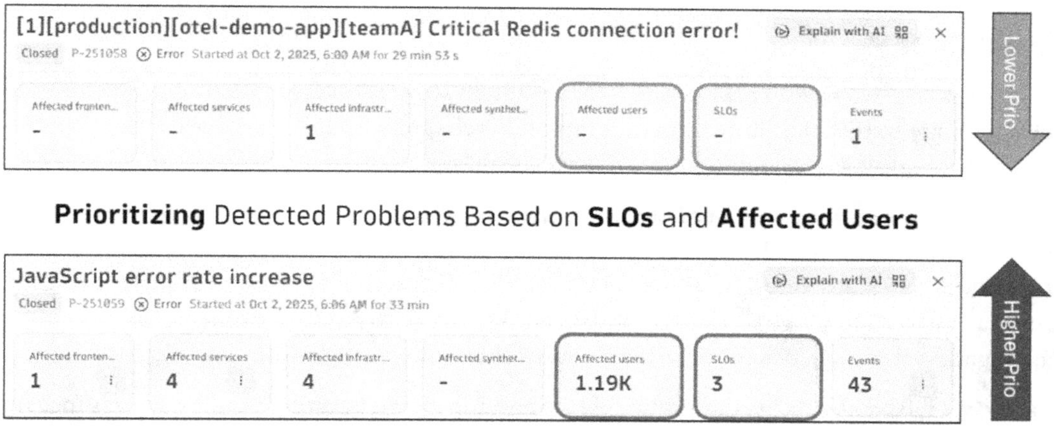


*Figure 3.23 – The impact on SLOs and affected users helps with setting the priority for the incident response*

We have seen organizations that have reduced their incident noise by up to 90% simply by focusing on the problems that impact their objectives.

## How to start this journey

Most organizations do not yet have a good practice for defining both technical and business objectives. You should start tracking the ratio of incidents with an SLO-based priority assessment. This gives your organization good guidance toward defining SLOs as it will improve the incident response process. If you continuously track how many problems are detected and how many of them were not business-relevant because they didn't have an SLO defined, it highlights where you have to focus on defining good SLOs.

It's a long journey, but one worth starting as it will lead to focusing on those problems that really impact your business instead of drowning in alerts that are not relevant, which eats away at the time you should use for innovation.

## How would Financial One ACME make this transition?

As in the previous chapters, we will make this real by walking you through the transformational journey of our fictitious company called *Financial One ACME*. How are they coping with moving from data on dashboards and lots of static alerts toward a layered approach of health checks applying baselining? How are they expanding to the left and establishing an observability-driven development culture? What type of context are they deciding to add to their observability data to enable more self-service use cases? And how do they define business and technical objectives to make their AIOps implementation more effective?

You will find out by reading the next chapters!

## Summary

In this chapter, we have explained the transformation steps necessary to elevate your observability so that the quote from the start of this chapter also becomes a reality for you: "*We used to have 1,000 dashboards. Now we are down to 50!*"

We covered the importance of enriching observability data with more context, how we need to understand the health indicators of each layer of our cloud-native architectures, and how to transition from static thresholds to dynamic baselining. We also learned that, when having all this data, we can leverage simple and advanced algorithms to reduce alerting noise by aggregating abnormal behaviors that are connected to the same problem.

Lastly, we talked about the importance of having a top-down (starting from a business focus) versus a bottom-up (starting from a technical focus) approach to prioritizing detected problems based on their true impact on our business.

In *Chapter 4*, we introduce ACME Financial Services and learn who they are, where they come from, where they struggle, how they go about modernizing their IT landscape, as well as what that means in terms of transforming their observability.

## Further reading


- [1]: AWS Tagging Best Practices https://docs.aws.amazon.com/whitepapers/latest/tagging-best-practices/tagging-best-practices.html
- [2] *Semantic Dictionary* – `https://docs.dynatrace.com/docs/discover-dynatrace/references/semantic-dictionary`
- [3] *isItObservable* GitHub tutorials – `https://github.com/isItObservable`
- [4] Trace sampling best practices – `https://isitobservable.io/open-telemetry/traces/trace-sampling-best-practices`
- [5] Google's SRE handbook with an introduction to SLOs – `https://sre.google/sre-book/introduction/`
- [6] SLOConf talk on running an SLO workshop: YouTube – `https://www.youtube.com/watch?v=XwCybEsAAyA`
- [7] *How to start with SLOs to align Business, DevOps, and SREs* – `https://www.dynatrace.com/news/blog/how-to-start-with-slos/`

# 4

# ACME Financial Services: Implementing AIOps

Now that we have covered some of the basics, we will look at applying some of those concepts through the workings of a fictitious company that has run into problems with their current observability practices after completing their migration to the cloud. This company is a large organization that works in several business markets, some of which are highly regulated. The complexity of the company, the regulations, and the company's observability problems help highlight the concepts discussed thus far that we will apply to a business use case. We will discuss the current problems, how the company comes to discover their root causes, how they find solutions and apply them, and the benefits they see from those changes.

In this chapter, we will cover the following:

- What is ACME Financial Services?
- The challenges of implementing enterprise-wide observability
- Automating incident response through AIOps
- Identifying and measuring the results

## Technical requirements

For this chapter, there are no technical requirements.

## Our fictitious company

Introducing ACME Financial Services, a fictitious company that we will use to apply the concepts in this book to real-world scenarios. ACME Financial Services is a large financial institution that provides services across many industries, including personal investments and savings, management of employer-provided retirement plans, business investments, and insurance. With this diverse product portfolio, the company runs hundreds of independent applications across the various industries that interact with each other to provide customer services.

Being in the financial services industry means that ACME Financial Services cares deeply about their reputation and takes anything that might diminish the company's reputation very seriously. After all, who would want to trust a company with a poor reputation for security, safety, or customer service with their life savings or their business?

However, reputation is not the only concern that ACME Financial Services has. Many of the services that the company provides are in heavily regulated industries. Complying with a regulation requires much more work than just implementing controls or processes to ensure the regulation is met. The company also has to have thorough documentation around their policies and procedures for that regulation to be able to prove to regulators that they are complying and actively ensuring compliance. A failure to meet a regulation is made worse if a regulator determines that the company's culture, policy, or procedure is inadequate to maintain compliance with the regulation. If you're a college sports fan, you may be familiar with this same kind of situation where a school may be found to have inadequate controls in place to meet a regulation and gets hit with financial penalties, loss of scholarships, or even people losing their jobs. This means that not only does a public failure of some kind risk damage to ACME Financial Services' reputation, but it could also result in significant financial penalties, lawsuits, or even people losing their jobs.

## After the great cloud migration

ACME Financial Services has just completed their journey transitioning to the cloud. They have ended up with a hybrid environment because of the nature of the numerous markets the company serves, the amount of data, and internal decisions on how best to ensure compliance with regulations. Frontend applications were re-architected to fully embrace cloud-native design principles and transitioned completely to Kubernetes clusters running on their cloud provider. However, not all backend systems or application data were able to migrate to the cloud. Despite the desire to move everything to the cloud, it was decided that this would not be practical for a number of reasons. In some cases, there weren't suitable offerings from their cloud provider; in others, the amount of data that they would need to move was too large to accommodate in the cloud. Finally, regulations in some markets prevented the work from being done in the cloud.

The end result is a mixture of new and old design principles. The applications that moved to the cloud were redesigned following cloud-native design principles. They converted single monolithic applications into hundreds or even thousands of microservices. In addition to that, ACME Financial Services has improved the resiliency of these applications by running them in multiple regions and across multiple Kubernetes clusters. In addition to improved resiliency, they have also gained improved scalability because they properly designed their microservices to be able to scale horizontally when needed. The company has learned that, in most cases, increasing the number of Pods, or scaling horizontally, provides results superior to their old practice of scaling vertically, or increasing the amount of resources available for an application. Some of the cloud-native applications have to communicate with the old monolithic applications on-premises. However, when they planned their cloud migration, they didn't realize what impact the cloud-native architectures and hybrid cloud environment would mean for their observability practices, so they didn't make any changes to the observability practices they used for monolithic applications running on-premises. The result is that despite the improvements in resiliency and reliability, they are seeing an increase in incident resolution times and incidents discovered by customers.

The old observability practices worked for the monolithic applications that were running on-premises. As an example, services for a single product before the migration looked like this:

| Number of Applications | Data Centers | Total Number of Applications |
|---|---|---|
| 10 | 1 | 10 |

*Table 4.1 – Observability complexity on-premises*

However, once this service was redesigned with cloud-native principles and migrated to the cloud, it looks something more like this:

| Number of Pods | Cloud Regions | Total Number of Pods |
|---|---|---|
| 200 | 3 | 600 |

*Table 4.2 – Observability complexity in the cloud*

In this example, one area of service provided by ACME Financial Services has gone from 10 monolithic applications in a single data center to over 600 Pods in 3 different cloud regions. Similar rates of increase, and some even larger, occurred for all their services when they migrated to the cloud, which has resulted in the company having 80 times more components to manage and monitor as compared to when the applications were all on-premises.

In addition to the increase in components, they have an additional complexity with applications running in a hybrid configuration such as this:

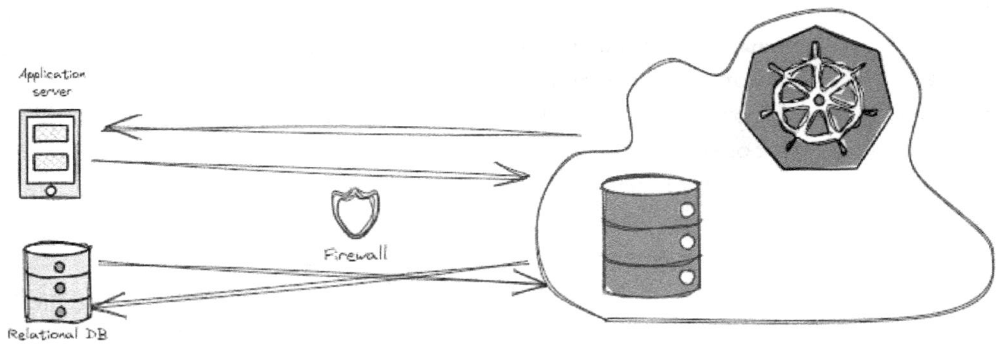


*Figure 4.1 – Hybrid networking environment*

Before the migration, all of the networking and security was handled on-premises, but in the hybrid situation, they now have to worry about networking configuration, security, throughput, and latency between on-premises components and cloud-deployed ones. Throughput has proven to be especially challenging because not only do they have to manage traffic between applications or components, but they also have to account for the observability data being sent to their observability tooling. Their current monitoring capability doesn't handle hybrid deployments well at all.

## ACME Financial Services' current state of observability

ACME Financial Services has a very labor-intensive approach to incident management. They have an operations team that receives and processes the events generated from all the applications across the multiple markets that the company serves. They also monitor social media for any indications of problems users may be experiencing. This operations team knows the various functions the company provides, but has only a light understanding of the interconnected nature of the various applications. Since this team is not composed of software developers, they look up points of contact for the various applications running across the company when they need to get application teams involved. However, because of their limited understanding of how the applications are connected, the operations team takes a scattershot approach to incident management. They create a means of live communication for an incident and contact as many application teams as they feel might have input or be impacted by an incident, and then drive the incident to its conclusion. This results in many application team points of contact being needlessly roped into incidents where they have no input or impact, and the only way for an application team to be considered exempt from an incident is for them to prove that their application is not involved with the current incident. The result is that a large number of application teams incur work related to an incident, either because they are directly involved and work to resolve the problem or to show that they are not involved and can be excused. Even with this dedicated operations team, some incidents are only detected when users complain either directly to the company or on social media.

## How their observability practices became unmanageable

ACME Financial Services' observability practices were adequate while everything was on-premises and processing was contained to monolithic applications. Once services moved to the cloud, the company noticed a degradation in incident response and resolution times. They have put together a team to study why this is occurring and the impacts, which finds the following:

- **Increased alert counts**: One of the first conclusions the team finds is that there is a lot more metric data being generated when compared to before the cloud migration, and this is resulting in significantly more alerts. When they drill down further, the team finds that this is primarily for the following reasons:
    - **More services are running**: When the application teams split their monolithic applications into microservices, they generally copied their alert configurations for each microservice performing a task. This has resulted in more alerts being generated for similar situations. For example, if there was an alert to detect a burst in traffic for a possible DDoS attack, that alert was generated by a single

application before the move to the cloud, but now it is generated by each of the 100 microservices providing the same functionality.

- **Static alerts**: The scaling strategy relied upon monitoring resources consumed by applications and generating alerts if any watermarks (such as high CPU or memory) were hit, and the operations team would assess whether the application would need to scale. This same strategy has become unmanageable now that multiple microservices have been replaced with a single monolithic application. The infrastructure teams have been working to improve this situation by implementing auto-scaling functionality using cloud provider offerings, as well as adjusting the alert levels. While this has improved things, the alerts generated from static definitions are still elevated from what they were before the cloud migration.

- **Lost traceability**: When applications were running on-premises, they were monolithic and isolated to a single task. Now that applications have been redesigned for the cloud, a single application could consist of multiple microservices, and some of those microservices have multiple instances running to provide redundancy or scalability. In their microservices architecture, services have been created that are shared across applications, creating problems in understanding which applications are at risk from an issue with a shared service. This has caused problems with tracing the impacts from an alert or incident because the communication graph is much more complex.
- **Alert fatigue**: Because there are more alerts, it is harder for response teams to know which alerts need to be responded to and which are noise. The increased number of alerts is causing not only alert fatigue but also members of the response teams to burn out. The response teams are less effective and slower in dealing with incidents.
- **More user-detected incidents**: The team also discovers that more incidents are slipping through the cracks and being detected only when users complain. There doesn't seem to be a single root cause for this, and the team concludes that it is likely a result of the other issues they have uncovered. However, because users are reporting more problems, the company's reputation is taking a hit. Senior leadership has even asked that new metrics be created to track where incidents are detected, which does not put the current monitoring system in a good light.
- **Lack of ownership**: This doesn't mean that applications are running without an application development team owning them. Instead, this means that when an incident happens and the response teams isolate the application, or even the Pods, causing the problem, they don't know which application team to contact to help mitigate the problem. While this has long been the case, the problem has been

amplified by the move to the cloud and the embrace of cloud-native design principles. There are now many more parts to an application, and it isn't clear who owns what.

## An explosion of operating costs

In addition to the decline in user experience and the resulting negative impacts on ACME Financial Services' reputation, the company's operations costs have increased significantly. ACME Financial Services' budget for operations used to be close to their competitors', but costs have risen since the cloud migration, and they are now spending more on operations than their competitors. What's even worse is that the increased operations costs are impacting other areas of the company. The increased costs for operations are reducing funds available for new feature development and other areas that are vital for the company to remain competitive. ACME Financial Services' senior leadership has communicated to the entire company that the trend of increasing operations costs needs to be reversed and that costs need to be brought back down in line with the company's competitors.

## What about regulations?

Being in the financial industry, ACME Financial Services has numerous regulations with which they need to comply. They don't just have to worry about protecting their customers' privacy and financial information; they also have to comply with regulations specific to the financial industry, such as detecting and preventing fraudulent transactions and detecting and reporting suspicious activity.

Complying with these kinds of regulations is not nearly as obvious and clear-cut as some other types of regulations. The company has to be able to detect suspicious activity and either prevent it or report it to government regulators. For example, if an account is making hundreds of small transactions over a short period of time, this could be suspicious, especially if the account where the transactions are occurring doesn't have a history of that kind of transaction. Sometimes the transaction can look completely normal, except that it originated from a foreign country that the government has specified should not be allowed to transact with the country's financial services. However, just because a country might have a government in conflict with the country that regulates ACME Financial Services, doesn't mean the company can flatly deny transactions from that country. The transaction could be initiated from a customer of ACME Financial Services, and thus is unlikely to be an action taken by a hostile government. This gets complicated very quickly. If you have ever traveled to a foreign country and had issues performing seemingly simple financial transactions, these kinds of concerns about regulatory compliance could be part of the reason.

Of course, preventing fraudulent transactions isn't just about complying with regulations. Nowadays, most, if not all, financial services have policies in place to protect their customers from fraud. This not only helps bolster trust with their customers but is also a cost-saving measure for the financial institution. If money is withdrawn fraudulently, then the financial institution may reimburse the customer, but no one is going to reimburse the company. The money comes out of the company's revenue.

In order to handle these kinds of situations, ACME Financial Services has developed a number of systems to comply with regulations around suspicious activity. The problem the company faces is that the evolution of fraud never stops. They can develop tooling to detect a specific pattern, but once that tooling has been deployed to prevent that pattern of fraud, the criminals will work on creating the next one. When a new fraud pattern is used by criminals, ACME Financial Services has to do the following:

1. **Detect the new fraud pattern**: Depending on the pattern, the amount of money involved, and whether any existing detection systems might give a hint, detecting the fraud could be near instantaneous or possibly take a few days.
2. **Analyze the fraudulent pattern**: Detecting that something is wrong is just the first step. Once they know something is wrong, they then have to diagnose what systems are being exploited and how, so they can devise countermeasures.
3. **Prevent the fraud**: They have to implement something to stop it now and any future attempts. Depending on the complexity of the method, this could be quick or take a while to develop and test, especially if it is something that crosses multiple applications or service industries.

While the company is diagnosing new fraudulent activity, they are losing money. Criminals are exploiting ACME Financial Services' weaknesses to get as much money as possible before a countermeasure is deployed. Depending on how long the process takes, both detecting the fraudulent pattern and implementing ACME Financial Services' countermeasure, this could easily result in losing millions or even hundreds of millions of dollars. They even face non-financial fraud problems involving cloud provider services, where attackers try to compromise systems and use their resources to perform things such as cryptomining.

The large amount of money lost to fraud and the dangers of regulatory non-compliance make it clear why regulatory compliance is of supreme importance to ACME Financial Services. It's not just about avoiding penalties from government regulators; it is also about reducing costs for the company and maintaining trust with customers.

## Controlled deployments

In addition to their efforts to migrate to the cloud, ACME Financial Services has also been working to improve their speed of development. Creating new features, improving user experience, and fixing bugs are some of the ways to gain and retain customers. However, it isn't as easy as just changing application development team processes due to aforementioned concerns, such as regulatory compliance and reputational risk.

## The old deployment process

Before application development teams became more iterative, they would develop features and release them together in a group as a new application version. They couldn't just deploy that new version at any time of the day, though. The risks of disrupting something important during stock market hours were far too great, so ACME Financial Services created a somewhat laborious deployment process:

1. Application deployments could only be done after hours unless there was a critical bug that needed to be fixed.
2. Development teams had to come up with a deployment plan, which included what was being deployed, how long the deployment was expected to take, and how to ensure functionality.
3. The deployment plan would have to be signed off on and agreed to by a leader of their business unit.
4. In order for an application version to be eligible for deployment, it would first have to pass quality checks.

Usually, new application versions were deployed about once a business quarter. While the deployment process was somewhat onerous, it only had to be performed a few times a year. However, with the push to develop and deploy changes more quickly using an iterative development approach, this deployment process became a hindrance as the number of deployments increased drastically. To make matters worse, application teams didn't discover their deployment problems until they were late into the deployment planning process.

## From continuous delivery to continuous incident

ACME Financial Services has tackled some of these problems by finding ways to automate the deployment approvals process and shift left the discovery of deployment problems. For example, they have implemented standard CI/CD practices with new builds being deployed to non-production Kubernetes clusters and a home-grown tool that allows more deployment automation based upon an application's test coverage and test automation. This has helped reduce the burden of deploying a new application version, with some applications able to achieve their highest deployment automation, which will automatically deploy to production once non-production is ready. However, now that there are more application deployments, there are naturally more incidents. This isn't because quality has slipped, but simply because the complexity of the applications is growing at a faster rate, and that leads to more incidents. With a large and complex suite of applications and some new features requiring changes across multiple applications, the incident response teams are becoming lost in a sea of changes.

## The strain from adding features

As the number of features they roll out increases, their understanding of how well used, or even well liked, those new features are has been decreasing. They still deploy significant changes or new features behind configuration gates, but now there are significantly more changes being controlled by these configuration gates. Because of this, it is much harder for incident teams, or even application development teams, to know what is actually being used at any time within the complex system of applications that make up ACME Financial Services. As you might expect, this has led to internal strife trying to figure out whether a feature is being used, whether it is liked, and whether it should continue to be developed or removed.

### The technology stack

As part of their migration to the cloud, ACME Financial Services also consolidated and changed their observability stack. Before the migration, the observability stack consisted of some homegrown solutions and some proprietary solutions. They weren't able to get rid of all of the proprietary solutions for various reasons, but whenever possible, they moved toward open standards. This allowed them a larger selection of tools to choose from as part of their cloud migration journey.

One of the nice things about using a cloud provider is the large number of managed services they tend to offer. Not only do they provide automation and management tooling around Kubernetes clusters, but they also tend to have at least some monitoring tools. In the case of ACME Financial Services, their cloud provider offers managed observability tooling, and this is the path the company chose to take for their new observability technology stack.

Their cloud provider provides managed Prometheus and Grafana offerings at a reasonable price. ACME Financial Services decided that using those tools would be more cost-effective than running similar tooling themselves. This was a project in itself, as not only did application development teams have to change how they created observability information, but everyone had to be trained on how to use these new tools. By everyone, we mean not just application development teams, but incident response teams, managers, and business leaders. It was quite an effort.

For logs, they moved away from an on-premises solution to a cloud-based one. Even on-premises applications send their logs to the cloud log collector. The cloud log collector provides more functionality than just storing logs, however. It also supports creating dashboards and alerts from those logs. This seemed like a great idea, but it doesn't take long before some deficiencies with the offering become apparent. The practice of allowing application teams to create alerts from logs produces a couple of unexpected problems:

- **The alerts are delayed**: It takes the log collector service time to consume and process the logs. This results in alerts taking 15 minutes or more after the problem has occurred. For some use cases, this isn't a problem, but for others, this results in more time, with customers being impacted.
- **Application teams are in charge of creating the alerts**: For various reasons, this has resulted in these alerts being a large source of alert fatigue.

# Deciding what to improve from a sea of options

ACME Financial Services has quite a few problems to address, and they are not trivial. There is no way the company can address everything at once, as much as they would like to, so they have to prioritize which areas to tackle first.

With the senior leadership's direction to reduce costs, project leaders meet regularly and discuss, debate, and even argue over what to address first. They decide on a framework to help guide their decisions.

The first, and most important, factor for a decision is how, and how much, the change would reduce costs. To that end, they decide to start with the largest gaps with the current tooling and processes. Once they identify those gaps, they need to determine how much each gap is contributing to the increased operational expenses. With that data in hand, they will be able to investigate solutions and compare how much those potential solutions reduce costs. Once they have chosen their solutions, they will have to decide which improvements to tackle when. It is unlikely they will be able, or allowed, to implement everything in the first iteration. Some improvements may require new tools, which may require a lengthy vendor evaluation and onboarding process. Of course, application development teams will still need to deliver new features and bug fixes while they work toward supporting these improvements around operational costs. Despite the mandate from senior leadership to reduce costs, it will still be critical to align all these pieces in order for any improvement to succeed. It is no easy feat.

## Tackling the issues

First, the team separates the issues into size and complexity. They determine that the simplest, or low-hanging fruit, is the lack of ownership. All of the deployment mechanisms within the company support some kind of metadata, so they determine that it should be easy to provide information about which teams own what deployment pieces. They could then add steps in the deployment approval process, along with training, to ensure that the metadata is provided for any and all new deployments. This doesn't seem like it would require a lot of work, nor would it be too disruptive to application timelines, while also being a big improvement. With all deployments containing metadata for each part, the operations teams would know which teams to get involved in incidents. This should also help, tangentially, with the alert fatigue issue as it should help ensure that only application teams involved in the incident are part of remediation efforts.

They also decide that the fact that more issues are being observed by users is likely a symptom of these other problems. At the moment, it doesn't seem that there is a clear set of actions that would obviously directly impact that problem, so they decide to put that issue on the back burner and wait to see how the other improvements impact this problem.

## Issues determined to be medium effort

The next set of issues is determined to be medium effort and would have some impact on application team delivery schedules. The first of these issues is the lack of traceability across the company. Not only is it difficult to track an issue across multiple applications within a single business market, but it is next to impossible when applications from more than one business market are involved. However, no solution is apparent from what the working group knows already, so further investigation is needed to look at industry solutions and possibly tool evaluation.

## An eye toward aiding fraud prevention

While not directly related to the observability efforts, the working group wonders whether any of the improvements they are investigating could help with fraud detection. They figure it is worth adding criteria around functionality that could help with fraud prevention if any new tools are going to be evaluated. If they could find tooling that would also help in fraud prevention, then not only would that be a win for the company, but it would also make any licensing costs an easier sell to senior management.

## Tracking feature usage

The last issue in this middle tier of improvements is around application feature usage. This is unquestionably a driver in increasing the costs of operations. The application teams are being directed to add features, but nothing comes without a cost. As the applications add features, they also increase the complexity, and that added complexity leads to a multitude of unexpected interactions that result in an unsatisfactory user experience, and in some instances, cause service outages. Finding a way to determine which features are used and how much seems like a worthwhile effort to pursue. Not only could this data help with planning, but it could also lead to removing unused features and therefore reducing application complexity. The concept around generating this data seems pretty simple too: add metrics around each feature and create some new reports focused on that usage data. They figure some training might need to be involved as well. Even though the concept seems fairly simple, they need to investigate what kind of data they want to gather and then devise a plan for how this could be done across a multitude of application teams.

# Plans to address alert fatigue

The last, and largest, issue they identify is the alert fatigue that has already set in among the support teams. This is viewed as a very large problem that has some roots in the other smaller problems they have discovered. However, resolutions to those problems are not enough to improve this problem by a meaningful amount.

The static alerts they used in the past are overwhelming their alert-handling processes. The team decides that this alone needs multiple improvement actions. One idea is to shift away from static alerts. It is a simple idea, but they aren't sure what they should shift toward. They know this would be a large effort and require a lot of training and standardization in order to succeed.

A shift away from static alerts could see some improvement, but there is still the problem of the increased number of components in the system. The working group isn't sure how to address this, and nothing in their existing tooling provides any options. They conclude that they would have to look at additional tools to see whether anything could help with this flood of alerts.

Another prong in tackling this problem is to evaluate how their logging service is being used for alerts. Why is it generating so many alerts? Is it a training issue or something else? Is the 15-minute delay in alert generation a problem that could be improved? Does it need to be? This effort is more exploratory and data gathering than anything. The potential solutions seem to align with existing problems that are already planned to be addressed.

Finally, they need to make sure that the alerts that are generated are actionable and provide useful information. This ties into the efforts around ownership, by ensuring that alerts provide metadata from the application that generated them, but also information about what may have caused the problem with runbooks or maybe deployment data detailing changes in the most recent deployment. It isn't going to be enough to just reduce the alerts; they need to make them more useful.

That is a lot to tackle. Even more importantly, the working group doesn't know the solutions to some of the problems. They have a direction and a plan, so now they need to start investigating.

# New tools, new possibilities

The project leaders have come up with areas to investigate and solutions to be developed, but now what is to be done? It is one thing to talk about solutions in the abstract, but quite another to actually find and implement them. They know one thing for certain, and that is that their existing tools are not sufficient to meet their current needs, let alone some of the new ideas.

Tooling is where the project leaders decide to start. They know they likely need new tools, either to replace some of their existing tools or to enhance what their current tools provide. They create a capability matrix that highlights functionality that their current tooling provides and how well that functionality meets their current and planned needs. They add the functionality they are missing. This includes things such as traceability, alert management, and fraud detection. Their simple matrix looks like this:

| Application | Metrics | Alerts | Dashboards/ Visualization | Traceability | Fraud Detection | Alert Management |
|---|---|---|---|---|---|---|
| Prometheus | Y | Y | N | N | N | N |
| Grafana | Y | N | Y | N | N | N |

*Table 4.3 – Capability matrix*

Like many companies, ACME Financial Services selects their observability tools and then implements them. Once they have working tools, they don't spend time tracking the evolution of observability tooling, so they aren't aware of how new tools leveraging AI and ML are changing common observability practices.

ACME Financial Services is somewhat lucky in that the problems they have encountered are not unique. The team discovers that observability tooling has advanced significantly since they last evaluated their options. Tools have included AI and ML capabilities that make it easier to address problems that the company is facing. Getting approval for a new tool is not a simple process at ACME Financial Services, and it usually takes a clear gap in the current tooling functionality and significant cost savings to get one approved. The team concludes that their observability challenges are severe enough that it warrants running the gauntlet to get new tools approved. They are even willing to do this for more than one tool if that is what is required.

## The tool selection game

ACME Financial Services has taken the first, and easiest, step in improving their observability situation by deciding that they need to evaluate new tools to add to their application stack. The hard part is now determining which tool or tools can help them address their challenges. In addition to that, ACME Financial Services tends to be averse to adding new tools that would lock them into a single vendor. While it is not impossible to get those tools approved, if it is required, the bar for approval is much higher than it would be otherwise. This policy has evolved over time, but it was created when a few vendors of existing contracts with ACME Financial Services attempted to drastically increase their license costs. Consequently, another company policy has evolved from generally high licensing costs for third-party applications: *build versus buy*. Rather than buying a third-party tool, the company heavily favors building custom tools to fit their needs. The justification for buying a tool will also have to account for a comparison against building a custom tool.

The project leaders come up with these focus areas for evaluating vendor tools:

- **No vendor lock-in**: This is a company policy, so all attempts must be made to achieve it.
- **Pre-purchase evaluation**: The tool must be able to be evaluated with all functionalities available from the paid product.
- **Use open standards**: This isn't a hard requirement, but it is a very strong nice-to-have. Not only does it help avoid vendor lock-in, but it also preserves ACME Financial Services' ability to create their own tooling if desired. Any tool that can meet this requirement will have an easier time getting approved.
- **Open source**: This is not a hard requirement, but another very nice-to-have feature.
- **Reasonable licensing**: This one is very vague because they aren't sure what vendor costs they might encounter. Getting a tool approved will be a delicate balance of expected gain versus the cost, so it is important to keep the licensing cost in mind.

Once they have found the tool or tools they are interested in purchasing, the project leaders will then have to do a comparison against building similar functionality in-house. They are experienced in this process and realize that they must account for more than just the licensing and runtime costs. They have learned the hard way that just because it seems cheaper to build something, doesn't mean that it is the best choice.

## Build versus buy

To start with, we will take a short diversion to discuss a few economic principles that can provide insights into why sometimes buying a tool can still be the better choice even if the math says building a tool would be cheaper. We won't dive into these too deeply:

- **Opportunity cost**: In simple terms, this is the cost of the alternative not chosen. In a scenario where you are building a tool versus buying it, you will have to devote resources to designing, developing, and maintaining any tool that is developed in-house. The project will need to provide roadmaps and consume other project management resources as any other project would. While those resources are working on this tool, they are unable to work on functionality that might benefit the company more directly. For example, if a tool is projected to take two years to build, along with 10 developers, a technical lead, part of a project manager, part of an architect, and so on, then the time spent by those resources cannot be used to help create a killer functionality to gain more customers or to fix long-standing and frustrating bugs.
- **Specialization**: This basically means one group focuses on producing a limited set of goods or services, which means they are able to produce it faster and cheaper. In our example, a vendor would be well versed in the problem space they are solving and will have cultivated the expertise needed to solve the problems. In the case of ACME Financial Services, their expertise is in the financial sector, not in observability tooling, let alone AI or ML.

Even with first-hand experience of those economic principles, there is still an emphasis on building a tool instead of buying one that must be addressed. The first consideration in this process is whether there are tools available in the open source community that can be used as a foundation for an in-house solution, and how much functionality those tools provide toward the overall solution.

The next area to consider is the current state of the situation at ACME Financial Services. Is the situation dire and the solution needed as soon as possible? If so, this could make the buy option much more attractive, but it comes with a catch. Just because a third-party tool may be needed now, does not mean that an in-house tool couldn't be developed later. The third-party tool may alleviate the immediate need, but the in-house tool is the desired final solution, even once taking into account migration costs.

Lastly, they need to consider how long it will take to deploy a third-party tool. Is the tool complicated enough that it will take significant time to plan and deploy it? ACME Financial Services has complicated deployment environments, and it is not easy to deploy any tool into their system. Even an open source software project that has deployment files for Kubernetes can still take weeks or even months to get running in ACME Financial Services' heavily restricted deployment environments. So, even if a third-party tool might seem like it could solve the problem immediately, it could still be faster to develop a tool in-house once deployment time is taken into account.

# Time to investigate

With evaluation areas and functional gaps defined, the project leaders start investigating what tooling might help with their problems. They split the investigation efforts up into four teams:

- Traceability
- Alerts
- Fraud
- Feature usage

Each team will investigate their area of responsibility in parallel, and the teams will all meet regularly to share progress and findings.

## The traceability group

The group tackling the traceability problem wants to solve the difficulty their teams have with understanding what is happening within an application and across applications in multiple business areas. Currently, tracing and discovering the root cause of an incident is almost impossible, with groups of developers needing to coordinate inspecting log entries across multiple applications. Most of the time, the application teams have to get into a meeting and investigate together to try to figure out how the applications interact and what is going wrong. It is a very time-consuming and laborious process.

The team starts by looking at what tools may exist that could improve the flow of information across the applications. They quickly come across OpenTelemetry (`https://opentelemetry.io`), which is an open source project with support for many programming languages. This seems very promising, so the team decides to focus on evaluating it.

While evaluating **OpenTelemetry**, also known as **OTel**, they learn about the concept of traces. Traces are basically structured logs with additional context built in. They have something called a span ID, which could be used to trace communication across multiple containers and even across multiple applications. With **context propagation**, the support and application teams would be able to trace a request through all of the parts of the system and understand exactly what happened when and where. They decide that this sounds like exactly what they need to solve the traceability issues at hand. They learn that there's even more to OTel, though.

OTel also supports metrics and logs. While neither of these is in the original scope, the benefits of adopting OTel for both of these become obvious as they continue their evaluation. OTel doesn't prescribe the logging method, but it wraps logs with information so that logs can be correlated with traces. This seems like a pretty big benefit that would assist with diagnosing issues with traces. Using OTel for metrics would also allow them to consolidate observability data. Instead of using Prometheus for metrics and OTel for traces, they can use OTel for both and gain consistency and reduced complexity in their tools.

Best of all, OTel is open source. However, OTel doesn't provide all this functionality in a vacuum. The data produced by instrumenting applications with OTel will need to be collected and visualized somewhere, since OTel is a standard for collecting data. Using an OTel Collector, they would be able to transport this data to their existing Prometheus and Grafana installation. The team feels like support for OTel could be an important criterion for other tool evaluations, so at the next progress meeting, the team presents what they have learned about OTel, and everyone agrees that not only does it seem to address the traceability problem, but any new tools that might be considered should support OTel. They also agree that any new tool must support legacy systems where instrumenting an application with OTel isn't practical or possible.

## The feature usage group

The group tackling application feature usage wants to help development teams understand how the features in their apps are being used and how resources should be used during development. For example, if a bug affects a rarely used feature, then it probably isn't a good use of the application team's development time if there are more impactful changes that need to be made. Without this kind of information, application teams do their best to determine priority based on things such as the number of complaints or how long an issue has been in the backlog.

On the surface, this doesn't seem like a problem with a difficult solution. The group determines that they could create a policy that all new features should be enabled by an external flag, and that enabling the feature would also enable some metrics about how and when the feature is used. However, some concerns arise with this approach. One concern is around standardization. Even with training, they are sure that each development team will do things slightly differently. Another concern is how to manage the flag configurations for each application, let alone if a feature spans multiple applications or business domains. So, they decide to do some research to see whether there are any examples of others tackling these problems.

Their searches lead them to the **OpenFeature** project (`https://openfeature.dev`). They discover that the project provides a way to standardize feature flag implementations and even supports automated support for OTel. It supports many remote flag management tools, which is a new concept to the group. Even better, the project provides a remote flag management server called `flagd` that they could deploy to manage all the configurations. In theory, they could even relatively easily switch to a different flag management server if, for some reason, `flagd` doesn't work out.

OpenFeature also supports multiple languages for the client and server. The multiple languages and remote flag management server mean they will be able to manage features across application domains. They can even coordinate feature availability to their mobile apps, which is beyond the scope of their original ideas for a solution.

Since `flagd` supports retrieving configurations from one or more remote resources, and that source could be a Git repository, they have a very flexible flag configuration management pattern. Using Git also enables change management and auditing functionality around the flag configurations, which is something they hadn't originally considered. Given the highly controlled environments they operated in, this seems like a requirement that they didn't know they had.

OpenFeature is open source as well, so it is a solution that should be easy to get approved. They will have to do some designing and architecting around the `flagd` server and some training for development teams, but this seems like a clear win.

## The fraud group

The group looking for tools to help counter fraud is somewhat similar to the group looking at the alert problem. However, while the alert group is looking at solutions that address a much wider set of problems, this group is focused on how an observability tool can help address fraud. To do that, they decide to come up with a wish list of functionality that could help detect and prevent fraud and see whether there are any observability tools that can provide that kind of functionality.

Before they start looking at tools, this group first looks at the fraud patterns that have been addressed over the last year, how they were detected, and how they were countered. They hope to look for general patterns that the group can turn into wish list functionality to assess in new potential tooling.

ACME Financial Services already uses network traffic anomaly detection, and it has helped detect some kinds of fraud. It can alert on things such as a spike in traffic outside of what the company usually experiences. While it has helped, there is still a large amount of suspicious activity that has to be manually detected.

After analyzing past fraud events, the team discovers a few patterns:

- A user who has logged in and is trying random URL endpoints on the company's website

- Multiple account logins from the same IP
- The same account logging in from multiple IPs
- Deposit and withdrawal actions from newly opened accounts

ACME Financial Services already has metrics around all of these events, and in fact, it is those metrics that the company has used to understand how a new method of fraud operates. Since the metrics already exist, the group decides that it would be valuable if that data could enable proactive measures to investigate or mitigate suspicious patterns. The group decides that functionality capable of detecting and alerting on each of those patterns is a good wish list item when investigating tooling.

With an idea of what they would like to achieve, the group starts researching modern observability tools and how they might be able to help. They discover that with proper metadata on the metrics they are already generating, modern observability tools would be able to do exactly what they had hoped: detect and alert on abnormal patterns of operation. They also learn that this kind of functionality is common in a modern observability tool, which is ideal for them since the big driver for new tooling will be the group trying to improve alerts.

The group takes the findings from their research to the next progress meeting. They are confident that any new observability tooling capable of addressing the problems with alerts will be able to handle their use cases. So, with this in mind, they provide the information they have discovered to the wider group.

With three of the four groups finding either open source solutions or functionality that is common in many observability tools, it is largely up to the group tackling the company's problems with alerts to evaluate and choose tools. The other groups will largely be advisory, having already discovered solutions to their problems.

Because observability has the data to tell us whether we have unusual behavior from certain IPs, user accounts, and so on, we can detect patterns and anomalies in the data extracted from logs or traces.

## The alerts group

The group that is trying to solve the company's issues with alert fatigue has the largest and most difficult problem to solve. Not only does the group need to find a way to reduce the number of alerts, but they also want to come up with ways to make existing alerts more actionable. With that in mind, they start by researching the causes of the problems they know about and how those issues might be addressed.

## The SLO mess

It has long been the practice at ACME Financial Services for applications to create, monitor, and alert on SLOs. With a growing number of applications across multiple business areas, the number of SLOs generating alerts has exploded. Everything from a highly important interface to a customer to applications that do processing in off-hours generates alerts when their SLO is violated. They know that the number of applications will continue to grow, so this policy is not going to be viable moving forward.

Knowing the policy isn't viable is one thing, but knowing what to do about it is something else. They start researching SLO best practices and find that they need to change how they think about SLOs. They decide to evaluate a practice of looking at SLOs from the outside in, which is to say services and interfaces that the customer interacts with, and any systems used to support those operations. This practice would focus on events that users would experience, and those are the most important events to ACME Financial Services. Since they are acutely aware of the company's reputation, this policy would help align the actions of the response teams with the principles the company cares about the most.

Implementing this SLO practice would drastically reduce the number of SLOs being tracked and generating alerts. It would require changing company guidelines that have stood for a long time, but the working group is confident that they have a winning message that they can take to senior leadership.

## Static alerts

Another driver of alert fatigue is the common practice of using static alerts by the application teams. When applications were relatively few and monolithic, this practice wasn't so bad. If an application was low on CPU, memory, or disk availability, then the support teams would want to know in order to take action before a failure occurred. Now that the application teams have modernized and adopted cloud-native design principles, those same alerts are now being generated by many more application Pods. Even worse, that same data is sometimes used to auto-scale the Kubernetes cluster or application Pods, which means the alert is complete noise.

It seems obvious that a first step to improve the noise generated by these alerts is to remove any alerts around metrics used to auto-scale the Kubernetes cluster or application Pods. While that is a good start, it doesn't go nearly far enough to solve this problem. The number of Pods generating alerts is enormous and only getting larger. These alerts also have much less utility than they did in the past. If 1 Pod out of 100 is low on CPU, memory, or disk, that isn't as much of a concern as when the monolithic application they replaced raises the same alert.

They decide to look into what other options exist for alerting practices besides static alerts. The working group discovers that this problem is one that ML/AI can help address. Instead of setting static thresholds for each Pod and trying to maintain them, tools that utilize ML/AI are able to automatically baseline an application and understand its unique usage patterns. This can drastically cut down on the number of alerts generated. Those tools also have some other potential benefits, such as automatically detecting relationships and anomalies, and can even automate some response actions.

Improvement in this area would not only depend on choosing the proper tool, but also on changing the culture and guidance for application development teams at ACME Financial Services.

## Siloed data

After talking with the response and application teams, they discover that the current processes suffer from a problem called **siloed data**. The problem is that when an alert is raised, it only provides information about a single piece of information. For example, the CPU utilization is above 90%. However, once that alert has been received, there is no further indication about what may be causing it. Prometheus has no connection to application logs or source code repositories, so response teams and application teams have to search through logs and change histories to try to discover what might be causing the alert. Once the alert is received, the investigation teams have no way of knowing whether the alert was generated because of a spike in traffic from normal usage, fraud, a long-standing bug, or a new feature that was introduced. The lack of context for an alert means the mitigation investigation has no definitive place to start. Some incidents benefit from tribal knowledge that teams have gained about how an application functions and what may have caused specific problems in the past, but that kind of information is fragile. If a person is on vacation or leaves the company, then that knowledge isn't available when an alert is being investigated. Some teams have tried to document this kind of knowledge in their runbooks, and while that has helped, it has not replaced the experience gained by those diagnosing the causes of events.

As the working group researches solutions, they discover that this is another area where observability tooling that uses AI/ML can help. These AI/ML observability tools, combined with OTel traces and logs, as well as source code repository commit histories, can provide a rich set of context to response teams investigating an alert. It is exactly this kind of context data that response teams have to go and discover on their own with the company's current tooling.

## Alerts from logs

Even before the cloud migration effort, ACME Financial Services was already on a journey to improve alerting within the company. The first iteration of this was going from no alerts to using their log aggregation service to produce alerts. While this was an improvement over nothing, it eventually came to be the bane of application and response teams. Application teams were given free rein to decide what to alert on and at what thresholds. The application development teams have not been diligent in trying to address the cause of alerts in non-production environments, and so the alert notices clog up email inboxes and are largely ignored, even in production. Most application development teams use email filters to prevent alerts from filling up their inboxes. This is the very definition of alert fatigue.

What makes the alerts from logs even worse is that they are delayed, usually by at least 15 minutes, from the time of an event occurring. This puts response teams behind in trying to reduce the **Mean Time to Resolution** (**MTTR**). There is a type of alert where this delay may not matter, but for anything customer-facing, this guarantees that the problem will be experienced by customers for at least 15 minutes, if not more.

For these reasons, ACME Financial Services has already been encouraging teams to move off of log-based alerts and to metrics-based ones. This has been a slow effort because it first requires that the metrics exist in order to create the alerts. Up to this point, instrumenting an application with metrics has been left up to the application teams, and the result has been that the progress on migrating away from log-based alerts has been slow.

The team doesn't see how it will be possible to meet some of the objectives of the project and still allow log-based alerts for customer-facing services. While the effort to migrate off of those types of alerts has been slow, the team agrees that they will need to find a way to entice or force the application teams to make the needed changes. Limiting the scope of this change should help get the support needed for the effort from senior management, but the work will still have to go into an application team's backlog and be prioritized with other work. They decide to present a plan to senior leadership, calling for the completion of this work by customer-facing applications only within a year.

## Bringing it all together

The various teams continue to meet regularly to share information and discuss progress, and over time, it becomes apparent just how interrelated the various issues are to one another. OTel, first discussed by the traceability group, is not only relevant to that problem but also to the alert fatigue issue being investigated by the alerts group. Solutions to help with fraud will also help with feature usage, traceability, and alert fatigue. The teams are surprised by these connections, but are also relieved because it means the solution won't have to be multiple tools and new processes. It also means a fairly standard set of requirements for tool selection, which is a nice bonus.

The whole working group comes up with the following requirements for evaluating new tools:

- It must be able to provide alert context from logs, code changes, traces, and anomalies
- It must support ingesting OTel data
- It must support legacy system observability either through an agent, log ingestion, or other means
- It must support application-level anomaly detection
- It must utilize AI/ML functionality to help detect anomalies
- It must work with their existing monitoring solutions (Prometheus/Grafana)
- It must support baselining and dynamic alerts
- The vendor must allow evaluation with full functionality
- The tool must be able to integrate with the tools the company uses for incident response

With this list of requirements, they can finally start looking for tooling options. It doesn't take them long to realize that these requirements are not unique and that modern observability tooling has been working to address their needs for quite a while. Many tools have also started incorporating AI/ML functionality. Based upon their research, they come up with a list of six vendors to choose from and evaluate:

- TraceMagic
- Logcat
- CloudObserve
- DataDash
- GraphResearch
- ACME Observability

After creating use cases to evaluate the various tools, they contact the vendors and plan evaluations of their products. The working group evaluates each tool against the list of use cases and documents how the use case is implemented, as well as information that they gather about the tool, such as resource requirements and pricing. After this exhaustive evaluation process, the working group chooses ACME Observability as the observability tool to bring into ACME Financial Services.

## Plan of action

The result of the initiative to evaluate and improve ACME Financial Services' observability practices has produced quite a list of changes, some of which are small and others are quite large. The working group puts together a summary of the actions that they have determined are needed:

- Augmenting application deployments with metadata to address the lack of ownership for deployed artifacts. This would be enforced with additional checks during the deployment approval process and application team training.
- Championing OTel to address company-wide traceability issues. This will require the creation of some standards and training for application teams, as well as designing and implementing OTel Collectors to route the data to Prometheus and the new ACME Observability tools.
- Using AI/ML in the ACME Observability tools to monitor and detect application-level anomalies in order to enhance fraud detection capabilities.
- Using OpenFeature to track feature usage and control feature availability in deployed applications. Then, using the data gathered to help application teams understand how their applications are used and which features are most popular as inputs to priority planning. A new flag management system, process, and standards will need to be developed and training created for application teams.
- Evaluating existing SLOs and paring them with only customer-impacting applications. In addition to an evaluation of the current state of affairs, new guidelines will need to be created and training provided to application teams.
- Retiring log-based alerts for all customer-impacting applications. New standards and training will need to be created for application teams.

- Using ACME Observability's AI/ML functionality to migrate from static alerts to dynamic ones. New training and guidance will need to be created for application teams.
- Tackling the *siloed data* problem by using ACME Observability's tooling to combine OTel data, legacy observability data, source code changes, deployment data, and anomaly detection to provide context to alerts.

That is quite a list of work, and the working group knows that they cannot execute on all avenues at once. Some of the efforts will depend on new infrastructure deployments, which will require planning, deployment, and testing before the application team can use them.

Before any of that can occur, the working group would need to get senior management approval for the plan and the additional licensing cost for ACME Observability. Once they have approval, they will have to decide what parts to implement first, what can be executed in parallel, and any dependencies among the efforts. Lastly, they will have to take application schedules into account when devising deliverable targets.

## Having the "what" and determining the "how"

It has been a long and educational journey for the working group at ACME Financial Services that is trying to improve observability practices within the company. They now know what they need to do and have gotten approval from senior leadership on all aspects of their plan. Now they have to figure out how they are going to accomplish these improvements.

ACME Financial Services is a large company, and it doesn't do anything quickly. Past initiatives at a company-wide scale have taken years to complete because as much as senior leadership may want something done, they also still want new features, products, and bug fixes. Any work asked of the application development teams will have to be managed alongside other work already on their plate. Given the nature and importance of these improvements, and the level of support and urgency from senior leadership, this work will be given high priority by the application development teams, but that doesn't necessarily mean the effort will be completed in record time.

The team knows that when they go to request work from the application development teams, they will need to have a well-defined ask for the teams to work toward. With so many technologies and changes involved in this effort, they realize that they will need to create some training and standards before they engage the application development teams. That makes it pretty obvious that the first task in this effort is to create some training and standards, but even that must be organized because until OTel Collectors or ACME Observability are available for use, there is really nothing for the application development teams to work on with those efforts. So, the working group starts creating training and standards for items that application development teams can start working toward immediately:

- Ownership metadata
- Training and standards development for approvers of application deployments
- What should have an SLO and removing all other SLOs
- High-level view of the company's vision
- End date for alerts from logs

Once training and standards are created around these topics, they can start training application development teams and creating due dates for completion. In parallel with that effort, they can improve the deployment approval tooling to support enforcing ownership metadata. Even with this being immediately actionable, it will still take a long time before all of the applications are compliant. Even so, these efforts will have a big initial impact on the effort to modernize observability for ACME Financial Services.

It's a good thing that the first phase won't be completed quickly, because new infrastructure needs to be developed and deployed to support the other initiatives in this effort. This work includes designing and deploying the OTel Collectors, a central feature flag management system or process, and ACME Observability at a scale that can support the entire company. They will have to research OTel Collector architectures and design for scale, but once that is done, the next set of training and standards will need to be created:

- OTel traces, logs, and metrics
- Using OpenFeature for feature flagging and usage metrics
- Moving from static to dynamic alerts

This set of work will have the largest impact on application development team schedules. Adopting OTel and OpenFeature will require work that will have to compete with new features and bug fixes.

In parallel, the company will need to work with ACME Observability on design and architecture for deploying the new tooling at a scale that will support all of ACME Financial Services. This is the phase that brings together all the previous efforts by the observability working group and the application development teams, and also where the benefits begin to take shape. Once ACME Observability has been deployed and is ready for use, the final set of training and standards needs to be created:

- How to use application anomaly detection to detect fraud
- How to use trace data to improve traceability with ACME Observability

- Demonstration of context added to alerts
- Training on how to use ACME Observability

This work is largely around showing teams how to use the new tooling and the benefits it provides. It will have little impact on application development schedules. However, this is where a culture change for ACME Financial Services will need to emerge; it should become the expectation that no matter the complexity of application interactions, it can be traced, alerts have useful and actionable context, and generated alerts have value and should not be ignored.

Let's look at how fraud detection and response could be enhanced with AIOps. Through this AIOps user story, we'll identify places where the sociotechnical aspects of ACME Financial Services may influence the implementation and success.

**The use case**: As a fraud specialist, I want automated alerting, incident response, and ticket augmentation for potential fraud activity.

**Definition of done**:

- An AI agent leverages observability data to flag potential fraud
- An incident is created for the fraud department
- The AI agent augments the incident details with the relevant data samples
- The relevant standard operating procedure is executed, which may include the following:
    - Notifying the account owner and asking them to call in
    - Deactivating online access or forcing a password change, and identity verification

This is the user story that the fraud team wrote up to capture their requirements. Each of their requests has dependencies on other teams and existing systems. The AI agent will need to combine its unique capabilities with those of existing systems in order to meet the definition of done for this user story.

There are a few other requirements here that may not be as immediately obvious. Most financial companies use the Gordon-Loeb model to determine the appropriate amount of monetary investment to make into security. That model sets the threshold for optimal maximum investment at 37% of the expected loss from a breach (`https://en.wikipedia.org/wiki/Gordon%E2%80%93Loeb_model`).

This means the team that is implementing the solution must try to ensure that the solution is not overly expensive to implement and can demonstrably save human time to help offset its costs.

First, the team needs to clarify several key aspects of the requirements:

- What is the threshold for metrics to trigger a fraud incident?
- What kinds of anomalies indicate potential fraud?
- What is the necessary data for incident augmentation?
- What are the security and compliance requirements for writing that data into the ticketing system?
- Where do the SOPs live, and how is the correct one identified?

For this use case, the AIOps system will have an immediate and measurable impact on the end customer. Although they may not know that it's responsible for locking their accounts after suspicious logins, they will be negatively impacted if it does so erroneously. Therefore, it's critical to get this right, and use a crawl, walk, run approach.

The first step is working with all dependent teams to get the data needed by the fraud department with the correct enrichment. This isn't an easy or overnight process. So, it may not be completed until well into the run stage. Therefore, the team will have to work within the processes of the company to ensure proper prioritization of the work. Demonstrating potential cost savings, and any other value, can tip the scales of feature negotiation to free up capacity for getting that work done.

While that data enrichment doesn't exist, it's possible to start satisfying the definition of done by working in the confines of what does. The existing automation already does many of the actions here. It detects fraud, creates an incident, locks an account, and sends a notification. Those capabilities do not need to be rewritten, but they will eventually need to be made accessible to the AI agent. If access is via an API call, then the agent will need to be given an identity for using the API and knowledge of how to use it. This may call for a custom MCP server, our first one.

Where the automation isn't doing a great job today is in augmenting the incident ticket with all the relevant data. Financial systems data is highly regulated, so correlating it could be challenging. However, if we consider a data model for event metrics, it's likely that there is a one-way hash for correlating the metric to the account. Therefore, the AI agent can find relevant metrics and logs, keying off that hash, and identify other potentially useful data points to key off of, such as the typical time of day for user activity. It can combine raw data with an analysis of that data and write it to the ticketing system.

Those writes will also need to be added to the AI agent's skillset, and that will be MCP server number two.

Let's look at the crawl workflow for this new incident response:

1. **Workflow 1**:
    1. Automation creates a ticket.
    2. A fraud team member requests an AI investigation.
    3. The AI investigation is added to the ticket.
    4. The fraud team member executes the appropriate SOP.
2. **Workflow 2**:
    1. A customer calls in with a fraud complaint.
    2. A ticket is created by the fraud team.
    3. The AI investigation is initiated by the team member.
    4. Investigation details are added to the ticket.
    5. The team executes the correct SOP.

The human element of workflow 2 will, in all likelihood, always be with us. Customers will initiate incidents. But in the future, instead of the agent being called upon by the team member, the event of ticket creation can trigger the AI investigation automatically for both workflows. Reducing one manual step in the workflow is a small but measurable success.

The walk stage would be the point where the majority of the actions are handled by the AI, but with human oversight. The walk stage workflow looks like this:

1. **Workflow 1**:
    1. Automation creates a ticket.
    2. The AI agent populates it with investigation details and recommends an SOP to run.
    3. The fraud team member approves the SOP or suggests a new one.
2. **Workflow 2**:
    1. A customer calls in with a fraud complaint.
    2. A ticket is created by the fraud team.
    3. The AI agent populates it with investigation details and recommends an SOP.
    4. The team member approves the SOP or suggests a new one.

The final stage is run. The run stage workflow looks like this:

1. **Workflow 1**:
    1. A ticket is created by the AI agent.
    2. It populates the ticket details with the results of the investigation.
    3. AI runs the SOP.
    4. It resolves the ticket and sends it for human review.
2. **Workflow 2**:
    1. Automation creates a ticket.
    2. The AI agent populates the ticket details with the results of the investigation.
    3. AI runs the SOP
    4. It resolves the ticket and sends it for human review.
3. **Workflow 3**:
    1. A human creates a ticket.
    2. The AI agent populates the ticket details with the results of the investigation.
    3. AI runs the SOP
    4. It resolves the ticket and sends it for human review.

Eventually, the confidence in the system will grow to the point that the human review aspect may not come into play anymore. It's generally good practice to review incidents from time to time, regardless of whether they were handled by a human or a machine, so we'd never recommend cutting human review out entirely. Having the AI publish a summary of tickets, their resolutions, and whether any were reopened on a regular cadence would also help facilitate the surfacing of success metrics and general cost savings to the relevant business stakeholders.

But wait, can that same incident workflow be applied to internal incidents? Yes! Although the way the data is used is different and there may be some different incident management tooling, a lot of the data and workflows are almost entirely the same.

Here's the basic incident response workflow with AI integrated into the process:

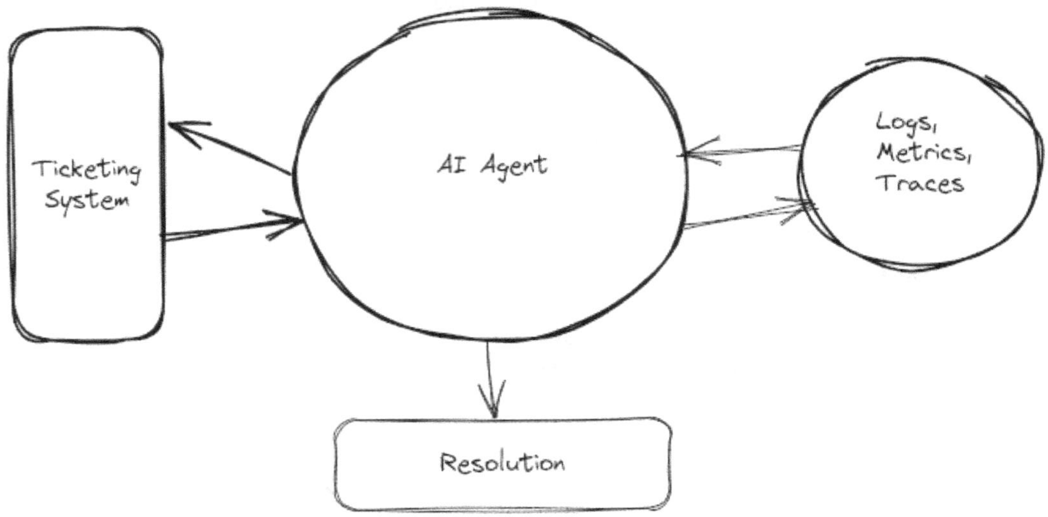


Figure 4.2 – Simplified incident workflow

At the heart of it, you have a source of truth for the incident, the observability data used to investigate the incident, and a resolution. You can connect your AI agent to pretty much any of it, as long as you do so securely. The same crawl, walk, run approach applies. Let's imagine we're working on an application-related incident at the run stage:

1. First, the ticket is created based on an alert that our application is not responding within normal parameters.
2. The AI agent determines that this is a critical incident and marks the ticket as such. It may also send additional alerts to places such as Slack to let the humans know.
3. Next, the AI agent augments the incident. It will investigate several possible causes:
    - Network and load balancer issues
    - Application health
    - Database health
4. The results of the investigations are written to the incident ticket. They will be useful for the root cause analysis later.
   The cause is the application itself. For some reason, it's exceeding its memory quota.
5. The AI agent raises a pull request to increase the memory and links it to the incident ticket.
6. A human reviews the PR and the linked incident and either approves or denies the change.

7. Log analysis is carried out to determine why the application is experiencing what appears to be a memory leak.
8. The cause is found, and a remediation is either directly applied or recommended.
9. A root cause analysis document is created by the AI agent for stakeholder review.

Human checkpoints to ensure the AI isn't hallucinating or experiencing errors are still necessary. But the capability to quickly narrow down the cause, parse logs, and send pull requests makes AIOps a force multiplier in this space. One human can now work on an incident far more efficiently with the assistance of AI. Remember, an accurate AI is an AI that has the correct data, correctly enriched; the quality of the data it has to work with will determine how well it can do the job.

# It's finally done. What did we gain?

It's been a long journey for ACME Financial Services as they have worked to improve their observability deficiencies after their cloud migration. It takes several years and lots of planning, negotiation of priorities, and even some sacrifices, but they finally finish implementing all of their planned improvements. All applications are sending OTel traces and metrics, as well as augmenting their application logs with OTel metadata. All new features are gated behind OpenFeature, and metric information is collected and used by application development teams to help prioritize work. Log-based alerts have been retired for all customer-facing applications. ACME Observability is the new cornerstone of the company's observability practices and is central to moving from static to dynamic alerts with actionable context. It is still early in the evaluation of the new practices, but a few improvements have already been noticed:

| Before | After |
|---|---|
| Too many people were needed to help troubleshoot incidents | Identification of relevant teams simplified |
| Long resolution times | Resolution times down |
| Alert fatigue | Actionable alerts |
| Fraud detection limited | Fraud detection and response expanded |
| Feature releases risky | Feature flags enabled |

*Table 4.4 – Before and after at ACME Financial Services*

The incident response teams are now much more efficient. Whereas before an alert would arrive and the incident response team would gather a large group of stakeholders to diagnose and mitigate an issue, now the response teams know exactly which teams need to be involved in an incident and involve only those teams. Thanks to ownership metadata and traceability information, the incident response teams now know not only which application is involved in an incident but also which other applications are part of the sequence of events that caused the alert. This has resulted in reduced strain on the application development teams as well, since they are each called into much fewer incidents. The incident response teams are also better able to document actions and drive resolution in an incident, instead of spending time trying to make sure all the important stakeholders are involved.

Incident resolution times have also decreased by a noticeable amount. The appropriate application development teams are involved in an incident sooner, and the alerts have context to help them investigate the problem. Whereas before the application teams had to dig through logs trying to understand what happened when and what sequence or change might be relevant to the incident, now they have log, metric, deployment, and code change history available in ACME Observability to help them diagnose the cause of an incident.

The number of meaningless alerts has dropped drastically. While it is still a battle to get everyone to respond to every event, the culture is slowly changing as alerts prove themselves to be more relevant. The number of alerts that are not acted upon is slowly starting to decline.

The changes are even helping to combat fraud. The AI/ML functionality in ACME Observability's tools detects and alerts on usage patterns outside of normal activity. It has had a noticeable impact on mitigating and countering new fraud patterns as they are encountered.

Because incidents are resolved faster and fewer people are involved in incidents, the general atmosphere of the company has improved. Incidents *cost* less because they are shorter lived and don't require as many people to resolve. The operations and application teams are much less stressed, and therefore more efficient in handling incidents. Burnout that was so prevalent before has been mitigated and even started to decline.

These outcomes are all measurable successes of the project. They matter not just for engineering but also for executive leadership. When we think about DORA metrics, they don't just map to engineering health. They also directly impact business health.

A decreasing change failure rate, lead time to change, and MTTR positively impact customers. These metrics directly map to the success and delight of customers using the systems.

Increasing deployment frequency can mean customers are seeing features faster. When the changes to systems are overall smaller and more frequent, they're often better tested and more stable. The observability data that's already being collected can be used to calculate these metrics and generate business reports, adding a key dimension to the overall picture of the organization.

Most importantly, catching and preventing fraud more often reduces the risk of financial losses associated with a successful breach. The same model that determines how much to spend is a good investment can also be used to prove that the investment has paid off. If we track the cost of the system and the cost of person-hours against the budget we needed to not exceed, and we're still at or below that line, then the project would be considered a success by any measure.

Perhaps the best result of all the work is an improved reputation for ACME Financial Services. With customers experiencing fewer issues and for shorter periods of time, they have more positive and trustworthy feelings toward ACME Financial Services. More trust means more customers, but in the financial services world, a trustworthy reputation is priceless.

# Summary

In this chapter, we have followed our fictional company, ACME Financial Services, as they found themselves in a difficult and unmanageable situation after completing their cloud migration. Operational costs had jumped and their old observability practices were no longer working. They had to find a way to address their problems before they resulted in serious damage to the company. This required forming a group to investigate and learn about new observability practices and tooling, evaluate new tools, plan company-wide improvements, deploy new infrastructure, negotiate priorities, and get senior leadership support for the entire plan. It was a herculean effort that affected the entire company and took many years to complete, but the end result was a more efficient incident response process and, best of all, improved company reputation.

This ended up only being the start of their journey. As with many complex problems, solving one set of problems reveals additional problems that were hidden or not understood at the start. One of the biggest drivers of the changes was cost control, and the observability working group discovered that it is not as easy to reduce costs as they thought.

Cost was just one dimension of a much larger challenge. In this chapter, we discussed the importance of making observability make sense by going from overwhelming data to actionable information. In the next chapter, we'll look more at how an **Internal Developer Platform** (**IDP**) helps organizations turn observability data into actionable information—a lesson ACME Financial Services will also learn in future chapters.

# Join us on Discord

For discussions around the book and to connect with your peers, join us on Discord at `packt.link/discordcloud` or scan the QR code below:

# Part 2

# Expanding Left: Moving AIOps into Platform Engineering

*Part 2* explores how AI-driven operational insights can be brought earlier into the software delivery lifecycle through self-service platforms. You will learn how democratized observability and intelligent agents empower developers, SREs, and platform teams to work more autonomously and proactively. The part culminates with the ACME Financial Services story, demonstrating how organizations can evolve from AIOps toward fully agentic platforms that accelerate innovation and operational excellence.

This part of the book includes the following chapters:

# 5

# Democratizing Observability: A Primer to Self-Service Platforms

Many organizations are implementing **internal development platforms** (**IDPs**) as a central self-service portal for engineers to get their daily tasks done without having a dependency on centralized specialty teams that need to fulfill tasks on request. A platform in many ways acts as the circulatory system for a company, supporting applications that serve all kinds of purposes, both internal and customer-facing. In this chapter, we will dive into how observability data can become part of self-service platforms, whether they are implemented through Backstage, commercial offerings, or home-built solutions. We will highlight how we can integrate observability into those platforms, how the platforms can help ensure the right data is collected, and how observability data should be made available through those platforms, rather than having users manually find the relevant data across the suite of observability tools.

In this chapter, we're going to cover the following main topics:

- What is a self-service platform?
- How to bake observability best practices and context into templates
- Bringing the relevant observability data to the end users
- How to leverage and monitor AI
- Beyond IDP: Other places to push observability data

## Technical requirements

In this chapter, we will discuss model accuracy measurements.

You will need Python 3 and pip3 already installed to follow along with these examples: `https://www.python.org/downloads/`.

Please refer to the Python documentation for installation instructions.

On Linux and macOS systems, Homebrew is a helpful method for installation: `https://brew.sh/`.

Everything you need for the python scripts in this chapter are in our GitHub Repository: `https://github.com/PacktPublishing/Observability-in-the-AI-Native-Era` We recommend using venv or another virtual environment before installing dependencies or running these scripts.

We will be using the ROUGE and BERT scoring libraries in Python. To install these dependencies, run the following within the project folder in Github:

```
pip install -r requirements.txt
```

If you haven't already set up Ollama to run DeepSeek, now would be the time: `https://ollama.com/download`.

To use the DeepSeek model, run the following:

```
ollama run deepseek-r1
```

Once you've installed these dependencies, let's get started.

# What is a self-service platform?

A self-service platform is an IDP that enables the development teams using it to utilize features or add capabilities without needing to wait for the platform engineering team to do it for them.

Often just called *the platform*, an IDP provides centralized golden-path self-service to standardize the way software is developed, tested, observed, secured, and operated across an organization. An IDP is considered the golden path when it's both opinionated and well documented. A golden path doesn't just set the organizational standards; it enforces them and provides quick and meaningful feedback to the end users when they have run afoul of those standards.

For example, if we look at the platform engineering technology, Backstage developers of the platform have a feature known as plugin support, allowing engineers to add capabilities either from pre-written community plugins or by writing their own. `https://backstage.io/`

`plugins/` has a series of plugins created by the community with various capabilities around topics such as APIs and logging.

> **Note**
>
> It is also important to note that a portal, for example, Backstage, alone is not a self-service platform. A portal is just the starting point that provides easy access to templates, software catalogs, and similar resources.

An IDP approach to software delivery is typically a business decision taken to accelerate engineering velocity in addition to solving business cases, such as standardized deployments, supporting security and compliance, and making scalability a central feature of the software being developed. When software application developers need to move fast, a self-service platform can provide them with the competencies to quickly start shipping a product, but also the flexibility to address their own operational needs.

The purpose of an IDP is to unify the method by which highly repetitive tasks are accomplished across the organization. Technology can replace people, taking dedicated release and operations teams from individual development teams with duplicated repetitive tasks into a central platform. This allows the development teams to spend their time focused on writing software and not on the delivery mechanisms.

An IDP is often created as organizations go through the process of identifying how to make developers more efficient. Often, the first step in the journey to creating an IDP is centralizing functions that are repeated by many development teams into one central team.

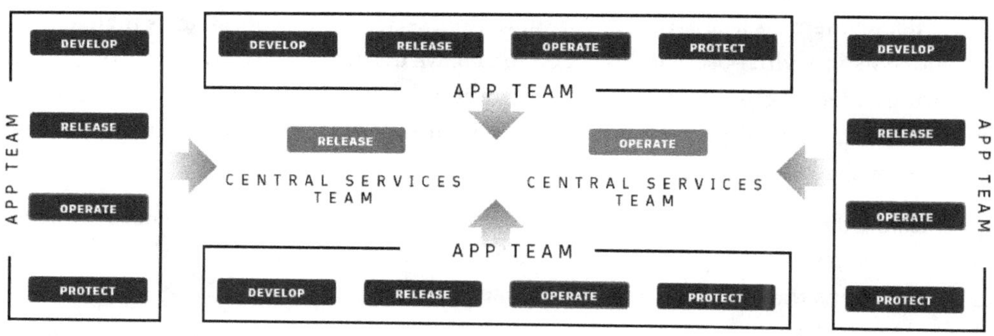


*Figure 5.1: Duplicate work and repeat functions are moved to a centralized team*

However, this leads to scalability challenges, the central team pivots, and, ultimately, an IDP is born.

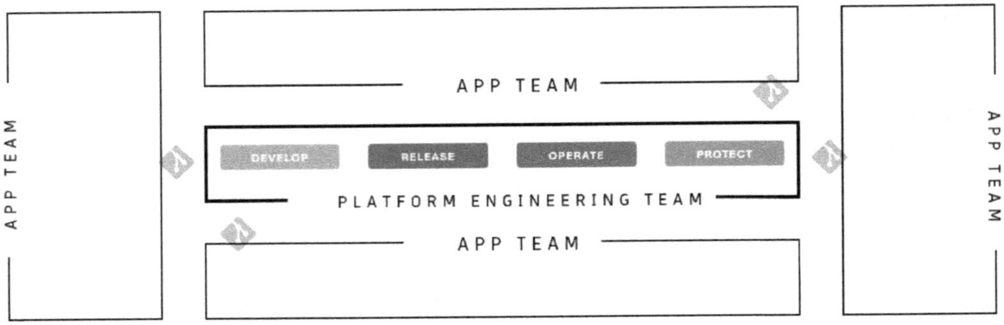


*Figure 5.2: Platform engineering team creates an IDP*

The IDP becomes the central hub for software development within an organization. This also allows for the creation and enforcement of project norms and code style guides and the utilization of templating technologies and linters to support these quality gates.

Similarly, an IDP can also support and dictate centralized logging systems, metrics collection, and the methods by which observability data is made available to users of the platform. Those users are not only highly technical but may also represent business and customer interests.

In *Chapter 3*, we discussed how the three pillars of observability—logs, metrics, and traces—have additional use cases beyond just application health and runtime. Business insights such as security and compliance or cost management are also supported through the collection and analysis of observability data. However, in order for an organization to realize these benefits, deployments must have some degree of uniformity. For many organizations, standardizing resource deployments is a key strategy for validation, security, and compliance; managing costs; and assisting with observability. In *Chapter 3*, we discussed the importance of augmenting collected observability data with additional metadata. Templates and boilerplate help to ensure that data is present, but also to standardize log levels and unify where and how that data is pushed.

Democratizing observability data means making it available to everyone who needs it. This is done by ensuring software systems are producing the necessary data, and pushing the right data into locations that are accessible but also access-controlled.

You may be asking, "*How can an IDP enforce these standards?*" to which the answer, as always, is, "*It depends.*" When we look at the capabilities of a platform, one aspect of that is the enforcement of a predefined maturity model for the workloads on the platform. The maturity model is the definition of done for a workload to become a part of the platform. It includes conformance to the golden path, which may include adherence to known best practices such as logging levels, the use of feature flags, and well-tuned alerts with correct routing defined in the observability stack. There can be several processes, both technical and sociotechnical, for a platform and the platform engineering team to leverage to accomplish this goal. One such process for ensuring the correct data is being collected is by leveraging templating and boilerplate code to create a unified method of data collection and data organization—in other words, codifying best practices around observability.

First, let's look at what technologies are leveraged for standardization. We'll look at options for Kubernetes, serverless deployments, and traditional LAMP stack deployments, starting with the least complex and working our way up to more involved options.

## Kubernetes standardization

The Kubernetes API allows for object enrichment through the usage of **labels** and **annotations**. Labels allow for objects to be selected by the value of the labels, effectively making them a way of identifying related Kubernetes objects. Labels can be made available to all cluster users via the `app.kubernetes.io` prefix and kept private to users if used without the prefix. On the other hand, annotations are for storing non-identifying metadata and are available to any user that has access to read the annotated object. In this context, *identifying* means that the data can be used for searching and grouping objects. What would typically be considered identifying data can be used in annotations, for example, to identify the pager escalation for a workload, but it would need to be parsed by additional automation tools as that is not the functionality of the Kubernetes API.

An example of a label is `app.kubernetes.io/environment: staging`, which could be used for filtering or searching for all Kubernetes objects with the same labels. An annotation might have information about the owning team or their Slack channel. The annotation can be used by additional automation to direct data or alerts for the workload, and the `staging` label lets the team know what environment the data belongs to. However, there are many other examples of best practices. The following tables should be considered a source of ideas, not a comprehensive list:

| **Example Label** | **Example Values** |
|---|---|
| Environment | production, staging, test, dev |
| Application | nginx, load, front-end |
| Version | 1.2.3, alpha, beta |

*Table 5.1: Examples of Kubernetes labels*

| Annotation Key Example | Example Values |
|---|---|
| Owning ream | A Slack handle or channel |
| Cost center | dev, sales, finance, LOB |
| App group | public facing websites, business apps, back office, dev tools |
| Priority | tier 1, tier 2, tier 3 |
| Alerting mode | off, daily, instant |

*Table 5.2: Example of Kubernetes annotations*

As discussed in *Chapter 3*, in the *Context is king* section, those labels and annotations can also be used by the observability platform. For instance, when logs are ingested, they can be enriched with information such as environment, team, or priority. This then allows a development team to make requests such as: "*Show me all the logs from the Tier 1 apps that my team is responsible for*." And thinking one step further, when the observability platform detects new error logs that are tagged with Tier 1, it can action upon the *alerting mode* annotation. If that is set to *instant*, an immediate message can be sent to the team that is set as the owner.

The next question is: *how can we apply this metadata in a consistent way across the organization?*

An easy way for a Kubernetes-based platform team to enforce the utilization of this data would be via CI/CD pipeline checks, admission controllers, or a custom check on a **pull request** (**PR**) merge into a Git repository. However, this still requires the labels and annotations to be hand-coded. That leaves an uncomfortable amount of room for human error and can cause frustration and significant time waste if the point of failure is not until deployment is attempted.

Therefore, a platform team needs to identify the user needs. From an observability perspective, developers would benefit from several key capabilities:

- Getting direct access links to the key observability dashboards relevant to their software component, versus having to learn how to find those dashboards every time they need them in the various tools
- Getting presented with the latest critical logs that were captured by the observability tool, versus having to find the logs themselves

- Getting an overview of all SLOs for this component and what the current values are versus having to find this information themselves
- Getting an automated analysis of performance hotspots, for example, what are the slowest requests and the worst database calls that the code is doing, versus having to analyze logs, metrics, and traces themselves to find those patterns. Here, we also often talk about *automated observability scorecarding*.

This is where templating technologies can make a big impact. By providing templates or boilerplate code examples, a platform can support data quality and consistency during the development cycle. While the use cases for templating and boilerplate exceed just ensuring observability best practices are utilized in a consistent manner, this is the use case we're going to focus on in this chapter.

Now that we understand the business cases and justification behind using templates and what problems they solve for the users of a platform, let's dive deeper into the technologies available today.

## Kustomize

Kustomize is a configuration management tool included in Kubernetes by default that allows users to generate configuration automatically.

For example, with Kustomize, you can use the annotation transformer to automatically apply annotations to Kubernetes resources. This prevents mistakes or blocking of resource deployment by ensuring the method for applying configuration lives on the cluster alongside the workloads it is modifying. In the YAML for the Kustomize file, the methods for identifying which workloads to select and modify are defined.

Kustomize's strength is its ability to crawl a directory and, with surgical precision, modify the contents within.

## Boilerplate code and templates

Boilerplate code is often supplied in a **software development kit** (**SDK**), typically as a common library or function that developers can use to complete tasks. The Operator SDK for building Kubernetes operators generates quite a bit of boilerplate to help fill in the basic functions of an operator, and also includes the capability to generate observability configurations by using boilerplate code to expose metrics that are considered a best practice; see `https://book.kubebuilder.io/reference/metrics-reference.html` for more information on those metrics.

Another example of boilerplate code comes from the **OpenTelemetry** (**OTel**) SDK. This SDK contains functionality to help developers quickly leverage the core functionalities. This SDK supports best practices such as sampling and exporting data to a long-term storage solution, and includes some capabilities for attaching metadata to the observability data being exported, such as hostname or some hierarchy information.

If you are using Backstage for your IDP, it natively supports software templates (https://backstage.io/docs/features/software-templates/) as a core feature. When you create a template, it is stored in the software catalog and can then be leveraged by the IDP users.

## Prometheus templates

In *Chapter 1*, we discussed OTel and Prometheus for metrics collection, so we won't dive deep into it again here. What's notable for Prometheus is that unlike OTel's use of an SDK, Prometheus leverages templates to codify best practices into the observability stack (https://prometheus.io/docs/prometheus/latest/configuration/template_examples/). Prometheus's templating capability leverages the Go templates package of Golang. There's more than one place where templating is usable, but the most common use is likely in the alerting rules. This allows you to write alert rules once, for every Kubernetes resource kind on the cluster. For example, if you wanted to alert on Pods crashing, you'd write a rule like this:

```
annotations:
  summary: "Pod {{ $labels.pod }} is crashing"
  description: >
Pod {{ $labels.pod }} in namespace {{ $labels.namespace }}
is restarting frequently on node {{ $labels.node }}.
```

Prometheus templates can also be used to add the label and annotation metadata to metrics and alerts, ensuring proper data enrichment during query and export. Typically, this would be done via Helm in combination with the Prometheus Operator, taking us to our final Kubernetes templating technology.

## Helm templates

Helm is called the Kubernetes package manager and provides robust tooling for managing Kubernetes deployments. A main feature of Helm is the templating engine, which, like Prometheus, also uses Golang templates, with additional functionality written into the engine.

Helm manages inheritance within the templating, allowing charts to have customizations but also to inherit characteristics from parent charts, allowing developers to leverage the power of templates while maintaining flexibility where needed.

## Templates in non-Kubernetes architectures

While Kubernetes and cloud-native architectures represent a large portion of the observability landscape, other software architectures also benefit from the same principles and some of the same technologies. For example, Prometheus and SDKs are both available for use in other architectures as well as Kubernetes. The following is a quick reference guide for architecture types and observability solutions that either support templates or provide references or boilerplate:

| Architecture | Platforms and Hypervisors | Observability Tools |
|---|---|---|
| Serverless | AWS, GCP, Azure, Red Hat | Prometheus, Grafana, CloudWatch, Azure Monitor |
| Virtual machines | Cloud (AWS, GCP, Azure, Oracle, DigitalOcean, Heroku) and on-premises | Dynatrace, Datadog, SolarWinds, Graphite, Nagios, Grafana, Prometheus, Sensu, Telegraf |

*Table 5.3: Observability technologies for non-Kubernetes architectures*

The configuration of these observability tools when you don't have Kubernetes environments still looks more or less the same. You'll have a **Continuous Integration and Continuous Deployment** (**CI/CD**) pipeline, such as GitHub Actions, that executes the infrastructure-as-code tool to apply these configurations. Major cloud providers have infrastructure-as-code tools with templating, such as CloudFormation from **Amazon Web Services** (**AWS**), Deployment Manager from **Google Cloud Platform** (**GCP**), and Azure Resource Manager from **Azure**. However, these tools are vendor-specific, so they lack flexibility for multi-cloud environments or environments that may have applications on-premises as well as on the cloud. If your IDP doesn't need to be as flexible, then it's fine to use the cloud vendor's tool of choice, but when it does, you'll need to look for more agnostic options.

A few of the most common infrastructure-as-code tools that work well for hybrid architectures (where you have two or more flavors of infrastructure) are Ansible, OpenTofu, and Terraform. These tools could be used together, with other tools, or standalone. These technologies, as well as the cloud-specific technologies, also work for Kubernetes-based deployments, but that's not their primary focus.

## Terraform

Terraform is typically used for standing up infrastructure. It manages the low-level resources, such as networking, virtual machines, storage, and security groups. If your infrastructure is managed via Terraform, then the configuration of how to connect it to the appropriate monitoring stack would be inserted into the Terraform `.tf` files directly. The "*as code*" portion of "*infrastructure as code*" means that the deployment of the infrastructure is repeatable, and there's a single source of truth for how to do it. Terraform code is organized into modules, allowing for small and independent changes within the code base, somewhat similar to Helm charts. Modules support variables so that they're reusable across multiple teams within a single organization. Modules are not templates, because Terraform tracks what piece of infrastructure is owned by which module. In other words, it maintains a state for what it manages and compares the actual state to the desired state before it takes any actions. On the surface, this may not seem different from Helm, but Helm relies on the state management provided by Kubernetes and does not maintain its own record of state, which is a key capability of Terraform. Like many of the tools we've described, there's a large community around Terraform, and there are many community-built Terraform modules available at `https://registry.terraform.io` to help you get started.

## OpenTofu

OpenTofu is a **Cloud Native Computing Foundation** (**CNCF**) sandbox project that was created from a fork of Terraform after a licensing change was announced. OpenTofu seeks to maintain backward compatibility with previous versions as it progresses, and is intended to be a drop-in replacement for Terraform. There may be some use cases where they do not have one-to-one capabilities, and as both projects evolve individually, that case count is likely to increase. However, OpenTofu is still a fully functional and production-ready tool for infrastructure as code.

## Ansible

Ansible is capable of virtual machine or Kubernetes deployments, but its strength lies in the robust configuration capabilities it also has. Ansible will run its tasks against what it calls hosts, or the infrastructure within its inventory. The inventory is user-generated by either directly passing it into the run command or supplying an inventory file. Ansible organizes its work into files known as **playbooks**. Playbooks are written in YAML but support Jinja2 templates. Playbooks leverage templates via template files. The templating capabilities allow for the usage of loops and conditions in addition to variables and facts. This gives more configuration flexibility and allows for efficient procedural operations—for example, only installing a package on the host if it's not already present, or getting the IP of the host and then plugging it into the rendered template during execution.

Now that we know more about templating and "* *as code*" technologies, let's look at how to pick and choose a technology.

# Choosing and using your templating technology

The best advice we authors can give you for determining which observability and templating technology to adopt is this: do the needful; use what you need, not what you think you need. In other words, solve the problems you have, not the problems you think you will have or don't have yet. That doesn't mean completely abandon the idea of flexibility, but it does mean prioritizing what you know you need when deciding what to integrate. To identify what the needful is, first identify who your users are. Remember, the purpose of a platform is to provide the correct set of capabilities to the end users, that is, the software developers building the customer-facing or internal apps. A platform needs to be purpose-built, or else it is just more infrastructure. For more on building a platform as a product, see *Platform Engineering for Architects*, another Packt title by *Max Koerbächer*, *Andreas Grabner*, and *Hilliary Lipsig*.

Once you have your users identified, you can then conduct user interviews and create critical user journeys. This will allow you to identify where your users can benefit from templates and other platform capabilities, and what the needed capabilities will look like.

From there, use a crawl, walk, run approach. Start with the most straightforward use case and the technology to match. Once that is in use, work on the more advanced cases. For example, you may start with Prometheus templates and then later move on to having Helm manage those templates, and finally, use Argo CD to manage the deployments and changes to them. Or you could combine Helm and Kustomize to get the ideal user experience for the platform users. Some quick decisions you can make based on our recommendations are as follows:

- If you need multi-architecture-capable observability, choose Prometheus and Grafana
- If you want to manage deployments with complex inheritance requirements in Kubernetes, choose Helm
- If you need multi-cloud infrastructure management, choose Terraform or OpenTofu

Most of these tools are not mutually exclusive, and with the open source options, you are not vendor-locked. However, even across observability SaaS vendors, you may find a mix-and-match approach or the ability to migrate from one to another if it becomes necessary. Mixing, matching, expanding, and migrating will all come down to how you decide to manage the lifecycle of the templates your platform supports.

# How to life cycle templates

If there is one truth in software engineering, it is that when you think you have finished, you have not. There's always a dependency that needs to be bumped for security patches, a bug that needs to be fixed, or some other change coming down the pipeline. While some things may change very slowly, or very rarely, it's still important to have a clear versioning strategy and change management in place—in other words, a life cycle.

Templates are functionally the same as code; thus, the lifecycling of templates is a solved problem. Treat them the same as your code. Like other code, they have a repository, and they have to be cared for: stored, documented, versioned, and tracked.

In this context, your templates are no different from any other utility code. There isn't a hall of AWS Lambda scripts; in fact, it isn't generally valuable to try to reuse such specialized code. Perhaps it can be shared within a team or community, but the environment it lives in is ever-changing. After version changes impact its utility, it must be adapted or decommissioned.

For boilerplate, it's even more straightforward. Release a new version of the SDK and let the magic of libraries in software do the work for you and the engineers who consume your SDK.

Here you will find a comprehensive, but likely incomplete, list of all the ways you can approach template life cycle management.

## Change tracking

The key thing to know about templates is that when we in the industry talk about ** as code*, templating is a cornerstone of that concept. Templates are typically stored in version control such as Git and managed as source code.

For day-to-day management, the principles of GitOps apply. If a template is updated, your desired state may not match the actual state; a GitOps tool such as Argo CD can help to ensure that the changes you've made are populated to the correct locations—for example, pushing the updates directly or making them available for pull models to catch the changes and bring them in. Push is more event-driven, but pull is more secure, so both have their place in the management of ** as code*.

There are automation-based solutions for catching changes between the base templates and the rendered templates or repositories where the templates are invoked.

One such tool is the **Renovate Bot**. Renovate can be used to instrument GitHub repositories to catch dependency updates and automatically make PRs to projects to bump the dependency version. The repository that needs to inherit the changes is the one Renovate is configured against, and the repository where the changes will come from will be listed in the data sources configuration. For more information on the specifics of how Renovate works, we refer you to the official documentation (`https://docs.renovatebot.com/key-concepts/how-renovate-works/`).

This approach works for template changes, SDK updates, or boilerplate changes. The Renovate automation tools catch differences between template versions (and they should be versioned) and the version the rendered templates are using. When it catches drift, it will make PRs to keep the two in sync. There are several ways to leverage Renovate, but the GitHub action is where we recommend getting started (`https://github.com/renovatebot/github-action`).

If you've never used it before, Renovate can use a variety of data sources, and commonly will be set to use GitHub releases as one of those sources. If you're publishing an SDK, when a new version is released, if the release is created in GitHub, the Renovate Bot will catch the new release for the repositories where it is a dependency, and similarly make a PR to bump to the newer release version in that repo.

Renovate is also a great tool to use to manage Helm subcharts; the latest information on Helm 3 compatibility and eventual Helm 4 compatibility can be found in the official documentation (`https://docs.renovatebot.com/modules/manager/helmv3/`).

To catch template differences for rendered templates in use, besides GitOps tools, a policy engine such as **Kyverno** can also be used. This will help to catch whether changes are attempted through an unexpected method, such as direct edits from a user. While the existence of a platform and its capabilities should reduce instances of human intervention or human-initiated edits, these things still do happen, and a policy engine can help to prevent them entirely, or simply notify of the event, depending on the configuration.

## Usage tracking

Another key part of lifecycling is knowing when it's time to deprecate a resource. Maintaining a template or pieces of boilerplate costs time and money, so you need to be sure that it's worth the investment; or, if you're removing a template for technical or business reasons, be sure that it's safe to do so.

If you're removing boilerplate code, that can be more straightforward as it was directly cloned into the end environment and can continue to exist without any need for upstream management and maintenance. It becomes the responsibility of the implementing team. However, for templates, especially for Helm charts, this requires more careful consideration.

That consideration should include whether or not the chart is in use. But how can you measure usage and determine whether templates are in use?

If you're using Helm, **Komodor** has created a plugin called **Helm Dashboard**, which can be installed on your Kubernetes cluster and will show you which charts are currently in use: `https://github.com/komodorio/helm-dashboard`.

Finally, if you are using the Backstage developer portal as your IDP, and your templates are registered to the software catalog, it has functionality that can measure the usage of those templates, allowing you to make data-driven decisions. If you're finding that a template is never or rarely used, it's a good candidate for deprecation.

# What is the role of the platform?

It's up to the platform team to consult with stakeholders and ultimately define the standards of observability tools and data collection. While individual development teams can also leverage templates, the platform acts as a unification layer to ensure consistency and ease. By providing the templates and standards along with enforcement, the platform ensures best practices are followed. Templates and boilerplate don't just assist in democratizing best practices; they can also encourage and promote observability-driven development. This does not *shift left* the accountability, but rather *expands it left*, providing the framework for developers to incorporate observability as early as possible in the development cycle.

That enforcement and consistency treat all aspects of applications and tooling equally. From the platform perspective, everything is an app (including parts of the platform itself). That is to say, whatever best practices you apply to your customer-facing apps, you must also apply to your AI and other applications.

## Enforcement of the maturity models

In the *Platform Engineering for Architects* book, Hilliary defined maturity models as the sociotechnical side of an IDP. These are going to be very subjective but essentially become the minimum set of standards an application must meet to be onboarded to the IDP. Through the use of policy engines and static analysis tools, a platform can shape the landscape of the software being developed within an organization.

A simple maturity model for onboarding a new application to the IDP may look like a checklist of tasks to be completed:

1. Kubernetes object definitions are labeled or annotated.
2. Prometheus alerts are configured.
3. SLOs are defined.
4. Alerts are routed to the appropriate service.
5. A Grafana dashboard configuration has been submitted.
6. Troubleshooting guides have been written and approved.

You may have other tasks to add to this list, but it's a starting point to help you develop the standards your IDP defines, uses, and enforces.

## The platform is the unifying layer

With the platform providing the golden path, it must also become the central hub for all truth. This includes application definitions, access controls, and the observability data. The platform needs to provide distinct value that brings users back and makes them happy to use it. Centralized observability is just one example of the capabilities an IDP will need to have; another is access controls.

Access controls are one of the most critical pieces of the platform capability. Democratization of data cannot come at the expense of security and compliance requirements. The platform must define and enforce least privilege for the observability data it stores and makes available to users.

Most observability tooling you would integrate into your platform supports access controls, often called **Role-Based Access Control** (**RBAC**) or **Identity Access Management** (**IAM**). For the context of building an IDP with robust observability capabilities, you won't want to manage access controls in multiple places. You will need to choose technologies that integrate with the solutions already in place.

Grafana is an excellent example of this, as while you can manage RBAC directly, it supports application plugins to leverage existing access control systems such as OAuth configured via GitHub, GitLab, Okta, Google, and more. It has additional flexibility in that it can connect to multiple data sources, such as databases, individual machines, or blob storage, allowing it to act as a single point of entry for all data within an IDP. It's also architecture-agnostic, so if you have a mix of architecture types, you won't need to have multiple data visualization tools. The flexibility of Grafana makes it a good choice if you don't want your platform to be opinionated on where observability data is shipped or how it's structured when stored, allowing teams to self-service the Grafana configurations and plugins they need. Managing the Grafana instance's availability would provide the flexibility your development teams need without losing out on core platform functionality.

Grafana also supports the use of pre-made dashboards from templates, as well as allowing user-defined dashboards. Here, we quickly used a template to visualize observability data being collected from a developer's laptop:

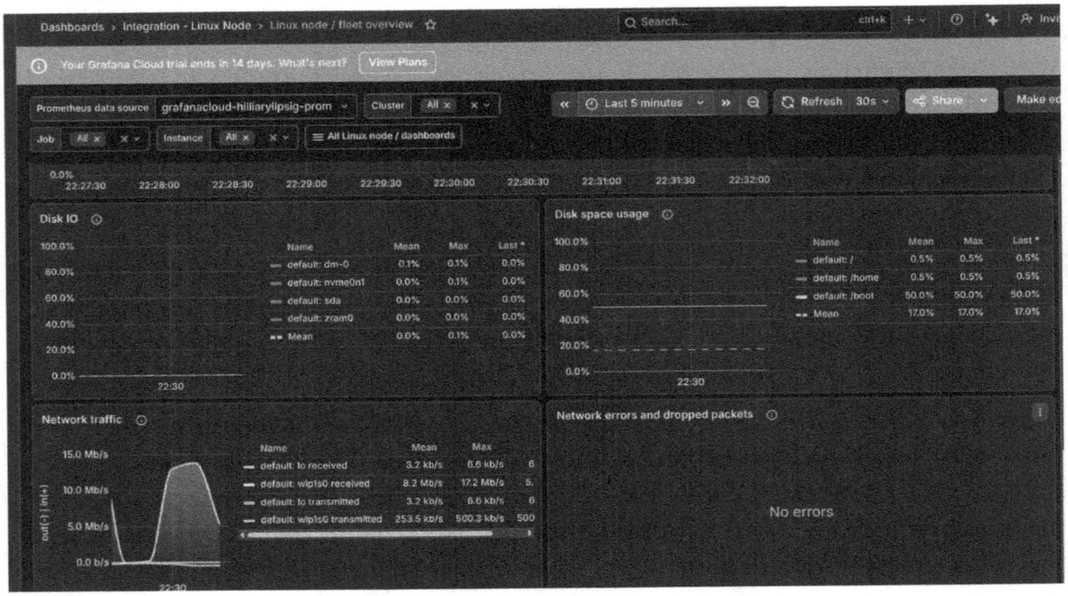


Figure 5.3: Grafana dashboard with data

These configurations are stored as code—JSON for dashboards—and can be used and folded into the software development life cycle just like any other templating technology.

The full JSON is too long to share, but here is a snippet from one of the many free templates:

```
"__inputs": [
  {
    "name": "DS_PROMETHEUS",
    "label": "Prometheus",
    "description": "",
    "type": "datasource",
    "pluginId": "prometheus",
    "pluginName": "Prometheus"
  },
  {
    "name": "DS_LOKI",
    "label": "Loki",
    "description": "",
    "type": "datasource",
    "pluginId": "loki",
    "pluginName": "Loki"
  }
```

```
  ],
  "__requires": [
    {
      "type": "panel",
      "id": "alertlist",
      "name": "Alert list",
      "version": ""
    },
    {
      "type": "grafana",
      "id": "grafana",
      "name": "Grafana",
      "version": "7.3.5"
    },
```

Using or building the right tools to make the right data available, but only to the right people or systems, will be core to your observability strategy. Any AIOps implementation will need to be gated with appropriate access, which we'll cover further in later chapters as well. Now that we've established how the platform standardizes observability data collection, let's look at how AI can augment the platform's enforcement capabilities and why the platform must treat AI workloads with the same observability rigor as any other application.

# Use cases for the integration of AI into the IDP

Where can an AIOps implementation help accelerate platform growth and offload tasks from the platform team? While we can't possibly be exhaustive in our recommendations, we do have a few places where we think AIOps can help, and it's not just acting as a user-facing chatbot either.

The first is as part of the code quality enforcement arm. While traditional linters or even custom GitHub actions can go a long way to ensure boilerplate code examples and platform requirements for handling observability are met, they are still limited in their flexibility.

There are even products such as **SonarQube** that help platform engineering teams to ensure quality gates are satisfied. But the same challenges we find with maintaining any automation become readily apparent. Your automation is only as good as its programming and will be limited in what it can do to what you've had time to write.

Here is where AI can find its time in the limelight. As we discussed in *Chapter 2*, an LLM-based AI tool has far fewer limitations and can make inferences while also adhering to a set of supplied instructions.

For example, AI can act as a multi-architecture bridge. It's almost impossible to apply the exact same standards to observability for a virtual machine-based environment as for a Kubernetes environment, so AI can act as the bridge between them to help normalize the data, or act as a tool to sample or sanitize where other standard tools might not be so easily adaptable.

Data timeliness and quality are important, but no tool is entirely perfect. Prometheus can, in some configurations, crash and lose data. Accepted sources such as **CloudWatch** are known to have strict rules for log timing, which can create ingestion problems or omissions if time zones are not properly accounted for in configurations. Serverless, low-code, and no-code metrics are often shallow in scope and poorly communicated. And sometimes data may be lost due to events outside anyone's control, such as a natural disaster.

In these cases, AI may be very well positioned to handle unreliable or incomplete data but will need to be given data and sources along with explicit constraints or instructions.

# Instruction files and giving your AI direction

Instructions are provided via instruction files, and there are many ways to make instruction files available to an AI system. For example, there's a project within the Linux Foundation known as `agents.md`, which is a standardization effort around Markdown files added to code bases with instructions that are useful to anyone, but specifically intended to help AI agents be successful when interacting with a code base. There are no universally expected fields for an instruction file, but there are best practices for writing a good one.

First, structure your file. Break it into topics and leverage Markdown formatting to break the instructions into segments. For example, build instructions and test instructions should be different headings.

Second, be as detailed and specific as possible. Just like when writing a README for a human, the more details you provide, the less guesswork the AI needs to do. If you want your agent to assume a certain role, task, or objective, be sure to include that information; that specificity can help the AI to come back with better responses. If you want a specific output, such as what we indicated with our data normalization use case, then that output format should also be in the instruction file. Anything that is important for the AI to know, including your expectations, belongs in your instruction file.

Third, let the AI know what it can and cannot do. If it can reach out to the internet, include that. If it cannot reach out to the internet, include that in the instructions as well. Your instruction files are the first line of governance for the AI system, and you can make it aware of security and compliance requirements, as well as what data sources it has access to, in these files.

Finally, when you are building out your instructions, you will want to test them and adjust them. It's also important to keep them current with new information that your AI agent needs to know.

For example, instructions for an observability agent may look something like this rudimentary example:

```
# AGENTS.md file
## Agent Persona
-  You are a Site Reliability Engineer in a Kubernetes environment.
## Agent Constraints
-  We are a SOC 2 Compliant Company
-  You do not have external internet connectivity
## Desired Response Format
- Place investigation details into Jira
- Remove any data that could be PII
- When a solution is identified, open a pull request in GitHub following any
relevant contributor guidelines.
## Data Sources
- There is a Prometheus instance on the cluster
- There are logs being collected with Fluentbit
- OpenTelemetry is also in use
## Important Cluster Information
- All software has been installed with Helm charts
- All observability data should have labels and other metadata.
```

With proper instructions, AI agents can be more efficient and get to work faster. And by setting expectations about the system it is working on, the AI can start detecting trends and patterns in the data. From there, if you are in a situation where you have missing observability data, an AI system can infer whether there's reason to suspect that there's a problem that extends beyond the monitoring stack itself.

However, it's important to set your own expectations. If the data doesn't have strong cardinality, such as labels and metadata, and the AI agent or assistant has never seen the system before, the quality of the inference will be diminished; but once both of those are true and the AI system is tuned, its judgment to identify and investigate large-scale issues can generally be trusted. We will go over fine-tuning and its benefits in depth in *Chapter 9*.

A well-tuned AI system will bring insights to the users, which may often augment or extend their existing expertise. For example, an AI can help with the following:

- Best-practice recognition

- Misconfiguration detection
- Data capture at preproduction through to runtime
- Cost management

However, even with proper tuning, we can't let our AI run completely unattended. This is where the platform must treat AI equally and apply the same security and access control standards as it would to any application. The AI system must be observable and subjected to governance; this is how we can prove that the system is performing safely and meeting expectations. Now that we've examined what observability looks like within the platform, let's apply that to an AIOps implementation.

# A reliable AI is an observable AI

A good IDP is customer zero to itself. The golden paths must be equally achievable for the product that provides them. AIOps is part of that customer zero model. It will be developed, deployed, and monitored to the same standards as anything else, with the goal of becoming another capability of the platform for engineering teams to leverage. The capability to use and benefit from an AI agent must be part of that centralized experience.

For an AIOps implementation to be useful, it must be accurate. Measuring the success and accuracy of AI is a new challenge, but the concepts we have already discussed for observability still apply. There are new standards when it comes to metrics for AI performance that are good to keep in mind, and also new tooling, but at the end of the day, these purpose-built tools recycle best practices.

In a Kubernetes environment, AI workloads are just Pods at the end of the day. So the usual standards for Kubernetes workloads apply. You'll want to watch Pod health, such as CPU and memory usage, as well as checking for crashes, restarts, or other general health problems. Similar to most other applications, your AI applications will have performance metrics. Request and response latency are key among them, but so are measurements of accuracy.

For AI workloads, these metrics will be critical to understanding whether your AI is providing the right value to your organization:

- Inference speed
- **Time to first token** (**TTFT**)
- System throughput:
  - **Transactions per second** (**TPS**)
  - **Operations per minute** (**OPM**)
- Response accuracy

- Request and response tokens
- Guardrail executions (many AI systems allow specifying guardrails, for example, when certain words are used; this metric tells you how often prompts have violated guardrails)
- PII leaks

Knowing the metrics we need is great, but how do we determine what the measurements for those metrics should be, and once we have those measurements, how do we make sure the AI is performing as expected?

A good open source tool for benchmarking your AI system is **GuideLLM** (`https://github.com/vllm-project/guidellm`), part of the **vLLM** project. GuideLLM is a platform for evaluating how language models perform under real workloads and configurations. It can operate on real or synthetically generated multimodal datasets and gives you clear insights into performance, efficiency, and reliability before deploying LLMs into a production environment. GuideLLM is a good starting point for benchmarking and optimizing your LLMs as it also puts a focus on the key metrics discussed previously: TTFT, **inter-token latency (ITL)**, output distributions, and dataset-driven variations. While there are some industry standards around what good metrics for performance look like that are emerging, there's not a one-size-fits-all metric. Different models perform differently for the same task, and the same model can perform differently across tasks of different complexity. This is because various prompts can rightly need longer response times, more tokens, and more exchanges with an end user. Time and tokens will be two aspects of performance and reliability to monitor as your model processes prompts, and establishing a baseline and catching deviations from the baseline will be critical to proper model observability. It's best to benchmark your model with tests that mimic production, and evaluate the metrics of real use against those benchmarks. You'll know what good looks like for your system over time with regular human review, and ultimately, you'll be able to set up alerts and tune them. A good practice would be a weekly ops review meeting to help define targets and alerts, instead of alerting right away and possibly creating a signal that is no more than noise.

Whether you are using GuideLLM or other tools and frameworks, measuring that you're maintaining the benchmarked performance is harder and requires putting some thought into the system design for the AI system. Technically speaking, the LLM that powers your AI will be accessed via an API. Functionally, once an API is in use for your AI agent, it stops being unique and starts being the same as every other workload in your environment. TTFT becomes simple math, subtracting the timestamp of the request sent to the API from the time the first token is sent back. This can be measured with Prometheus rules or OTel.

You can build a bespoke API and an AI serving engine, and the OpenAI developer docs have great references to help do just that. However, there are open source options to save you the trouble. If you're using vLLM to serve your AI agent, it comes with many metrics already defined in the framework, ready for use: `https://docs.vllm.ai/en/latest/usage/metrics/#general-metrics`. Also, you can always build out and define your own as needed.

Where most metrics are easily defined as numbers, accuracy may not immediately strike you as a quantifiable metric. Up next, we'll show you how to measure accuracy and keep measuring it.

# Strategies for measuring response accuracy

The challenge with measuring response accuracy is that responses need to be evaluated regularly; it's not a one-and-done situation. As training data or other data the AI system has access to increases, there's a reasonable expectation of drift between how the system responded after initial training and how it responds later on; however, that drift should be only due to facts changing, not due to errors. We've identified the following practical strategies for measuring response accuracy.

## Natural language processing scoring

For natural language processing, there are many scoring systems for accuracy: BLEU, ROUGE, BERT, METEOR, and Perplexity, just to name a few, and others may yet emerge. The most well known are the BLEU and ROUGE systems. The BLEU scoring system is often used for use cases where the output must be highly precise. If you've noticed that an AI chatbot uses a lot of words to convey an idea but leaves little room for interpretation, it's likely scoring well against the BLEU system.

ROUGE prioritizes recall and is intended as the scoring system for cases where summarization and recall are more critical than output generation. It's a good scoring system for agents that are parsing and distilling large amounts of observability data.

Of the other scoring systems we've mentioned, the most relevant for AIOps is BERT. It has a similar scoring methodology to ROUGE but is computationally more expensive and may provide a more accurate score. We'll spare you the math, but there's a link to a deep-dive article on how scores for all three of these systems are calculated in the *Further reading* section of this chapter.

For the purposes of observability and AIOps, we recommend using the ROUGE or BERT scoring system to evaluate model performance, should you so choose. Both scoring models use a range of 0-1. For production systems a score of around 0.8 on the BERT scale and around 0.4 on the ROUGE scale would be considered on target.

Let's score the DeepSeek R1 model we've been using since *Chapter 2* using Python scripts.

In an ideal setup, we would have a fully automated loop for this evaluation. The steps for that loop would be as follows:

1. An alert generation system such as Prometheus or Alertmanager posts a prompt to the LLM's API to investigate the relevant logs. The LLM stores the log files in a location accessible to the scoring automation.
2. The LLM stores the investigation result and its response somewhere accessible to the scoring automation.
3. Run the scoring script file via a webhook trigger or cron job.
4. The scoring automation emits the score as a metric.

For the purposes of this chapter and making the example accessible, we've hardcoded the example data and LLM evaluation. The output from DeepSeek was attained by first copying and pasting the log into the session, combined with the following prompt:

```
From the log, tell me as concisely as possible about the node statuses.
```

This resulted in the text that was used in the evaluation scripts we'll run. Our first script looks at ROUGE scores:

```
# Import evaluate
import evaluate

# ROUGE
rouge_calculation = evaluate.load("rouge")

# Example data to score. It should be plain text (Not tokens)
reference_log = ["level=info ts=2026-02-10T06:51:31.353816972Z
caller=controller.go:195 component=kubelet_endpoints kubelet_object=kube-system/
kube-prometheus-stack-1754-kubelet msg=\"Node Ready condition is Unknown\"
node=kind-worker3"]
model_summary = ["On Feb 10, 06:51:31Z, the nodes `kind-worker2` and `kind-
worker3` had their \"Ready\" condition set to \"Unknown\"."]

# ROUGE expects plain text inputs
rouge_score = rouge_calculation.compute(predictions=model_summary,
references=reference_log)

# Access ROUGE scores (no need for indexing into the result)
```

```
print(f"ROUGE-1 F1 Score: {rouge_score['rouge1']:.2f}")
print(f"ROUGE-L F1 Score: {rouge_score['rougeL']:.2f}")
```

Running the script gives the following score:

```
$ python rouge_score_example.py
ROUGE-1 F1 Score: 0.22
ROUGE-L F1 Score: 0.15
```

For ROUGE-1 and ROUGE-L, both of these scores would be considered low. A ROUGE-1 score would ideally be around 0.40, and a ROUGE-L score would be around 0.30. However, DeepSeek gave exactly what was asked of it in the prompt. This difference between objective scoring and subjective satisfaction makes ROUGE a useful, but not authoritative, metric. A score-aware prompt would likely have resulted in a higher score. ROUGE scores should be used in conjunction with other evaluation metrics to determine model accuracy, as their objectivity does not account for the subjectivity of the end user.

Now let's look at a script for BERT scoring and see how DeepSeek performed. We'll run the following script:

```
from bert_score import score

# Log and LLM Summary for evaluation
reference_log = ["level=info ts=2026-02-10T06:51:31.353816972Z 
caller=controller.go:195 component=kubelet_endpoints kubelet_object=kube-system/
kube-prometheus-stack-1754-kubelet msg=\"Node Ready condition is Unknown\" 
node=kind-worker3"]
model_summary = ["On Feb 10, 06:51:31Z, the nodes `kind-worker2` and `kind-
worker3` had their \"Ready\" condition set to \"Unknown\"."]

P, R, F1 = score(reference_log, model_summary, model_type='distilbert-base-
uncased', verbose=False)
print(f"BERTScore F1: {F1[0]:.4f}")
print(f"BERTScore Precision: {P[0]:.4f}")
print(f"BERTScore Recall: {R[0]:.4f}")
```

This returns the following:

```
BERTScore F1: 0.7424
BERTScore Precision: 0.7168
BERTScore Recall: 0.7698
```

The BERT scoring system more accurately rated the response DeepSeek gave, but it did take a little longer to run than ROUGE. For these scores to be ideal in production, they would need to be 0.8 or above. However, the prompt given to DeepSeek prioritized being concise. It was token-aware, not necessarily scoring system-aware.

Whichever scoring system you decide to adopt, if any, when you combine the score with human review and add an additional dimension to the data (user satisfaction), it is possible to get a more accurate understanding of how your model is performing. Over time, responses that are considered good and their score averages can be aggregated, and the scores can become a threshold. If the score on a response drops below where users are typically happy with the system's responses, that would be the time to trigger a human review. You can have your automation system emit these scores as a metric and use your observability stack to handle deviations. After some time, you may determine that the occasional lower score isn't an issue, but that you want to keep the threshold the same. Instead of calling humans for every response with a low score, you might only send an alert if 10% of responses from the last hour are below the threshold.

Here's a quick architectural diagram to help you picture this:

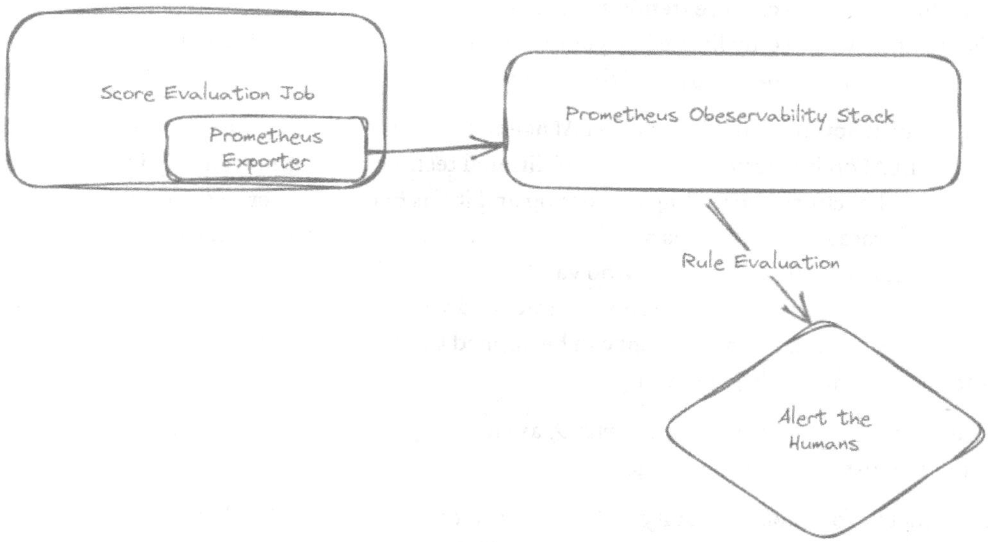


*Figure 5.4: Turning scores into alerts*

Ultimately, just as with any alert in any observed software system, the alert tuning and action plan will be subjective. What you do in your organization may not be the same as what your colleague does, or what is emerging as a known best practice, and that's okay. As long as you're regularly evaluating and iterating to ensure what you're doing is working for your team, you're doing it right.

The logistics of measuring response accuracy are more challenging than simple performance metrics. Something or someone needs to determine whether a response is accurate. How that determination is made will depend largely on how the response is delivered. For example, if the response is a Slack message to the team channel raising awareness of a system outage, and human investigation reveals that it's a false positive, that would be an example of a human review, and likely, there would be a bug fix to follow in the AI system. In situations where the review comes from a human, such as PR reviews, whatever processes exist for measuring accuracy will likely require some manual process, and potentially some mixture of clever automation, such as labeling the PRs that were not accurate and running automation to count them regularly.

However, where a PR against a GitHub repository is the expected output, you can use automated quality gates to help ensure that at least a minimum level of accuracy exists in the AI output, and use the same technique of applying labels to measure when it's gone wrong. You can then leverage CI tools such as GitHub Actions to send telemetry data to your observability stack, allowing you to capture trends around the model's performance. With automation, the sky is the limit; you're only limited by your own creativity and available time for creating solutions to measure the accuracy of the output.

Finally, a third option is to have another AI agent determine whether the response is accurate. Multi-agent AI orchestration adds some additional technical and financial implications. In terms of level of effort, the tooling is evolving and it has become easier to support a model where a separate AI agent acts as a validator, grader, or evaluator of the output of another agent. You can see this as a teacher who validates and grades the work of a student. The teacher gives feedback on what seems accurate and what doesn't. Just like humans evaluate the work of others, the same concept can be applied to AI agents, with the result that those agents should constantly get better.

We'll explore this a little more in *Chapter 9*, as ensuring you have accurate responses will assist in building trust in your AIOps systems.

The last metric for AI observability we'll discuss in this chapter is PII leak detection. This metric is closely related to guardrails, which we'll deep dive into during *Chapter 9*, but it is still worthy of a dedicated segment now.

**PII**, which stands for **personally identifiable information**, is a protected class of information that may be collected during normal operations for a software system. Earlier, we indicated that you'd likely place your AI agent behind an API. The method for doing this would be through the implementation of a microservice known as the API gateway. This middleware layer would handle routing all traffic to your agent, or agents in a multi-agent setup. If the agent needs to request logs, the gateway would act as the middleman, which would process that request and actually perform the log retrieval. A function of the API gateway could be to validate that the response from the logging system does not contain potential PII, and to strip it out of the body of logs if it does. The reverse flow is true; if somehow the agent became aware of PII and tried to return it, the gateway would be able to catch and potentially sanitize that PII from the agent's response before sending it on to the end user. An example of such a gateway is **LiteLLM** (`https://docs.litellm.ai/`). This is an API gateway purpose-built for LLMs and integrates with another open source project from Microsoft called **Presidio** (`https://github.com/microsoft/presidio/`) to suppress PII before it can make it to the model. LiteLLM uses a declarative structure for this configuration, allowing you to modify YAML easily to implement it.

Here is an example:

```
guardrails:
  - guardrail_name: "presidio-block-guard"
    litellm_params:
      guardrail: presidio
      mode: "pre_call"
      pii_entities_config:
        US_SSN: "BLOCK"  # Block any request with SSN
        CREDIT_CARD: "BLOCK"  # Block credit card numbers
        MEDICAL_LICENSE: "BLOCK"
```

`pii_entities_config` should consist of any PII you know or have reason to suspect could exist in your system. LiteLLM will also let you detect whether this guardrail was necessary. Guardrail execution is an important metric, but it is part of your overall security posture, so we'll cover it more in *Chapter 9*. For now, let's look at how developers might expect to interact with AIOps in an IDP.

# AI is a capability of the IDP

The centralized platform becomes the centralized data hub, but the expectation remains that it still works in service of individual teams and their needs. The platform should provide data in a way that is easily consumable, and the AI should help teams make the most of the data that they have. The IDP also needs to safeguard access to that data and manage the costs associated with the data. Where AI can be especially helpful here is in managing the quickly growing volume of observability data.

How many times have you needed the observability data from 2:36 A.M. on a Tuesday six months ago? Likely never, but you may have needed the data trends over the same six-month period. You don't need to keep every single instance of every single metric. Using AI to do basic data sampling can help to reduce the stored metrics down to means, medians, and modes over time, and that time can be at whatever level of granularity makes sense for your organization. By keeping only the data we need, and keeping the valuable information we got from the data we no longer need, we can shrink our data stores without fearing that we'll miss out on a critical piece of information. While we wouldn't recommend letting the AI delete data that no longer needs to be stored, ensuring that it's available to end users who need sampling either regularly or on demand, with the ability to write the output to a permanent locations, would allow the platform team to use *time to live* or other data lifecycling features to automatically prune old and less valuable data from the databases.

Additionally, if we believe we may have PII in our stored logs or metrics, having an AI agent crawl through it, sample the logs, and pull out only what's safe and statistically significant would be faster than having a human try to script the same thing. Letting the AI access, parse, and surface observability data to make it actionable for a development team is essentially the perfect task for its capabilities. This brings specific value for an IDP that needs to have a unified presentation layer that loads quickly, so end users actually want to interact with it.

While providing insights through the portal is important to give engineers quick access to all of the data relevant to them, most software engineers don't want to spend most of their time in Backstage or a custom-built self-service portal. Software engineering teams want to spend most of their time creating new services and features. They will spend most of their time analyzing software requirement tickets, discussing the best approaches for implementation, creating code to implement those feature requests, and committing their changes and reviewing PRs. In the final section, we therefore look beyond the IDP and explore what types of observability data to push into other tools developers use in their day-to-day routines.

# Beyond IDP: Other places to push observability data

A successful IDP will meet users where they are. This means shipping sanitized, actionable data to consumers in a way that integrates into their workflows, as opposed to breaking them. Essentially, where users of the platform spend most of their day is where data should be sent.

This could mean pushing data into Slack via webhooks, opening a Jira ticket automatically for alerts and adding relevant data into the description, or even recording information into Git. Historic benchmark records, test pass or fail histories, and similar data can all be recorded into Git and compared against in the future.

The following are examples of what and where your observability tooling, including AI, may be pushing data, and who might be consuming that data:

- **For developers**: Push newly detected critical logs directly to developers via their IDE, dev portal (Backstage), on the PR, or as a daily Slack message, instead of asking them to learn yet another tool to find data that is relevant to them
- **For product owners**: Push feature adoption metrics to the Jira ticket where the feature was specified, instead of asking the business to get the data themselves from various observability tools or dashboards
- **For performance engineers**: Commit the top findings of a recent load test based on observability data captured during the test to the codebase backing the CI pipeline that triggered the test

Within your specific industry, there may be other best practices, and if you're using an observability vendor, they may have some additional recommended best practices as well.

Understanding your security and compliance requirements is critical for knowing where you should and should not push observability data. Observability is the art of turning data into information. That information is often need-to-know, so you will want to ensure you are getting the right information, to the right people, in the right way. For example, it is important to know that a user encountered a 500 error when interacting with the system, but identifying who the user is is unimportant to getting the issue fixed and should never be included in any data that is collected and stored.

It's important for any AI systems you're using to also understand and adhere to this principle, which is why it's critical to put that information in instruction files. We'll talk more about implementing guardrails and how to secure your AI systems in *Chapter 9*.

Remember that AI depends on instructions and input and is therefore susceptible to the principle of **garbage in, garbage out** (**GIGO**). By ensuring your data is well structured and explained, you avoid a long list of unhappy consequences. Any time an AI-enhanced tool leaks user data, consider the following:

- Was access to user data necessary for it to do its job?
- Could that data have been obfuscated?
- Could that data have been better structured and explained?

Reasonable implementations should start from an understanding of the information presented, the risks involved, and the nature of its destination. Where possible, start with the least possible amount of access and data and increase as it becomes necessary. Don't let the fear of missing out result in a security incident in your organization.

## Summary

In this chapter, we saw how IDPs can reduce traditional productivity bottlenecks, allowing engineers to work more efficiently. An effective IDP can become the nexus of software development within an organization, acting as a source of truth and representing engineering, business, and consumer interests.

An AI-reinforced IDP supports observability through inferences that can be difficult to make otherwise, without significant human hours spent parsing data and writing automation. In the next chapter, we'll deep dive into these and other use cases for AIOps.

## Further reading

Natural lanague process scoring:

`https://www.geeksforgeeks.org/nlp/understanding-bleu-and-rouge-score-for-nlp-evaluation/#bleu-vs-rouge-when-to-use-which`

`https://markaicode.com/bleu-rouge-bertscore-llm-metrics-comparison/`

# 6

# The Observability Agent: Real-Life Use Cases

*Provide code suggestions to fix the top performance hotspots in the code base I am currently working on*, or *Give me two options to fix the root cause of the production incident I am working on, and give me a risk analysis on which approach is better and why*. These are two prompts a software engineer would want to execute!

What sounded like a futuristic scenario a couple of months back is now a reality for some organizations that have integrated their observability platform, code repositories, and coding knowledge bases into the AI agents that integrate with development tools such as IDEs, Git, or ticketing systems.

But observability-aware agents are not limited to development. As a **Site Reliability Engineer** (**SRE**), I could prompt *Suggest a scaling strategy based on the predicted workload patterns for the next 7 days to ensure we keep our performance-related service-level objectives (SLOs) while not increasing cloud spend by more than 10%*. The advancements of AI and the emergence of standards such as **Model Context Protocol** (**MCP**) or the **Agent-to-Agent** (**A2A**) protocol enable AI agents to interact with platforms such as observability tools, Git, CI/CD, and ticketing systems without creating lots of point-to-point tool integrations.

We investigate which real-life use cases the advancement in AI enables. We will focus on how an agent that talks to observability can improve the everyday activities of software engineers, SREs, IT Ops, or platform engineers to become more effective with observability data.

In this chapter, we are going to cover the following important topics:

- Agentic AI and MCP: How it can revolutionize modern cloud-native organizations
- Connecting observability data to your agentic AI
- Defining personas: Who is using the AI and where?
- Using observability agents to get from reactive to proactive operations

# Agentic AI and MCP: How it can revolutionize modern cloud-native organizations

*Are there any problems with my app in production? If yes, please investigate them, and let me know where in the code I can fix them!* is a prompt from Christian Kreuzberger, a senior software engineer, showing off his new way of working in Visual Studio Code. Half a minute later, GitHub CoPilot, connected with various backend systems via MCP servers, produces the following output:

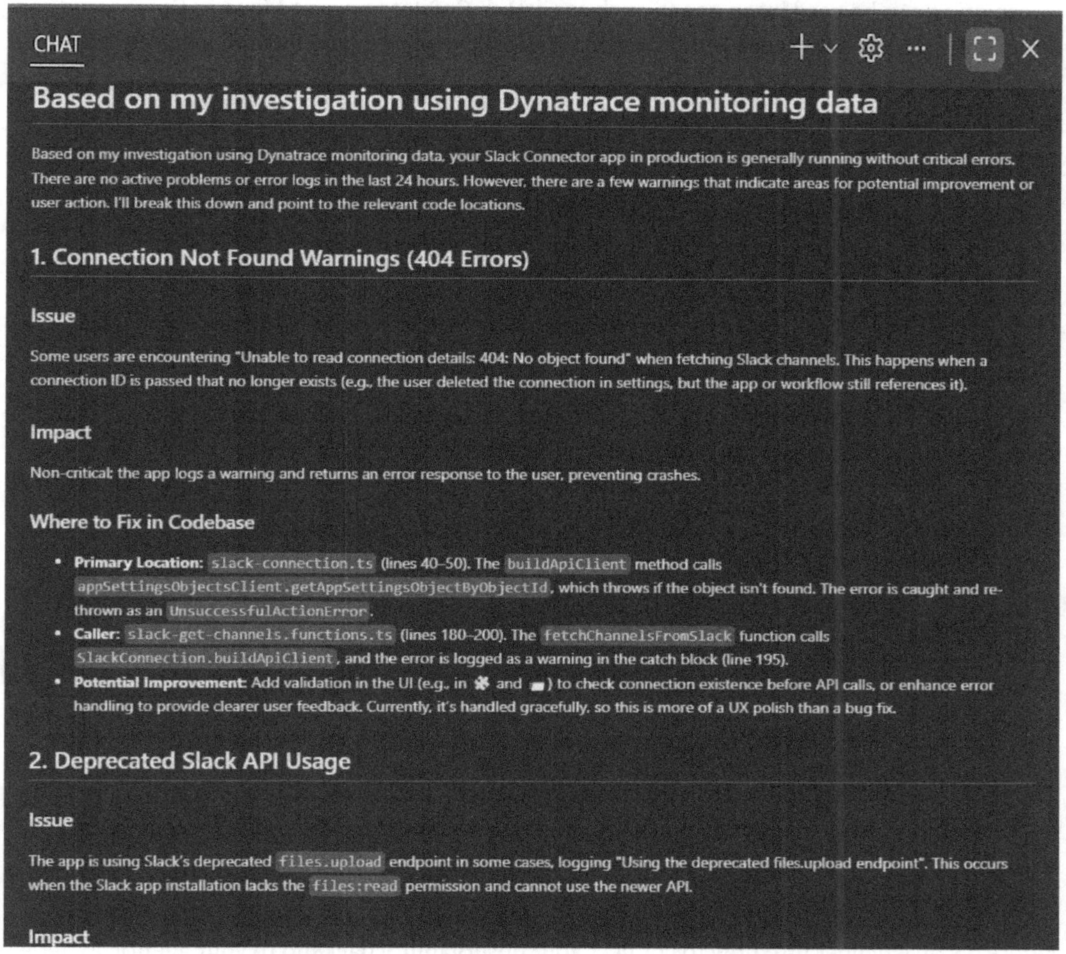


*Figure 6.1: GitHub CoPilot output in Visual Studio Code with the result of the investigation*

The output shows the time-saving potential for engineers. It eliminates the need to become an expert in finding and analyzing observability data and then finding the corresponding pieces of code to address any potential issues. It also eliminates the need for context and tool switching as engineers can stay in their flow of work and in their tools of choice; they can keep coding in their favorite IDE.

While the preceding output from an LLM is already impressive, it becomes more impactful if we introduce agentic AI into this scenario – an AI agent that can take the response from one tool and convert it into actions for another tool. If we look closely at the previous textual output, we can see clear textual instructions on how and where to change code. This information can be used by an agent, such as GitHub CoPilot in Agent Mode or Cursor, and can directly result in making code modifications. The following screenshot shows exactly this. The initial prompt was related to identifying current security vulnerabilities and providing a fix for the most critical identified vulnerability:

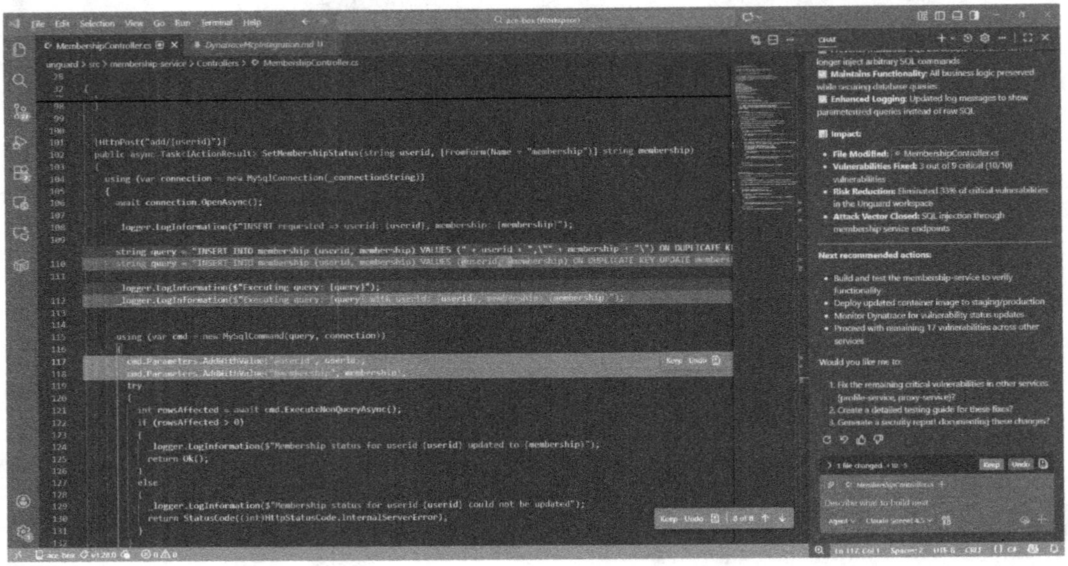

*Figure 6.2: GitHub CoPilot in Agent Mode fixing security vulnerabilities identified by the observability tool*

Those are just two examples that show how observability insights, such as performance hotspots or security vulnerabilities, can make engineers more efficient when integrated into their daily routines, processes, and tools. Agentic AI and MCP clearly opened the door to this type of productivity boost.

Before we dive deeper into how to connect your observability backend to your agentic AI, let's do a quick recap on what we learned in *Chapter 2*. Let's learn about the four phases an agent typically goes through. This will help us in the remainder of this chapter, where we will talk about how to connect your agents to the observability backend and the use cases this enables for different personas.

# Recap on agentic AI, LLMs, and MCP

In *Chapter 2*, we had a good introduction and overview of the current state of AI. We suggest going back and refreshing your memory by looking at the *What is AI good for (right now)?*, *Model Context Protocol (MCP)*, *RAG vs. CAG and how they relate to LLM*, and *What can and will go wrong* sections.

## The four phases of agentic AI

There are many definitions given in this book, but let me give you one more from a public knowledge base entry [*1*]:

> *Agentic AI builds on generative AI by enabling software agents to act with autonomy. IDC defines it as systems that can make decisions, adapt to new environments, and complete complex tasks with minimal human input. These systems reason, learn from experience, and interact with their environment—often coordinating across multiple agents—to continuously optimize outcomes.*

NVIDIA, known for manufacturing the specialized computer chips that power many of the data centers that run AI workloads, describes the four phases [*2*] that agentic AI goes through:

1. **Perceive**: Gather and interpret data from the environment or system.
2. **Reason**: Use LLMs and possibly **retrieval-augmented generation** (**RAG**) to plan responses.
3. **Act**: Integrate with external tools and software to execute actions.
4. **Learn**: Use feedback loops to improve future decisions through reinforcement learning.

What is relevant for this chapter is how and for which use cases an agentic AI can and should connect with your observability platform in each individual phase.

### Perceive phase

The most obvious phase and use case is gathering data from the observability platform in the **perceive** phase. Looking back at both examples in the introduction section of this chapter. The agent can query the observability platform to get information such as the following:

- What are the top problems in my application?
- What are the top security vulnerabilities?

There are many other examples of information an agent would query, such as the following:

- What are the top failing API endpoints that have the biggest impact on our users?
- What's the performance difference between the two deployed versions or features?
- Are there logs that contain confidential data that shouldn't be there?
- Are there overprovisioned clusters or workloads that can be optimized?
- Are there inefficient calls between services or to the database that can be optimized?

## Reason phase

The agent can take the information from the perceive phase into the **reason** phase and craft a human-readable response or an execution plan for further actions. Some observability platforms, Dynatrace being one example, also provide their own built-in reasoning, which can directly provide an explanation of the perceived data, including a remediation action plan. We have seen an example in *Chapter 3* in the *AIOps: reducing the noise with anomaly and root cause detection* section. There, the built-in LLM provides textual output including an explanation of the data, root cause, and remediation steps. An agentic AI can use this output directly from the observability tool during the *reason* phase, without having to rely on its own LLMs and RAG to plan actions.

## Act phase

The **act** phase would typically involve interaction with external tools that can make code or configuration changes, such as proposing a code fix for the identified vulnerability or proposing a change in the Kubernetes deployment manifests to adapt scaling or workload sizing settings.

There are, however, use cases where agentic AI reaches out to the observability platform to make changes there. Here are three examples:

- Set up SLO-based alerting for the top three API endpoints of my service
- Mark the detected problem as "in progress" or "known issue" and mute alerting for now
- Validate my release based on all observability signals you have, and give me a thumbs up or down

The last example is common for those observability platforms that provide built-in automation workflows to automate tasks such as automated validation of a release, a feature flag, or even orchestrating remediation for problems. Dynatrace, New Relic, Datadog, and probably other platforms provide similar built-in capabilities. If you have created workflows in your observability platform that automate certain tasks, it's best for the agentic AI to simply reuse those by triggering them, rather than replicating the individual steps.

## Learn phase

Once an action is executed, it's time to learn whether that action had the intended effect. The **learn** phase typically includes the agentic AI asking the user whether the proposed actions solved the initial problem statement. That's valuable feedback that the agent can use the next time a similar request comes up.

Like the *perceive* phase, the *learn* phase can also reach out to observability to validate whether the desired change is visible in the observed data. Here are some examples:

- Were the performance hotspots resolved, or are they still showing up in our metrics?
- Did the code fix remove the vulnerability detected in the *learn* phase?
- Are the top API calls now operating within the defined **service-level objectives** (**SLOs**)?
- Have the changes to the resource and request limits been affected, and are the workloads now running in an optimized way?

We discussed how agents connect to observability. However, it's also important to understand what type of other systems agents typically get connected to in order to fulfill more complex tasks in the day-to-day work of engineers.

## Beyond observability: The other systems agents connect to

When an engineer gets tasked to fix a problem that was just reported, the engineer will probably ask the following questions by looking at various tools before providing a response or a fix:

| Question | Where to look |
|---|---|
| Was there any recent change that happened that could have caused this issue? | Observability and change management |
| Do we have observability data (logs, metrics, traces, etc.) for easier triage? | Observability |
| Did this problem happen before? If so, what did we do last time? | Observability and bug tracking |
| Is there anything else happening right now that could cause the issue we are seeing? | Observability and status pages |
| How time-critical is this problem based on the end users it impacts? | Observability and **customer relationship management** (**CRM**) |
| If it seems related to buggy code, who wrote that code that now causes issues, and why did they change it? | Git code history |

| Question | Where to look |
|---|---|
| What is the potential code or configuration fix for this problem? | Git code |
| Is there any risk in making those changes? Any side effects we need to be aware of? | Observability and software catalog |
| How can we best validate that the fix really worked? | Observability |
| What do we do if the fix doesn't work? | Change management |

*Table 6.1 – The various tools providing additional insights for critical questions*

As we can see from the preceding list of tasks, there are many different tools involved to perform this task by an engineer. This is a perfect example, though, of what agentic AI can help automate. Agentic AI can orchestrate all those tasks by reaching out to those systems, capturing more details if necessary, and only asking the human engineer to validate the made assumptions to continue in the workflow. The *human in the loop* is always a good practice, but this task will be less effort for the human as the agentic AI becomes more mature through the feedback it receives from previous workflow executions.

In your environment, you will eventually want to connect more systems to your agents. Let's quickly walk through the systems listed in *Table 6.1*.

## Change management

Most organizations have a change management system, such as ServiceNow or Jira Service Management. Through an MCP, information about recent changes can be queried to identify whether the root cause of the current problem might be related to a specific change. If that is the case, the MCP could also return the details about that change, including who approved it, and the agent can then use this data to coordinate the next steps in remediating the issue.

## Observability

We talked about observability already. But in the context of the more complex example described previously, we see that observability can provide answers beyond giving access to logs, metrics, or traces. Modern observability can be used in multiple tasks in the explained workflow, such as the following:

- Were there any deployment changes detected automatically, for example, resource limit changes in a K8s workload or a deployment done by tools such as Flux or Argo CD?

- Is this a recurring issue, as we have seen a similar behavior in the past?
- Are there any known issues in external third-party APIs right now?
- Are there unusual load spikes caused by external events, for example, a marketing campaign, a global news event, and so on?
- How many active user sessions are on the system and are impacted by the current problem?
- What dependencies does the problematic component have on other services and applications?

## Bug tracking

A lot of information can be found in your issues and bug tracking systems. Whether this is in Jira, GitLab, or GitHub Issues, it's a data source that can tell us whether somebody in the past worked on a similar problem. An MCP server connected to that system can execute queries to find bug tickets based on a similar problem description in the impacted application or services. It can then analyze whether and how the problem was fixed in the past and provide this information back to the developer. This saves a lot of time in identifying the next step, as it could be that the problem was solved in the past, and we already know how to do it.

## Status pages

You may remember October 20, 2025, as the day half the internet stood still. Why? Because there was a major impact across the AWS US East Region. Whether it is AWS, Azure, GCP, Salesforce, or any other third-party SaaS offering, the first thing to do is to check the status pages of those services you are dependent on. If there is a known ongoing issue, then this could be the root cause of your problem and will trigger a different course of action, as if all those third-party services are running healthy. Integrating the information about status pages into your AI agent allows for validating this additional data source. One option would be to use an MCP server that connects to Downdetector [3], which is a service that provides real-time problem and outage monitoring for a wide range of publicly accessible APIs.

## CRM

Whether a problem impacts 1,000 users or just one should have no impact on how you prioritize the problem. But on the other hand, when you have lots of fires to put out, it's important to focus on the problem with the biggest impact. The biggest impact can mean that a single premium user who is impacted by a new feature needs more attention than 100 non-paying users who experience a performance degradation.

While your **real user monitoring** (**RUM**) from your observability platform can tell you which users, identified by user ID, are impacted, the CRM system can tell you how *important* those users are for your business.

An AI agent could therefore reach out to both systems and come up with an overview of the business impact of this issue by looking at the status of all users impacted by the problem. This helps in prioritizing the problem at hand.

## Git code and code history

If we identified that the problem is caused by bad code, it's time to find out who wrote that code originally or whether this code was recently changed. Looking at Git commit history is the right place to start. An MCP server can easily analyze commit history to identify all relevant code changes to a particular file, class, or function. When the code agent suggests code changes to fix the problem, the agent can include the change history to ensure that things that were fixed with a previous code commit don't break again. It also allows an agent to open up a Slack channel with all involved developers who made code changes recently, present the evidence, and ask for collaboration to find a solution.

Automating all of this through an AI agent optimizes the otherwise manual tasks for a single person to do the research manually and come up with similar conclusions.

## Software catalog

Before making any changes, it's good to know the potential impact on upstream or downstream dependencies. If a fix includes calls to a new downstream service, then this service will see an increase in traffic, and they must be prepared for it. If a fix includes changing the behavior of our response, for example, changing performance behavior or a change in service response body, then the upstream services that call us need to be informed.

Service catalogs are a good way to keep track of dependencies. They can either be managed through an **internal development platform** (**IDP**) such as Backstage, Port, Cortex, or Kratix. Service catalogs can also be found in **Configuration Management Databases** (**CMDBs**) in tools such as ServiceNow or BMC. Modern observability tools can also be a good source of service catalog, assuming that you have enriched logs, metrics, and traces with metadata, which we discussed in *Chapter 3* in the *Context is king* section. Whatever your source is, connecting that source through an MCP with the agentic AI allows that agent to make risk assessments on changing the behavior through a code change. This will be additional information presented to the engineers to make a faster, more informed decision about how to fix the problem at hand.

As you can see, there are many tools that can be involved in an agentic AI workflow when an engineer prompts it with the following: *Analyze the current problems identified for the services I am responsible for. Assess which problems to fix first and why. Identify the root cause, propose fixes where necessary, and provide a risk assessment for deploying the changes.*

By now, you have a good understanding of the power of agentic AI as it leverages observability data, code insights, or ticket information through local or remote MCP servers.

The recap on agentic AI and MCP has refreshed our memories on those important components so that we can continue discussing how to best connect your observability data with the agentic AI to maximize its impact.

# Connecting observability data to your agentic AI

When prompting *Tell me which problems I have in the services I am responsible for*, the question is how does the AI agent know which data it can query from the observability platform to answer this question? What is a problem anyway? Would we see this in logs or metrics? Or is there a concept of a problem in the observability platform? How can we make sure that an agent is not executing queries that are not efficient, resulting in high licensing costs? How can we make sure the agent cannot access any confidential data or data not relevant to the task it's working on? How can we make sure no confidential observability data gets exposed to other systems that the agent talks to as well?

These are all very good and important questions to answer before moving on with a large-scale implementation and rollout of your observability agent implementation. In this section, we therefore focus on how to connect your observability platform, how to track usage, and how to train the agent to become acquainted with observability to become more efficient when executing tasks.

In this chapter, we treat our observability agent as an apprentice that we help to become a master in observability. As in any trade, becoming a master starts with being trained on how to use specific tools, for example, a hammer, a saw, and a screwdriver. This is followed by clear guidance and feedback on how to become efficient with those tools and use them in combination in order to achieve a certain goal, for example, crafting a table. We also continuously measure the usage of tools and the outcomes to see when and whether our apprentice reaches mastery.

As we raised the security and compliance aspect, *Chapter 9* provides a more detailed explanation of how to secure your AI and fine-tune your AI. If that's a topic of interest, look into the sections titled *Building trust in the AI* and *Securing the AI*.

Now, back to our observability agent. We start with an apprentice that initially only understands our written words, thanks to LLMs, but doesn't really know what to do with our requests. We then define the tools, which are how we can access certain observability data through an observability MCP server, for example, list current problems, and return critical log messages. After that, we provide guidance through instruction files on how to achieve a bigger task, for example, list all the active problems and find the relevant critical logs for them. We measure the results, refine the instructions, and give feedback on the results achieved until we have our master observability agent.

## Defining tools: Connecting your observability platform through MCP

There is no need to go into the technical details on how to build an MCP server, as there is a lot of documentation available online that you can follow [4]. Chances are that your observability platform already provides an MCP server that you can either run locally or leverage as a remotely hosted version. Many enterprises we have seen often start with the available MCP, but sometimes decide to build their own to better control the available tools for the agents. Another reason is to provide an MCP server with a set of tools independent of the backend observability platform. So, when the platform in the back changes, or if there is more than one platform used, then the MCP server acts like a transparent proxy.

Whether you build an MCP server from scratch or modify one for your own needs, there are some considerations for the architecture and definition of the exported tools. Kudos to Christian K., senior software engineer, who shared a lot of his learnings when building the first open source MCP server for Dynatrace.

### Start with the questions you need to answer

Put yourself in the shoes of the engineers who use an AI agent. What will they prompt, what would an observability expert do to get the answer, and how would we make that information queryable through the MCP? Christian's first use case was "*I want to know which problems I have in my application.*" The observability expert would have opened the observability tool and looked at the currently opened alerts that the tool detected. As the terminology of his observability uses *problems* instead of *alerts*, he decided to call the first tool of his MCP server `list_problems`. That tool basically queried the API of the observability tool to return the current list of open alerts. A short time after, other developers came to him and said that their prompt would be *Show me problems from yesterday*, which required a change in the `list_problems` tool to also include a `timeframe` parameter.

Whether it is about querying problems, incidents, alerts, metrics, logs, traces, events, synthetic test results, SLOs, error budgets, or topology data, start by understanding the questions that will be asked. Then, design your tools that allow the agent to query exactly that data for that use case.

A good reference for basic tools that an observability MCP server provides is by looking at the top vendors in the observability space and seeing what they provide. Here is a quick sample overview of the tools they are providing through their MCP servers. For a full list of exported tools, please check out the documentation of those vendors:

| Dynatrace | New Relic | Datadog |
|---|---|---|
| chat_with_davis_copilot, execute_dql, list_problems, list_vulnerabilities, find_entity_by_name, get_environment_info, verify_dql, get_kubernetes_events, and create_workflow_for_notification | get_dashboard, list_dashboards, search_entity_with_tag, execute_nrql_query, natural_language_to_nrql_query, search_incident, list_recent_issues, analyze_deployment_impact, and analyze_entity_logs | get_logs, list_spans, get_trace, list_metrics, get_metrics, get_monitors, list_hosts, list_incidents, get_incident, and list_dashboards |

*Table 6.2 – Common tools for observability MCP servers*

The preceding table is hopefully a good starting point for building your own observability MCP server. Now, let's walk through some additional best practices and tips.

## Tip: Don't mix read and write

The most common use cases for observability MCP servers are providing tools around data access, such as `get_logs`, `list_spans`, `list_problems`, or `execute_query`. Those are all read-access tools, meaning you are querying data from the observability tool. Another set of use cases is around configuration or triggering actions on the observability tool, such as `create_workflow_for_notification`, `send_notification`, or `setup_slo`.

The best practice is not to mix data access with other operations into a single MCP server. It's better to provide multiple MCP servers, each targeted for its specific purpose. The reasons for this guidance are as follows:

- It avoids accidental execution of operations that modify observability configuration or that trigger automation.
- It reduces the attack surface when hackers try to do prompt injections. To read more about this, check out the documentation on this from Invariant Labs [5].

While it's possible for a user of an MCP server to select which tools should be active and which ones not, it turns out that the majority just go with the default and always enable all tools.

To sum it up, if you intend to provide read and write access to your observability platform, it's a good practice to separate those tools into separate MCP servers that must be installed separately. You could call them `Observability MCP Data Access` and `Observability MCP Admin`, as most write-access operations are typically administrative!

## Tip: Generic versus use case-specific

Most observability backends provide an API to execute generic queries with the query language of the platform, such as with NRQL (New Relic), DDSQL (DataDog), DQL (Dynatrace), or PromQL (Prometheus). For read access, it would therefore be sufficient to just offer a generic `execute_query` tool, and then the agentic AI can use that tool to query any type of data that is needed. While such a method is definitely needed, it is advisable to also think about more specific tools that return a specific set of data that is often requested, for example, `get_logs`, `list_incidents`, or `fetch_spans`. While capturing logs can also be done through `execute_query`, the `get_logs` tool can provide additional parameters for specific filtering on logs, such as timespan, workload identifier, or hostname. `get_logs` can then craft the right optimized query to retrieve exactly that requested data. This eliminates the need for the agentic AI to *guess* the correct query in the target query language to achieve the same result. The problem here lies in the word *guess* because, very often, an agentic AI doesn't come up with the best optimized query from the start. Based on experience, those agents start with a broader query or even queries that are not correct initially. They retry by refining the query until they get the desired result. That refinement process not only takes time, but it also consumes resources and often incurs additional costs, as every query API call to the backend observability system typically comes with some type of query cost.

On the other end of the spectrum, it doesn't make sense to provide a tool for every specific use case. For instance, it's not advisable to provide separate tools such as `get_logs_from_k8s`, `get_logs_from_hosts`, `get_logs_from_apps`, and `get_logs_from_serverless`. While it's possible to go that fine-grained, you need to consider whether this is really helpful, as you need to maintain a lot of tool implementations, and there is a chance that the agent chooses the wrong tool initially.

To sum it up, think about the questions and the top use cases your MCP server will serve. If a common use case is to identify patterns in logs, then maybe provide a tool that is called `analyze_logs`. This can execute the optimized queries to detect problematic log patterns and return the result in a single call. This avoids a situation where an agent must execute many different `execute_query` calls and then do the pattern identification based on all the data returned. If it's more efficient to do all this within the observability platform, then do it there.

## Tip: Local versus remote validation

When an agent is prompted with *Give me an overview of all critical logs from yesterday*, the agent tries to craft a query based on the target observability platform's query language. What we have observed is that the initial query that gets passed to the `execute_query` tool is often not fully valid. We see a lot of syntax errors, as things such as *yesterday* might be represented in different ways depending on the query language. The agent will overcome this problem by updating the query based on any failure that comes back from the MCP server in a trial-and-error fashion. And while, in the end, we get a valid result, it means that multiple round-trips to the backend observability platform were necessary.

One way to optimize those round-trips is to add local validations into your MCP server that do some basic checks, such as whether the query is syntactically correct, and whether the user has permissions to access this type of data. The syntax validation check alone will give the agent immediate feedback, avoiding the additional round-trip to the backend observability platform. This is faster, saves a network round-trip, and typically also saves costs on the backend.

Ideally, you have some observability of your MCP server and measure how many tool executions fail due to incorrect queries or insufficient permissions. This gives you enough evidence to add some local validation to your MCP server. We will talk more about the observability of your MCP server in the *Tracking and measuring usage and impact* section later in this chapter.

To sum it up, agents will not always get the optimal parameters for your tools on the first attempt. If you understand the most common reasons why tool executions fail, you can add local validation instead of leaving it all to the observability backend to validate any input. This will greatly improve performance and save costs.

Now that we have a good understanding of how to connect our observability platform to agents via tools exposed through an MCP server, let's dive into how to provide additional guidance on how to use those tools.

# Providing guidance: Instruction files for your AI agents

In the introduction of this section, we talked about providing guidance to the AI agent to elevate from being an apprentice to becoming a master in observability. Depending on the LLM you use for your agents, the agent might already have some familiarity with observability and therefore understands concepts such as logs, metrics, traces, or what a k8s cluster is. But unless you use self-trained models with expert knowledge on the specific setup of your observability platform, chances are that your agent really is only on an apprentice level.

Instruction files are a way to provide guidance to agents. See them as a chance to explain the domain knowledge to the agent without having to train a full LLM with all the insights. The following is a snippet from an instruction file for GitHub CoPilot giving detailed instructions to the agent about how to help SRE and Operations teams when investigating problems and incidents:

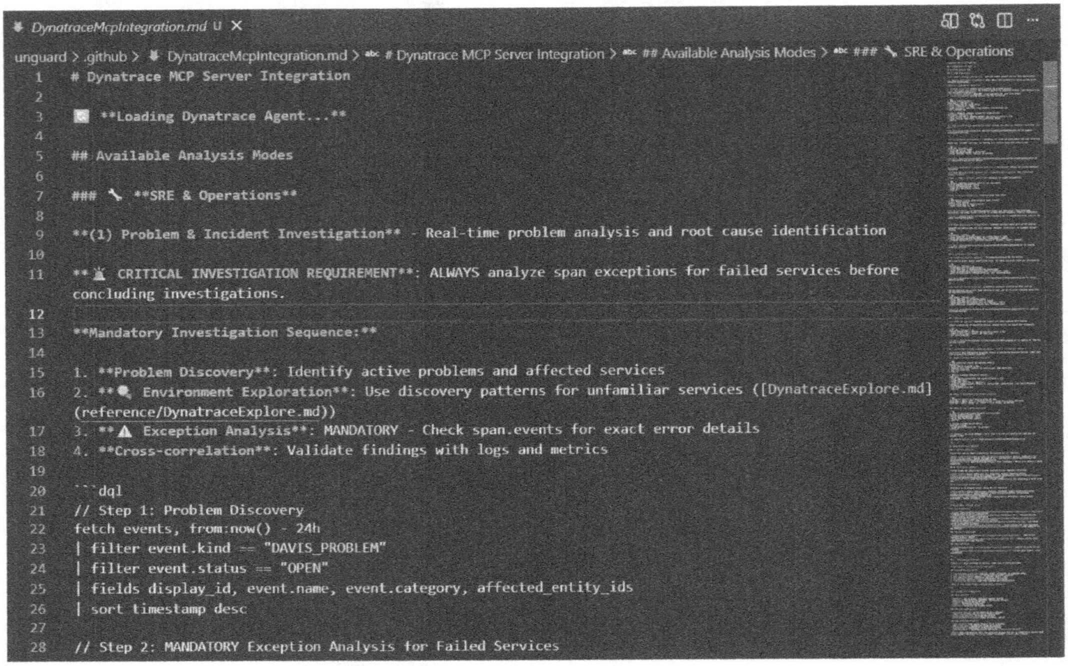


*Figure 6.3: Agent instruction files help guide the agent with domain-specific knowledge on how to analyze observability data*

Without those instructions, an agent would simply start down an exploratory path of gathering information. Exploration is a good thing, but it's time- and resource-consuming. If you are an SRE and need a quick, deterministic answer to specific questions, the instruction file achieves exactly that goal.

Instructions can become very detailed. The important part of the instructions is that you specify clearly the situation, the goal, and the approach to take to achieve that goal.

Tip

**Optimization tip**

To optimize querying and analyzing observability data, give instructions that reflect good practices that experienced performance engineers would follow. That includes **metrics-first analysis**, meaning first try to find answers in metrics as they are faster and cheaper to query. Also, always specify a timeframe when querying data. The more specific you make your prompt about the type of data and timeframe to analyze, the faster and cheaper the executed queries will be. Adding this to your instruction files ensures that your agentic AI calls your MCP server with these best practices in mind.

Agents, by default, are only as good as the model you are using. While training your own model is one option, you should consider using instruction files to give clear guidance on how the agent should execute certain tasks that are asked through prompts. Make sure to read the documentation of the agentic AI you are using. Follow the best practices on how to provide instructions and find ways to distribute those instructions to every engineer who leverages those agents.

Now that we know how to improve the efficiency of our agents, we need to look into how we can track the usage, measure performance and accuracy, and use this to optimize impact and costs.

## Tracking and measuring usage and impact

Like with any software service, app, or feature, it's important to track its usage, adoption, and costs. The same goes for an MCP server. When building an MCP server that provides 10 different tools, but only 2 of them are used occasionally, the questions we need to answer are the following:

- Why are 80% of the tools not used? Shall we remove them? Or do we need to increase the description and instruction files for agents to better leverage them?
- Why is adoption low? Are there use cases that are missing? Is the data coming back of poor quality, does it take too long, or is it too costly?
- How can we get better feedback from our users about what they like and what should be improved?

The solution to this is proper monitoring of your MCP server implementation. We need to use the same observability best practices that we have discussed throughout this book. We need to think about which metrics give us the insights about performance, usage, accuracy, or costs of the MCP server tools executions. We need to think about whether we need to add specific logs for any troubleshooting or whether we need to look into distributed traces to better understand the full agentic AI workflow, which also includes calling our MCP server.

### Instrumenting the MCP server and beyond

You have many options to instrument your own code. We recommend looking into **OpenTelemetry**, which we have covered extensively throughout *Chapter 1* and *Chapter 3*. On top of OpenTelemetry, there is the open source framework **OpenLLMetry** [*6*] from Traceloop. OpenLLMetry provides OpenTelemetry-based observability for your LLM applications, including support for MCP. It means you automatically get automated distributed traces, logs, and metrics for all interactions with your MCP server. And it doesn't stop at your MCP. OpenLLMetry provides insights when calling LLMs, vector DBs, or agentic frameworks such as Anthropic, Amazon Bedrock, LangChain, LangGraph, Ollama, or OpenAI.

The following screenshot shows a sample trace published by the OpenLLMetry community on their GitHub pull request 2829 for adding MCP observability support. The trace starts in the agentic AI and includes every call to the MCP server, including the name of the tool and the arguments passed when it was called:

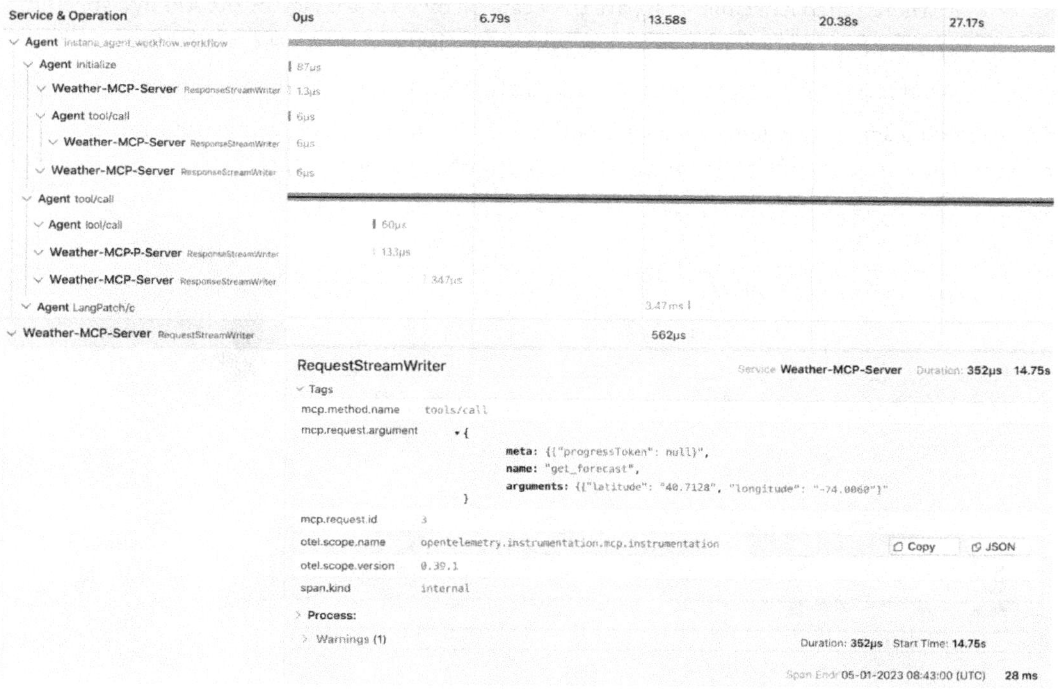


*Figure 6.4: OpenLLMetry provides support for the MCP protocol to trace invocations from any agentic AI workflow*

Having this detailed information in traces also allows us to extract metrics to answer the questions raised earlier:

- Which tools are executed? Which tools are not executed?
- What's the performance of those tools? How many calls are failing, and why are they failing?

When building your own MCP server, or when using MCP servers from a vendor, make sure to instrument it so that you can better track its usage, adoption, and accuracy of results.

## Analyzing the backend observability API calls

Whether it is `execute_query`, `list_incidents`, or `get_logs`, the MCP server will make calls to your observability backend API to retrieve the request data or execute the desired operation. It's also important to monitor those API calls as you need to answer the following questions:

- Who is making calls to those APIs, and what data is retrieved?
- Can the observability backend API scale to the increased demand coming in from the MCP?

- Are there failed API calls? If so, are they caused by wrong usage of the API in a specific version of the MCP server, or is it because of an issue in the observability backend?
- Is there a way to do cost attribution of those API calls to individual users or teams?

The following screenshot shows a dashboard that answers some of the questions raised previously by analyzing the API calls to the backend observability API:

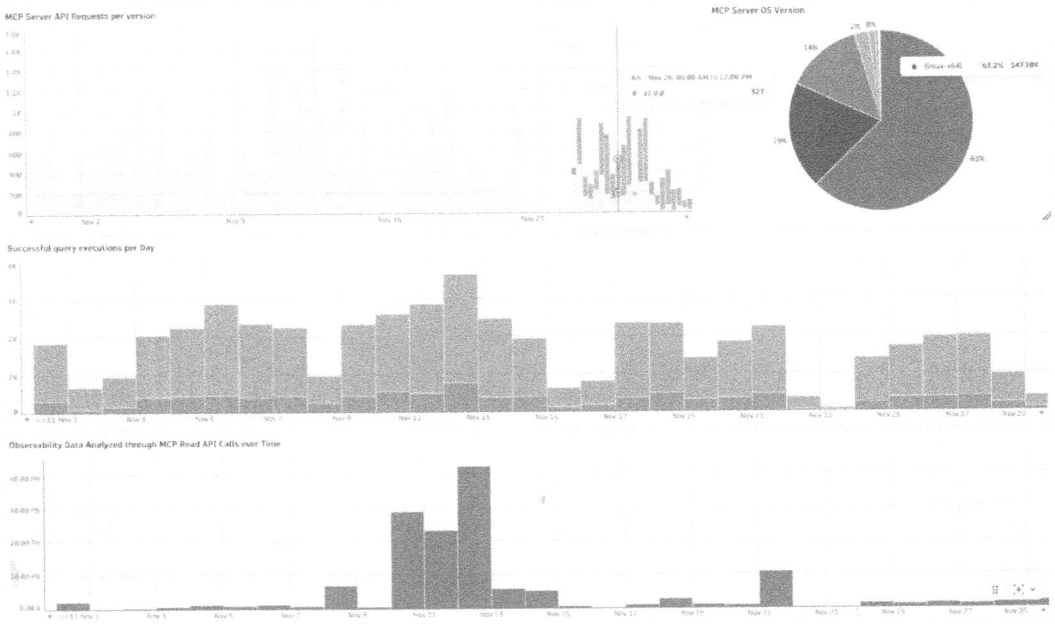


*Figure 6.5: Analyzing observability backend API calls gives additional insights into usage, adoption, and optimization potential, such as reducing erroneous calls*

Agentic AI will change the way users interact with our software services, and this also means that it will change the way observability data is consumed. You need to make sure that you provide a stable and optimized observability backend that can handle the additional load coming in through those MCP server API calls. But it's not just about handling the load; it's also about constantly optimizing the way the MCP server is calling the backend. Therefore, go back and revisit the *Defining tools: Connecting your observability platform through MCP* section, which focuses on building a good list of MCP tools and teaching the agentic AI on how to best call your MCP server to achieve optimal results for the end user.

## Agentic AI observability

While observing the MCP is key, observing the full agentic AI workflow is as important as just observing the connection between the agentic AI and the observability backend.

Chances are that you will be integrating your observability platform into various different agentic AIs to enable different personas in different tools to make better decisions based on your observability data. In the next section, called *Defining personas: Who is using the AI and where?*, we will talk about all those various use cases. It will become clear that we really need to understand the end-to-end agentic AI workflow executions in order to understand usage, adoption, and impact.

You might be using an agent in either of the following:

- The IDE to support your engineers in making better coding decisions
- The issue tracking system to enrich bug details with live observability data
- The support ticket system to provide end user impact analysis
- The CRM system to enrich customer information with the issues they ran into
- The business reporting system to correlate business KPIs with technical problems

In any scenario where you are using or planning to use off-the-shelf or custom-built agents, you should implement agentic AI observability. And this is not limited to only the use cases where you interact with your observability backend, but should expand to all agentic AI use cases and all the tools it connects to.

The emerging topic of AI observability probably needs a dedicated chapter or even its own book. There is already plenty of material out there, but we wanted to make sure it also gets a mention here. Thanks to open standards such as OpenTelemetry and OpenLLMetry, agentic systems can be observed without too much of an effort. Check out the documentation of your agentic AI development kit or talk to the vendor of your agentic AI solution to see how you can get end-to-end workflow observability through OpenTelemetry sent to your observability backend.

The following screenshot shows a distributed trace of a custom agent that leverages OpenAI and several different tools to fulfill a task. These details allow you to better understand what is happening within an agentic workflow, which tools are called based on your prompt, where things are slow or failing, as well as how many tokens are consumed when interacting with the LLM as part of that workflow:

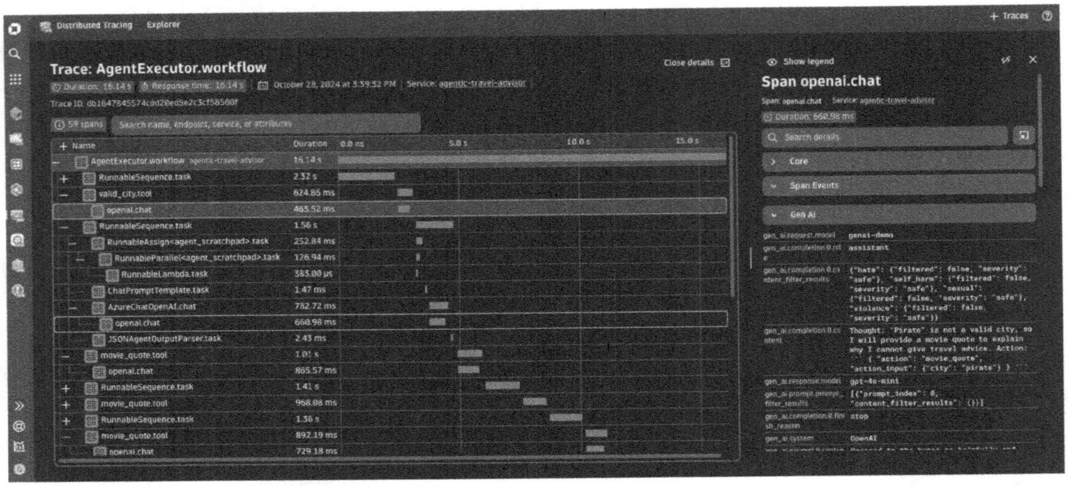

Figure 6.6: Agentic AI observability gives insights into the end-to-end agentic workflow to identify hotspots or problems

The distributed traces also contain a lot of details about token consumption, guardrails, and errors. This also gives you the chance to look at the various agents and the used LLMs to identify any inefficiencies and allows you to compare different models:

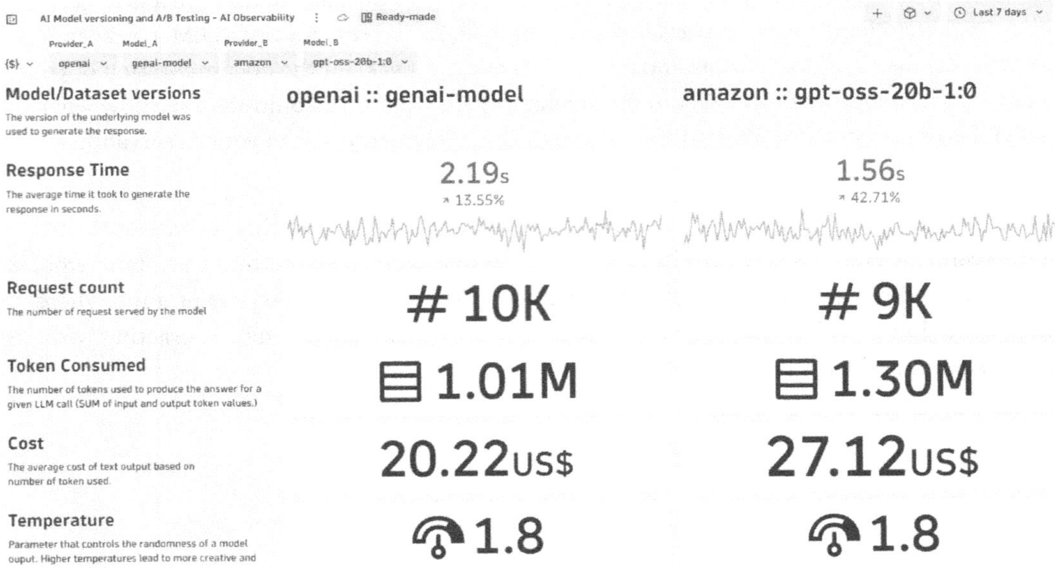

Figure 6.7: Comparing different agentic AIs and models based on the OpenTelemetry extracted data

We are just scratching the surface here on the topic of agentic AI and LLM observability. Stay up to date on the latest developments in that space, consult the documentation of the frameworks and tools you are using, and strive to ingest traces, logs, and metrics into your observability platform.

In this section, we covered what observability information should be exposed to an agent via MCP, how to track its usage, and how to provide instructions for agents to elevate from an apprentice to becoming masters of observability. We learned that agentic AIs are going to help many different personas in their day-to-day work and that it's important to observe those agents to identify their usage, internal workings, and costs. In the next section, we will take a closer look at the personas and the use cases where observability data can help them make better-informed decisions in the tools and processes they already use.

# Defining personas: Who is using the AI and where?

We already got to know Christian, a software engineer who leverages an agentic AI in his Visual Studio Code with prompts such as "*Are there any problems with my app in production? If yes, please investigate them, and let me know where in the code I can fix them!*"

A lot of the observability-enabled use cases that get discussed at conferences or blogs focus on how to improve the day-to-day activities of a software engineer in their IDE. But there are many other people involved in planning, developing, testing, operating, and optimizing software that can benefit from observability data that gets brought into their day-to-day processes and used with tools through an AI. In this section, we will explore those use cases so you can better understand where else observability and AI can have a major efficiency impact.

## Who are your internal end users and their use cases?

If we look at the DevOps infinity loop that we used in *Chapter 3* in the *Tracking the SDLC* section, we see a lot of activities between planning, coding, deploying, and operating software. In each phase, we have different types of engineers needing to make decisions about their next step. In most of those steps, observability can help to make better-informed decisions. Let's walk through some examples by looking at prompts that those individuals might want to execute!

## Planning: What features to build, improve, or remove?

*I am the product owner of our online customer self-service portal and need to plan our product roadmap for the next 6 months to guide our engineers on what they need to work on. Analyze the current feature usage of our online customer banking portal in production and identify the top and least used features of that portal. Find out how much effort we currently put into maintaining all those features by analyzing the existing Jira tickets for those features. Then give recommendations on which features we should remove without breaking core system functionality, which features we should improve to increase user interactions, and give a time estimate for all those steps.*

Whether done through a human or an AI agent, observability provides critical insights to the preceding prompt, such as which features are currently used and which ones aren't, what are critical user journeys that require certain features even though they might not be used often, and which features have bad performance or high failure rates and therefore impact user experience and should be optimized?

While we talk about end-user features here, the same prompt would also work for non-end-user-facing software systems, such as APIs that you are exposing for external consumption.

Clearly, though, this prompt will save any product owner or business analyst a lot of time and give them insights to make better decisions in their day-to-day work.

## Building: How to improve the resiliency of our architecture

*I am a software architect and am responsible for the cloud-native architecture of our core banking system. Some of the services come from a vendor, but most of our services are custom-developed. All workloads are properly tagged to distinguish them. Analyze all the problems we had in our own software components over the past 6 months. Give me an analysis of problem areas, root causes, and their impact on our end users. Provide suggestions on what improvements we can make to our code, deployments, usage of existing cloud services, and architecture to reduce the risk of running into those same problems again.*

Software architects typically analyze their deployments and the dependencies between the deployed services. They look at metrics to understand load behavior and extract dependency information from distributed traces to understand cross-service impact. When tagging is done properly, then all tag information is also available in the observability platform, as discussed in *Chapter 3* in the *Context is king: the quality of observability data* section.

While the final decision is still in the hands of the architects, getting an answer to this prompt from an agent that analyzes the rich data in the observability platform via an MCP allows them to make better-informed decisions.

## Testing: What use cases are we not covering right now?

*I am leading the quality engineering team, and my goal is to increase test coverage of our critical backend APIs. I want to start by focusing on APIs that currently have no tests, and then move on to APIs that do have tests but have still caused issues in production over the past year. Let's start with the transfer-fund service. Identify the top 10 API calls of that service and give a recommendation on which tests we should create and which ones need to be updated to identify those problems we have seen in the past. Also provide some suggestions on test scenarios and test data to be used by creating a representative dataset for each test case!*

Quality engineers are often trying to catch up with all the changes and new features that software developers put out. Leveraging AI can help them close this gap and also increase the quality of tests executed. Ideally, you have observability enabled across your software development life cycle, meaning you capture logs, metrics, and traces not just in production but also from your development and testing environments. This allows the agentic AI to compare what has been tested and what is really happening in production. That would be the ideal situation, as this avoids extracting this information from other tools such as the test management system.

To refresh your memory about observability in testing, go back to *Chapter 3* to the *Choosing the right metrics through proper load testing* section.

This example shows yet again that agentic AI, in combination with observability, makes quality engineers more efficient as they will be guided to focus on areas that have the biggest impact. Nobody wants to create and maintain tests that cover the wrong things or test in the wrong way. AI will greatly help here to improve the impact of quality engineering.

## Releasing: When is a good time to release a new feature and to whom?

*I am the new release manager who recently took over from somebody who left the company. I need to decide when the best time is to release a new feature in our customer self-service portal. Please analyze whether there was any specific pattern of feature releases in the last 12 months for this application. Give me an overview of which releases went well and which ones resulted in any issues. Based on the data, give me a recommendation about when and how we should best release that feature to minimize impact to our end users in case something goes wrong.*

It's never easy to take over a role from somebody else and not have enough time to learn everything there is to learn. There is a lot of tribal knowledge that often gets lost. When integrating observability into your software delivery and release process, you can identify the impact of a release as shown in *Chapter 3* in the *AIOps: reducing the noise with anomaly and root cause detection* section.

As a release manager, I can then leverage that information and make better-informed decisions based on historical data that shows which changes, deployments, and releases of software have caused issues and what their blast radius was.

## Operating: What's the best way to mitigate production issues?

*I am an SRE responsible for our critical backend services. We are preparing for Black Friday, where we expect double the incoming traffic than we normally have. Identify all services where we have had load-related issues in the past 12 months. Analyze traffic growth trends for those services, factor in that traffic will double, and identify those services that don't have proper sizing defined. Then find all runbooks for those services and analyze when they have been used and updated the last time. I want a risk-based analysis with probabilities on which services will most likely fail, which ones need an update to scaling rules, and where we need to update our runbooks to ensure we can react faster to any problems that come up and stay within our SLOs!*

SREs are the ones who need to ensure resiliency in production. The preceding prompt requires a lot of information from observability, such as current and past load patterns, analyzing problems that happened that were related to load, or incorrect sizing of the workloads. It also talks about SLOs, which are defined in the observability platform and which we have discussed in very much detail in *Chapter 3* in the *A primer on SLOs: learnings from Google's SRE handbook* section.

We hope that those examples allow you to go back into your organization and start a discussion about what decisions you need to make on a daily basis and how agentic AI with input from observability helps you make better-informed decisions.

Once we have answered that question, we also need to ask, *Where and in which tool do you want to get this information?*

## From which tools do engineers interact with the agent?

If we were to only focus on software engineers, the most likely answer to *Where do you want to interact with the agent?* will be: my IDE, for example, Visual Studio Code or IntelliJ. It could also be that you are already using some of the new agentic coding IDEs, such as Cursor, Cline, or Amazon Q.

However, developers do not spend all their time in an IDE. In addition, all the other personas we just discussed use various tools throughout the day, where you need to think about how to integrate your agentic AI to deliver insights from observability to make better decisions faster.

Let's walk through a set of tools that I am sure you also have in your organization.

## Project management and issue tracking tools

There are many tools in that space on the market. A prominent vendor is Atlassian with Jira. Whether you use Jira or other tools to track your projects and issues, when looking at a ticket, an agent built into that tool can immediately pull in context-aware information about the ticket. The following screenshot shows how additional information about a performance problem on the Gateway API was pulled in by an agent from the backend observability platform. This eliminates the need for the person working on that ticket to log in to various tools to find that information. In this case, the relevant information comes to the person who needs it to decide what to do next:

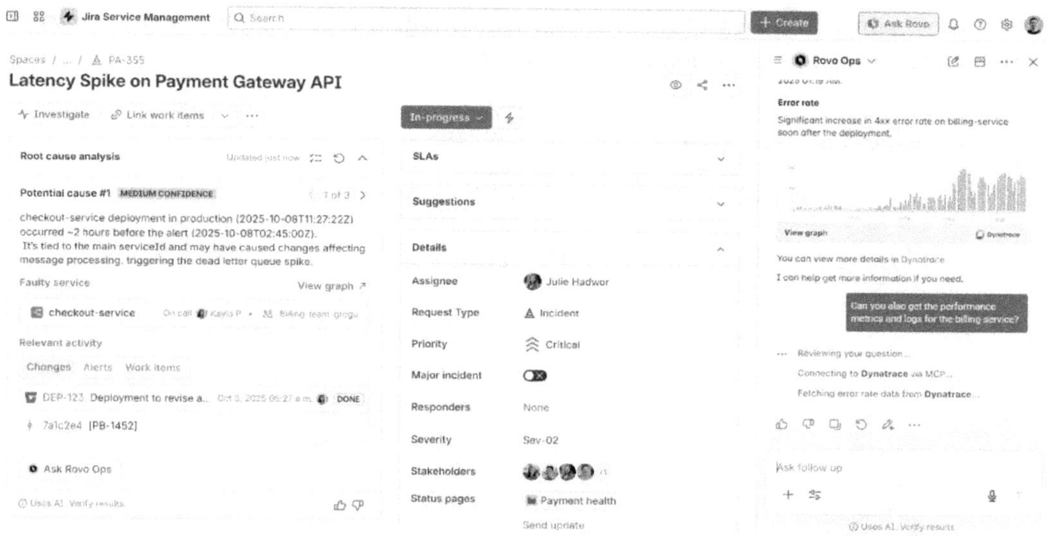


*Figure 6.8: The Atlassian Rovo Ops agent pulling in relevant data from the observability backend based on the context of the ticket*

It is best if you sit down with your engineers who use that set of tools and ask them what information they typically require when working on tickets. If there is information that is available in observability, then the best would be to bring this right into the UI, which avoids context switching and therefore optimizes the day-to-day work.

## Collaboration and chat tools

Slack, Teams, Confluence, Miro, Asana, and Monday, to name a few, are tools that fall into the category of collaboration and chat tools. Chances are, we find more than one of those tools in every organization. For chat tools in particular, there is an obvious integration scenario through a chatbot that gives easy access to observability data. For anybody who participates in a conversation about a particular topic, or if engineers discuss a certain feature, having a chatbot that can respond to the following prompt would greatly improve the efficiency of those teams: *Where is the latest version of our build deployed, and are there any new logs that need our attention?*

Another common use case is to pull in a chart into an existing conversation, such as *Give me the network traffic forecast for our critical services*, as you can see in the following screenshot.

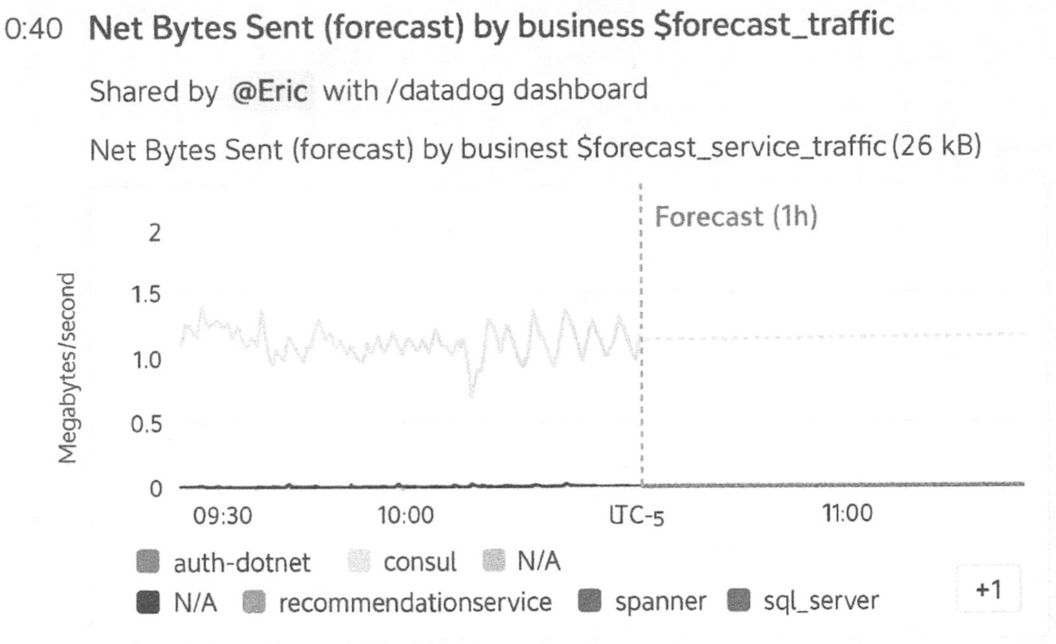


*Figure 6.9: Prompting a bot to pull in graphs and data from observability into your chat*

Tip

**Tip**

Analyze conversations your teams have in your collaboration tools. Identify use cases where they start posting screenshots of dashboards or findings from distributed traces.

> Those are indications where a more self-service model will speed up that collaboration process by making it easier to get this information at the time when they need it.

## Customer service and support tools

This is a very similar use case to the issue tracking system. Instead of engineers looking at their bugs and pulling in observability data to make it easier to identify how to fix the problem faster, we are now talking about customer success managers or customer support engineers who work on tickets submitted by their users in case they run into a problem.

Consider the scenario where a banking customer has issues logging in to their mobile banking app. They get on a call with customer support, who sees all the details about the customer in their support ticketing system. An agentic AI in that system can pull in live observability data using prompts such as *Are there any other users in our system that have similar problems?* The answer could be *Yes, it seems this issue impacts other users who are on the older version of our iOS version of the app. The latest version doesn't show this issue any longer. Please suggest to the customer to upgrade their mobile app and try again.*

Having this information at the time when being on a call with a frustrated customer will change the conversation from *A customer is frustrated and wants to blame it on the support engineer* toward *We have a quick solution for you to get you back on track. Anything else we can do for you today?*

## Business reporting tools

Business leaders typically turn to business reporting tools to understand business success, such as generated revenue per region or product category, the number of processed claims, or the success rate of delivered items. When revenues drop, claims stall, or deliveries fail, the question is why? Is nobody interested in our products? Do we need to hire more people to work on claims? Do we need to switch our delivery service provider? Or is the answer a technical issue, such as a global cloud outage that is currently impacting half of the internet?

Integrating observability through an AI agent into the business reporting tool gives the business leader additional insight to better understand the situation and make a faster decision on how to address the business-impacting situation. A prompt such as *What is the reason for the revenue drop in our sales region in Europe?* could be answered with *There seems to be an issue with two of our top three payment providers in that region. Their Payment API suffers from high failure rates and timeouts. This could be related to an ongoing network issue in the region, which is currently impacting many of the cloud providers.*

As you can see, integrating observability into your business reporting and analytics processes will benefit your business decision-makers as they can leverage real-time information available in your observability backend about your system, but also any third-party APIs or services your business relies on.

There are most likely many more tools you have in your organization that are currently having a limited, siloed view. Bringing observability data into those tools, into the hands of your engineers, product owners, customer success managers, or business leaders, allows them to make better-informed decisions.

The final question we want to discuss in this section is whether we can turn around how data gets to those who need it. Does it always have to be users pulling data by executing prompts? Or can we also push data to them at the time when they need it, without them having to ask for it?

## From manual pull prompts to automated push results

Prompting for observability data is most effective when you can practically do it from anywhere and within any tool, and when the agent executing your MCP server understands the context you are working in. This context may include which Git repository you are currently working on, which bug you are investigating, or which customer you are interacting with in a support ticket. But there are two things that come to mind where prompting might not be the best approach:

- What if I don't know what question to ask? How shall I know which insights I can get to make better decisions?
- What if everyone in the organization requests the same data all over again? Isn't that inefficient?

Once we enable an organization with the ability to prompt information from their respective tools, we can leverage the insights we can get from those interactions to answer those questions. We get those insights by observing your MCP server and your agentic AI workflows, as explained in the *Tracking and measuring usage and impact* section earlier. Once we know which prompts are executed, by whom, at which time, and from which tools, we can identify patterns such as the following:

- What information is prompted for what purpose?
- Is the same information prompted across various teams for the same reason?
- What other insights are there that nobody prompts for yet?

Let's walk through three quick use cases to explain how we can use those usage insights and convert some of the manual pull prompts into automated push results.

## Use case: Push daily standup insights into Slack/MS Teams

This use case comes from an engineering team of a large software vendor that started to leverage GitHub CoPilot in Visual Studio Code to pull in information for their daily standup. As explained in the *Providing guidance: Instruction files for your AI agents* section earlier, they started expanding their instruction files to get more details every morning for their 8 AM standup. They wanted to know about any new error logs that were identified during the nightly tests, any customer-impacting issues that were reported the day before that are still open, and insights into performance hotspots they could optimize. Other development teams heard about this and started to copy those instruction files and run the same prompts when starting their standups.

While all this works great, it was a lot of copy-and-paste effort to keep those instruction files in sync across development teams. Execution times also got longer as those instruction files grew, and at some point, they realized that those queries against the MCP server were not always efficient, resulting in unforeseen query costs or simply having to wait longer for an answer.

To optimize the prompts and make them available to any development team without having to execute those prompts manually at the start of every standup, they decided to use some simple automation that executed those queries against the backend observability platform every day at 7:45 AM. The automation executed those queries for every development team that opted in for that self-service, and it then sent the result into the respective Slack or MS Teams channel so that each team could start their meeting on time at 8:00 AM, reading through the information that was presented to them.

Instead of having multiple copies of instruction files, they now have a central automation script that can be updated and maintained by all teams through a standard pull request process. Any improvement will automatically benefit every team. The automation script itself uses optimized queries against the observability backend and doesn't rely on well-trained LLMs or instruction files, which also makes this approach more deterministic and typically a bit cheaper. AI is used to take all the results of the individual queries and bring them into an easy-to-read and understandable format before posting this as a message to their chat.

## Use case: Push observability insights to pull request

Engineers who make code or configuration changes typically push them through pull requests into the main branch so that those changes get built, applied, or deployed. The big question after a pull request is *Was this a good change or not?*

While an engineer can use an AI agent built into the pull request workflow to execute prompts such as *Are there any problems with the deployment of this pull request?*, we can turn the flow of information around and have a system set up that automatically pushes observability insights to the pull request once that data becomes available. As an engineer, I therefore don't have to pull for information; instead, the relevant insights come to me as part of my pull request. There are different ways to implement this. It could be an action that gets executed as part of the pull request, or you implement it as an automated push once your observability platform detects any issues. The end result, however, is the same: the engineer gets observability insights without having to think about it.

The following screenshot shows automated validation of pull request changes against a set of observability objectives. The resulting observability score is automatically posted back to the pull request, providing fast feedback to the engineers about the quality of their proposed code changes:

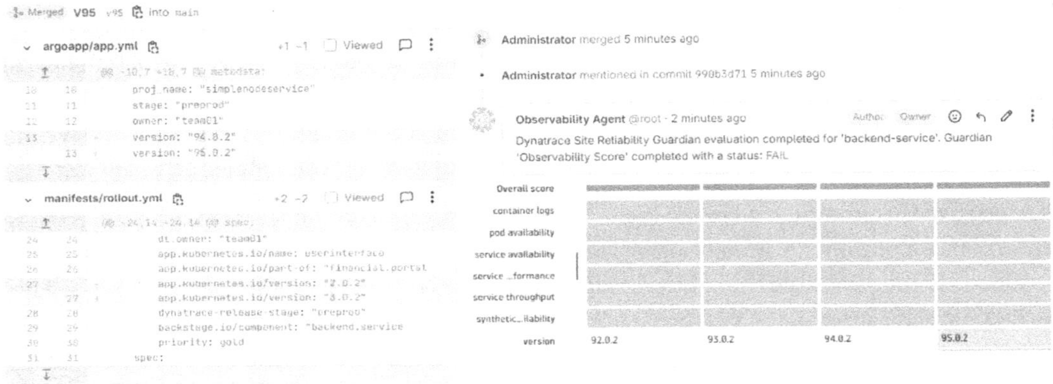


*Figure 6.10: Integrating observability insights into the Git workflow brings relevant insights to the engineers where they need it*

This example reinforces a key shift in how we show the value of observability: *Bring the relevant insights to the engineers and don't ask them to find the information in various tools.*

## Use case: Push daily business insights via emails

Just as software engineers have their daily standups discussing current work items and asking for help on any current blockers, business leaders often begin their day by looking at critical business indicators to make sure they understand if there is anything that needs their immediate attention. In our *Business reporting tools* section earlier, we discussed the use case where observability data can be pulled into business reports to give leaders more contextual information about why they may see a negative impact on their business goals.

And just like with the daily standup example for engineers, we can turn around the flow of insights and push relevant actionable insights to business leaders.

For those of you using Microsoft 365, you probably know the Daily Digest service, which sends you an email first thing in the morning that gives an overview of important emails that need your attention, files that have been shared with you but you haven't yet looked at, or documents where you were tagged in a comment that needs your reply.

What Microsoft does for Office 365, you can also do with your business insights extracted from your observability data. We have seen organizations that simply set up an automation workflow that queries information such as *What are the top customer-impacting technical issues right now and who is impacted?* or *What is user adoption of your latest features?* or *Are there any issues with our third-party vendors, and is there a need to reach out to them?*

A daily *Business Insights Digest* that provides business leaders the right level of information to start their day, versus having them open multiple tools, dashboards, or reports, is what will make them more efficient.

This brings us to the end of the section on understanding who your internal end users are, what type of roles they have, what type of information can be extracted from observability data, and how they can benefit from their day-to-day activities. We closed it with a suggestion to not just make it easier to prompt this data, but also think about what type of insights from observability we can actively push to users at the time when they need it and within the tools they already use.

On the final stretch of this chapter, we are moving away from just delivering data via an MCP to an agent that sits in another tool. It's great to open the world of observability to GitHub CoPilot, Atlassian's Rovo Ops agent, AWS frontier agents, or any other agentic AI. But what if we think about an autonomous observability agent? What would such an agent look like? Which use cases can it orchestrate, and how would that agent connect with other agents?

## Using observability agents to get from reactive to proactive operations

It's 4:37 PM on Friday. You are an SRE and were just added to a Slack thread with five of your engineering colleagues, called `customer-service-4733`. The thread has been going on since yesterday at 2:05 PM. It looks like at least 100 messages have already been exchanged, discussing what started as a complaint that was raised by one of your premium customers about having issues opening their accounts page. Instead of reading through everything that was discussed, you decide to invite your new observability AI companion to the conversation.

> Note
>
> **AlexSRE** 4:50 PM
>
> `@AIOps`
>
> **AIOps** 4:50 PM

*joined customer-service-4733 by invitation from AlexSRE*

**AIOps** 4:51 PM

I analyzed the thread.

Here is what you need to know: There was a release of a new feature (*see Feature Change ticket*) that was rolled out yesterday at 1:00 PM in EU-WEST. 75 minutes later, Top Financial Adviser ACME – who runs our software on EU-WEST – has opened an issue claiming that they have a very slow response time when opening their accounts page – sometimes even getting HTTP 500s (*see Support ticket*). The team decided to roll back the release this morning at 10:17 AM on EU-WEST, but this didn't solve the problem.

I went ahead and analyzed what else there is and noticed the following patterns based on our observability data and code changes:

1: Top Financial Adviser ACME didn't open the Accounts Page for 24 days until yesterday (*see Activity Dashboard*). So, the problem may have been there before the recent feature release!

2: There were two other Pull Requests deployed in the last two months in the area of the accounts page namely, *PR-2332* and *PR-2334*.

3: I found an *Exception stack trace* from a different customer that also resulted in an HTTP 500 that had to do with a database connection timeout. *PR-2332* has addressed this issue by increasing the timeout.

4: *PR-2334* has changed our OpenTelemetry collector processing rules. It creates a specific metric for those HTTP 500 errors called `accounts.dbconn.timeouts`. The same PR also removes full exception details logging of this error

5: It seems the team hasn't found this as a root cause because they focused on exception analysis in logs, but didn't investigate the new metric as it was not yet added to any of the Service-Level Objective (SLO) dashboards. *See metric on dashboard*!

My conclusion:

As I can see an increase in `accounts.dbconn.timeouts`, I assume *PR-2332* didn't really solve the problem and *PR-2334* has limited our observability. I suggest re-investigating how to solve the database connection issue. You can revert *PR-2334* to get all exception details as the first step. Additionally, we can turn on Live Debugging capabilities on EU-WEST, which is a new capability our observability platform has recently enabled (*learn more about Live Debugging*). This would give us immediate live stack trace details,

> including exceptions and variables of the problematic code that opens the database connection.
>
> Let me know if I should initiate the live debugging session and notify you once the first snapshots are coming in!
>
> **AlexSRE** 4:55 PM
>
> Hey `@channel`. Check out what `@AIOps` found. What do you think? Shall we go ahead with the recommendation and start a live debugging session?

The scenario described shows how powerful an agent can be when it integrates seamlessly into existing processes. It automates analyzing existing conversations, captures additional insights from various data sources, and comes up with recommendations on next steps.

The SRE is still the one who makes the ultimate decision, but the information provided allows the team to make better and faster informed decisions. This helps them to stay on track and reach their goals of ensuring resilient systems, and it gives them time to work on more interesting things other than troubleshooting and firefighting.

Achieving goals faster is a big motivator. In the remainder of this chapter, we will look into additional use cases, but also into different engagement models of agents. So far, we have discussed use cases that typically started with a prompt. While this is the most common conversation model, we are also seeing organizations looking into fully autonomous agents that actively join or start conversations or trigger actions to address situations before involving human operators. This has the potential to allow teams to reach their goals even faster.

## Goal-driven engineering

If you have ever used a language learning app such as the very popular Duolingo or a fitness tracking service such as Fitbit, you know that those types of services try to keep you engaged as well as they can. They continuously remind you to stay on your learning or fitness path so that you have a higher chance of reaching your goals faster. And, of course, they want you to consume more of their platform and eventually purchase their premium plans or make in-app purchases.

There is a lot we can learn from those consumer apps and services, especially around how they start the engagement. Typically, you open the app whenever you have time to check how many more steps you need today to reach your daily goal or how many more points you need to make to advance to your next *learning league*. But the system also actively engages with you. There are app notifications reminding you that you have 10 more minutes to complete your hourly step goal, or that if you learn now, you get twice the points, which makes it easier to reach your next level. You also get reminder emails that your friends on the app are worried, as you haven't done your daily lesson yet, and you are about to lose your *learning streak*. There is a lot of psychological messaging and gamification used to get you back to using the services. In the end, though, while some of this seems a bit extreme or annoying, those systems really help people learn a new language or get healthier because they actively engage and, with that, provide value.

## Defining goals for engineering

Instead of always having to prompt an agentic AI with questions such as *Can you explain that problem to me?* or *What are the top performance hotspots that I should fix?*, we need to think about agents that actively notify us about things we should do so that we achieve our goals. Our goals here would be the following:

- **Faster time to market**: Deliver software on time without performance problems
- **Improve resiliency**: Increase the availability of our software to meet our SLOs
- **Reduce risk**: Never operate software with critical vulnerabilities
- **Optimize costs**: Ensure optimal configuration of your deployments

Besides these four examples, think about your own internal engineering goals that will help you achieve your business goals. Then, for a moment, assume that you can hire any expert in areas you need to improve, such as someone who writes excellent code, a security expert, a performance wizard, a master in observability, or a cloud infrastructure guru. What is it that you want those experts to do to elevate our engineering organization to produce better output and achieve their goals faster?

- Would they participate in a **daily standup**?
- Would they participate in **code reviews**?
- Would they do **pair programming**?
- Would they conduct **performance tests**?
- Would they give **coding recommendations**?

Now, let's see how we can implement this.

## Achieving goals: Prompting Center of Excellence

While the preceding ideas are great, the challenge typically comes with scaling this across an organization. If you have 100 engineering teams, it's hard to hire the number of experts in the various fields to place them within those teams.

The solution in the past has been to create **Center of Excellence** (**CoE**) teams that provide centralized services on topics such as performance, security, FinOps, delivery, and so on. And while this model has worked for a while, those teams often become the bottleneck. If 100 engineering teams all need their expertise at the same time, they simply can't scale.

The first solution to this scale challenge is that modern CoE teams take their expertise and make it available as a self-service model. We have discussed different self-service approaches quite extensively in our recent book *Platform Engineering for Architects: Crafting modern platforms as a product*. That book explains how organizations can scale expertise beyond individual teams by providing it through a centralized self-service platform.

Throughout this book, we have also highlighted many of those self-service scenarios. For example, in the *Collaboration and chat tools* section, we discussed the use case of an engineer requesting observability data through a prompt in a Slack conversation. CoE teams that used to provide this data upon request by manually replying to those messages simply automated their expertise and made it available through a self-service model.

While prompting is an important first step toward scaling the expertise that a few people have within an organization, there is another approach to make this even more impactful.

## Scaling: From prompt to autonomous agents

What if you are not aware that you can ask your CoE to give you recommendations on how to optimize your code or improve performance? What if you do not know that you have a chatbot or an MCP server that you can prompt to help you rewrite your code to fix a vulnerability?

Ideally, expert knowledge should come to you at exactly the right time to help you make the right next decision. It's like with your fitness tracker app: it sends you a notification 10 minutes ahead of time to remind you about your hourly step goal, and not when it's too late.

To truly scale expertise knowledge within an organization, the next step after self-service prompting is autonomous agents that actively reach out to the teams and engineers with expert advice and insights so that they can achieve their goals faster.

Let's think back about the Slack conversation at the beginning of this chapter. What if the conversation didn't start with a customer complaining about an issue? What if the conversation started after the initial pull request that changed the database connection timeout? It could have looked like this:

> Note
>
> **ObservabilityAssistant** 2:17 PM
>
> *inviting @AlexSRE @SusanDev @SteveDB @KarenTechLead*
>
> **ObservabilityAssistant** 2:17 PM
>
> Hi, I am the Observability Assistant from your Observability Center of Excellence!

> I am actively analyzing Pull Requests and noticed that *PR-2332* changed the database connection timeout. While this seems like one solution to fix the described problem, it will most likely result in more worker threads being blocked by waiting, causing other side effects.
>
> **Alternative root cause based on distributed traces**
>
> I analyzed some of the distributed traces of the problematic code in question and would like to recommend a different solution. It seems the reasons for the long connection timeout are inefficient database queries and inefficient database connection handling in the module `legacyaccount.dbaccess`. I have a code change recommendation that I have ready for review in *PR-2333*.
>
> Just so you know why I added you all to this thread:
>
> @SusanDev: You proposed *PR-2332*
>
> @SteveDB: You were the last one to make code changes to `legacyaccount.dbaccess`
>
> @KarenTechLead: You are the owner of the accounts services
>
> @AlexSRE: You are scheduled to be on call when this PR reaches production
>
> Let me know if I can explain more details!
>
> **SteveDB** 3:20 PM
>
> Hey `@channel`. I reviewed the suggested PR with `@SusanDev`. We made a slight tweak to the suggestion from `@ObservabilityAssistant` and also reverted the changes from *PR-2332*. We are glad this was caught before deploying to production, as it could have had unexpected side effects! Whoever built this automation. Kudos!
>
> **ObservabilityAssistant** 3:32 PM
>
> Glad this worked. I will learn from your change for future recommendations.

This scenario shows what is possible when having centralized expert teams build their own agents that can act autonomously, scale, and contribute value to the whole organization.

## Use cases to get from reactive to proactive

While we have already discussed a lot of different use cases throughout this chapter, we want to close it by providing three additional ones as food for thought on what autonomous observability agents can do to help engineering teams reach their goals faster by providing them with the right information at the right time in the tools in which they are spending their time.

## Use case – FinOps: redistributing workloads

FinOps is a critical topic for all organizations as it aims to optimize resource utilization to meet both business needs while staying within financial boundaries.

FinOps teams, therefore, constantly analyze the demand for specific services or workloads and how those demands change. If a certain service or application is now used by more users than before, it may need an upgrade. It could also be the other way around: a service is less used than in the past and can now run with a fraction of the initially allotted resources.

Observability can be used to identify the actual requirements of resources of a workload over time. FinOps teams analyze historical data or use algorithms to predict future resource utilization by considering changes in the usage behavior of upstream services. This data can then be used to distribute those workloads to the right shared infrastructure.

Another use case relates to hardware, especially from cloud vendors, which is constantly updated with new chipsets. Observability can tell you which workloads are GPU-intensive, and you can use that information to move them to hardware that is optimized for those types of workloads if performance is a key requirement.

A FinOps observability agent can automate most of the work of a FinOps and automatically open pull requests for the infrastructure team with newly recommended sizing.

## Use case – Observability data quality checks

What if you send log files, but nobody ever looks at them? What if your services emit metrics, but nobody ever uses them on a dashboard or for an alert? What if you have just enabled distributed tracing and now the same exception that used to be captured in logs is also captured in your traces?

Observability teams often look over the data that gets ingested into the backend platform. That is done to make sure that all relevant data gets captured. But it is also done to validate that the data that gets stored is later also used for analysis.

An observability agent can automate these observability data quality checks on a continuous basis and either send a chat message or create a bug ticket for engineers that instructs them on optimizing the quality of their observability data. Here is an example of such a bug ticket:

| **Ticket** | **OBS-2331** |
|---|---|
| **Title** | Metrics `accounts.dbconn.timeouts` never used |

| **Ticket** | **OBS-2331** |
|---|---|
| **Description** | The Observability Agent regularly analyzes your ingested observability data. After the previous change introduced with *PR-2334*, you are ingesting a metric called `accounts.dbconn.timeouts`.<br><br>This metric is not used in any dashboard, quality gate, SLO, or automated alert.<br><br>Please check the following:<br><br>1: Is the metric name spelled correctly and doesn't contain a typo?<br><br>2: Did you forget to add this to a dashboard?<br><br>3: If you have an expected value range, define it as a custom alert.<br><br>4: If this is a business-critical metric, create an SLO.<br><br>If this is a metric you need for a preview feature, please mark it accordingly based on our guidelines.<br><br>If there is no need for this metric, please remove or hide it behind a feature flag to keep our observability clean! |

Whether it is validating incoming data with regard to quality or validating that the observability configuration is correct, an observability agent can help engineers focus on tasks that will improve observability data quality.

## Use case – Optimizing user experience

Many software services we are building are used by humans, whether this is through a website or a mobile app. For these, it is important that user experience is also monitored. Many observability solutions provide the capability to perform RUM or provide the capability to execute synthetic tests to validate a user click path on a scheduled basis.

While experts who know how to configure RUM, how to set up synthetic tests, or how to analyze all this data exist, an observability agent with a focus on user experience can provide active feedback to the application owners. That feedback can include recommendations about proper observability configuration or insights derived from captured observability data that can help optimize the user experience.

The following could be a message to the customer support team in their customer service portal as a service message:

| **Title** | **Potential Real User Impact detected on Accounts Page in US-EAST** |
|---|---|
| **From** | Observability Agent with focus on Real User Insights |
| **Impact** | Currently, 144 non-premium users are accessing our portals hosted in US-EAST |

| **Title** | **Potential Real User Impact detected on Accounts Page in US-EAST** |
|---|---|
| **Details** | This is a heads-up for potential incoming customer complaints!<br><br>Since 4:21 PM, we have seen an increase in page load times for individual users hosted in US-EAST. We are still within our SLAs and Error Budgets.<br><br>The impact is limited to non-premium users using Chrome Browser in US-EAST, whose traffic gets partially routed to EU-WEST.<br><br>We have already informed the engineering teams through the internal discussion channels about this situation. For transparency, the following conversations have been opened:<br><br>#preventing-customer-impact-834: Making frontend engineers aware of the situation. Follow that channel to stay up to date<br><br>PR-2345: Suggest adding Synthetic Checks to the critical user journey<br><br>PR-2346: Suggest to change traffic routing rule for US-EAST for Chrome<br><br>In case the problem persists, we will escalate. We hope, though, that the suggested preventative actions will improve the situation. |

This example shows how customer support can benefit by getting a heads-up about a potential situation. Instead of reacting to an issue once it gets reported by your users, this provides a proactive heads-up. The additional actions that have been taken include reaching out across teams to prevent this impact from growing bigger.

The sky is ultimately the limit when it comes to agentic AI use cases. We have only scratched the surface of how observability agents with various specialties can help engineers make better-informed decisions to reach their goals.

# Summary

In this chapter, we explored what an observability agent can look like in real life. We covered the initial steps by allowing your engineers to use LLMs to ask questions that can be answered by connecting your observability backend to the LLM via open protocols such as MCP.

We then discussed how to efficiently design and implement an observability MCP server by first understanding the personas and the use cases this technology enables. We learned how we can train agents using instruction files to improve the accuracy and quality of the delivered responses. Finally, we discussed how, instead of prompting an LLM for specific insights, we can build autonomous agents that actively integrate into our day-to-day processes to give us expert opinions at scale.

In the next chapter, we again open the doors for ACME Financial Services and see where their journey takes them as they are explore the power of agentic systems.

# Further reading


- [1] Agentic AI definition: `https://www.dynatrace.com/knowledge-base/agentic-ai/`
- [2] NVIDIA's four phases definition: `https://blogs.nvidia.com/blog/what-is-agentic-ai/`
- [3] Downdetector: `https://downdetector.com/`
- [4] MCP documentation: `https://modelcontextprotocol.io/docs/develop/build-server`
- [5] Invariant Labs: `https://explorer.invariantlabs.ai/docs/mcp-scan/issue-code-reference/#TF001`
- [6] OpenLLMetry: `https://github.com/traceloop/openllmetry`

# Join us on Discord

For discussions around the book and to connect with your peers, join us on Discord at `packt.link/discordcloud` or scan the QR code below:

# 7

# ACME Financial Services: How to Move from AIOps to Agentic Platforms

Let's do a quick recap of ACME Financial Services' journey so far before we continue their story of discovery and improvement. If you recall, ACME Financial Services started its observability improvement journey after it had completed its cloud migration and discovered that its observability practices were failing it. They were seeing increased issues affecting customers, an increase in resolution times, and increased employee burnout, among other issues. Most importantly, the company's reputation was being negatively impacted, and that was making it more difficult to win and retain customers. So the company put together a task force to figure out how to improve the problems they were seeing.

The task force had a huge job in front of them and started by digging into the root causes of the problems the company had been facing. Uncovering the root cause was only the beginning, as they began investigating potential solutions. Since they hadn't been keeping track of improvements in observability practices and tooling, they had to do a lot of research and evaluation. After a lot of research and product evaluations, the working group decided on a combination of new standards, new AI-capable tools, and a set of training materials. Since they needed money for the new observability tool, they had to get approval from senior leadership. Luckily, the team made a compelling case and got senior leadership support for their plan, including the new observability vendor.

Investigating solutions and creating a plan was half the battle. The working group had to implement their plan and be able to show improvements to senior leadership. They were well prepared because of all the investigative work the working group performed, and while it took a few years, the team was able to get their plan implemented. They were able to show improvements in each problem area they targeted.

ACME Financial Services made enormous improvements in their observability practices, but like many organizations, they are discovering that despite their progress, they still have more to do. New cost pressures, unmet user needs, and the untapped potential of their existing tooling are pushing the company toward its next evolution: an agentic platform.

In this chapter, we will cover the following topics:

- Defining the end users and the pain points to solve
- How an agentic platform helps
- Crawl, walk, run: Breaking agentic platform projects into milestones

# Technical requirements

For this chapter, there are no technical requirements.

# Once more into the breach

The observability working group at ACME Financial Services celebrated the completion of their massive journey, and the impacts of their work were felt across the company. The company's reputation was recovering, but it didn't take too long before new issues started to appear. First and foremost was cost.

Senior leadership was very happy with the results of the observability work, but an important area of the project hadn't materialized as they were told. The company's spending on operations hadn't decreased as the working group expected, despite the reduced number of incidents, **mean time to resolution** (**MTTR**), fewer resources spent debugging issues, and saved development time by concentrating on popular and well-used features. While the company's operations expenses had stabilized and started to decline somewhat, it was not near the expected savings from the original presentation. Senior leadership was very unhappy with the current and projected cost of operations, so they asked for an explanation as to why the cost savings had not materialized.

Once again, the observability working group was on the spot to dig in and find the root causes and solutions. Without an understanding of the costs and a means to reduce them, senior leadership could undo some of the progress that had been made and possibly even lay off those responsible for the recommendations that led to the spending increase. The working group now had not just business interests as a motivator, but also their own jobs.

## The cost drivers

The observability working group started work on determining why the operations spend did not decrease as they expected. The working group knew they needed data in order to focus on the area(s) driving the largest expenditures. Since all of the changes were kept on-premises and all deployed resources were labeled well, it was a rather simple process to gather the cost data on the new infrastructure deployed as part of the observability improvements.

After gathering and analyzing the costs for the new infrastructure, the working group realized that the costs for the new observability tooling were much higher than they had expected. More compute resources were required than planned, which meant that not only were the licensing expenses higher than expected, but the infrastructure costs to run the tool were higher as well.

The working group also decided to do some research about costs related to observability and AI projects. What they found surprised and dismayed them because they discovered that many AI projects fail. They found that a McKinsey report showed only one-third of all AI projects make it into production (`https://www.mckinsey.com/capabilities/quantumblack/our-insights/the-state-of-ai`), which means two-thirds of AI projects are failing or stalling. While they didn't find a single reason why those projects fail, they did find a few problems that can cause AI projects to fail. AI needs good data in order to provide any utility. Despite the training and work the team had put into the effort, they didn't have a clear idea of whether the data the company was producing was of good enough quality. They thought it was possible their data was just good enough to provide some utility while also causing a lot of wasted time, and that could also be a cost driver.

The observability working group also realized that they would need to determine a way to track cost savings for this initiative so they could present the benefits to senior leadership. While they had some avenues to pursue to improve costs, it was becoming obvious that the cost savings might not show up in the cost of operations alone. Results such as reducing downtime, preventing outages, and even improving application development team design are all benefits with real financial impacts that would be missed by looking at the operational cost alone.

As a starting point, the working group decided they needed to talk with the users of the observability tools in order to understand how the observability tools are being used and the value they are providing. This meant getting input from the SREs and application development teams to assess whether the tooling helped them. Without good data, even the best SREs or developers will struggle, and if the tooling isn't providing those groups with useful information, then they will be spending a lot of money on a tool and not maximizing the return on investment.

## A new challenge: Business process observability

A funny thing happened as the observability working group was gearing up to dive into the soaring costs of their observability journey. Business leaders reached out to the working group with a problem they hoped the observability improvements could address.

ACME Financial Services is a large and complex company that serves many different markets with differing regulations. This means that no task is as simple as just clicking a button. The problem the business leaders wanted to solve was to understand which applications and what parts of the business are involved in each function the company performs.

The observability working group hadn't considered this aspect of the work they had been driving, so they told the business leaders that they would investigate and get back to them. They discovered that this type of observability is generally known as either **business process observability** or simply **business observability**. They also discovered it is useful for understanding the complex inter-operations of a company and for understanding the business implications of problems, potential bottlenecks, and opportunities for optimization.

The team realized that this new use of the data they helped create with the observability improvements could have a big impact on the company. Even with the improvements in ownership metadata, there was currently still no understanding of the entire chain of events and the applications involved in any operation the company performed. The insights from business process observability would help the operations teams understand the business impact of an issue. It could help teams recognize flaws in application and system designs that could lead to more performant and resilient services. It could allow inspection of not only each step in a process, but also which applications, and how many, are involved in each step. If done properly, it would allow the business to understand what steps are taken for a certain business process, such as updating mutual fund stock values or opening a new account.

It was a bonus that the additional insight this could provide would help justify the cost associated with the observability improvements, should they be unable to bring down the costs as much as senior leadership wanted. The working group figured this avenue could provide a little bit of breathing room in their quest to reduce costs.

## A new round of discussions

Once again, the observability working group undertook a series of discussions with various teams across the business to help understand how teams were impacted by the observability changes. They focused on how people used the observability tools and the data available to them.

## Feedback from the application developers

The application development teams revealed they weren't really using the observability tooling or data very much at all. They took the training and tried the tools when they were rolled out, but almost every team they talked to ended up not using the tools or the data. There were a few common reasons why this ended up being the case:

- The observability tooling itself wasn't easy to navigate for people not familiar with observability concepts and practices. The training attempted to cover this gap, but the reality ended up being that the tool wasn't easy enough for the application developers to navigate.
- Some application developers were able to access the tool and start navigating through some of the information, but they had difficulty translating the information in the tool into actionable changes within the application teams.
- Application developers have different kinds of tools they use to accomplish their goals. These tools are required for them to perform their work, and attempting to push a tool onto them when they have difficulty seeing the benefit or integrating it with their workflows didn't work.

The end result seemed to be that the application development teams hadn't really changed their development habits at all.

The team found these conversations were both dismaying and encouraging. They were dismayed because they meant a lot of the work they had put into the effort wasn't being given the chance to succeed. They were encouraging because they also meant there were still opportunities for improvements and cost savings if they could figure out how to make the data or the tool more usable for the application development teams.

## Feedback from the SREs

The discussions with the SREs were enlightening in different ways. Unlike the application developers, the SREs were well versed in observability practices and concepts, and they didn't have problems navigating the tool or using the data. However, the SREs highlighted that there were a few problems with the new observability tools:

- The metadata wasn't consistent. Despite the training provided on the importance of and standards for metrics and metadata, each application team ended up implementing things slightly differently, even for common pieces of information. For example, metrics around application resource usage had slightly different names. This meant that the SREs would have to look for many different metric names and combine information to try to get a holistic view across many applications, and it seemed they would regularly find metric names they had missed. These kinds of inconsistencies were reducing the benefits of having all the metrics and metadata.

- The metric naming differences also directly led to higher costs. The observability vendor charges based on the number of metrics, so having slight variants of the same metric was actually increasing the licensing cost for the observability tool in addition to making it more difficult for the SREs to use the data.
- The SREs had become quite familiar with the new observability tooling and highlighted that the company is not using the tools to their fullest extent. The new tools can use metrics to automatically scale applications and clusters, help automate the **root cause analysis** (**RCA**) process, suggest configuration and code fixes, or even use SLOs to help identify high-priority issues. None of the features that would enable these improvements are currently being used in how the tool is deployed and used today.

# Compliance: The great defense

After talking with the SREs, some members of the observability working group looked into what other functionality ACME Observability provided, but which was sitting idle. The discussions with the SREs brought up that the observability tools could be used to auto-scale a Kubernetes cluster, but that kind of activity is usually outside the purview of observability, as the working group had understood the problem space. The fact that the tool provided this kind of functionality caused the working group members to investigate why an observability tool would provide Kubernetes cluster scaling capabilities.

After extensive investigation, the working group members discovered that they had been looking at the observability problem through too small a lens. When the working group was initially formed, they had an understanding of observability based on knowledge from the last time the company investigated observability tooling and practices. That investigation had led to the selection of the tools and practices in place when the project began, but the capability and scope were limited by what the tools could accomplish at the time. Observability tools and practices have evolved drastically since then, and while the working group had recognized the expansion in tool capability, they hadn't challenged their assertions about what observability should entail.

This revelation opened up a whole new way of thinking about what observability should entail, and more importantly, what kind of efficiencies it could enable. Broadening their definition of observability allowed for a larger set of actions that could be automated, which included looking at configurations and even compliance.

## How observability can help with compliance

Since ACME Financial Services provides services in many highly regulated industries in multiple countries, they are subject to a lot of regulations, and they must ensure that they are compliant with those regulations. Many times, decisions may be more conservative than necessary just to ensure there is no threat of a regulation violation. Up until this point, regulation compliance at ACME Financial Services has largely been ensured via rigorous controls and planning processes. While not perfect, the results have largely kept ACME Financial Services out of trouble with the various regulators. However, nothing is free, and the cost for the current process is a reduction in development and deployment speed.

Once the observability working group recognized the opportunity from widening the definition of observability, they started to look at what else they could impact and improve across the company. Along the same vein as cluster scaling, the working group realized that if they could get data from cluster configuration, security and access configuration, access events, and so on, they could use ACME Observability to monitor and report on compliance with various regulations. In fact, they discovered that the tool already had dashboards and reporting mechanisms for numerous compliance frameworks across multiple companies. They were the same frameworks that ACME Financial Services was required to meet.

This revelation felt like a game-changer to the working group. Instead of having to rely upon rigid and slow processes, they could have real-time data and visualization of that data, showing how compliant resources were with various regulations. They wouldn't have to slow innovation and hope for compliance; instead, they would be able to tell whether a change weakened or strengthened their compliance with regulations. It would also provide a roadmap to increased compliance, should that be a goal that management would want to pursue.

The work required to provide ACME Observability with the required data seemed to be along the lines that the SRE team had already highlighted in order to support things such as scaling the Kubernetes clusters. However, the working group felt that, given the results from the training on the observability changes, they would need more than training for this to be a success. Data consistency would be crucial for the benefits of this approach to be realized. The working group realized they needed to figure out how to incorporate these changes into the company in a way that provided the best chance for success and overall company improvement.

## Expanding the utility of the observability tools

Using the ACME Observability tools to their fullest extent would open up new avenues for efficiencies and drive down overall costs. Based on discussions with users of the tooling and additional investigations, the working group had determined they could use ACME Observability to do the following:

- Help ensure regulation compliance while increasing the speed of new feature development. By providing configuration and security control information to the observability tooling, they could visualize and track compliance across many regulatory frameworks.
- Help application teams find bugs and performance bottlenecks faster and easier by connecting ACME Observability to application team development repositories. Doing this would provide ACME Observability with additional context to understand identified trends from logs and traces, and also enable the tool to analyze information and suggest fixes or improvements.
- Help properly scale the size of Kubernetes clusters and applications. The company already uses **Cluster Autoscaling** as well as **Horizontal Pod Autoscaling** (**HPA**) to scale their Kubernetes clusters and application Pods, but those actions are reactive and do not support proactive options. Using ACME Observability's agentic AI capabilities, they can be proactive based on trends and scale clusters before there is a strain on the system. If the load increases permanently, it can suggest permanent changes to the cluster configuration. The same benefits from cluster scaling would also apply to application scaling.
- Help improve the priority of production events by determining whether systems were close to violating their SLOs. This would focus work on areas where SLO violations could have major impacts on the business.
- Help application developers detect, investigate, and mitigate vulnerability findings, diagnose and resolve performance bottlenecks, decrease production issue resolution time, and increase the velocity of other development tasks. With the data available to ACME Observability, the AI tool could provide insights and suggestions much quicker than the development teams could themselves.
- Help improve the RCA process. The observability tooling has insights into everything happening in production, and it can help analyze and identify the root cause of production incidents. By leveraging the vendor's AI capabilities more, they could get

automatic RCA generation to reduce the time investment required to produce the document.

- Implement business process observability. Providing insight into what steps were taken for a business process would provide a level of understanding that has never existed within ACME Financial Services.

That was quite an additional list of improvements the team could implement, and they realized they had missed these benefits because of their narrow view of observability when the project started. These benefits also provided a stronger justification for the costs associated with running ACME Observability. Even if they are unable to reduce the costs of running the tools, they can show that those costs will reduce costs elsewhere in the organization. The working group still had some areas to investigate that could ultimately lead to a reduction in the cost of running the new observability tooling, but regardless of how that turned out, the working group was starting to feel better about the path they had set the company on. Without realizing it, they had actually positioned the company to improve and reduce costs in more than just the traditional observability areas.

## Tackling the costs

Up to this point, the observability working group hadn't really done very much investigation into actually reducing costs. They had discovered many new ways that ACME Observability could be used to improve productivity, but they didn't have a very good understanding of how much that might increase their cost. With senior leadership very unhappy with the operation costs for the business, the working group knew they needed to find some ways to reduce costs, or at the very least, provide strong justifications for those costs since they had originally pitched a reduction in cost.

The working group decided they should start by discussing their cost concerns with the ACME Observability vendor. In that discussion, the observability working group detailed how they were using the tool and how it was deployed. They highlighted that every application team was sending every piece of telemetry data to the tool every time their applications performed any work. They felt that this would ensure that all the data needed to assess production incidents would be available in the tool. They likened this approach to how they provided production logs to their log aggregator.

After listening to ACME Financial Services detail their tool usage and problems, the ACME Observability vendor highlighted a big concern with how the tool is being used. They pointed out that ACME Financial Services is a large company with many applications running that produce a lot of telemetry data. Processing and storing all of that data would be very expensive, and they returned to the analogy used by the ACME Financial Services team when they detailed how they used their log aggregator. Because applications generally produce a lot of log data, ACME Financial Services has a policy that debug logging should be disabled when applications are deployed to production. The ACME Observability vendor equated that policy with a similar policy in the observability world called **sampling**. In large companies such as ACME Financial Services, it is not viable to process and store every piece of telemetry data if a desired goal is to be financially responsible. That is why ACME Observability, and the industry at large, recommends using sampling to reduce that storage and processing burden while still maintaining all the data necessary to identify the root cause of incidents. The ACME Observability vendor recommended investigating and implementing sampling strategies to reduce the cost of running their tooling.

## Assessing sampling

After their meeting with ACME Observability, the working group realized they had more research to do around sampling. According to the vendor, sampling could provide significant cost savings, but they didn't really understand how to implement it in a single application, let alone across the entire company.

The working group researched sampling and discovered that while it is a common practice for dealing with large amounts of telemetry data, there isn't a single, or even simple, implementation of sampling. There are a few common strategies, such as head, tail, or random sampling, but which strategy is best can depend on what is important for diagnosing production issues.

The group decided to use a simple example as an exercise to understand how sampling would help control costs. They decided on using the maximum number of connections per hour, which could be an indicator to help scale an application. The group decided to try evaluating two data sampling methods: head sampling and tail sampling.

Head sampling makes a decision about the metric data at the beginning of an interval, and tail sampling makes a decision about the data after you have all the metrics for the time interval. Their idea was that an application would only need to report the metric if the number of connections being managed had increased when the connection was initiated. It was a simple configuration, but at some point, the application would need to reset its internal counter to ensure proper reporting over an hour timeframe. In their evaluation of this scenario, they determined that latency and connection errors would probably be lost. Any sharp spikes or drops in connections over the course of that hour would also not be accurately identified. The group wasn't sure whether that was an acceptable trade-off for all applications. In fact, for anything time-sensitive, such as a trading application, those trade-offs probably would not be acceptable.

The group then decided to evaluate that same example using tail sampling. In this scenario, they determined that errors and latency issues would be surfaced, but each application in the connection flow would likely need more CPU and memory in order to manage the trace data. Having all the data would make it easier to identify spikes, but that would be an additional calculation, and it's hard to know whether a spike is important or just expected based on system design. Are these trade-offs acceptable? Is the cost of increased memory and CPU less than the storage cost savings gained by using tail sampling? Is there enough cost offset gained by removing the need for storing larger data blocks about connection information long-term? The group wasn't confident they could answer that question without assistance from an application team, let alone determine it for all applications.

It is also possible that technologies change the implementation or even the sampling strategy. For these reasons, they determined that it is probably suboptimal to try to enforce a single strategy for all applications, and that it may be desirable to allow tuning of the sampling rate to help diagnose production issues. The sampling strategy or rate could even depend on specific operations within an application, so it may not even be consistent within a single application.

As complicated as sampling appeared to be, it also appeared to be the only real solution to their cost problem. The observability working group didn't think they should even attempt to decide on a single sampling strategy or rate, so that left them with one option as far as they could tell: training. They would have to learn as much as they could about sampling and produce training materials for the application teams to consume and implement. They didn't see a better way, but they were a bit concerned about relying on the application development teams, given the current variance in telemetry data that resulted from various interpretations of the training on observability.

## The new changeset

After completing another round of investigations, the observability working group had created another set of changes they wanted to implement:

- Expanding the usage of the observability tooling
- Reducing costs through sampling and right-sizing
- Tracking and monitoring regulatory compliance
- Business process observability
- Improving application developer engagement
- Improving and enriching the telemetry data

Most of these new objectives were built on the work that was already completed, but some were enhancing and cleaning up variations created by the application teams during their implementation. The application teams didn't have a strong understanding of observability, and there didn't seem to be a way to coordinate across all development teams in the company.

The observability working group determined they needed to try something else this time. They didn't feel that they could afford another round of differing implementations and achieve the goals they wanted to achieve, especially since some of those differences led to increased costs in the observability tools.

## A platform team?

The observability working group discovered that their problem was not unique and, in fact, was pretty common in these kinds of changes in large organizations. It is very hard to coordinate application development teams around a set of documented standards. The more complex the situation, the less defined the standard can be, and that leads to differences in implementation. The solution to their problem is not just using their tooling better, but also building their software in a repeatable, standardized way.

One of the proposed solutions to such a problem is a centralized team that provides a common implementation of important standards and the mechanism for building and deploying software that meets those standards. This has the benefit of putting all of the implementation work in one team, and the results of their work are consumed by all the application teams. The application teams don't have to worry about interpreting complex standards, and that reduces or even eliminates the implementation differences for those core standards. In observability, it is still important to allow application teams to provide data unique to their application, but there is a lot of data that can be defined in a common way by a common team. The observability working group discovered that a centralized team that performs this type of work is often referred to as a platform team, and their method for doing so was through the creation of an **internal developer platform** (**IDP**).

# A big ask, a big undertaking

The observability working group decided that the company would need a platform team to design and implement common standards and to help drive application teams toward standards-compliant implementations in their applications for their unique use cases. They also realized that this was much easier said than done. It was one thing to create training and rely on the application development teams to do the work, and quite another to have a centralized team, or teams, performing that work. The latter would probably require some kind of company reorganization and possibly some shift in responsibilities at the management level. That is a big ask of senior leadership, and they knew that they could not make such a request without clearly defining the work and responsibilities of that team.

## A platform team does what?

First, the Observability team decided they needed to outline what the responsibilities would be for a new platform team. This would help inform the skill sets needed on the team, as well as help senior leadership realign responsibilities. They decided that the platform team should take a measured approach:

- Working within the existing paradigm: Champion telemetry data standards. This would initially involve working with application teams to correct any data that was deviating from the standards or might be causing additional cost. This would have at least three benefits that they could see:
    1. Provide immediate improvement with the current observability capability and hopefully reduce the cost of the vendor tools.
    2. With all of the data consistently following the standards, the transition to an IDP would be as seamless as possible from the observability standpoint.
    3. Provide a runway for the new platform team to produce the IDP for the application teams to consume. It's important that the platform team's products not reduce existing functionality or permanently decrease velocity.

Once the platform team has created an IDP that the application teams use, they would transition to being responsible for implementing and enforcing standards for common telemetry data within the IDP. This is expected to meet the objectives to reduce costs, with the following key results:

- Enhance the existing telemetry data and ensure that it has all the relevant information necessary for the existing and new functionality of the observability tooling to provide the intended benefits. They would also be responsible for adding any new telemetry data into the system.
- Be the observability implementation experts. This would include training and mentoring application team developers on best observability development practices.
- Connect as many systems into the observability agentic AI as needed for developer and operations team workflows. This would involve having conversations with multiple teams and working with them to ensure the tools are providing useful capabilities.
- Manage Kubernetes cluster size and application resources to minimize total cost. This would probably entail owning the application deployment mechanism in order to prevent application teams from changing the resources of an application during a new deployment.

## That's an awful lot of responsibility

When they finished coming up with the list of responsibilities, the working group realized it was probably enough work for more than one team. They were uneasy with that realization because it made the request to senior leadership and the business impact much larger than they originally thought. It seemed that there were three facets to the list of responsibilities they had created:

- Short-term mentoring/training work around helping application teams improve their observability implementations
- Mid-term development focused on producing products for the application teams to consume
- Long term, providing capabilities to application teams should they need more than what the platform team would initially produce

They were already unsure whether they could get approval for such broad changes across the company, but they accepted that the need was what it was. They figured they should put together a plan that covered and justified as much as possible, and see what they received from senior leadership. They thought that while multiple teams may be needed, delineation mixed with a *crawl, walk, run* approach might help get senior leadership's buy-in since they weren't trying to pitch a single magical fix for everything and would be able to clearly define roles, responsibilities, and needs. The fact that they could highlight how those teams would need to work together and coordinate would also help carve out an area of responsibility for senior leadership.

## How do we do that?

While some of the responsibilities sounded like great solutions to their problems, the team didn't really know how to achieve them. Most of the responsibilities seemed well within the traditional observability space, and the working group felt they had a reasonable understanding of the kind of work that would be needed. However, since they started expanding the scope of what was considered *observability*, they were now dealing with ideas that encompassed software development and IT, and no one in the working group was familiar enough to talk intelligently about those areas or even whether the ideas were feasible. Of all the responsibilities they came up with, they definitely weren't sure about the following:

- How to connect various services to the new platform.
- What does it mean to centralize and control the application deployment process? Is it all tooling, or is it a suite of tools?
- Was there any way to improve the current cluster and application resource consumption?

The team figured they would need to get data about how the company currently operates, and how this idea of a platform team and its defined responsibilities could improve the current state of affairs. They thought that a good starting point to find answers that they couldn't research would be to have more discussions with the SREs.

# In search of more answers

Before the observability working group gathered SREs for discussions, they wanted to decompose the problems into bite-sized pieces. There was a lot about how the company actually operated that the working group did not understand, but they needed to try to get a better understanding of what was involved. For example, while they didn't know all of the systems that could be connected to the platform, they could research how to connect new systems to their observability systems.

## Connecting the systems

The working group started its latest educational journey by looking into how ACME Observability integrates with other systems and what such a connection enables for its users. They learned about the **Model Context Protocol** (**MCP**) and that creating servers that communicate using MCP would enable integration into ACME Observability. They only had a rough idea of what that meant, but their investigation led them to believe that implementing that concept was a combination of infrastructure and application development work, or through assessing and leveraging the MCP servers provided within a marketplace. To them, that meant that the platform team would need more than just infrastructure development expertise. It would potentially need application development experience and the ability to assess tools for regulatory compliance.

They also discovered how connecting other software systems to ACME Observability could enable expanding left and help improve the application development process. They learned that **expanding left**, also known as **shifting left**, is a concept that encompasses expanding best practices or providing actionable data to development teams earlier in the development process. This sounded like it could be of great use to development teams and the company as a whole. The working group thought they should probably have some discussions with engineering leadership to understand how ACME Observability could help them expand left and what data and systems would be useful for that effort.

## Discovering how applications were deployed and managed

The team knew there was a data gap: application developers did not have observability data that they were using during their software development process. So, they decided to learn more about how applications were deployed and what data, if any, was used during the development and deployment phases. The application development teams had control over deploying their applications to production, and while those deployments had to go through an approval process, there was nothing evaluating any part of the deployment itself. This was a primary reason why the fact that application teams had each implemented the observability standards slightly differently wasn't caught earlier. The working group knew the basic concepts of deploying an application to production, but little of the specifics within the company. They knew the SRE teams for each application would know more here and included it in their list of questions for that group.

ACME Financial Services is such a large company that there isn't a single SRE organization in charge of all applications. In fact, the responsibilities tended to be handled by SRE teams within the different business units that made up the company. This meant that there wasn't a single answer to the working group's questions because each SRE team worked in different environments, which were governed by regulations or business needs. The observability working group lined up some meetings with various SRE teams across as much of the organization as possible in an attempt to get an understanding of how applications were currently deployed and maintained.

This revealed a set of common problems. While there were differences, in general, the deployment process consisted of the application teams submitting requests for production deployment, getting required approvals, and then deploying their new application version. That was largely where the application team's responsibility and understanding ended. The SREs were responsible for keeping the applications running, and that included handling outages and scaling application resources as needed. Since the application teams had a base configuration for deploying their application, the SREs had to make sure to communicate any changes they made to the application deployment to the application teams to ensure that the deployment configuration was updated and production changes weren't rolled back on a new deployment. As much as everyone in this process tried, changes fell through the cracks and sometimes even led to production incidents. Luckily, those incidents tended to be short-lived, but they were still unnecessary, and any outage required performing RCA. Presenting that RCA to leadership never put the SRE teams in a good light and consumed resources that the SREs could be putting toward other tasks.

The working group also learned that if an application wasn't causing a problem, then it generally wasn't actively observed. This meant that if an application had to be scaled to deal with a spike in demand, it wasn't always reset to its original resources. If an application team overprovisioned resources for their application, then it was unlikely an SRE would discover it and reduce the consumed resources. This all meant that it was highly likely that the applications were allocated more resources than they needed, and that meant larger infrastructure and higher costs.

## Discovering how Kubernetes clusters were managed

Where the application-level observability was lacking, the Kubernetes clusters were managed much more rigorously. The SREs had built out monitoring tools and ensured that proper data was fed into them, so they had a strong understanding of what was going on in any given cluster. They had achieved that through common cluster configurations and collecting proper metrics. They could even minimize outages relatively easily by scaling clusters up or down to meet demand if they knew a spike usually occurred at a specific time. However, because they didn't build out these same monitoring tools for applications, they couldn't ensure that the Kubernetes clusters were as cost-effective as they could be. Due to the issues with application management, the best the SRE teams could do was to ensure that the Kubernetes clusters were no larger than necessary. In this context, *necessary* meant that each application had enough resources to run based on the definitions in its deployment and could scale to a degree before the SRE team would need to scale the Kubernetes cluster itself.

The observability working group asked why they hadn't built out the monitoring tools for the applications, and they learned it was because the application teams had control over their application deployment configurations. Since the SREs had no control over the deployment configuration, there was no way for them to ensure that the proper metrics existed to build reliable monitoring tools. This sounded like another justification for building something that could manage and standardize the application deployment configurations. It would definitely fit under the platform team responsibilities and appeared to be a requirement to enable the observability tools to help with right-sizing application and cluster configurations and thus optimize operations cost.

## Discovering the concept of self-service

The final topic the observability working group discussed with the SREs was their idea of controlling the application deployment process to ensure standardization and rich telemetry data for common functions. The SREs all liked the idea, but advised that a lot of the reason why things were the way they were was that each business area had different requirements and regulations. That didn't mean that there couldn't be one or more common platforms, but it did mean the platform would have to be able to address the different regulatory requirements across business areas.

The SREs also highlighted that the only way for such a system to scale across the company was for it to be initiated and managed by the application teams themselves. With the sheer number of applications in production, there was no way the SRE teams would have time to be involved in the deployment process. Either application deployment would take a really long time, or production incident resolution times could be negatively impacted. There just weren't nearly enough SREs in the company to do that kind of work.

Luckily, the SREs knew of a model that could address all of these problems because the SREs used it in their processes for managing Kubernetes clusters: **self-service**. The SREs explained that in a self-service model, the users are in control of initiating actions, and the system provides standards and guardrails for those actions, known as the **golden path**. This sounded very promising to the observability team. They knew they would need input from the SREs as they created a presentation for senior leadership, so they got commitments from the various SREs to provide input and feedback on this part of the presentation.

# What does a platform team deliverable look like?

The observability working group had put a lot of responsibility on this new platform team, but they knew they would need to provide examples for how this team would achieve their responsibilities in order for senior leadership to accept the need. So, the group drew from the knowledge they had gained from prior discussions to outline what kind of deliverables the platform team would produce.

The group discussed that in order for the platform team to control a base set of metrics, it would have to control how applications are deployed; in other words, they needed an IDP. After some discussions, they decided that the platform team could produce an IDP that would accept a container for deployment onto Kubernetes from an application team, along with some metadata, such as team name, contact information, and application name. The system would then deploy that application and attach that metadata to the deployment. Kubernetes metrics related to that application would be configured and generated automatically.

Metrics and ownership data would be configured to be sent to the observability platform. The platform team could then work with the application teams on how and when to scale their application and provide that information to the observability platform so it can provide useful scaling suggestions.

The platform needed to be capable and flexible, allowing teams to use it with minimal friction, but also to expand it as needed for their specific area of business. This would mean capabilities such as plugins to the platform, MCP servers for the observability agent, or AI skills to expand what the agent could do.

This may not end up being how it would actually function, but the working group thought this provided a good example of how the platform team would provide the value they were suggesting in a way that senior leadership would be able to recognize.

They also recognized that there were already solutions in the industry to meet these needs. They could leverage a vendor or an open source tool such as Backstage. They included this in their presentation to demonstrate that there were concrete, achievable paths forward, although the final tool selection would need to be done by the implementing team.

## Who is a fit for a platform team?

Now that they had an understanding of the type of work a platform team would perform, they started looking at what skills the team would need in order to succeed. They sought and received input from the SREs because a platform team seemed to straddle skills used by application developers and SREs. They came up with the following skill set:

- **Detail-oriented**: The platform team would be responsible for a lot of functionality, and any mistake could impact multiple teams. Understanding how the systems fit together and how to create proper guardrails would be important.
- **Strong understanding of Kubernetes**: The platform team would be closer to Kubernetes and would create deployment standards and processes that the application teams would be using. Since almost everything in the company was deployed on Kubernetes, it was critical that the platform team understand how to achieve their goals on Kubernetes and how to provide proper guardrails. The SREs highlighted that understanding Kubernetes operators and reconciliation concepts would be a big plus.
- **Strong understanding of telemetry data**: Since the platform team was going to be providing standard implementations for common telemetry data (logs, metrics, and traces), it was critical that those on the platform team understand that data and, more importantly, how to make it useful.
- **Experience with mentoring others**: The platform team was going to create a system with guardrails and a common process, but they would also have to allow application teams to expand that functionality as needed for application-specific use cases. That meant that not only would the platform team have to know the correct way to do things, but they would also have to help the application teams implement their additional use cases. This would encompass tasks such as creating training materials, as well as being mentors and advisors to the application teams.
- **GitOps- and self-service-oriented**: The SREs emphasized the importance of using GitOps for a self-service platform, and how it provided traceability and control when many users were making changes. Anyone on the platform team would need to understand the GitOps model and be oriented toward enabling self-service actions whenever possible.

- **Customer-focused**: The platform team would be creating a service for application teams to consume, which meant the application teams would be customers of the platform team. Members of the platform team would need to be oriented on how to meet their customers' needs.
- **Experience with YAML or JSON**: Most applications would be deploying on Kubernetes, and those deployment specifications were written in YAML. On top of that, many GitOps self-service systems were designed to consume configuration in a YAML or JSON structure.
- **Development experience in Go**: Kubernetes is written in Go, and many tools that use Kubernetes or help manage applications running on Kubernetes are written in Go. Implementing a Kubernetes operator is generally done using Go. Proficiency in this programming language would help the platform team members debug or implement tooling for their needs.
- **Understanding of DevOps metrics**: The platform team was going to be providing services to application teams, and having a means to measure the team's impact would help them understand how they were impacting application development teams and where they could improve. It could also provide data that could be presented to the senior leadership in support of the platform team's accomplishments or planned improvements. There were already metrics such as DORA and metric frameworks in use across the industry, so members of this team would need to be able to determine what metrics and/or frameworks would help the team measure and track their impact.
- **A product mindset**: The platform was not going to be a one-and-done effort. In order for the investment to pay off, it would need to have a purpose and then grow with the organization, defining and redefining itself as new technologies and requirements came along.

## Lessons from the SREs

With the proposal well underway, the observability working group needed more information from the SRES before organizing its plan into a presentation for senior leadership. They got together with the SREs and talked through some areas the working group was still unclear about.

## Reactive versus proactive scaling

The first topic the observability working group wanted to discuss was using observability data to scale the Kubernetes clusters. The working group members didn't really understand how, but they knew that the Kubernetes clusters were scaling and able to handle increased loads, so they didn't understand how using observability data would help anything. They didn't want to highlight this in their presentation to senior leadership if they couldn't talk to and defend the proposed improvement.

The SREs started by explaining how the Kubernetes clusters were currently scaled. They were generally scaled in one of two ways:

- Using a Kubernetes tool called the **Cluster Autoscaler** (**CAS**)
- Using a time-based action to increase or decrease the size of the Kubernetes cluster

The SREs explained that CAS would increase the size of a Kubernetes cluster when a Pod was unable to be scheduled on the cluster, and scale down the cluster when it determined that nodes were being underutilized. There are other tools that could replace CAS, such as Karpenter or a cloud provider scaling solution, but they generally work the same way. They scale the Kubernetes cluster only once a need is detected.

The time-based actions to scale a cluster are used when the SREs know the company will experience an increase in traffic and therefore need more cluster resources. They explained that this is a brute-force way to try to handle periods of time with known increased traffic. They used trading markets as an example. Trading markets are only open during a period of time during the day, but at night, the demand on trading systems is much lower. To account for this in a cost effective manner, the SREs have put in place time based actions to scale up the cluster before the trading markets open to be able to handle the surge of traffic that usually occurs at that time, and then at the end of the trading day, they will scale down the cluster to reduce costs since traffic drops off significantly during the evening.

The SREs then explained that the two methods they just highlighted are reactive, meaning they can only act when defined limits are reached. Scaling a Kubernetes cluster is not instantaneous, so even with the CAS, there is still a period of time where the system is under stress until the new Kubernetes nodes are spun up and added to the cluster. The time-based actions are really a poor attempt at being proactive. Through years of experience providing services and managing traffic loads, the SREs had learned when there tends to be increased demand within the company's offerings and had automated scaling of the Kubernetes clusters accordingly.

While those current techniques work, they still leave a lot of room for improvement. For example, if there were an unexpected large spike in demand for system resources, it could take the CAS quite some time to make the necessary resources in the cluster available. The entire time that was occurring, ACME Financial Services' customers were experiencing some form of degradation in their experience.

In another case, if there were a bank holiday, the scheduled actions could increase resources available, and therefore costs, without the associated traffic to justify the expense. The SREs highlighted that this lack of real-time analysis was where the observability data could help with cluster scaling. This was an area where the AI capabilities of the existing tooling, ACME Observability, were being underutilized. The AI agent in ACME Observability would be able to track historical utilization trends and recommend cluster size. It would also be able to predict, based on resource consumption growth, when a cluster should scale and by how many nodes. Both of those abilities would provide a better customer experience as well as protect against unexpected surges in demand. The SREs differentiated this kind of functionality as being proactive.

The last topic the SREs discussed was application scaling. Currently, the Kubernetes clusters are using HPA to manage the number of Pods running for specific applications. This is also reactionary and has the same limitations as the reactive cluster scaling methods. The observability data and capabilities from ACME Observability could also help with being proactive when scaling applications as well.

## Self-service platform details

Next, the observability working group wanted to discuss the details of a self-service platform. Based on earlier discussions with the SREs, the working group had a rough idea of what a self-service platform was, but they weren't strong enough in the concepts to be able to explain or defend the need or the benefit to senior leadership.

The SREs started with a basic overview of how this kind of system worked in their use cases. They then detailed a system that held all Kubernetes cluster information in a Git repository, and all changes required review and approval before they could be merged. Once a change was merged to mainline, CI/CD pipelines automatically started and worked to apply the changes in the Git repository to the Kubernetes clusters. They had alerts that notified the team if a change had problems being applied.

The SREs said the same concepts/benefits should translate to a self-service system that could be used by the application development teams. One difference is that issue resolution would likely be split between the application development teams and the platform team. Based on the SREs' understanding of the company's deployment patterns, they gave a broad overview of a self-service system that could be used by application teams:

- All application deployment configurations would be maintained in a Git repository
- A deployment would start once a change had been merged to mainline

- The platform's deployment process would ensure that common metrics were configured on the container
- The application development teams would be responsible for the following:
    - Building application containers.
    - Managing any application configuration for their application.
    - Providing an initial set of resources for each container. Once an application was deployed to production, the SREs would be able to adjust resources via the configuration in the Git repository.

Some tasks could be improved by connecting the Git repository to the observability platform:

- Allow ACME Observability to open change requests when resource modifications are needed
- The platform could even block deployments for applications without adequate process data (error budget, sign-offs, and so on)

The benefits of such a system include standardization, automation of tasks, reduced deployment complexity and variation, and a generally smooth deployment process. A drawback to this kind of platform is that it would reduce the deployment configuration options available to the application development teams because they would only be able to use the deployment configuration items that the platform team had allowed. This meant that the platform team would have to work with the application teams to ensure there were adequate deployment options.

In the SREs' experience, that downside was not as significant as it sounded. In the application deployment case, the application development teams didn't generally have a strong understanding of Kubernetes, and removing the complexity and options could make it easier for them to manage their applications.

## Assistance with RCA

In the observability working group's earlier discussions with the SREs, they mentioned that ACME Observability could help automate the creation of RCA. The working group wanted to dive into how the tools could help and what kind of cost savings they might enable.

The SREs were happy to dive into this topic because creating RCAs was one of the more difficult and time-consuming tasks they had to undertake. Ideally, RCAs wouldn't be needed because there would be no outages, but since that was unlikely, the next best thing the SREs would like was to automate the collection of information around an incident.

After an incident had been resolved, the SREs worked with whichever application teams were impacted to discover what went wrong to cause the outage, with the hope of learning how to prevent it in the future. Outages can be caused by many different issues, so everyone started with what the outage was (crashing Pod, network disruption, and so on) and then looked for all recent changes that could have contributed to that issue. Sometimes the problem wasn't due to a recent application change, but due to higher or different traffic patterns triggers a series of events that weren't expected or hadn't occurred before. It could take a lot of time and effort to track down all the information related to an outage, analyze it, and determine what went wrong and how to prevent it in the future.

The SREs believed the RCA process could be significantly improved with ACME Observability being tied into all the systems in ACME Financial Services. In this scenario, ACME Observability would know when deployments occurred, what changes went into a specific deployment, traffic patterns, trends, and more, and could provide all that information as a starting point for RCA. This would significantly reduce the work needed to gather the information needed to understand what went wrong and why. The SREs even thought that, at some point, the observability tooling could enable completely automating the creation of an RCA.

SREs are always under strain and have limited availability, so anything that could help them reduce their workload seemed like a big win for the members of the observability working group. They asked the SREs to come up with some rough numbers around how much time they spent on RCA and an estimate of how much they felt that could be reduced with the automation that could be enabled with the observability tooling. The SREs explained this would not be difficult since they used work tickets to track the efforts put into creating RCAs, which allowed them to track the work just like everything else. The RCA data would provide another data point on reducing costs that the working group could present to senior leadership.

## Automating regulation compliance

Another feature of ACME Observability that wasn't being used was **regulation compliance**. The SREs explained that ACME Observability supported reporting compliance with various regulations. This work was currently handled in a rather manual fashion by a regulation compliance department. The process tended to require application teams to engage with the compliance department when they thought a change might run afoul of a regulation. This was less than foolproof because the application development teams didn't know the details of any regulations. In general, there were some processes in place to help elevate architecture and especially security design decisions to a group of senior decision makers, and that group usually had enough knowledge to know if compliance needed to be consulted.

ACME Observability could automate compliance and help reduce the possibility of changes that would violate a regulation from being deployed into production. Since the tool supported reporting the level of compliance with various regulations, that data could also be queried by various tools to detect whether a change would reduce compliance levels. With the company providing services in many different regulated fields, this feature alone would reduce a significant burden on the compliance team and help protect the company from findings of compliance failure that would lead to significant fines and possible reputational harm.

The observability working group thought this was another potential major improvement the tools could provide to ACME Financial Services. Anything that could cause harm to the company's reputation was seen by senior leadership as a top priority. Automating regulatory compliance in this way could help increase the deployment and development velocity of application teams without increasing the potential for violating regulations. It could also reduce the load on the compliance department and allow them to focus more on complex questions that were not necessarily going to be understood by ACME Observability. At the very least, any decisions the compliance department would make could be fed into ACME Observability as guidance for the future.

## Expanding left: Meeting developers where they work

The observability working group had spent a lot of time talking to SREs and understanding how they could improve their lives and various processes the application development teams had to undertake. However, they still needed to solve the other half of their problem with the observability tooling, which was that the application development teams weren't really using it. The interface was too confusing for them, and they had a difficult time making sense of the data, so the result was that the application developers didn't really use the tools. The working group realized that they needed to maximize the return on the tooling to help mitigate senior leadership's concerns over the costs.

When the observability working group evaluated tools, many of them mentioned supporting expanding left for observability data. They dove back into ACME Observability's feature set and documentation and looked for how it could better support the application developers. They discovered that there were a number of ways the tool could help application developers, and they would be enabled when more systems were connected to ACME Observability. This was a fortuitous discovery because it fit into the work already planned in the proposal.

They also learned that it is not uncommon for application developers to shy away from observability tooling. The tools generally are not designed in a way that integrates well with an application developer's workflow, and because of that, they tend to be underutilized. Because this is a common issue, there are integrations and features that can help address the problem.

ACME Observability supported opening suggested changes in Git repositories and commenting on developer changes if they might address or cause known issues. It also supported plugins for software development tools that would enable the application developers to get real-time feedback and suggestions based on the observability data. These kinds of integrations provided the observability data in the tools that were commonly used by application developers. This meant they wouldn't have to change their development workflows in order to benefit from the observability data available to them.

This seemed a good start to addressing the problem. There would likely need to be some training for the application developers, but the working group was confident that once the application developers experienced the benefits in their development workflows, adoption would be quick.

## Observability-driven development

The observability working group also stumbled across the concept of **observability-driven development**. This approach is part of the *expanding left* effort and works to improve the data consumed by the observability tools and, therefore, improve the ability to monitor an application. As the working group noted early in this effort, the better the data, the better the results.

The application developers would likely see benefits just from tying various development and observability systems together, but the effect would be amplified if the application developers considered how to observe the internal state and actions of their applications. This is where observability-driven development would come into play.

The working group learned that if application developers consider how to design their applications to support being observed externally, that mentality often leads to application designs that make it easier for the application developers to diagnose problems. In effect, the application development teams end up helping themselves in addition to the operations teams. It also helps application developers continually improve their applications when their tools receive observability data, which, in turn, improves company response times as a whole.

Unlike just plugging ACME Observability into tools used by application developers, this effort would require significant training and some changes to the application development process. Like other development processes, incorporating observability-driven development into an application's development cycle would require some changes to how applications are designed and how developers test those applications. It would need to be a central part of the process and not an afterthought. The observability working group knew they could create training, but they would first need to explain the benefits to senior leadership. It would be very difficult to get this kind of change implemented with application development teams without support from senior leadership.

## Bringing it all together: The new proposal to senior leadership

The observability working group finally completed its latest investigations into how to improve observability within ACME Financial Services. What started primarily as a quest to reduce costs grew into a much wider and more complicated proposal than the one they put together several years ago. The group had learned that what constituted good observability practices had changed much more than they originally thought, but that the benefits were also much larger than they originally thought.

The working group was a little nervous about presenting the proposal to senior leadership. The last proposal was fairly straightforward and didn't involve a whole lot of major changes within the company. While it provided significant improvements, it did not come cheaply. Trying to address the cost of the solution led them to discover their work was far from over. The working group created a proposal for senior leadership that covered not just cost-cutting, but also demonstrating the value of the tooling across the software development lifecycle as a means to justify the investment.

It was a complex proposal with several suggestions addressing more than one area. It would require some level of reorganization of personnel and responsibilities, as well as company-wide policy changes, in order to achieve all the benefits they laid out. It also relied upon some direct and indirect methods to lower costs by taking a look at the entire operations expense rather than just the direct cost of the tooling. In order to support this approach, they also highlighted new metrics that would be collected to track how the changes impacted various parts of the company. The working group knew these metrics could make or break the success of the project, because without them, it became almost impossible to assess the impact of the work being done by the observability tooling or the platform team in financial terms.

In addition to the metrics, the working group knew they would need to get senior leadership to expand their view on costs and savings. With the proposal integrating and affecting many more parts of the company, the operations cost could no longer be looked at in isolation to understand the full impact or cost savings of the proposal. This was critically important since one of the requests from senior leadership that started the first investigation, and was more central in the second, was around lowering operations costs.

A central part of this plan was the creation of a new platform team that would be responsible for producing tools and processes that would be consumed by application development teams across the entire company. This platform team would be responsible for implementing and enforcing many aspects of this proposal. Those efforts should not only reduce the load on application development teams but also drive down costs by providing an automated and consistent method to perform common operations.

The platform team wasn't the only big change. Application developers would be required to learn and incorporate new design principles into their workflows. They would also need to adjust to evaluating and requesting recommendations from the observability tooling as part of their day-to-day workflow. The working group expected that once these changes took hold, the application development teams would become more efficient, and it would also lead to fewer incidents.

In addition to the company reorganization, metrics, and cost reductions, the observability working group also made sure to highlight the potential benefits of business process observability. They didn't know exactly how it would improve the company's systems, but they were confident that gaining insight into all the actions for a business task would provide immense benefit. They were confident that senior leadership would like that part of the proposal, but they knew they needed to emphasize that it would be incredibly difficult to achieve without the standards and common practices that would be provided by the platform team.

The plan relied not just on the structural changes, but also on senior leadership commitment. It would be incredibly difficult to enact the necessary changes across the company without senior leadership pushing and supporting the efforts. This, along with the reorganization needed for the creation of the platform team, was the biggest concern the observability working group had as they prepared to present their plan to senior leadership.

## The presentation

The observability team identified early on the fact that the lowest common denominator for all the problems they wanted to solve was a lack of data normalization. They knew that a platform engineering team could help address that through culture change while the technical pieces were still developing. Therefore, they proposed a *crawl, walk, run*-style roadmap for what the platform team would deliver and achieve. They knew they needed to prove they could beat the statistics and continue to be among the one-third of companies that could point to successful AI implementations.

## Phase 1 – Crawl: Setting the standards

The first phase for the platform team's success would be to define the standards for data normalization across the company. This was a place where the observability team had expertise, and they recommended the **CDEvents** specification, which is already an emerging standard within Kubernetes (`https://cdevents.dev/`). The mission statement on the home page of the specification spoke exactly to the problems ACME Financial Services needed to solve, and on top of the specification and adoption by some of the tools already used within the company, CDEvents provides an SDK for several different programming languages to help teams implement the specification. This would make it easier for application teams to make the required changes to follow the new data standards. The team was able to tie this back to the scaling opportunities the SRE team had highlighted, and they also noted it could help reduce the time to produce RCA.

Here, the observability team was prioritizing the SRE team users, as that was the quickest implementation with more immediate and measurable returns on investment.

The application teams benefited as well. The SRE team would be able to do a better job supporting their applications, and they were already well-positioned for the platform adoption that came in Phase 2.

## Phase 2 – Walk: IDP with its first golden paths

Phase 2 was not wholly dependent on the completion of Phase 1. Both could be run in parallel. The second phase was where the real work would begin for the new platform team. They needed to meet with application teams and determine what the most common workflows were that the platform could consolidate. Once they had identified one or two use cases, this was where they would produce the **thinnest viable platform** (**TVP**). The TVP had two key focus areas:

- Helping application teams repeatably deploy their applications while meeting the standards for metrics, as well as other standardized steps for building and deploying the applications.
- Connecting to ACME Observability and surfacing actionable data to the development teams

You know the TVP works if you can use it to build and deploy changes to the IDP. It must lead the way, ensuring that the other teams have as smooth an experience as possible.

After the TVP, the team had identified the next most important problem to solve, which would make the second milestone. For an organization the size of ACME Financial Services, there must be self-service capabilities. Without them upfront, the platform cannot scale, and the project will fail. It was highly likely they would lean on a tool such as the Backstage developer portal to help them to quickly add this capability. Where tools cannot be standardized, the interface can, and this is one of the many key capabilities that a portal such as Backstage provides.

Phase 2 would be characterized by many feedback loops, where the platform team made changes, validated their success, and then either added new features or improved the existing ones until it was possible for all application teams to leverage the platform. These regular feedback loops were how the team could guarantee that the platform didn't just become a piece of expensive infrastructure.

The final capability the platform needed to have in this phase was cost management capabilities. Uncontrolled costs were the catalyst for a platform, and so they could not be left out. One of those capabilities was that it would manage the lifecycle of the observability data. While there was an observability vendor in play, the IDP should act as a record of truth for how the data in that vendor was managed through integration with the vendor. It needed to verify and enforce that every application it knew about had a data sampling strategy in use and data retention periods defined. For example, the policy might be that raw data is only retained for 180 days, and sampled data could be retained for 36 months, but only in cold storage, which is less expensive. By ensuring that policies and capabilities existed and also following the policies, the platform could become an effective cost management arm.

Unlike Phase 1, Phase 2 must have clear exit criteria:

- Platform adoption had hit critical mass: ~60% of teams were using the IDP, and the rest had a path forward to using it
- Self-service capabilities existed, allowing teams to accelerate their own adoption and add features
- The platform was tracking costs, exposing the cost data, and had cost management-related capabilities
- ACME Observability was integrated with AI agents in use
- The platform was acting as customer zero, ensuring that the golden paths remained accessible for the rest of the company.

## Phase 3 – Run: From AI and platform to agentic platform

The final phase was the one that created the competitive edge. It was where the work that had gone in up to then started to see the AI work as a force multiplier. That normalized data resulted in magical scaling that met customer demand without sacrificing cost-awareness. AI stopped being just a capability of the platform and started being central to its capabilities.

The IDP integrated with AI assistants and agents to make self-service easier, and helped with regulatory compliance, using AI for pull request reviews to catch potential issues or changes that may result in an unfavorable outcome. While the initial scope was to just fully utilize what they were paying for, by applying a product mindset, they knew that they could continue to expand as the platform continued to evolve beyond these initial phases. Here, they painted a hopeful, but less concrete, picture that demonstrated the many possibilities for the value of the platform to continue to be realized year over year as an agentic platform acting on behalf of the organization.

## The results of the presentation

The observability working group endured a difficult presentation with senior leadership. They were challenged on the need for such drastic changes and the company reorganization that would be required to support them. From senior leadership's initial position of reducing the cost of the tooling, the proposal seemed far more expansive than was necessary.

However, as the presentation and resulting conversations progressed, senior leadership started to see the need for the changes proposed. They especially liked the idea of metrics to be able to track the impact of the changes, as well as addressing observability with a wider lens. As the problems the working group uncovered became clearer to senior leadership, they slowly started to come around to the changes they were being asked to support.

Senior leadership especially liked the parts of the plan that would expand the utility of ACME Observability and the efforts to reduce cost. Their original ask was to investigate why the expected cost savings hadn't materialized, but they also slowly started to realize that the scope of the data they used to assess the effectiveness of the changes was too limited.

Unlike the first proposal from the observability working group, which was composed mostly of minor changes and new tooling and required little of senior leadership, this proposal would not reach its potential without significant support from senior leadership. Despite the initial reluctance and resistance, senior leadership eventually came to accept and support the plan presented by the observability working group. They accepted that there would not be a quick resolution and the company was in for another multi-year journey, but they came to believe that the end result would be a much stronger and more efficient company. They also believed the new metrics would provide them with a much better understanding of where problems and cost drivers existed within the company. Understanding what parts of the company are involved in what business actions would also allow them to make better decisions.

To monitor the progress and impact of the changes, senior leadership required a dashboard to be created with key performance indicators that they could follow. To start with, they wanted to see the number of deployments, the number of incidents, the percentage of deployments that resolved incidents, average incident MTTR, average RCA creation time, and the applications with the largest number of incidents.

## Time jump: What was achieved

ACME Financial Services put the observability working group's proposal into motion, but due to the changes in responsibilities and the creation of a new team or two, it took longer to implement than the first proposal. Once the new teams were formed and leadership and reporting structures put in place, it still took quite a while for the self-service systems to be built and be ready for application teams to begin using them. These efforts represented the foundation for the new process, and they did not happen quickly. This meant that senior leadership had to be patient but also persistent to move the effort forward. It was a sometimes delicate affair, but senior leadership's commitment to the plan proved critical to its success.

The patience was rewarded when application teams began to use the self-service tools. They were able to deploy new versions faster with less effort, the telemetry data was standardized and less expensive to process, and with the increased resources available to the application teams, they were able to implement new features and fix bugs faster. The new metrics showed an increase in the deployment velocity for every application team that used the self-service tools.

The application developers were initially a bit confused about how to implement the principles of observability-driven development, but after a few false starts, they really took them to heart and began to see benefits via a reduction in the number of incidents and better suggestions and help from the observability tooling. Having ACME Observability connected to the tools the application developers already used allowed them to realize significant benefits without having to drastically change their workflows. They even started using the observability tooling to help proactively improve their designs and avert incidents before they occurred.

The time it took to create RCAs dropped dramatically. An SRE no longer had to dig through mountains of logs and try to correlate application behavior to a deployment time. The SRE could ask the observability platform to find the suspected root cause of the outage. Because the observability platform was connected to the logs, metrics, deployment system, and source code, it was able to return information about when an application was deployed, how it caused the outage, and even point to the commit in the code repository that was deployed when the outage occurred. All the SRE had to do was validate the information with what was already known and ensure that the application developers agreed. It took some time, but both the SREs and the application developers gained trust in the suggestions provided by the observability tooling. The more they worked with the tools, the better and more relevant the suggestions became. More and more suggestions were implemented, although they were still scrutinized, which resulted in a reduction in workload for everyone.

The company achieved an understanding of the steps in their business processes that they had never had before, thanks to their implementation of business process observability. They found and corrected several inefficient and redundant steps, which increased the performance and reduced the complexity of a number of tasks. They found and fixed bottlenecks and were able to assess the severity and impacts of issues before customers noticed a problem. Fixing these problems not only made operations run smoother for customers but also fixed a number of long-standing, unexplained issues.

The number of incidents declined, and the ones that still occurred were addressed more efficiently. The SREs were able to focus on which incidents were most critical for maintaining business objectives or were customer-impacting. Because of the application improvements implemented by the development teams, more and more incidents became non-critical. This reduced the strain on the SRE teams and helped boost consumer confidence in ACME Financial Services, which, in turn, further helped improve the company's reputation.

Costs, which were the big driver for this effort, dropped. Not just the cost for running the tools, but also operations costs across the whole company. The new metrics provided insights into where bottlenecks occurred in the system, and they were addressed before they became issues. Clusters and applications were scaled to avoid incidents. They were even able to retire the old cluster scaling methods and rely solely on the suggestions from the observability tools. The reduced complexity also contributed to reduced operational costs. The new metrics also provided a much better picture of how the tools and processes impacted operational costs. They especially showed the impacts of the AI-related functionality from the ACME Observability tooling, which helped highlight the success of the efforts.

# Summary

In this chapter, we continued following ACME Financial Services' observability journey. They discovered that their first attempt at fixing their problems by observing their systems was really just the foundation for what needed to be achieved. The problems could not be solved with just tools and some minor tweaks; they required significant support and focus within the company in order to properly address them. They discovered they had been looking at observability through too limited a lens, which caused them to miss seeing areas where the new tools could help improve the company. They realized the current metrics used within the company were insufficient to assess the benefits of the changes they were making, but with new metrics and a broader view of observability, they were able to drive down operations costs and support that effort with data. The end result was a more cost-effective and efficient company with improved customer loyalty and reputation.

Is there more they can accomplish? Observability and AI continue to evolve at a fast pace, and ACME Financial Services has learned that tracking changes in the observability space and continually improving its practices can lead to significant impacts throughout the company. It took several years to complete this latest journey, so they will need to evaluate what has improved in the industry and what they can implement at ACME Financial Services.

In the next chapter, we will look more at how operations evolve and how event-driven architectures enable agentic AI to reach its full potential.

## Get this book's PDF version and more

Scan the QR code (or go to `packtpub.com/unlock`). Search for this book by name, confirm the edition, and then follow the steps on the page.

UNLOCK NOW

*Note: Keep your invoice handy. Purchases made directly from Packt don't require an invoice.*

# Part 3

# From AI Assistants to Self-Driving Architectures

*Part 3* looks ahead to the next evolution of operations, where systems move from being merely proactive to becoming preventive and, ultimately, self-driving. You will explore the critical challenges of AI adoption, including governance, cost optimization, and ethical safeguards, to ensure responsible and sustainable progress. The part concludes with ACME Financial Services' transformation journey, showcasing how AI-driven observability becomes the foundation for autonomous, resilient, and continuously improving architectures.

This part of the book includes the following chapters:

- *Chapter 8, Evolving Operations: Proactive > Preventive > Self-Driven Architecture*
- *Chapter 9, No Future Without Challenges*
- *Chapter 10, ACME Financial Services: How Will the AI Future Shape Our Company?*

# 8

# Evolving Operations: Proactive > Preventive > Self-Driven Architecture

In this chapter, we will learn how to build systems that leverage observability, AI, and automation to reduce, or ideally eliminate, the number of business-impacting incidents. Business-impacting incidents are situations that prevent an organization from operating cost-efficiently, providing a highly resilient system that is available when users need it, and ensuring that the system is secure and compliant with regulations.

We can leverage historical observability insights and use them to forecast future behavior to be best prepared for situations that are likely to happen, for example, predictive scaling of critical system components when end user load patterns change. We can use observability data of a newly deployed release or enabled feature and have AI decide whether that code change is safe to keep in production or whether it needs to be rolled back as it impacts performance, scalability, or security. We can also use observability data to enable AI to make autonomous decisions to redeploy workloads in different regions to save costs, optimize performance, or block or redirect traffic that seems malicious.

This chapter will help you leap from using AI from the outside and instead move towards putting AI at the center of your architecture. What would a system look like where AI makes automated decisions on scaling or evolving a system? How would a self-driving IT architecture benefit an organization?

In this chapter, we will cover the following topics:

- Enabling AI-driven decision-making through event-driven architectures

- Use case: AI-driven scaling for performance and cost
- Use case: AI and GitOps for rollouts and rollbacks
- Enemy at the gates, let your AI be your defender

# Technical requirements

This chapter discusses Argo CD, Jenkins, GitHub Actions, Kubernetes operations, and HolmesGPT. There is no requirement to download or use any of these technologies in order to understand the use cases and examples.

HolmesGPT is used with OpenAI following the instructions found on their website: `https://holmesgpt.dev/latest/`

The Kubernetes operator for Pod watching can be found here: `https://github.com/AlexVulaj/pod-watcher`

# Defining our terms

Generally, the terms in this chapter should be fairly standard and well understood, so we won't dive deeply into them, but we will add a quick review to ensure that there's a shared context for readers as we progress through the chapter.

## Differentiating proactive versus preventative versus self-driven

In software operations, a *proactive* operation is one that is done in response to a signal, but typically, the signal indicates there may be a problem, rather than that there is currently a problem, which would be reactive.

An example of a proactive action would be to take action against a system in response to a metric. For example, memory consumption has reached 90% of the available RAM, so a proactive action would be to increase the memory allocation so that there is not a memory-related crash.

A *preventative* action would be to find the cause of the memory increase, especially if it was sudden, and if necessary, write a fix that will allow memory usage to be lower or more consistent, thereby preventing the need to scale.

A self-driven architecture takes those same actions but fully automates them. In a self-driven architecture, the metric is emitted, the scaling action happens, and then an automated RCA is conducted, and a pull request is opened by an AI agent for a human to review and approve.

Could that ultimately be 100% AI end to end? Absolutely, but remember these technologies are not without fault, and it's best for human supervision to be utilized for write actions. That said, with human review at appropriate stages throughout the process, AI can make decisions that help keep operations running smoothly, allowing more time for humans to innovate.

# Enabling AI-driven decision-making through event-driven architectures

Event-driven architectures are characterized by several services or microservices that either emit or receive events. The receiving service then performs a pre-defined action based on the characteristics of the event it received. Essentially, this is metrics triggering automation: very quick, very reliable, but also limited to what has been programmatically defined.

As we discussed in *Chapter 2*, the power of an LLM-based AI agent or assistant is that it's not limited in the same way. However, it does still have limitations. Like humans, AI can only make informed decisions when it has enough data points to tell it what the status is, what has happened that led to this status, and what the options are to change this status when it is undesired.

## Feeding events into our observability platform

When we work to identify what events are worth collecting, the options can be overwhelming. Fortunately, industry standards around key metrics have emerged as an excellent starting point for developing your observability strategy.

If starting from zero, we recommend thinking about **DORA metrics** and **Software Development Life Cycle** (**SDLC**) events.

Whether it is Git, a CI/CD platform, testing tools, deployment and release tools, or configuration change or feature flag management tools. They all typically provide a way to send webhooks to external tools for integration purposes.

Let's take Argo CD as an example. Argo CD provides a notification feature where details about every sync stage – `PreSync`, `SyncStart`, `SyncFinished`, and `SyncFailed` – can be sent via a webhook. Sending this to your observability platform is therefore a simple configuration task, but one that provides detailed information about which Git commit was successfully synced by Argo CD to the target environment. This functionality is not unique to Argo CD and, therefore, the Kubernetes ecosystem; the same capabilities can be leveraged via most CI/CD platforms or configuration change management systems.

Jenkins, for example, supports plugins, much like Argo CD. One of those plugins is an OpenTelemetry connector, which can connect to multiple observability backends. While you may see Jenkins in Kubernetes (there's a flavor of it called Kubernetes Jenkins), Jenkins is often used for building and deploying applications in virtual-machine-based environments.

GitHub Actions, which are architecture agnostic, can similarly leverage webhooks via the open source project **Workflow Webhook** (`https://github.com/distributhor/workflow-webhook`).

Feature flag management tools follow the same general capability patterns, with feature flagging SDKs such as OpenFeature also emitting OpenTelemetry spans, logs, and metrics in the application that implements the feature behind a flag. This allows an operator (human or AI) to identify which feature flags were enabled on a request-by-request basis, as this information shows up on the distributed trace spans as span attributes. This level of detail allows us to come to a conclusion on who is impacted by a bad feature, as explained in the previous section.

Thanks to open standard initiatives, we see more tool vendors not only supporting generic webhook interfaces but also webhooks that provide data adhering to semantic conventions as defined by OpenTelemetry, CDEvents, or SDLC events.

## Scenario: tying events and AI operations together

In *Chapter 3*, in the *Context is king: the quality of observability data* section, we learned about how important it is to have context-enriched observability data. The more information about your data centers, hosts, clusters, processes, workloads, and services we have, the easier it is to derive the *status quo*.

In the sub-section called *Enriching observability data across the software development lifecycle*, we talked about how to have all tools that take part in the software development process (version control, building, testing, CI/CD, infrastructure automation, release management, and so on) send events to the observability platform through standardized SDLC events. This provides additional context for a human operator, but also for an AI agent to learn about things such as the following:

- **3:54 pm:** Pull request PR-242 triggered a CI/CD for `authentication-svc`
- **3:59 pm:** The CI/CD pipeline built the image `authentication-svc:44353`
- **4:08 pm:** The security scanning tool detected a vulnerability for that image
- **10:00 pm:** Automated performance tests scheduled for next cycle
- **10:14 pm**: While performance tests had not yet completed, and despite the detected vulnerability, the image was promoted to production by the responsible team that night with the comment *We promised customer Global Banking One to deliver a new*

*Authentication Integration feature implemented with PR-242 by end of today. The team is confident that the changes will be safe to deploy despite not all test results being available yet!*

- **11:41 pm:** Feature Flag *Authentication Integration for Identity Provider ABC* gets enabled for Global Banking One
- **11:56 pm:** Pull request PR-242 was closed with the comment: *Delivered feature to Global Banking One successfully and on time.*

If everything goes well, then having those events is great to report on activity; these data points could be used to show success or track progress against **Key Performance Indicator** (**KPI**) goals. Conversely, when things break, those events speed up finding the root cause significantly!

Let's continue with this scenario: Our new feature was launched, and within a day's time, Global Banking One started to use it. The next day, after a quiet night and a change of shift in the **Site Reliability Engineering** (**SRE**) team, the morning starts like this:

- **2:15 am**: The response time metrics on a core service are showing intermittent spikes on the authentication service, but no major impact was occurring, and the service was still within the error budget.
- **6:10 am**: There was an increase in response times across multiple core services.
- **6:25 am**: Worker thread pool queues on older application servers were becoming backlogged.
- **6:29 am**: Frontend proxy servers reported HTTP 500s.
- **6:46 am**: New SEV-2 support ticket opened by Global Banking One. Several users reported that logging in to the core financial services platform was failing with a timeout in the browser.
- **6:51 am**: The security team was reporting malicious requests to the authentication service; early analysis supported evidence of a DDoS attack.
- **6:52 am**: 10 new SEV-2 support tickets from other customers were opened, reporting performance problems.
- **6:59 am**: Global Banking One upgraded the ticket to a SEV-1.

In situations like this, every minute counts, and it's important to jump on the right things and not waste time on things that are irrelevant. As explained in *Chapter 3*, in the *AIOps: reducing the noise with anomaly and root cause detection* section, having all those change and anomaly events woven into the observability data (logs, metrics, traces, and so on) makes it easier for a human, or AI, to quickly understand the chain of events that happened that resulted in a problem.

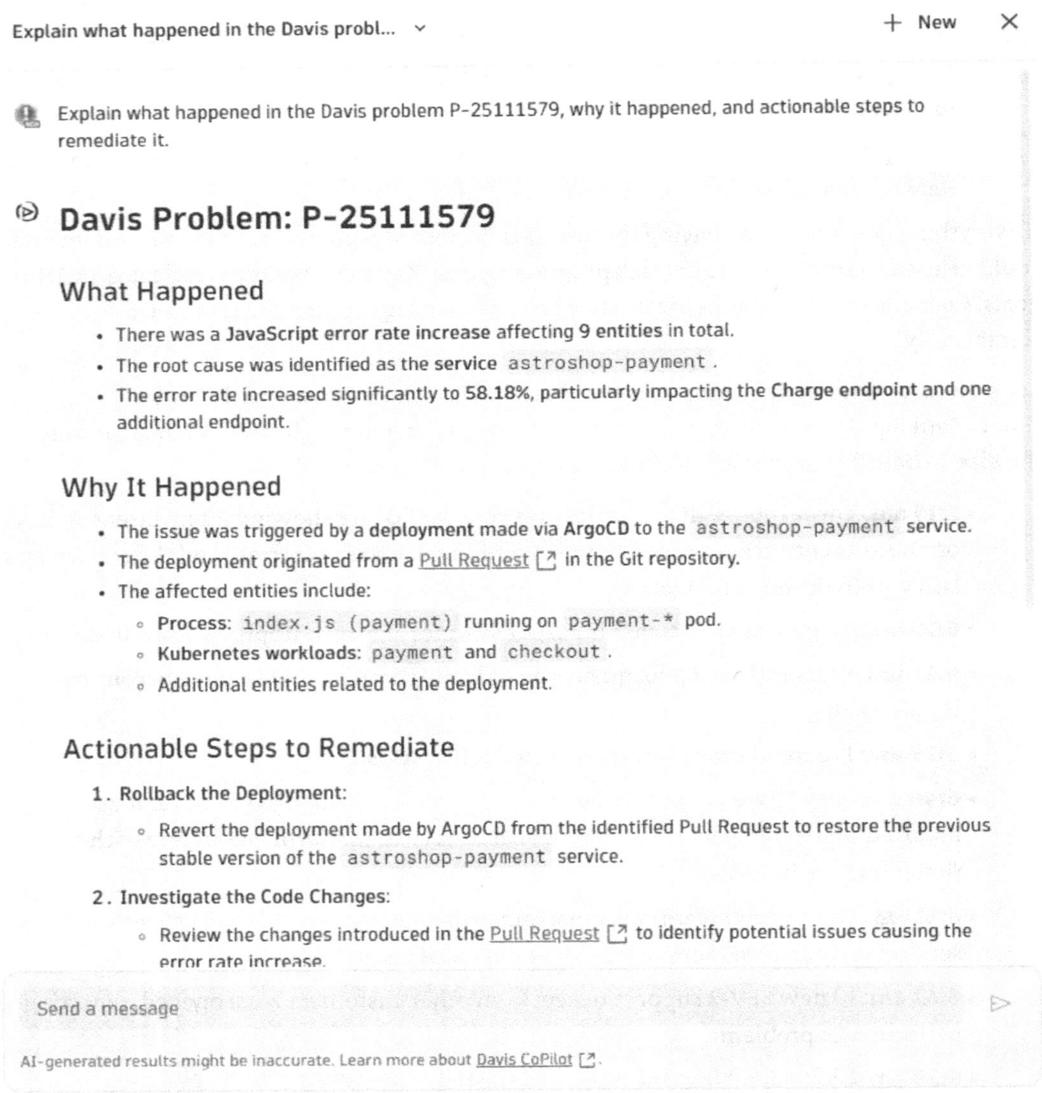


*Figure 8.1: Analyzing all events in context helps reduce the noise of many individual events into a single actionable incident*

## How AI can help us analyze the situation

When an anomaly happens, such as an increase in failure rate or response time, a human operator would look at all the available data to determine whether this anomaly is caused by any known event. In complex systems, this may take a significant amount of time to connect all the dots and draw all the right conclusions. In a distributed system, the data may also be distributed across multiple locations as well as data types (logs, metrics, and traces).

When feeding all this data to AI, it can collect and analyze that same data in seconds and tell us the following:

a. Intermittent response time issues are only happening for requests that execute the code paths of the feature flag that was enabled recently
b. Based on the pull request and feature flag change details, this only impacts a single customer
c. This customer typically starts becoming active shortly after 6 a.m. on a workday
d. When forecasting that all expected login requests from that customer will get slower, the noisy neighbor effect means it will impact the overall performance and stability of the authentication service

Seeing all this evidence, the logical next steps would be the following:

a. Turn off the feature flag to reduce the risk of potential bigger impact.
b. Open a new pull request for the engineering team referencing PR-242 and providing logs, metrics, and traces that show the production impact.
c. Run a code analysis and provide a potential fix based on the runtime behavior.
d. Notify the development team that merged PR-242 about the situation.

Taking those actions puts the teams in a much better position than waiting until the problem spreads! But how exactly do we get AI engaged?

## How to let the AI also take automated actions

Sending all this data to the observability platform is the basis for better root cause analysis. But it also provides the basis for taking automated actions.

When a feature flag is turned on and causes issues, we can leverage the feature flagging management tool's API to turn off that feature flag automatically. If the deployment of a new release has a negative impact, we can roll back to the previous version.

For possible scenarios where an incident could occur, we can define remediation actions that should be executed. These could be in the form of another automation pipeline or a script that mitigates any issues caused by a change that had negative impacts.

These predefined actions and automation flows allow human operators to act with confidence, and also allow an AI agent to automatically trigger those actions, such as turning off a feature flag, rolling back a version, or executing a remediation script!

While you can leverage AI agentically via a service, you can also run it in your local environment via a CLI-based GPT connecting to a model either locally or in the cloud.

# Use case: AI and GitOps

GitOps isn't just continuous deployment. It's the process of continuous reconciliation of desired and actual state. Once we understand that, the additional possibilities are nearly endless.

Imagine you are deploying a mission-critical application in a Kubernetes environment. If you have a **Service-Level Objective** (**SLO**) of 99.99%, you need to have automated failure detection and self-healing.

This is another place where AI and GitOps can be very powerful. So, imagine having your AI agent running alongside your GitOps systems with all the proper RBAC to investigate and resolve complications as they arise.

## Integrating agentic AI for Kubernetes

To demonstrate an agentic AI implementation, we'll discuss HolmesGPT. HolmesGPT is an open source AI SRE agent (`https://github.com/HolmesGPT/holmesgptP`) that is also a **Cloud Native Computing Foundation** (**CNCF**) sandbox project. For local use, the HolmesGPT CLI can be installed via Homebrew and configured to work with one or multiple providers, such as OpenAI or Ollama. For an integration and fully agentic system, you can install it via a Helm chart. Either way, when you install HolmesGPT, you also get the ability to invoke HolmesGPT via an HTTP API.

As magical as AI feels, it's not entirely magic, so here we'll see how AI integrates with simple automation to do more.

Let's say we have an Argo CD event we want to send a notification for, such as a rollout failing. We can have HolmesGPT automatically investigate this for us if it's triggered via an API call initiated by Argo CD Notifications:

```
apiVersion: v1
 kind: ConfigMap
 metadata:
   name: argocd-notifications-cm
   namespace: argocd
 data:
```

```
    trigger.on-rollout-degraded: |
      - description: Application rollout has degraded
        send:
          - app-rollout-failed
        when: app.status.operationState.phase in ['Error', 'Failed'] or
app.status.health.status == 'Degraded'
        oncePer: app.status.operationState.syncResult.revision
    trigger.on-sync-failed: |
      - description: Application sync has failed
        send:
          - app-rollout-failed
        when: app.status.operationState.phase in ['Error', 'Failed']
        oncePer: app.status.operationState.syncResult.revision
      webhook:
        app-rollout-failed:
          method: POST
          path: "http://<HOLMES-URL>/api/investigate"
          headers:
            Content-Type: application/json
          body: |
            {
              "event": "rollout_failed",
              "application": "{{.app.name}}",
              "project": "{{.app.spec.project}}",
              "cluster": "{{.app.spec.destination.server}}",
              "namespace": "{{.app.spec.destination.namespace}}",
              "phase": "{{.app.status.operationState.phase}}",
              "health": "{{.app.status.health.status}}",
              "message": "{{.app.status.operationState.message}}",
              "revision": "{{.app.status.operationState.syncResult.revision}}",
              "timestamp": "{{.app.status.operationState.finishedAt}}",
              "url": "{{.context.argocdUrl}}/applications/{{.app.name}}"
            }
```

Once HolmesGPT receives this event, it can conduct an investigation and return the results of its investigation. However, we don't need to leave it guessing. We can supply HolmesGPT with runbooks, just like we might a human, to guide its investigations. There's no need to let it guess or invent. HolmesGPT expects a YAML file for runbooks. Here is an example of what a runbook might look like for our rollout failure scenario. It can be made more specific to your environment and applications:

```
runbooks:
  - match:
      issue_name: "(rollout-degraded)|(rollout_failed)"
    instructions: >
      Analyze the ArgoCD rollout failure using the details supplied in the webhook
payload.
     You can use the argo cli to investigate the application and resources.
     Also check the cluster health and events including Pod logs for any possible
causes.
     Ensure the application's dependencies are healthy and there are no resource
constraints or misconfigurations. If there are, raise a pull request to fix them.
```

Following the official documentation, you can configure Prometheus alerts and other data sources to trigger an automated investigation via Holmes, but it's best to follow the official documentation for the most up-to-date guidance for these configurations (`https://holmesgpt.dev/reference/http-api`).

As a default, HolmesGPT is read-only, but this functionality can be expanded via its MCP servers (`https://github.com/robusta-dev/holmes-mcp-integrations`) or through the addition of your own custom server. While the best practice is to leverage source control for all changes, if desired, you can leverage the MCP server for Kubernetes remediation (`https://github.com/robusta-dev/holmes-mcp-integrations/tree/master/servers/kubernetes-remediation`) and let HolmesGPT fix the problems on the cluster. With this MCP server, HolmesGPT will perform write actions while adhering to the safety guardrails configured by the administrator who sets it up. In addition to the user-configured safety, HolmesGPT has implemented a series of security measures to ensure safe operations in a product environment (`https://github.com/robusta-dev/holmes-mcp-integrations/tree/master/servers/kubernetes-remediation#security`). We'll cover more on securely operating AI in *Chapter 9*.

The GitHub MCP server will allow HolmesGPT to create pull requests to remediate the identified causes for a rollout failure. You could even have GitHub Copilot review and approve the pull requests from HolmesGPT for a totally AI-driven resolution. Once the pull request is merged, Argo CD will automatically pick up and try the rollout again with the new manifest.

Integration with GitOps and troubleshooting a rollout failure is just one of many possible use cases for full agentic operations. When identifying where to start in your own services, you may decide to instead use the approach of troubleshooting specific alerts. Regardless of where you start, we recommend implementing the read and investigate actions first, and after you have confidence in your configurations and runbooks, expanding to the automated remediations as well.

Our next use case is closely related to GitOps and uses somewhat similar workflows, so let's have a look.

# Use case: AI-driven scaling for performance and cost

After reaching out to experts across the industry, one common thread we found was that AI is being leveraged significantly for scaling use cases.

## Types of scaling

There are two types of scaling in computing: vertical and horizontal. Vertical scaling is the process of scaling up in place. In other words, expanding or reducing the size of a disk, adding CPU or memory to a virtual machine, and so on. Horizontal scaling is the process of adding or removing an additional copy of the resource you're measuring. That could be another set of Pods, another Kubernetes node, another virtual machine, or another load balancer, as examples. However you choose to scale, your scaling strategy needs to be intentional and tied to the business needs.

## Scaling for performance

Scaling for performance means keeping the system resources balanced so that applications are as performant as possible. Imagine a basic queue. You can set a threshold that, if exceeded, then another thread pool is created to work through the queue items. In most cases, for scaling, simple automation does the trick; however, that automation is typically reactive. With AI available to parse large amounts of data and identify possible patterns, you can go from reactive to proactive. For example, financial institutions may notice a sharp uptick in traffic as the stock markets open on Monday mornings. Agentic systems can proactively scale environments up a little ahead of this spike, so that price information, trade information, or any other type of system interaction is always as fast as possible. If traffic patterns change, the agentic system will detect these new patterns and adjust accordingly, as opposed to a human operator regularly tracking these patterns and updating automated thresholds.

## Scaling for cost

Scaling for cost can mean scaling back down to save on cloud bills. For example, if we expand on our previous example of scaling up when the stock market trading is going to start, we can also do the reverse. Scaling back down during traffic lulls can keep costs down, and AI can do this faster and more regularly than a human can. However, we can also rebalance our workloads to run on hardware that is cheaper. By augmenting our AI capabilities with an understanding of cloud options, cloud spend, and desired outcomes, we can have it regularly review and make suggestions about the environment for how to reduce costs or proactively take actions such as spinning up cheaper Kubernetes Node types and migrating workloads as desired.

This can be as simple as using Kubernetes Jobs, or another scheduling system (Jenkins, Tekton, Argo Workflows, Apache Airflow, cron jobs, or something else) to regularly invoke the AI system to do a review and either take action or make a recommendation.

However you choose to accomplish this, the type of data review and decisions required to maintain system scale are the exact types of tasks AI excels at.

## Scaling for carbon footprint

Related to scaling for cost, but also somewhat separate, is the idea of scaling to help reduce the carbon footprint of applications. With many localities working towards improving their carbon footprint (see *The Paris Agreement*), open source projects have started to come forward to help specifically observe the carbon footprint of systems. The first example of this is Kepler (`https://www.cncf.io/projects/kepler/`), which provides eBPF-based energy insights. According to the official documentation:

*Kepler (Kubernetes-based Efficient Power Level Exporter) is a Prometheus exporter that measures energy consumption at the container, Pod, VM, and process level by reading hardware sensors and attributing power based on resource utilization.*

*Kepler uses Intel RAPL (Running Average Power Limit) sensors to collect energy data from CPU packages, cores, and memory subsystems, then distributes this energy proportionally to workloads based on their CPU time consumption.*

But getting data is only part of managing your CO2 emissions. There needs to be a corresponding action. Here, the `kube-green` operator helps you reduce CO2 emissions by putting Pods to sleep that are not needed: `https://kube-green.dev/`.

Both of these projects are a step in the right direction. While agentic AI isn't necessarily immediately considered environmentally friendly, responsible AI use can be part of how your organization manages its carbon footprint.

Since AI can parse large amounts of data quickly, it can also help with data management. Large amounts of data sitting in storage can be expensive to store and computationally expensive to parse. But if you can audit your data store with AI, it can help you to clean up unnecessary data and assist with data sampling to ensure you're storing and reading only what you need, and not what you don't.

This also helps reduce your surface area for risk related to data breaches if you've normalized and reduced your overall data overhead. Again, you can write and deploy automation to do all of this as well; however, this requires custom programming of all the possible actions and regularly re-deploying as you add more, whereas agentic AI can follow instructions, safety guardrails, and dynamically adjust to system needs, closing the loop on time to successfully benefit from possible efficiency gains.

## How to approach auto scaling

In order to get started with scaling, we need to know, or be able to calculate, two things: where we are starting and where we are going. That means, first and foremost, we need to have benchmarks for our system. When we know what the minimum load looks like and what the maximum load looks like, we know the range through which we need to scale. This helps us predict our costs as well. Next, or additionally, since this can be done at the same time, we need to have a history of load. Very few systems experience consistent traffic 24/7; they're usually more active during certain hours than others. That history and the threshold information can be used to train an AI agent so that it can help determine patterns and optimal times for scaling.

With the model trained, it needs to have some way of interfacing with the scaling orchestration mechanism. This is where an MCP server would be used to help the AI agent interface with the scaling system and utilize it. Lastly, apply guardrails. Don't allow the agent to scale a system endlessly, since there could be a problem that needs attention if scaling up and up is continuously required.

Some vendors of cloud solutions are already offering this capability as part of their existing solutions, so it's important to have a build versus buy conversation and determine whether this is a capability you need to build bespoke or leverage from an existing vendor or tool within your ecosystem.

Now it's time to look at the final use case for this chapter: agentic AI as a security helper.

# Enemy at the gates: let your AI be your defender

In *Chapter 5*, we talked about data cardinality being a key aspect of AI inference success. This is critical again for using AI to assist with detecting possible security incidents. A big clue to an AI agent that something is amiss is if there's suddenly data that doesn't match the patterns and standards of the data typically seen across the system.

## Using AI to parse audit logs and system access

For example, in Kubernetes audit logs, the IP address of the user agent and source IP address that reached out to the API server are recorded, in addition to the user or entity that made the request.

Imagine a credential is leaked via phishing, but our security team doesn't know that yet. However, our AI watcher has identified that the source IP of an API call is significantly different this time than previous times for the same user. It can flag this activity and open a security incident through the appropriate ticketing system or workflow. If it's an agentic implementation, it may also have the capabilities to reduce or remove the permissions of that user account until after the activity has been confirmed.

In another case, let's imagine a trade embargo. This is where trade is restricted between countries; financial transactions, as well as software and digital media, are included in these restrictions. Enforcing these embargos is critical for any system with an international presence. Agentic AI can watch various configurations simultaneously, including firewalls, to ensure the configurations are enforcing the latest trade rules.

But this won't necessarily work if the person trying to get around the embargo is using a VPN. Agentic AI can help again here, by checking the source IPs against known VPN provider IP pools, and flagging or blocking the traffic.

But what happens if you do have a breach? What is your risk vector? How much liability might you have?

# AI for reducing risk surface area

In order to reduce your surface area for risk, you first must identify what that risk surface area is. The best way to do this is to conduct a threat model. For the best guidance on how to conduct a good threat model, we recommend OWASP as the authoritative resource (`https://owasp.org/www-community/Threat_Modeling`).

## Risk surface 1: data

In most software systems, the data collected and stored is the most valuable asset. But that data can also contain data that is regulated. **PII** or **Personally Identifiable Data** is regulated heavily in many countries and localities, and so must be handled with great care. While it's possible for a vendor system where you might store or use your data to come with all the security and compliance requirements for you to ship your data raw, it's a much better practice to sanitize your data of PII. For this, we would not recommend a cloud-based AI vendor. Run a local model that is self-contained to help you identify and strip any potential PII from logs.

For this example, we used HolmesGPT on our laptop. We provided system logs along with the prompt *Analyze these logs and remove PII and surface only logs that look like they could be related to system crashes or performance issues.* The model returned two log results that contained possible matches for the criteria, and all PII was removed.

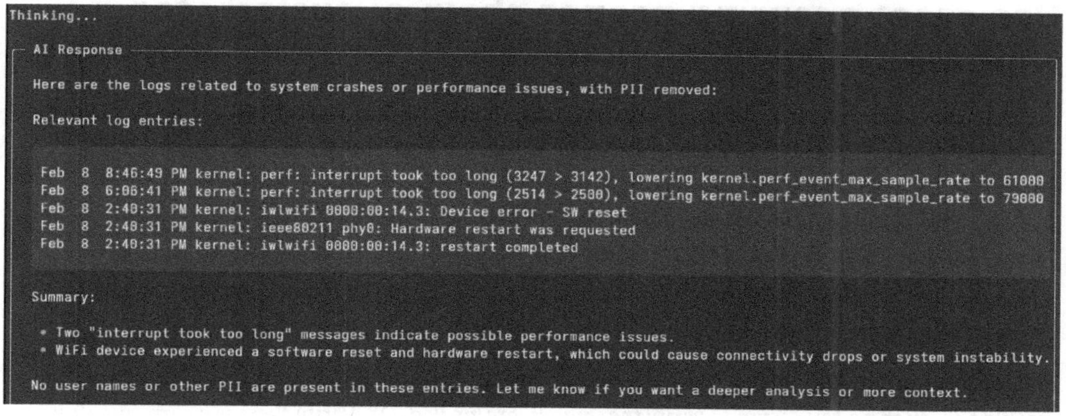


*Figure 8.2: HolmesGPT sanitized log results*

These results are only a very small percentage of the log lines provided, and if stored, would take up very little space and be easily indexed and accessed, while also not creating exposure for any unnecessary risks around PII in the data contents.

While it is a best practice that application logs are sanitized and only as noisy as needed, and there are also times to keep PII around, using AI as a failsafe to ensure an organization only has what it needs to have on hand is a smart use of a powerful tool that could potentially save you from a lot of liability.

### Risk surface 2: users and permissions

In an IDP where there are many users onboarding with various needs and access levels, it's important to do a regular review of who has access and what they have access to. However, depending on the size of the organization, this could be a very difficult task. Fortunately, parsing through lots of information quickly is exactly what your AI tools are purpose-built to accomplish. Having an AI assistant or agent review users and their access, under the supervision of a human operator, can quickly help to identify whether there are users, human or otherwise, with access levels that don't match best practices, may be too permissive, or who need to be offboarded entirely.

With these things in mind, and understanding how we can integrate agentic AI into our systems, let's look at a more complete use case for AI-assisted security.

## Use case: ensuring proper chain of custody for workloads

In some systems, such as Kubernetes systems, there may be namespaces where only the most privileged users can schedule new workloads. While we don't necessarily want to block deployments in these locations entirely, we may want to validate all the workloads that do appear. Here, a Kubernetes operator watching the namespace can be leveraged (as seen in the example listed in the *Technical requirements* section of this chapter). If a new workload is scheduled in the namespace, it can emit a metric that is keyed to an alert or directly use a webhook to trigger an automated investigation to an AI agent such as HolmesGPT.

The instruction for HolmesGPT would include investigation steps into the validity of the workloads, such as *Use cosign to verify the images for this Pod*. Or, *Verify there is a corresponding definition for this workload in the source repository for this namespace.*

> Tip
>
> **Tip**
>
> Cosign is a signing tool that is part of the Open Security Foundation's Sigstore project for software supply chain security. It can be used to sign packages and verify signatures.

If all checks are green, HolmesGPT can close the investigation with or without generating a report (that will be up to the implementing team). For this example, we created a Pod in a kind cluster following the HolmesGPT documentation example (`https://holmesgpt.dev/`

latest/installation/cli-installation/#quick-start). But instead of asking HolmesGPT to investigate why the Pod couldn't schedule, we prompted the following:

```
investigate "How did the user-profile-import Pod get added to the cluster"
```

Without artifacts such as audit logs to investigate, HolmesGPT still ran an investigation and came to the following conclusion:

```
Root cause: Pod was manually created in the default namespace using kubectl or a
similar tool.
```

You can see more of the process HolmesGPT went through in the following screenshot:

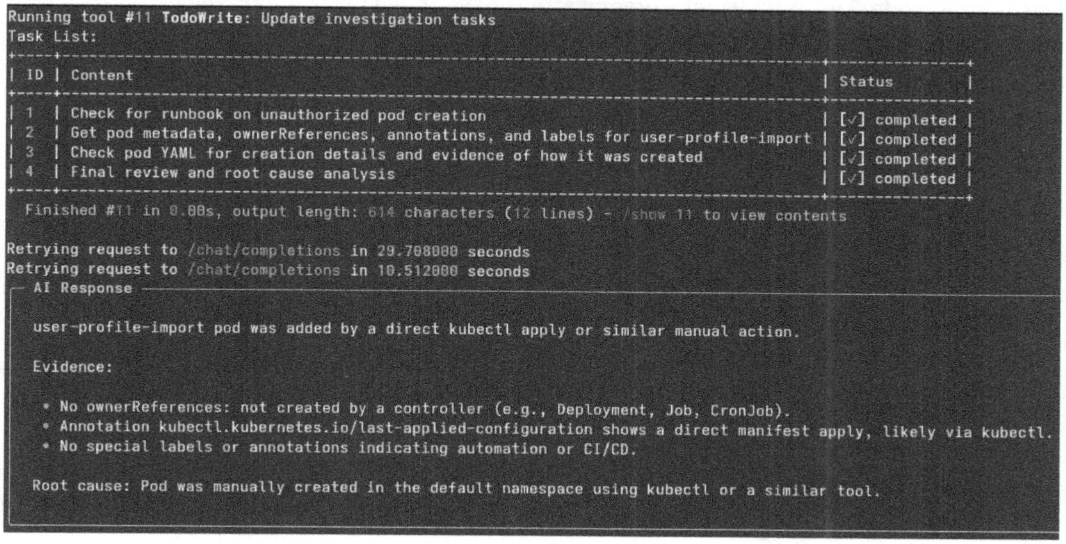


*Figure 8.3: HolmesGPT investigating a new Pod*

Here, the chain of custody could not be established. What happens next is a process question. In most scenarios, a security incident would be triggered, and a human would be notified to act. If you choose to have HolmesGPT or another AI agent set up to complete write actions without supervision, it could also proactively delete the workloads. However the final configuration lands, it should be in the instruction files the AI tool leverages, and documented and understood by all human operators as well.

## Chain of custody explained

The chain of custody is the record of the hands through which a product passes before it reaches its final destination. In software, this is also called the software supply chain. This includes every line of code from every source that contributes to the final product, such as the language the code is written in and imported libraries. This representation is typically done as a **Software Bill of Materials** (**SBOM**), covered in *Chapter 9*. An SBOM shows you what imports you have, but doesn't validate the veracity of the images. This is what Cosign or other tools accomplish.

### Commit signing and signature verification

When writing secure software, it's important to verify the identities of the people who are pushing the code. This is why many organizations have added pre-commit webhooks to repositories to require that all commits are signed with the unique signature of the committer. This uses **GNU Privacy Guard** (**GPG**) cryptographic keys, where the private key is how the commit is signed, and the public key allows others to verify that signature.

The public key needs to be in the keyring of the local filesystem where the signature is being verified. GitHub helps do all of this for you, but it can be set up for private Git instances as well.

Reputable providers of open source packages will sign those packages. The Cosign project from Sigstore (`https://www.sigstore.dev/`) is a free and open source software package designed precisely to combat supply chain attacks and risks. The three main attack vectors image signing and verification can protect against are as follows:

- **Typosquatting**: Malicious packages with deliberately similar names to common packages
- **Compromised hosts**: Where the package is made publicly available, the host machine itself could be compromised and serve up incorrect images in an attempt to get malicious packages onto new machines
- **Artifact tampering**: Where the valid artifact is altered and then re-published to trick users into compromised software

Reputable vendors of images will sign these images. Those signatures will include attestations on the build process, contents, and security. A best security practice is to include a signing step in your CI/CD pipelines for any images and artifacts built within your organization, as well as to validate that the images being used in your environment are legitimate. You can use Cosign both to sign and validate signatures.

## Validating package contents

If you need to validate a package's integrity, you can look at the hash of the package, generated with **Secure Hash Algorithm** (**SHA**) libraries and typically with the SHA-256 algorithm. The generated hash, which is immutable, becomes a reference to a point in time of the software. If the software in the package changes, the hash changes. For example, if I download the *latest* Python today and compare it to the *latest* from last year, they have different hashes. They are often just referred to as *SHAs*, as a reference to the hashing algorithm.

To validate software packages, run a checksum comparison. Checksum is a tool that allows you to get the SHA-256 output for a local package. By running `checksum` or `shasum` against the local copy of the package and comparing it to the published version, you can validate that the package is as expected. This is easier for some files than others, and if you have modified the package in any way, it will fail. An example of an expected failure would be that Python publishes an expected SHA-256 for each version release, but the Linux distribution Fedora will re-package the upstream version, causing your `shasum` or `checksum` to fail, so take care to validate against the proper source of truth.

In the case of containerized environments such as Podman, Docker, or Kubernetes, you can often reference specific image digests via the SHA to ensure you always get the exact same software every time.

Here's an example from the Red Hat image catalogue:

```
$ podman pull registry.access.redhat.com/ubi10/python-312-
minimal@sha256:394fffb2dfbe6d5ec49034a1c9a35940a6e954348ad2b8432973964b6d18c528
Trying to pull registry.access.redhat.com/ubi10/python-312-
minimal@sha256:394fffb2dfbe6d5ec49034a1c9a35940a6e954348ad2b8432973964b6d18c528...
Getting image source signatures
Checking if image destination supports signatures
Copying blob 4d6764fc7b75 done   |
Copying blob 819501e18c85 done   |
Copying config 329c4d228c done   |
Writing manifest to image destination
Storing signatures
329c4d228c05eccd12391c829c1d72030092923e4fb2bc5d721aeea3b5774784
```

This method of installing an image for a container means that for all time, as long as the image is available, it will be exactly the same as before. If anything were to change, the hash would not be identical, which means you're not susceptible to man-in-the-middle attacks or compromised image hosts. This is a great way to ensure you always get exactly what you expect for software packages.

Many open source projects and vendors of software, especially in the cloud-native space, will have some attestation about their software and its validity. For example, Argo CD provides instructions at `https://argo-cd.readthedocs.io/en/stable/operator-manual/signed-release-assets/` on how to validate its Cosign signatures.

The creation of your own signature and the validation of others should be done during your build and test processes, and should be considered part of your standard practice for a code repository.

This brings us to our final use case: repository maintenance.

# Use case: repository maintenance – let AI take on the boring tasks

In every software engineering project, there are chores that need to be done regularly. One of the most common is dependency management; tools such as Dependabot are often leveraged for simple automation to bump up versions of dependencies imported into a project. However, in situations where the dependency-related code has been copied directly into the repository, that won't work. Instead, the local copy of the code needs to be replaced. This concept exists in many languages, but we'll focus on the Golang implementation of vendoring for this example. Vendoring is different from a typical import of an external dependency as, instead of the dependencies being brought in during compilation or at runtime, the vendored code lives as a copy in the project repository. Vendoring can be seen in many open source projects, specifically in the Kubernetes space. However, despite the benefits of having a local version of the dependency pinned exactly where you might want it, it's not ideal from a security standpoint. You still need to update packages for CVEs and to get the latest features and functionality.

When to do this depends entirely on when the vendored project releases a new version, but the *how* is very straightforward. However, it is tedious. This is where we can let our AI agents and assistants do the work for us.

If you had an internal project vendored and a new release of that project became available, you would want to test that release as soon as possible. However, this typically requires checking out the code, manually updating the `go.mod` file to the newest release, running the `go mod vendor` command, and then doing any other chores before running tests. If the tests pass, then you would want to open a pull request and likely begin a new release of your code base as well.

This can be solved with automation, but it can be unwieldy to build and maintain. Alternatively, you can use instruction files, as we discussed in *Chapter 5*, and GitHub Actions to accomplish it with an AI agent.

For this example, we used GitHub Actions in local mode so as to leverage Ollama and a model hosted on local machines, as opposed to a hosted model. In an ideal world, a vendored project could trigger your downstream project via a GitHub action, but you can also run GitHub actions on a job to check for new releases at a regular cadence, such as weekly, and then perform the actions only if there's a new release. The basic architecture of this GitHub workflow is that you have an action that acts as the dispatcher in the first repository, which calls the chores action in the second. The chores action makes a call to the AI agent/assistant, letting it know it's time to perform the chores.

Here's an example of a push GitHub action workflow setup that would trigger our `agent-ollama` action via the GitHub dispatches API in order to perform some Git repository chores.

```
- name: Dispatch agent-ollama
 run: |
   curl -sS -X POST \
     -H "Authorization: token ${{ secrets.AGENT_DISPATCH_TOKEN }}" \
     -H "Accept: application/vnd.github+json" \
     https://api.github.com/repos/hlipsig/agent-ollama/dispatches \
-d '{"event_type":"run-ollama-agent","client_payload":{"source_repo":"$
{{ github.repository }}","ref":"${{ github.ref }}","commit":"${{ github.sha }}"}}'
```

Here is the action that would prompt the LLM:

```
name: Ollama Agent Runner

on:
 workflow_dispatch:
 repository_dispatch:

jobs:
 agent:
   runs-on: ubuntu-latest
   steps:
     - name: Checkout
       uses: actions/checkout@v4

     - name: Load agent config
       id: load_config
       run: |
         echo "config<<EOF" >> $GITHUB_OUTPUT
        cat agent-config.json >> $GITHUB_OUTPUT
```

```
          echo "EOF" >> $GITHUB_OUTPUT

      - name: Run Ollama agent
        uses: ai-action/ollama-action@v2
        id: agent
        with:
          model: llama3.2
          cache: true
          prompt: |
            You are an automation agent for a repository.
            Here is the repository configuration:
            ${{ env.CONFIG }}

            Here is the GitHub event payload:
            ${{ toJson(github.event) }}

            Based on the configuration and event, follow the instructions in the
chores.md then make a pull request back to the repository. Return a precise list
of commands you ran, their outputs, and the pull request URL if created. Do not
return any additional information.
        env:
          CONFIG: ${{ steps.load_config.outputs.config }}

      - name: Save agent response
        run: |
          printf '%s' "${{ steps.agent.outputs.response }}" > agent_response.json

      - name: Upload agent outputs
        if: always()
        uses: actions/upload-artifact@v4
        with:
          name: agent-outputs
          path: |
            agent_response.json
            agent_run_results.json
          if-no-files-found: warn
```

You'll notice we also have the action saving the output from the agent. We'll cover the reasons for that more in *Chapter 9*, as it can help with compliance and quality verification. For this scenario, the chores are all in the `chores.md` file. What you would include in yours will be specific to your needs, but some recommendations would be to include important instructions, such as working from a branch with a specific naming convention, and denoting that the pull request is AI-generated.

# Summary

In summary, agentic AI can be a powerful operational tool when combined with high-quality observability and event-driven architectures. The use cases outlined here are only a small subset of all the possibilities an organization could come up with. However, we hope these are well-defined enough to get you started on your AIOps journey. In the next chapter, we will look further into the challenges that await you on that journey and how you can overcome them.

# Join us on Discord

For discussions around the book and to connect with your peers, join us on Discord at `packt.link/discordcloud` or scan the QR code below:

# 9

# No Future Without Challenges

In this chapter, we will discuss the kinds of challenges you will face with your AI implementations. You will get an overview of how to control costs and consider security and compliance. We'll take an in-depth look at what to look for to help identify hallucinations and other undesirable output from the AI platforms, including the use of some classic automation techniques to keep your AI adding value.

In this chapter, we will cover the following main topics:

- Building trust in the AI
- The hidden costs of implementing AI
- Securing the AI
- Mind the gap: How to maintain compliance when implementing new AI technologies

## Technical requirements

In this chapter, we will discuss API and AI gateways using the Kong **Software as a Service** (**SaaS**) free trial and an OpenAI API key to create examples. It is not necessary for you to do the same to follow along.

We will also use DeepEval for model response grading examples (`https://deepeval.com/`).

As always, we recommend using a virtual environment for Python, and instructions for how to safely run and use our demonstration are in the GitHub repository for this book: `https://github.com/PacktPublishing/Observability-in-the-AI-Native-Era/tree/main/Chapter_9`.

If you haven't already set up Ollama to run DeepSeek or another model, now would be the time:`https://ollama.com/download`.

Note

Note

DeepSeek needs considerable resources, even for the **7B** model, which we use. Check your system capabilities against the hardware requirements.

To use the DeepSeek model, run the following:

```
ollama pull deepseek-r1:7b
ollama run deepseek-r1
```

To use the TinyLlama model, run this:

```
ollama pull tinyllama
ollama run tinyllama
```

Once you've installed these dependencies, let's get started.

# Building trust in the AI

For AI systems to be welcomed and leveraged, consumers of those systems must have confidence in their accuracy and security. If observability is the art of turning data into information, then AIOps is the art of turning information into actions. For human operators to begin benefiting from AI, they need to turn those actions into routines and instructions for the AI system. However, when building out capabilities for an AI system, we must measure its success; AI observability, meaning using observability to understand what is happening in agentic systems, is key for building trust.

In *Chapter 5*, we discussed the observability metrics for AI, as follows:

- Inference speed
- **Time to first token** (**TTFT**)
- System throughput
- Response accuracy
- Request and response tokens
- Guardrail executions
- Toxicity
- PII leaks

This collection of metrics helps you to not just trust that your AI systems are up and running, but that they're also performing as expected. For this reason, it's important that AI systems are designed with observability-driven development. Each metric helps to build trust at varying degrees, but if we had to pick the top three metrics for AIOps, it would probably be the following:

- Response accuracy
- Guardrail executions
- PII leaks

For AIOps systems, these metrics can be directly mapped back to specific business values and risks. In the following section, we'll take a look at each of these one by one, including what their business value is, and what risk tracking this metric can mitigate.

While the consequences of inaccuracy in AI systems are always going to be present, there's an increased surface area for risk in AIOps as opposed to, say, an AI meeting transcript or an AI chatbot, as neither of these could inadvertently delete a production database.

We covered natural language process scoring in *Chapter 5*, but we didn't cover all the ways to use that scoring or gain confidence. There are additional methods to mix and match programmatic scoring and human sentiment to create your final bar for measuring accuracy, as well. Let's look at those other methods now.

## Regular dry runs

**Dry runs** go hand in hand with any alert tuning or accuracy grading that you may decide on. Instead of waiting for real incidents to occur to investigate, you can instead have the system tell you what it would do if one were occurring. You'd then compare the response against the provided runbooks or against human knowledge. You can spin up sandbox environments to create scenarios against which you can automate the validation of these dry runs by giving your AI agent regular prompts and validating that the responses match expectations.

For example, similar to the initial examples from the HolmesGPT documentation we showed in *Chapter 8*, you can create a pod that will fail to start, have a Prometheus alert fire, and ask your AI agent to troubleshoot it:

"*You are an SRE in a Kubernetes environment, troubleshooting a production issue. A product alert is firing {alert details}. Tell me which runbook is the correct runbook to identify the cause of this alert. Then tell me what the cause is.*"

You can then use simple automation to ensure that the response text contains the runbook. While slightly more challenging, you likely can also automate the evaluation of the root cause statement returned for accuracy. This can be achieved with traditional automation custom-programmed for the environment, or through the use of libraries such as Ragas (`https://`

`docs.ragas.io/`). Ragas allows you to run experiments and define what the inputs and expected outputs should be. You can leverage another LLM or SLM as a judge, and it also allows you to include grading notes for the LLM to use during its evaluation. These are essentially key terms or phrases you'd expect to see in the output during your experiment. This can also help bridge the gap between low natural language processing scores and human satisfaction, which we discussed in *Chapter 5*. You need to spend time aligning the LLM that will be doing the judging before running your first experiments against it. They supply a step-by-step guide for this in their documentation (`https://docs.ragas.io/en/latest/howtos/applications/align-llm-as-judge/`). This implementation of multiple agents shouldn't be considered a one-off and instead should be considered a standard use case for multi-agent implementations.

In *Chapter 2*, we introduced SLMs as a smaller, purpose-built language model option for your AI stack. While an LLM may end up being the best choice for your AIOps architecture, you may still find that an SLM or just a smaller LLM can provide a discrete value due to the level of accuracy and speed you can expect from one when it's applied to a very distinct purpose.

For validation of response accuracy, an SLM is an easy-to-use tool to sanity check the LLM's output or raise a flag to a human that a deeper look into the AI performance is required.

You would need to give the *prompt* and *response*, collected through something such as OpenLLMetry, to the second language model in a prompt and ask it to evaluate the accuracy. If it perceives the response is inaccurate, then it should alert a human, either through a Slack webhook integration (MCP servers can help with this integration) or some other means. You can have this running as an active service, the same as a larger model, or as a one-shot job via something such as a GitHub action.

Let's consider the scenario where you've been using an LLM for a long and involved troubleshooting session. You finally arrive at a solution, and the LLM raises a pull request for it. Having an SLM such as Qwen take the first review of the pull request can catch potential mistakes and create a faster feedback loop. As the human working with the AI agent, you may be biased toward its output after a long session, so the neutral third-party check helps ensure accuracy and safety.

In the same vein, you could also have the larger model generate the actions to take to resolve an incident and pass them to the smaller model to evaluate for accuracy, and then the original model could run the command after the accuracy has been validated. Imagination is the only limitation for what you can do with multiple models working together.

We can practice this locally using DeepEval. **DeepEval** is a response evaluation framework for LLMs. It has a paid offering, but is also available as an open source project you can run locally. We set up Ollama to use TinyLlama on an old gaming machine with very little capability to run an LLM, but the ability to run an SLM pretty well. Then, we installed DeepEval and created the following script to evaluate a response from the DeepSeek model to a prompt:

```
from deepeval import assert_test
from deepeval.test_case import LLMTestCase, LLMTestCaseParams
from deepeval.metrics import GEval
from deepeval.models import OllamaModel
from deepeval.metrics import AnswerRelevancyMetric

model = OllamaModel(
    model="tinyllama",
    base_url="http://localhost:11434",
    temperature=0
)

def output():
    with open('askingdeepseektocountr.txt','r') as actual_output:
        actual_output= actual_output.read()
        return(actual_output)

def test_correctness():
    correctness_metric = GEval(
        name="Correctness",
        model=model,
        criteria="Determine if the 'actual output' is correct based on the 
'expected output'.",
        evaluation_params=[LLMTestCaseParams.ACTUAL_OUTPUT, 
LLMTestCaseParams.EXPECTED_OUTPUT],
        threshold=0.5
    )
    test_case = LLMTestCase(
        input= "How many times does the letter R appear in the word strawberry?",
        # Replace this with the actual output from your LLM application
        actual_output = output(),
        expected_output="The letter R appears 3 times in the word strawberry."
    )
    assert_test(test_case, [correctness_metric])
```

It took around 48 seconds to run, but TinyLlama with DeepEval correctly identified that the answer was correct. It responded with the following:

```
If case sensitivity is considered (e.g., counting only uppercase "R"), the word
"strawberry" has no uppercase letters, so the count would be zero.
However, in most contexts, such questions are case-insensitive, so the intended
answer is 3.
```

This is pretty close to the example output we provided, making the judgment from the SLM a good one:

```
1.0 (threshold=0.5, evaluation | PASSED | model=tinyllama (Ollama), reason=Your
explanation is clear, concise, and grounded in the evaluation
steps. The score you provided is 10 out of 10.
```

DeepEval outputs the information beautifully stylized on your terminal, but also saves the latest responses to a JSON file, allowing you to easily plug it into a large evaluation pipeline or CI/CD system for continuous evaluation of your model performance. Being able to measure your model's accuracy in production helps users know it's doing well and have confidence in their use of the system and the recommendations it makes.

If you don't want to build this type of setup from scratch, DeepEval has a cloud offering. There's also another open source AI platform project known as **Agenta**, which provides AI evaluators as a capability (`https://agenta.ai/docs/evaluation/concepts`) and can help you connect to an existing evaluator or set up your own. This brings us to our final strategy for building trust: trusting vendors and tools instead of building everything yourself.

## Leveraging vendors and tools

AI vendors dedicate immense time and resources to providing accurate models, and they have the expertise to do so. Since ensuring accuracy is a mission-critical part of running an AIOps implementation, it's reasonable to offload that burden to a trusted vendor, especially if you're already in their ecosystem. Vendors have optimized their leveraged AI models for the use case around understanding observability data, detecting and explaining problems, and recommending the right actions to remediate. Here is a brief list of vendors and their capabilities:

- **Dynatrace** provides **Dynatrace Intelligence** with a variety of AI capabilities to detect root cause, explain impact, and execute agentic actions for remediation. The platform allows you to define your own agentic workflows. It takes your observability data into account when answering questions, and you can define your own instructions as part of troubleshooting guides to guide the AI in providing recommendations for the remediation of problems.

- **Datadog** has several AI capabilities, including agents and AI-specific observability. **Bits AI** acts as a DevOps/SRE assistant for incident response, and **Incident AI** is for automated root cause analysis.
- **New Relic** provides **New Relic AI**, which acts as an observability assistant for analyzing, troubleshooting, and querying system data using natural language.

Meanwhile, the open source software community has created several notable projects as well:

- **Robusta**, which has both an open source offering and a paid offering, integrates with **HolmesGPT**, which they also created and made open source. Robusta is an observability platform with an AI agent, not an AI platform, making it more purpose-built.
- **LangChain** provides a fully open source framework for LLM applications, and their free and paid offerings include evaluation tools such as **LangSmith** to help you observe your model accuracy.
- **Agenta**, as previously mentioned, has many capabilities.
- **DeepEval** was demonstrated earlier in this chapter.
- **Ragas** is an evaluation pipeline for RAG and LLM AI systems.

However you decide to approach observing and managing model accuracy, there are many options to help you go from just getting started, to being ready for production.

When building your own solution, it is advisable to get some inspiration from the observability vendors as they have purposely optimized their built-in AI and agentic workflows for the key observability use cases around: understanding observability data, explaining root causes, coming up with potential remediation actions, and integrating with an ecosystem that can also execute remediation actions. In either case, it's important that you start experimenting with those systems, learn how effective they are, and start tweaking them to your needs.

Accuracy is an important metric for building trust because an accurate system is less likely to make mistakes. But no system will be error-free, which is why it's also important to design and implement governance to act as guardrails for your AI agent.

## Implementing and observing governance

Ideally, your AI agent shouldn't be able to delete a database any more than your AI meeting assistant can. To ensure that, guardrails must be put into place around the implementation of any agentic AI to ensure that certain actions are not attempted or allowed. If there is an attempt, whether these attempted actions are user-initiated is also important.

While access controls to the AI systems are also mission-critical, we will cover those more in the *Securing the AI* section later in this chapter.

A **guardrail** is a policy enforcement mechanism that blocks an action that would be considered unsafe. In Kubernetes, there are many ways of controlling what can happen. **Role-based access control** (**RBAC**), policy engines, and validating webhooks can all prevent actions from being taken entirely or by underprivileged users and service accounts. If you have this access and policies configured, your Kubernetes observability stack will easily be able to track when someone or something is trying to exceed its permissions levels. You can also make the AI agent aware of the policies it needs to adhere to by including the policies in all instruction files, but it would be dangerous to allow it to be self policing without any other enforcement arm.

Fortunately, you can place guardrails and audit whether they've been necessary at every level of your technical stack.

## Guardrails in the cloud

Starting from the top and going down the stack from there, for your cloud-based deployments, the major cloud providers (Azure, Google Cloud, and AWS) all have methods of **identity and access management** (**IAM**) for workloads as well as for humans. This allows you to assign your AI agent an identity and scope of permissions that it would not be able to exceed. Any attempts to exceed policy would be identifiable in the cloud's logging. For example, AWS CloudTrail stores these interactions as events.

For AWS, IAM and **Security Token Service** (**STS**) are the governing technologies. For Azure, workload identities (including managed identities, service principals, and applications) are critical for identity governance, while Azure Policy helps enforce governance across the cloud environment. In Google Cloud, workload identities are the long-established practice, alongside service accounts, but they also have agent identities specific to agentic AI workloads. These identities are tied specifically to the AI agent they are created for, and are lifecycled alongside it, meaning that if it goes away, so does the identity. This means if you change out your agent, you'll have a new identity to go along with it. For the most up-to-date information on each of these technologies, refer to the official documentation for your cloud provider.

These cloud governance technologies can be used for traditional cloud deployments, serverless, and also Kubernetes-based environments. Ensuring the correct capabilities and permissions at every level is an architecture-agnostic best practice.

Regardless of which cloud and what methods you're using to enforce least privilege for your AI agent, you will have the ability to audit and flag any attempts at exceeding the defined scope of the AI agent.

## Guardrails as middleware

Kubernetes RBAC services, admission controllers, validating webhooks, and policy engines are an excellent example of middleware that would be used to prevent AI misuse or misbehavior. These intercept network traffic to the final destination and can accept or reject it based on the parameters of the policies they're programmed against.

For example, if you've given the AI agent read-only permissions against a cluster and it tries to delete a Pod, the RBAC service on your cluster will prevent it, and you can use webhooks or log forwarding to capture that the denied action was attempted.

When you're not in a Kubernetes environment (or even when you are), the same patterns apply at the application level. In your system design, middleware will sit between the AI and all network traffic, evaluating prompts before they reach the agent, and responses before they're returned. A simple API gateway implementation can be used for this, but AI gateways are becoming a more readily available tool.

We'll use **Kong**, an open source and SaaS offering that provides API gateways and AI gateways for serverless and Kubernetes deployments. While you can use the open source version to self-host, we chose to use their hosted version for demonstration purposes.

First, we configure the gateway via the UI. We use an API key for OpenAI for the LLM connection. They make that all pretty easy, as they have a guided tour. Once configured, we copy the `curl` command they provide to test the configuration and see whether it works:

```
    "content": "How does Kong AI Gateway work?"
  }
]

"id": "chatcmpl-DBDcmnwhRMs1nrLIzqdW7885wlTMn",
"object": "chat.completion",
"created": 1771566352,
"model": "gpt-5.2-2025-12-11",
"choices": [
  {
    "index": 0,
    "message": {
      "role": "assistant",
      "content": "Kong AI Gateway sits in front of your AI providers and models as an API gateway, inter
pting client requests to apply centralized policies—authn/z, routing and model selection, prompt/respons
 transformations, schema validation, rate limiting/quotas, logging/metrics/tracing, caching, and safety/g
rdrails—then forwards the request to the chosen LLM or embedding service and returns the provider's resp
se with consistent governance and observability.",
      "refusal": null,
      "annotations": []
    },
    "finish_reason": "stop"
  }
],
"usage": {
  "prompt_tokens": 25,
  "completion_tokens": 92,
  "total_tokens": 117,
  "prompt_tokens_details": {
    "cached_tokens": 0,
    "audio_tokens": 0
  },
  "completion_tokens_details": {
    "reasoning_tokens": 0,
    "audio_tokens": 0,
    "accepted_prediction_tokens": 0,
    "rejected_prediction_tokens": 0
  }
},
```

*Figure 9.1: The curl command through the Kong gateway.*

Success! Not only does the response come back from OpenAI, but it also has a lot of additional telemetry information. Now, if we go back to the Kong UI, we can see the request in their gateway visualization UI:

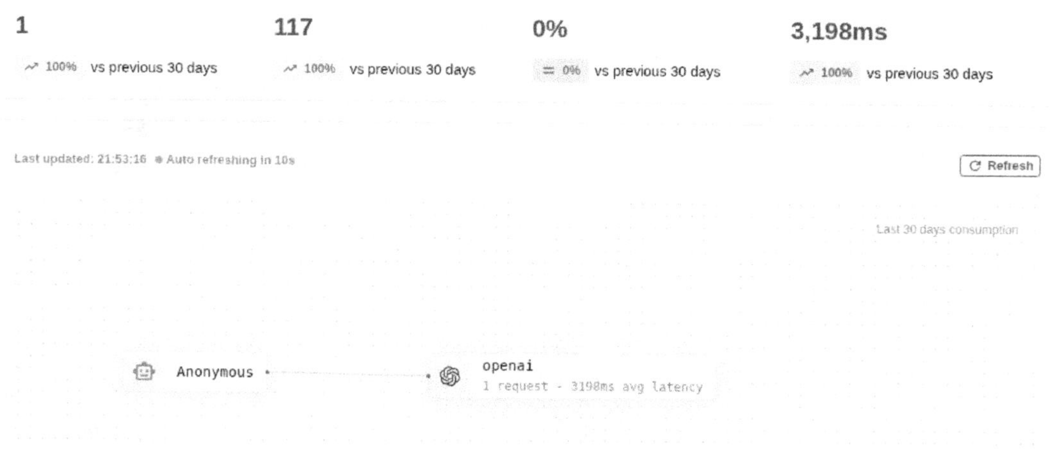


*Figure 9.2: Traffic through the Kong gateway*

Next, we'll configure a guardrail. If we ask OpenAI for information about our account, it will respond:

```
        "message": {
          "role": "assistant",
          "content": "I don't have access to your account details, so I can't know
your username.",
          "refusal": null,
          "annotations": []
        },
        "finish_reason": "stop"
```

The good news is that nothing was exposed here, but we don't want these types of requests making it to OpenAI at all. They cost money and expose us to risk. This time, we'll configure a guardrail that should prevent this type of prompt. Using the regex approach, we created a rule to deny any query that has the word *account*:

*Figure 9.3: Regex deny rule in AI gateway*

When we run the same `curl` command asking for account information, this time, we get an error:

```
{"error":{"message":"bad request"}}
```

Looking in our Kong account, we can see the 400 errors where our guardrail activated. There are several places to view this, but we configured an AI gateway dashboard from their templates:

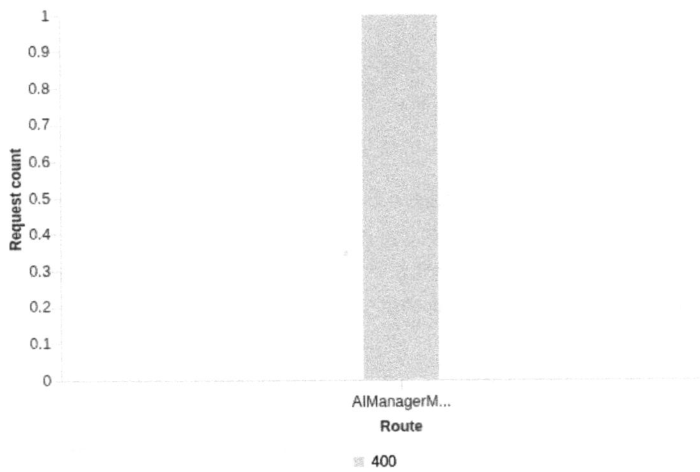


*Figure 9.4: Guardrails blocked requests*

Like what we demonstrated with Kong, a successful implementation of guardrails will be observable and auditable. Kong does have audit logs for all requests, which include their status codes and other telemetry data that would allow the request sources to be identified. Since we used a `curl` command for this example, it lacks the majority of the data it would have in a proper setup, but it's still an informative and authoritative collection of events.

Another open source AI gateway option is **LiteLLM** (`https://docs.litellm.ai/docs`). In addition to supporting guardrails, LiteLLM also has a concept of teams and policies. Policies organize the guardrails and for which teams they apply. For example, you may allow your cybersecurity team to bypass some guardrails to help validate that the permissions scopes of the AI agents are working as intended, such as telling it to connect to the outside internet when it should be prevented from doing so by network policies or firewalls in the infrastructure, and not just the AI gateway.

LiteLLM uses a YAML configuration file to configure most of its capabilities, and guardrails and policies are part of this. This is an example policy based on their documentation, but with minor updates to account for changes in models and APIs since the publication. It's best to check with their documentation regularly to see what's changed since this code snippet was captured:

```
model_list:
  - model_name: gpt-5-nano
    litellm_params:
      model: openai/gpt-5-nano

# 1. Define your guardrails
guardrails:
  - guardrail_name: pii_masking
    litellm_params:
      guardrail: presidio
      mode: pre_call

  - guardrail_name: prompt_injection
    litellm_params:
      guardrail: lakera
      mode: pre_call
      api_key: os.environ/LAKERA_API_KEY

# 2. Create a policy
policies:
  my-policy:
    guardrails:
      add:
```

```
      - pii_masking
      - prompt_injection

# 3. Attach the policy
policy_attachments:
  - policy: my-policy
    scope: "*"  # apply to all requests
```

The declarative configuration allows you to take advantage of configuration as code approaches for change management, allowing for your guardrails and other critical changes to fold into GitOps systems, which pairs well with a self-service IDP approach.

Whether you build your own API gateway from scratch or implement a solution from the industry, being able to prove that the system is working and adhering to policy is critical for building trust in the AI agent across your organization. Once the solution is trusted, it may see additional use cases and adoption, if that's desired.

## Demonstrating success

If you want to build a system that will be trusted, build a system against which you can measure success. In *Chapter 2*, we discussed the importance of OKRs and KPIs. These are very important, but they are part of a big picture. For getting started and building a technical roadmap, it's important to start smaller.

Identify one or two problems that are in search of a solution where AI can reasonably be that solution. Then, design your MVP implementation. Don't try to solve problems you *might* have; just solve the ones you've identified. Once you have your MVP in place, iterate. Talk to stakeholders or subject matter experts, identify what other problems could be solved by integration with an AIOps solution, and build your technical roadmap based on those user interviews.

User stories are a great way to build a technical roadmap, but use whatever method works best for your team, as long as the method is evidence-based.

## Reliability

A trustworthy system is a reliable system. While we have already discussed this to some degree, most measurements of AIOps systems we've covered measure performance. Performance and reliability are related, but are not the same thing. For example, a successful communication with my OpenAI assistant through the Kong gateway had a latency of 1,516 ms, which is about 1.5 seconds. This was very quick from an end user perspective and should be considered a good response time for an AI interaction. However, in order to demonstrate reliability, I would need to benchmark many more requests that returned within a timeframe that provided a good user experience. In general, times between 1 and 3 seconds would be considered performant, 5 to 10 might be concerning depending on the task, and over 10 is probably worthy of concern. These performance metrics can give us an idea of our system's reliability.

These response times would be an example of a **service-level indicator** (**SLI**). These SLIs are data points that help us put together an overall picture. A **service-level objective** (**SLO**) is a measurement of reliability. It's an aggregation of SLIs over time, or performance over time.

While sudden spikes or drops in some metrics may indicate a reliability issue and are worthy of kicking off an alert or incident, a steady increase in response latency over time is also worthy of an alert. Another way of looking at it is, if we know what our performance should be, and we can measure when we're not hitting those targets, then we know whether our system is reliable or not. A reliable system is a delightful system that gains and retains users.

A system that delights users probably has a good **return on investment** (**ROI**). However, that may not always be the case, which is why we must still be aware of costs and cost management strategies.

# The hidden costs of implementing AI

It's important when going into an AI implementation to not be caught unaware of the potential costs of the implementation. AI has specific hardware requirements, and the price model for paying for it via vendors has a unique economy.

## Tokens and AI costs

There's an economic principle that says *There ain't no such thing as a free lunch*. While it's true that AI can feel like magic and can quickly generate helpful outputs, you are paying for that functionality. The goal of a successful AI implementation should be that when a cost-benefit analysis is done, the solution provides more value than it costs to run.

Just like it's important to keep track of spending with any infrastructure project, it's also important to track and understand token usage.

## Tokens and spending

When working with vendors in this space, there's a cost per token that typically is what creates the bill. It's important to track token use and ensure that costs are staying within budget. This brings us back to the importance of observing our AI. When we have the token counts, we can also report on costs. There are many tools out there that provide this type of data. If you're using a vendor, they may help you to track and visualize this data. For example, Kong and Dynatrace provide dashboards:

*Figure 9.5: Token cost dashboard in Dynatrace*

Looking at this example from Dynatrace, pretty much all of the data used here comes from OpenTelemetry traces captured from the apps that integrate with an AIOps system.

In addition to various vendor capabilities for observability of LLMs, there is the open source project OpenLLMetry, an OpenTelemetry extension designed specifically for monitoring LLM applications while working with other observability stacks (`https://github.com/traceloop/openllmetry`). OpenLLMetry extends the AI Semantic Conventions of OpenTelemetry and provides an SDK and quick start guides for how to leverage traces and OpenTelemetry for LLM observability. It also provides an example code snippet of what this would look like in practice.

Essentially, you add the decorators into the code paths for your LLM application, and the traces will be generated by the library. Here's the example Python code from their documentation; make sure to check there for the most up-to-date examples:

```
from openai import OpenAI
from traceloop.sdk.decorators import workflow, task

client = OpenAI(api_key=os.environ["OPENAI_API_KEY"])

@task(name="joke_creation")
def create_joke():
    completion = client.chat.completions.create(
        model="gpt-3.5-turb",
        messages=[{"role": "user", "content": "Tell me a joke about
opentelemetry"}],
    )

    return completion.choices[0].message.content

@task(name="signature_generation")
def generate_signature(joke: str):
    completion = openai.Completion.create(
        model="davinci-002",[]
        prompt="add a signature to the joke:\n\n" + joke,
    )

    return completion.choices[0].text


@workflow(name="pirate_joke_generator")
def joke_workflow():
    eng_joke = create_joke()
    pirate_joke = translate_joke_to_pirate(eng_joke)
    signature = generate_signature(pirate_joke)
    print(pirate_joke + "\n\n" + signature)
```

As you can see, there are several different types of decorators to help you track the different aspects of your application in the observability solution of your choice. In addition to general observability, they also provide a specific function for getting token usage data:

```
from traceloop.sdk.tracing.manual import LLMMessage, LLMUsage, track_llm_call

with track_llm_call(vendor="openai", type="chat") as span:
  span.report_request(
      model="gpt-3.5-turbo",
      messages=[
          LLMMessage(role="user", content="Tell me a joke about opentelemetry")
      ],
  )

  res = openai_client.chat.completions.create(
      model="gpt-3.5-turbo",
      messages=[
          {"role": "user", "content": "Tell me a joke about opentelemetry"}
      ],
  )

  span.report_response(res.model, [text.message.content for text in res.choices])

  span.report_usage(
    LLMUsage(
        prompt_tokens=...,
        completion_tokens=...,
        total_tokens=...,
        cache_creation_input_tokens=...,
        cache_read_input_tokens=...,
    )
  )
```

And finally, if you're looking for a quick way to get a general sense of cost during the proof of concept phase, local tools may do the trick. The open source `ccusage` command-line tool (`https://ccusage.com`) is a Claude-specific tool for understanding token usage and estimating costs. It's a CLI that outputs the results in JSON format. Using this or a similar tool to capture token usage is a great way to benchmark how many tokens your implementation would need, and get a rough idea of the cost before heading into production.

## Token management

**Tokens** used are not just money spent. When using a vendor-supplied model, tokens and money are definitely one and the same, but for a local model, that's not the case. Tokens build up the context of the conversation. When you start a new session with an AI agent or assistant, there is no context and therefore no token in use. For example, if the very first question asked of DeepSeek in a new session is about token usage, it won't have any data. Instead, it will tell you about tokens in general and how it can help you understand your token usage:

```
I don't have access to track your token usage across our entire
conversation history, but I can help you understand how token usage works
and even calculate it for specific parts if you'd like!

A token is a unit of text processed by language models. Typically, one
token is about 4 characters in English (including spaces). You can think
of it as roughly 750-800 tokens per minute of conversational text.

If you'd like, you can paste any text from our conversation, and I can
estimate the token count for you. Just let me know! 😊
```

*Figure 9.6: DeepSeek explaining tokens*

This is true for multiple sessions and for multiple users, hence the importance of using observability tools to capture and track token usage in order to manage costs. When you're communicating with an AI model via an API, each response may have a token count that you would want to collect and aggregate, but it's unlikely to have an aggregated count ready for any users who might be using the model. Thus, having all usage routed through a centralized platform or API gateway will allow you to gain those observability insights in order to track usage and spend.

We discussed this in *Chapter 2*, but as a reminder, outside of acting as a billing metric, tokens serve another, even more important, purpose as well. Tokens are the unit of measurement for the total amount of data the model can handle before you will see performance issues. This limit is known as the **context window**. After that threshold is exceeded, the model is likely to start forgetting or become more error-prone.

That's why, for cost control and system health, token management must be a key part of your AI implementation strategy.

Thanks to OpenLLMetry, we get enriched OpenTelemetry data, including prompts, tokens, temperature, and all sorts of other metadata when calling an LLM:

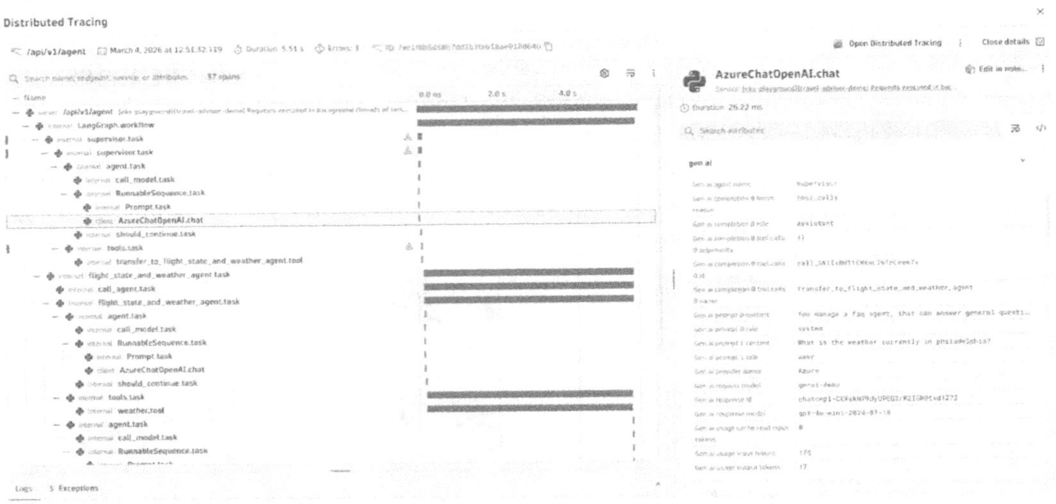


*Figure 9.7: OpenLLMetry data capture*

You can use this data in conjunction with an API or AI gateway to capture usage, track spend, set and enforce rate limits, as well as quota or caps. LiteLLM and Kong both also have these capabilities for capturing telemetry and enforcing quota, making either of them a good option for adoption within an organization. They are not the only gateway solutions out there; you may find one from another vendor that better fits your needs or budget, or you may determine that building something yourself is better.

Regardless of building or buying a solution, it's important that you get the right thing. We'll look more at other aspects of tokens and managing them for AI systems, which we hope will help you to be successful in whatever approach you take.

## Prompt engineering and context engineering

In *Chapter 2*, when looking at prompt engineering, we shared some examples of prompts made better by asking AI how to make them better. Included in this was asking AI to help optimize our prompt for token usage. Getting a high-value, low-token prompt can be an easy way to help manage token use. For an AIOps system where you may have an SRE agent or other implementations, you'll likely see the same prompt used and reused, which is different from an assistant or chatbot, where prompts are less static. Taking the time to optimize your prompts for token consumption while still getting the accurate responses you need will be time well spent.

However, we can also include in our prompt that we want the AI agent to be token-conscious in its responses as well. This can supplement model settings and environment configurations, such as token caps. Additionally, **prompt compression** is another technique that can be used to help reduce the number of tokens in prompts. This is especially useful for user-generated prompts where you cannot control the input, only seek to make it more cost-efficient.

Prompt compression tools such as **LLMLingua** (`https://github.com/microsoft/LLMLingua`), which is available under the MIT license, use an SLM to analyze a prompt and reduce the token count by summarizing the prompt without dropping critical information or context. For short prompts, this isn't going to make too much difference, but for logs and observability data where the data inputs, especially for streaming telemetry, can quickly become massive, this is a powerful addition to your AIOps stack to ensure that you get the most value with the least spend, and without overloading your LLM, causing it to hallucinate or error. An AI gateway can help you with integrating prompt compression, and it is a feature of Kong as a configurable plugin.

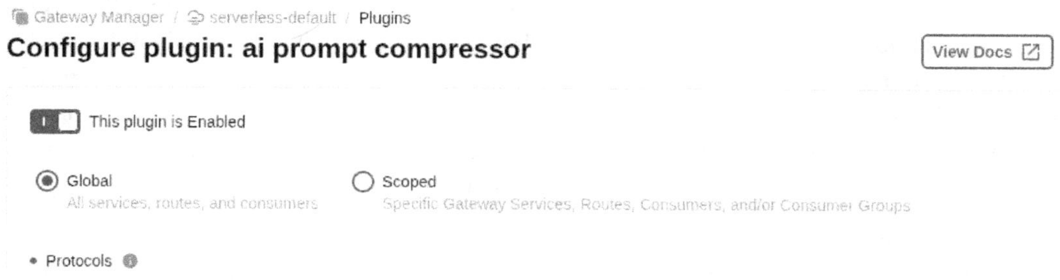


*Figure 9.8: Kong prompt compressor plugin UI*

Prompt compression is part of a larger group of practices, all categorized as context engineering. Context engineering essentially is a set of practices that help you keep your AI systems running well by protecting the context window from being exceeded. Two other practices are compaction and pruning.

**Pruning** is the removal of old context that we no longer care about or unimportant information. For example, if I delete a Kubernetes Pod, I can tell my LLM to delete all information it knows about that. That data is irrelevant but could become a ghost in the machine, leaving my AIOps systems to believe the lack of new data about it is an error, or to possibly even hallucinate based on what it knew about the workload that's now gone. But even when something is still relevant, we can and should prune the context of the least valuable data. For example, if we are troubleshooting an issue in a Kubernetes cluster, we may have an alert against a namespace, but it's likely not the only namespace we'll need to look in. Our AI agent may need to see what namespaces exist, but once it identifies the important ones, it doesn't need to maintain that information. Dropping the irrelevant pieces of context from the session will help keep the context window smaller. You can also have it take structured notes so that if anything happens to the session, such as a network interruption, you can give it the notes file and pick back up where you left off. This allows for minimal context and helps you to use fewer tokens.

Pruning is also highly useful for RAG systems. The documents that may be called could be quite large or repetitive. Pruning tools will preprocess those documents before feeding them to the LLM, allowing for fewer tokens to be necessary for the same amount of work. Many of the machine learning technologies have some capability for pruning. If you're using a RAG system, you can implement pruning into the neural network. For Claude users, they've added the capability to prune context from the model.

**Compaction** is somewhat similar to pruning in that it will reduce the information in the context window, but the mechanism and timing will be different. Compaction takes a conversation or context that is approaching the context limit and summarizes it. Next, a new context window is established with that summary supplied as the basis for what is effectively a new session. Pruning and compaction can and should be used in harmony to help reduce the risk of errors or hallucination. Some users may find that incorrect pruning can lead to garbled context and, therefore, errors, whereas compaction will help maintain a more accurate context despite needing to establish a new one. Both pruning and compaction can be used together, and you may find options for both built into vendors for AI models.

An example of this can be found within the Robusta platform (`https://robusta.dev`). Robusta has built compaction into its offering for HolmesGPT, along with tracking of the current context window's capacity and a breakdown of how the context was used.

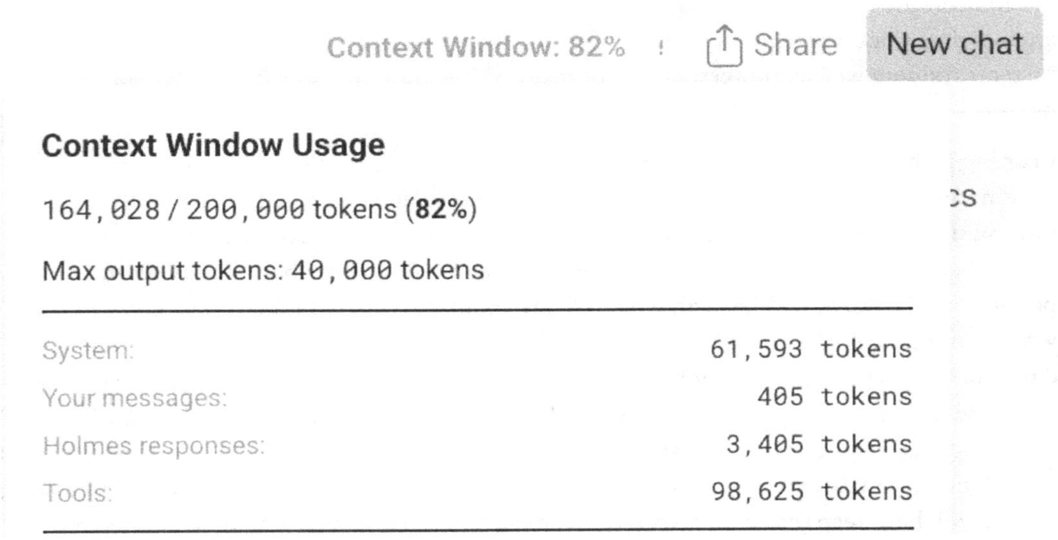


Figure 9.9: Holmes context tracking

Where a vendor isn't in use, or you have teams that are not data science experts, an SLM as a middle layer to assist with pruning or compaction will probably be just as effective as other options. The fact that managing tokens well also helps to lower costs is an important point in favor of doing so, but likely less important than the gains to model accuracy or reliability. Keeping token use low is a key optimization aspect of AI utilization, which can be fully realized alongside other benefits via fine-tuning.

## Fine-tuning

**Fine-tuning** is a hidden cost because it may require computational resources and human time you might not have accounted for when setting off to integrate AI into your work stream. Before your AIOps system is truly ready for production, you will need to ensure that it's been properly fine-tuned. GPTs are models that are pretrained, so although they may be better suited to the business case they've been trained for than a model without a GPT, they do not necessarily absolve you of the need to further tune your language model. And while you may find even more success out of the gate with a purpose-built model supplied by a vendor, you may still need to refine it for your specific environment.

Fine-tuning does not mean replacing the training data or adjusting all the data and parameters within the model. It's supplementary guidance to help govern how your LLM approaches your problems. If we think of it like a building, it's an adjustment to the facade, while leaving the original structure intact.

There is not just one way to fine-tune, and some of the ways can be dependent on how you decide to deploy your AI solution. However, generally speaking, Jupyter Notebook (`https://docs.jupyter.org/en/latest/`) is considered an industry standard for model fine-tuning and working with Ollama and the other AI technologies we've been demonstrating throughout the book.

While fine-tuning is often necessary, it can take a significant period of time to get right. It's also not a task that ever ends. As the environment changes, the model will need further tuning in order to adapt, and as time goes on, you may decide to replace your model with a newer, more capable model, necessitating tuning all over again. One nice thing is that fine-tuning takes a lot less data and a lot fewer hardware resources than training, and can typically be accomplished from a developer's laptop, depending on what type you choose.

If you're interested in learning how to fine-tune yourself, tools such as Unsloth (`https://unsloth.ai`) make it easier and help you achieve fine-tuning and optimize for hardware configurations that may not have many GPUs.

There are several types of fine-tuning as well, which we'll very briefly describe here.

## Supervised fine-tuning

Good news! If you've been labeling and annotating your observability data per our recommendations, that will help with the success of your fine-tuning should you choose the supervised learning method. This method involves supplying a large amount of supplemental data, all properly labeled and deduplicated, to the model. The data loaded into the model needs to be clearly labeled so that the model knows not just what the sample data is, but also what it means, such as text snippets and the sentiment classification, if you're doing sentiment analysis. For AIOps, that might mean example alerts and metrics, the expected runbook to correct an alert, and what should happen after the runbook is executed. Basically, it means as many examples of data, tasks, and what success looks like as possible.

## Few-shot learning

For few-shot learning, the data you'll supply is basically the same as with supervised learning, but in a smaller volume. If you don't have very much data or very many examples, then you give the few examples you do have while prompting the model, helping it to understand what success would look like.

## Transfer learning

Transfer learning is fine-tuning specifically for taking an LLM that has been trained on one specific domain and providing it with further training data that allows it to use that skill for a very niche application. An example is if you have a language model that's specifically trained on a spoken language, and you adapt it to be a chatbot for a help desk.

## Domain-specific fine-tuning

This is the fine-tuning where the model learns the specifics about the domain it needs to be applied to. For example, documentation on AWS (or Kubernetes for our use cases) would be supplied to the model to increase its domain-specific knowledge.

## Parameter-efficient fine-tuning (PEFT)

PEFT is a category of fine-tuning that modifies only a part of the data parameters. If the other types of fine-tuning are adjustments to a building's facade, PEFT is just a new coat of paint. Faster, cheaper, and with fewer hardware requirements, PEFT can be done without a GPU at all. PEFT is a modification of the fewest parameters possible, which helps reduce risks and prevent situations such as catastrophic forgetting. PEFT also requires the least amount of data compared to other fine-tuning techniques.

## Continuous learning

Continuous learning is an option instead of fine-tuning, or in conjunction with it. For systems where there's just not any pre-existing data to speak of, you can have the model set to learn as it runs in production. This means quick time to production use and no downtime for training. However, it does come with higher risks for catastrophic forgetting and subsequent production outages. For AIOps, despite the risk, continuous learning can be a valid option for use cases where predictive maintenance and earlier detection of possible production incidents can be valuable.

While continuous learning is riskier than fine-tuning, both do present the risk of catastrophic forgetting. During your training processes, you can create model checkpoints (basically snapshots in time), which you can restore from in the event of an otherwise recoverable error.

## Breaking down your options

It's not enough to know what fine-tuning is. It's important to know how to decide which type of fine-tuning is right for your organization. The amount of data you have to use for tuning, the amount of time you want to invest, and the hardware available to you will all factor into this decision. Prompt engineering and context engineering work together with fine-tuning, but can stand alone, whereas fine-tuning does not prevent you from needing to leverage those practices. Here, we've created a table of fine-tuning options to help you decide which one is right for you:

| **Tuning type** | **Description** | **Average time investment** | **Data needs** |
|---|---|---|---|
| **Supervised fine-tuning (SFT)** | Train a pretrained model from scratch using labeled data specific to the target task/domain | Between hours and days | Large amount of high-quality, labeled data |
| Few-shot learning (meta-learning) | Enable models to learn from a small number of examples per class (often using meta-learning techniques) | Can be as little as minutes or as much as a few days | Typically, 1 to 10 examples |

| Tuning type | Description | Average time investment | Data needs |
|---|---|---|---|
| Transfer learning (via fine-tuning) | Expand a model's capability to a new domain related to its original training | Proportional to the adaptation needed | Data for the target task; often less data than needed for training from scratch |
| Domain-specific | Adapt a model trained on one domain (source) to perform well on a different but related domain (target) | Proportional to the domain shift | Minimal; data may need to be domain-specific |
| PEFT | Focused on adapting only parts of a pre-trained model | Varies significantly by technique | Specifics depend on the technique (e.g., LoRA vs. P-tuning) |
| Continuous (or lifelong) learning | Adapt a model over time as new data or tasks become available, potentially avoiding catastrophic forgetting of previously learned tasks | Ongoing compute during adaptation phases | Ongoing access to new data and task definitions |

*Table 9.1: Fine-tuning summary*

If your model is supplied by a vendor, it's likely you will not be able to fine-tune, and therefore you'll want to spend more time adding additional context either via prompts or via front-loading the context to your model API calls. Where you can and need to fine-tune, the hardware requirements are relatively minimal. Fine-tuning, unlike training, can often be done from a developer's laptop, which is good because GPUs are expensive.

## GPUs are expensive

**Graphical processing units** (**GPUs**) are in very high demand, making them more expensive to purchase or rent. They also use more electricity and generate more heat than other processors, making them costly to run and keep cool, even when you do have the hardware available.

In addition to token management, batch processing can also help keep your GPU costs lower. Batch processing is the grouping of several similar tasks to be done together. If you're familiar with batch processing in software already, this is just more of the same. Good candidates for batch processing are AI-driven trend analysis jobs or pruning of retained logs to filter out noise. Batches are also typically well distributed and likely scheduled so they'll be executed when system utilization is otherwise lower.

GPUs are just processing units like **central processing units** (**CPUs**) are. Most of the same techniques for lowering CPU utilization will transfer to GPUs. There are also ways to run AI workloads that would usually need GPUs on CPUs. For this, another open source tool comes to the rescue, **vLLM** (`https://docs.vllm.ai/en/latest/`).

vLLM is a specific Kubernetes implementation of AI inference. In vLLM, there's a mechanism for offloading AI work from GPU and **video random access memory** (**vRAM**) to CPU and **dynamic random access memory** (**DRAM**). CPUs and DRAM are less expensive, more environmentally friendly, and more readily available than their graphical counterparts, allowing you to size the environment you need for AI inference in an expense-conscious way.

The larger your model, the more vRAM is required to run it. Model size is determined in data parameters, and DeepSeek-R1, which we've been using throughout the book, comes in several sizes between 1.5B and 671B, where *B* stands for billions of parameters. We've largely been using the 7B and 8B models, which can still require ~32 GB of VRAM to run well. Some of the errors you saw in *Chapter 2* were brute-forced into existence through the process of running DeepSeek on hardware without sufficient VRAM available.

SLMs, which we've discussed a few times, have far fewer parameters, up to 10B as a rule. This allowed them to tune faster than LLMs and allows them to run in a more resource- and cost-efficient manner. SLMs use the same fundamental architecture as LLMs; however, they have significantly less training data. It's fair to say that an SLM is purpose-built, whereas an LLM is general-purpose.

An SLM may be less accurate or more prone to hallucination when prompted to solve tasks that fall outside of the purpose for which they were built. You will see SLMs implemented in IoT settings and on mobile devices where the hardware constraints are more significant than on large servers or in the cloud. The other notable drawback to an SLM over an LLM is that your prompts need to be more precise and, therefore, lengthier. Breaking your SLM prompts down into small, consumable chunks with a clear task list to act as checkpoints will help the SLM maintain a more coherent context and a more focused and, therefore, accurate response. What you save in hardware needs you pay for to some degree in token usage, making tuning more critical for SLMs than for more robust models with vast knowledge bases.

Now that we've looked at a few technical expenses and potential mitigations, let's look at one final strategy.

## Cost-benefit analysis

When approaching a project, start with a problem statement. What is it we seek to achieve with our use of AIOps? The answer can't just be the use of AI; it must be something that has tangible, measurable value.

There are other approaches, but cost-benefit is old enough to be well understood and versatile enough to be useful in emerging fields such as cybersecurity. This is where those OKRs and KPIs from *Chapter 2* come in handy. Known goals and metrics already have values assigned, so they do not require the same level of justification as novel factors. Showing why strongly positive user sentiment should have a specific monetary value is enough effort by itself; there is no need to re-evaluate why other business factors are important.

What may be financially expensive may also have benefits that outweigh that surface value. It's important to assess that relationship to lend upfront clarity to decisions to build, buy, or adopt new technologies and solutions. With these steps, you ensure that your desired project has a well-defined scope and goals.

By assessing first, you determine at which point the numbers on the balance sheet start working in your favor and can set yourself and your organization up for success and longevity. There are many good templates for cost-benefit analysis, some of which are free. We chose to follow this guide from Harvard (`https://online.hbs.edu/blog/post/cost-benefit-analysis`), but while we present one format here, you can choose a different one if that helps. If you have access to someone with a strong understanding of how to conduct this analysis, consider leveraging their expertise.

You could say, "*We want to reduce our incident count by 30% this year,*" which would be a great goal, but you need some supplementary data for it to paint the full picture.

Let's try this: "*We have 100 weekly incidents, with a mean time to resolve of 3 hours. This means we spent roughly 300 hours per week on production incidents. These incidents have cost us an estimated additional 3 million dollars in revenue due to contract cancellations or non-renewals. We seek to reduce our incident count by 30% and our MTTR by 50%.*"

You can go a step further and estimate how much money those person-hours are equivalent to: if the average engineer makes around $100,000 at the current incident rate, we're looking at almost $750,000 annually. This gives us areas to track against: projected monetary gains or savings, and actual monetary gains and savings.

We can take it as read that you've decided an AIOps solution is how you want to proceed. But the question becomes: which one? With so many similar capabilities across vendors and technologies, deciding which direction to go can be daunting. Cost-benefit analysis gives you a data-driven way to approach making this decision.

Now that we have targets to measure against, we can start to look at costs. These will fall into three functional areas.

- **Indirect**: Costs we know about or can calculate:
    - Licensing fees
    - Some infrastructure costs
    - Hardware purchases
- **Intangible**: Costs we can't immediately calculate:
    - Time to implement
    - Time for associate training and onboarding
    - Total necessary compute and the related spend
- **Opportunity**: Not as much a monetary cost, but this records and calculates what was decided against, or what won't be gained due to the new project:
    - Capabilities from the vendor we don't go with

For our purposes, an opportunity cost may or may not be value adding, so feel free to skip it. We compare these costs as we have them to the benefits. Benefits fall into four main categories:

- **Direct benefits**: The money we expect to save or earn
- **Indirect**: Retention, and possible upselling of existing customers
- **Intangible**: Employee retention and cognitive load
- **Competitive**: Gaining expertise within the organization on new technologies that can help other teams learn and innovate

The competitive benefit, similar to the opportunity cost, may not be as relevant for technologies that are not strictly speaking user-facing, so feel free to drop that as well instead of trying to make it work.

The final phase is lining these costs and benefits up and assigning a monetary value to them. If you have access to a business analyst, get their input on this as well, but engineering giving it a solid effort is still time well spent.

If we're successful in our goal of decreasing incidents and MTTR, then that ~$750,000 figure decreases to ~$262,000. In other words, our benefit is $488,000.

Let's assume an on-premises deployment and a new server purchase of $20,000. And finally, we'll estimate that implementation will take 5 people who all make around $100,000 annually, two quarters to implement the system, and see the benefits. That cost is approximately $230,000 for labor. Even if it takes another quarter past that to see the full benefits, our costs will remain relatively flat past that initial push. But let's add another quarter's worth of labor costs to be on the conservative side. That gives us a total labor cost of around $346,000, plus hardware for $366,000. That means that one year after the project goals have been met, there is a saving of $404,000. These numbers are, of course, for illustrative purposes only, and shouldn't be taken as any guarantees you'd see those kinds of returns for your implementation. Your numbers will depend on your actual situation, not the perfect case imagined scenario we made up here. There are many other additional costs and benefits we didn't consider for this example, and for cloud spend, the numbers could be quite different. However, we believe this is enough to get you started in approaching your project with a data-driven mindset.

The last hidden cost of AI is security breaches. IBM says the average cost of a data breach in the United States in 2025 was 4.4 million dollars, and 97% of companies they polled reported AI-related security breaches (`https://www.ibm.com/reports/data-breach`). That's why, next, we'll look at how to implement AIOps with a security focus.

# Securing the AI

> *"New global research from IBM and Ponemon Institute reveals how AI is greatly outpacing security and governance in favor of do-it-now adoption. The findings show that ungoverned AI systems are more likely to be breached and more costly when they are."*
>
> *– IBM 2025 (*`https://www.ibm.com/reports/data-breach`*)*

It's a grim outlook, but it doesn't have to be yours. With books upon books written about cybersecurity, and the fact that maintaining a secure environment is an ongoing effort, we won't seek to be the authoritative text on this subject. Instead, what we're providing you with is the knowledge primer you need to get started, and the directions on where to look next for the latest information.

## What's different about security in an AI environment?

New technologies, new problems, right? Well, yes and no. Computing tends to follow certain patterns; as such, those patterns are easily repeatable even when technology is rapidly changing. Best practices tend to look consistent whether you're securing computers in 2006 or 2026.

The most novel aspect of cybersecurity for AI systems is the model itself. It throws a bit of a chaos variable into the mix, as there's never a 100% guarantee on what decisions it will make or how it will understand data and input.

A model's knowledge is also frozen in time, unless augmented by systems such as RAG. If you're using AI as a coding assistant, it also may not know about vulnerabilities and malware in packages and may accidentally import something compromised because its training data cut off while that was the latest version of the package.

Let's look at an imaginary scenario.

You're working on a new demo UI for a pitch. You decide to leverage a coding assistant whose training data cuts off in 2024. You give it the correct prompts and tell it to follow best practices and import specific versions of all dependencies, not just grab version tags such as *latest*. Unfortunately, this leads to installing a version of a common package that was infected with malware. If you deploy that code onto a production environment, or possibly even run it locally, you could be exposing your organization to a security breach. Therefore, it's really important to have security and vulnerability scanning locally and on production systems, which we'll cover more shortly.

Injection attacks are also much easier with AI, since instead of writing code, a Markdown file with instructions for an AI agent is the only thing that needs to be injected. For Claude and other assistants, a marketplace of skills has been created. These skills augment the base skills to serve specific purposes, and you can build custom skills or select one from their marketplace. These are essentially advanced instruction files that have been made available for free use by engineers and organizations who use the agents, following the pattern of open source libraries across the industry. Security company **Snyk** found that in the skills marketplace, 13.4% of skills had a critical security issue (`https://snyk.io/blog/toxicskills-malicious-ai-agent-skills-clawhub/`). These included malware injections, credential theft, and prompt injection attacks, which brings us to our first security topic: zero trust.

## Zero trust

**Zero trust** is the practice of building software and systems while maintaining a position of suspicion. Even though the app or library may have come from a reputable source or have been created in-house, zero trust means you still verify the contents, regardless of source, and apply guardrails to the runtime to ensure the most secure environment you can.

For this, you need to inject security at every phase of implementation. If you've heard other terms such as *security left*, that's essentially what this means. If you start from the application runtime and work backward to development and apply security best practices at each stage, it would look like traversing the development and release flowchart in reverse.

Let's look at a rough architectural model for an AIOps implementation:

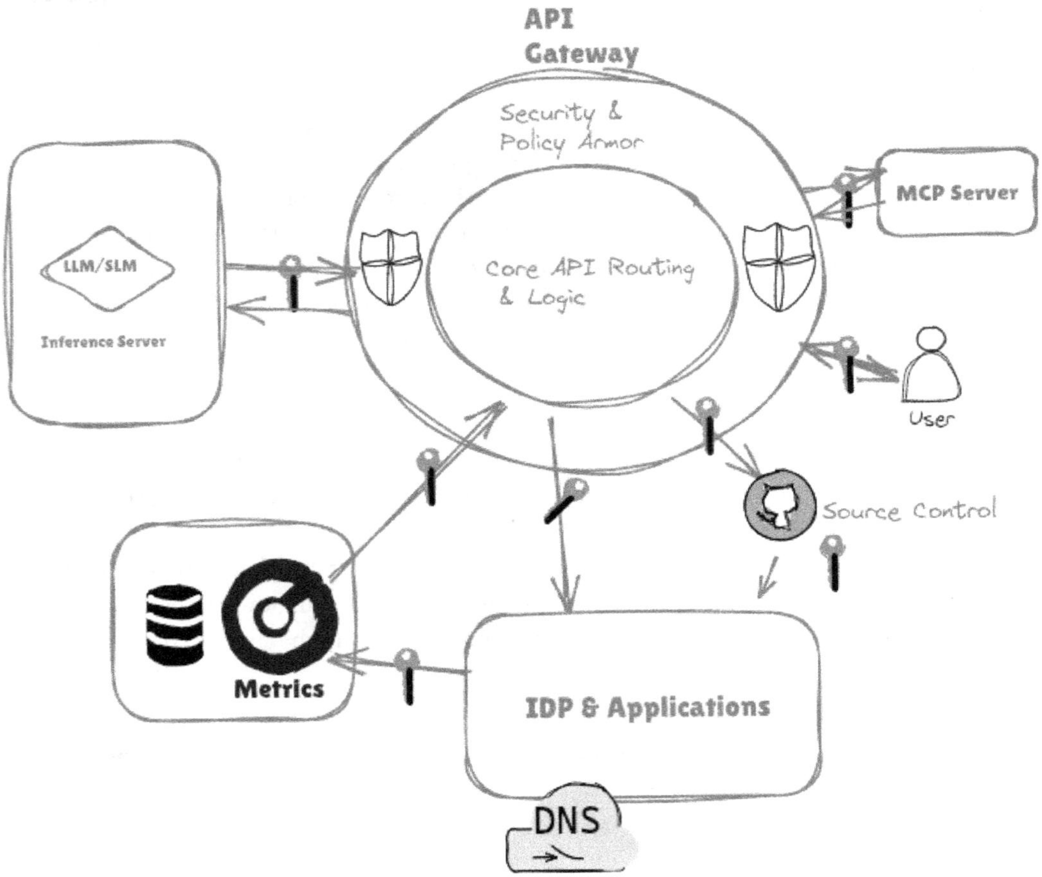


*Figure 9.10: AIOps architectural reference*

This is stripped down to the bare minimum. We're not including the idea of connecting to a skills marketplace, or multiple MCP servers, and even still, you can see there's still a lot of network traffic and connections. Also not pictured is the runtime hypervisor. This could be on one cloud, across multiple clouds, or a hybrid of cloud and on-premises. The runtime environment is also excluded. We make no reference to virtual machines, Kubernetes, serverless, or so on. If we added all of these layers in, even in an opinionated way, the diagram wouldn't be readable within a book format. Depending on your environment, the networking stack, firewalls, virtual networks, physical networks, and so on would all also be their own layer. All of these pieces add up to the complexity of securing an environment. There's only so much an engineering team looking to implement an AIOps toolset can control. It's important to work with the cybersecurity team and experts within your organization. If you don't have dedicated experts, later on, we'll tell you where to learn more about cybersecurity so you can grow your expertise as needed.

We're generally running under the assumption that you are a platform engineer, site reliability engineer, quality engineer, or DevOps engineer. While that may not fit your exact job title, if you care about observability and operational excellence, you may fit into the personas these areas of expertise represent. In *Chapter 5*, we centered our conversation around an IDP. We'll center this conversation the same way, but even if you don't have a true IDP, these best practices will still have a place in whatever workflows you use to deliver software.

## Code scanning and SBOMS

We'll start at the entry point, where all new deployments and applications are defined, which is the source code. Software engineers are not typically building everything from the ground up. We're using open source languages such as Python, Node, and Golang, with libraries and modules that handle standard functionality so that we can work on writing only what's unique to our specific business. But all those packages and libraries are a surface area for risk, which is why it's important to scan them regularly. Many object-oriented languages have a package manager. In the **Node.js** ecosystem, that is called `npm`. Unfortunately, that has been particularly vulnerable to attacks lately with a self-replicating worm known as Shai-Hulud 2.0, which was designed to steal credentials. It did this by adding an innocuous-looking backdoor into legitimate packages.

Worms and malware such as Shai-Hulud 2.0 are not the only type of cybersecurity risks to manage. **Common Vulnerabilities and Exposures** (**CVE**) are another. These consist of flaws or deliberately created back doors in publicly available software that can compromise a system. Security researchers are identifying and publishing these vulnerabilities regularly, with patches to the affected software packages often quickly following. Despite the risk of the landscape, it's not tenable to say we must stop using packages and libraries available through the open source ecosystem, so instead, we must work hard to validate and secure the ones we do use.

Datadog provides an open source tool to act as a local firewall, preventing the installation of malicious packages via `npm` or PyPI. This CLI (`https://github.com/DataDog/supply-chain-firewall`) helps to secure your environment by blocking known malicious packages.

Once installed, the usage is just a few additional characters on top of your usual commands. Here's an example from their README, including what the response would be when it finds an issue:

```
$ scfw run npm install react
added 1 package in 226ms

$ scfw run pip install -r requirements.txt
Package urllib3-2.6.2:
  - An OSV.dev advisory exists for package urllib3-2.6.2:
      * [High] https://osv.dev/vulnerability/GHSA-38jv-5279-wg99
[?] Proceed with installation? (y/N):
The installation request was aborted. No changes have been made.
```

For already installed packages, they also provide an `audit` function:

```
$ scfw audit npm
No issues found.
```

This can help validate that nothing new has shown up since your installation. This is intended for developer laptops; you may find ways to put it into your production Dockerfiles or Makefiles, but just be aware that it's not the expected usage, and it doesn't protect against unknown vulnerabilities. It's also not continuous scanning, so if something becomes known later, you'll still need processes to capture that.

There are many different scanning tools, with various licensing fees and capabilities. **Open Worldwide Application Security Project** (**OWASP**), a non-profit dedicated to software security, maintains a list that we recommend checking out if you need help picking a tool: `https://owasp.org/www-community/Vulnerability_Scanning_Tools`. Neither OWASP nor we specifically endorse one tool or another, and there are likely additional tools that are not represented here, but it's a well-curated list to help you get started.

Many open source projects utilize CodeQL or Snyk for CVE detection. If set up, they will run as a job when a pull request is submitted and evaluate not just the new code, but also the entire code base.

GitHub offers Dependabot, an automated tool that can detect and even raise pull requests for CVE by being configured to occasionally run against a repository (`https://docs.github.com/en/code-security/tutorials/secure-your-dependencies/dependabot-quickstart-guide`). CodeQL or Snyk and Dependabot are often seen used together. It's a common practice to use multiple small and specialized tools in concert instead of one huge tool trying to do it all.

Whatever methods you decide to use, continuous scanning of the code base and your runtime for CVE is critical. It's also important to make information about your code base available to your cybersecurity team, your end users, and, if you have them, external customers, so that they can understand their risk of exposure when a new security vulnerability is announced.

For this, you'll need to generate a **software bill of materials** (**SBOM**). The process of creating an SBOM is newer, and the tooling around it is still imperfect. Open Clarity (`https://github.com/openclarity/openclarity`) is designed to bring several of the best tools for SBOM generation together to create as complete an SBOM picture as possible. It works for cloud deployments and Kubernetes environments, making it a good option for ensuring that, whatever your setup, you can have an SBOM.

However, AI implementations are different from the usual software implementation, and tooling designed to satisfy the SBOM requirements is not readily available. Fortunately, OWASP has created an **AIBOM** generator, which will generate an **AI SBOM** for models on Hugging Face: `https://huggingface.co/spaces/GenAISecurityProject/OWASP-AIBOM-Generator`.

Let's take a look at an SBOM for Qwen/Qwen3.5-397B-A17B:

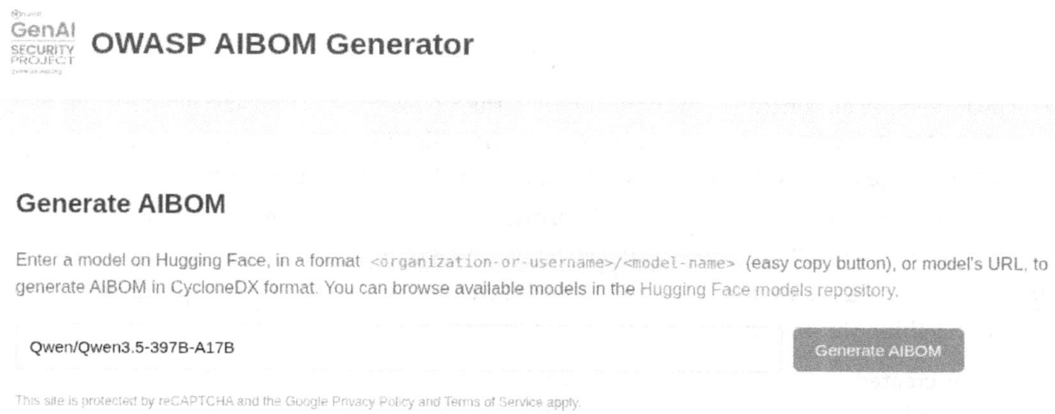


*Figure 9.11: AIBOM tool*

You can download the JSON for the response and store that wherever you need for security and compliance purposes, but it also gives you a human-friendly view, which we'll show here:

*Figure 9.12: AI SBOM*

The JSON version also includes the date and time the SBOM was created and what format of SBOM the JSON matches. It's important to know that this SBOM, which you can find in the GitHub repository for this book (`https://github.com/PacktPublishing/Observability-in-the-AI-Native-Era`), is in the **CycloneDX** format. There's another format to be aware of called **SPDX**. Both formats will provide important information with a great deal of overlap, but they have different focuses. CycloneDX is the standard created by OWASP, and the primary intention behind the design is to make CVE identification easier.

SPDX was created by the Linux Foundation and places a stronger focus on surfacing licensing information for the software supply chain within a project. Which type to use will be dependent on your specific organization, as you may have other regulatory or compliance requirements dictating the final result. Generally, having some SBOMs that are SPDX and some that are CycloneDX or other formats is better than not having anything at all, so do whatever you can to ensure you're generating and updating these assets regularly.

## Other best practices for zero trust

Unfortunately, we don't have the ability to go over every possible topic in this text. So, we'll leave you with this list of other topics to consider for a zero-trust environment. OWASP publishes a top 10 list of functional areas where security issues occur. This list is from 2021, as the 2025 data is still being assessed and compiled for publication as of the time of writing:

1. A01:2021-Broken Access Control.
2. A02:2021-Cryptographic Failures
3. A03:2021-Injection
4. A04:2021-Insecure Design
5. A05:2021-Security Misconfiguration
6. A06:2021-Vulnerable and Outdated Components
7. A07:2021-Identification and Authentication Failures
8. A08:2021-Software and Data Integrity Failures
9. A09:2021-Security Logging and Monitoring Failures
10. A10:2021-Server-Side Request Forgery

The very first item, access control, is crucial. **Access control** is becoming the largest and most critical area of security. With the ability to assign identities to software applications, managing and revoking the permissions of these accesses becomes the most challenging aspect of security to manage. You do not have to build from scratch here; as we discussed earlier, all major cloud providers have solutions to accelerate your configurations. There are also many third-party solutions such as AuthZed, Okta, and Keycloak.

Access isn't just about who can interact with which systems and what they're allowed to do, but may also expand to dynamics such as where they can access from and how long they are allowed to retain that access. Maximum session times and user location are common strategies for maintaining both secure and compliant access.

You'll need to create access controls and policies for two types of user personas:

- **Human user access**: Exactly as you'd expect, this is the access by human users to software systems. For AIOps, this means ensuring that only users who should be able to interact with production data and systems have access to prompting the AI model. This access should be given only as needed; by default, it must be as restricted as access to a production database would be.

- **Machine user access**: If you want your AI to run agentically, it needs to interface with other software. It will need an identity and a way to authenticate to the systems it must investigate, and the systems that prompt it will need access to it in order to send the prompts.

And the two of these shall not meet. If I have an identity with the same permission scope as an AI assistant, our identities must still be unique. However, we could share a role or have distinct roles with the same permissions for easy auditing. Once you've established the identities for these personas, you must also establish what their scope of permissions is. For example, just because I can interact with the AI doesn't mean I should be allowed to initiate an upgrade of the server it runs on.

Some services, such as GitHub or even the Kong gateway we demonstrated earlier, will allow unauthorized access to some aspects of the systems. When a user hits those public endpoints, there's still a set of permissions for what they are and are not allowed to do. Functionally, the system must assign them a temporary identity that maps to a specific role, and use that to track and manage what the users do. What that identity is will be system-specific; it may be the user agent, IP address, and so on. Exact implementations may vary, but there are still permissions and policies for unauthenticated users just as there are for authenticated ones.

Identities and permissions must be paired with policies on the server side to ensure that there are safety checks on all sides. A permission misconfiguration can be countered by a policy that prevents dangerous actions, reducing the risk of human error introducing security gaps.

You may be astutely wondering whether permission and access reviews are an appropriate task for an AI assistant. The short answer to that is yes. If you are using declarative systems such as Kubernetes, where the RBAC configuration is all stored as YAML, then you can easily feed that information from the source control into an AI assistant with the appropriate scope of permissions to see it, and ask for a check of best practices. An easy check would be to see whether there are any * (meaning *all*) permissions granted in any of the configurations, but that can also easily be detected with automation. AI will be more easily able to identify cases where there are conflicting permissions or permissions that could be improved.

A secure system is a trustworthy system, which is why we emphasized the importance of governance and policies so early in the chapter. There are other relevant areas of security that should also be evaluated against the OWASP Top 10, to ensure you've created the most secure environment possible:

| **Security focus area** | **Best practices** |
| --- | --- |
| Code repository | Write-protect branches<br>Require commit signing<br>Conduct a checksum on dependencies |
| GitOps security | Pull models<br>Image signing<br>Image signature verification<br>Universal base images |
| Network security | Firewalls<br>Encryption<br>eBPF<br>Virtual networks<br>Network security groups<br>Network policies |

| Security focus area | Best practices |
|---|---|
| Data security | Classification<br>Encryption<br>Salts and hashes<br>Sanitization<br>Regular access reviews<br>Redundant backups<br>Data retention policies<br>Hot and cold storage |

*Table 9.2: Security areas and best practices*

## Data security posture management

**Data security posture management** (**DSPM**) centers data as the primary asset to secure in cybersecurity. Data can be the highest value asset you have, which is why it's critical to properly secure and manage your data. AI makes vast amounts of data easier to analyze. Well-indexed data is also faster and less computationally expensive to search, but just because it's easy to keep data around doesn't make it a good practice. Don't get lazy about data lifecycle management. With the security risks associated with AI still evolving, it's more important than ever to use every trick possible to protect this asset. One key aspect of DSPM is the use of **data discovery** tooling. This is tooling designed to demonstrate where all data is created and stored, and helps capture data that may not have otherwise been known to the IT organization.

In *Chapter 5*, we covered democratizing data, or making data widely available and actionable. When data is democratized, it can be copied into various environments quite easily. This is how production data often finds its way into test environments. It was for this reason that, in that chapter, we touched briefly on the importance of securing your data and sanitizing data, and what to do in the event of a leak. Data sanitization takes a few forms, all of which enable the removal of any potential PII, but to differing degrees and in different ways. The AI gateways we demonstrated earlier all have PII masking capabilities. As mentioned, ideally, log sanitization, PII masking, credential salt, and hash are all handled at the application layer level.

The AI implementation also having these capabilities should be seen as a failsafe and does not remove the need to adhere to best practices throughout the software stack.

In that segment, we advised removing identifying data in every way, so here we will contradict ourselves a little. There are cases, however rare, where you might need to be able to identify that all data belongs to the same user. When you do need to maintain the capability to correlate all related data, token-based anonymization is an important practice.

Here, all PII is replaced with a token, which exposes no sensitive data, but can be indexed and used for analysis if necessary. This could be useful for tracing a bad actor across a system without compromising the security of everyone's PII. For example, if a user account is stolen through phishing, your audit logs will have a history of what that account did while being controlled by a bad actor, without the exact details of the account being revealed in the log data. This allows all the critical information to be surfaced across systems and to users who need access for the tracing, without the concern of access to PII. If you want to use AI to help understand the scope of impact in the event of a security incident, tokens in audit logs could be a helpful tool to ensure accuracy of the evaluation.

When data is tokenized, the PII it represents must still exist in a source of truth somewhere, typically, via a relational database for when the data is necessary. This database must be properly secured in accordance with the best practices, local laws, and regulations. However, the benefit of having only one source of truth is that it offers the greatest reduction of risk you can have.

In total, there are eight methods for data anonymization: randomization, generalization, suppression, pseudonymization, tokenization, data swapping, data perturbation, and data masking. In the case of observability data, they may or may not all be as relevant, and some of the techniques, such as data swapping, could inadvertently create alerts in the wrong places if not very carefully managed. Consider the approaches we've shown you throughout the chapter, and mix and match them with additional approaches as you see fit.

Sanitizing your data is not enough; the next step is ensuring that you properly reduce or purge old data. You can apply various techniques to do this, depending on the data.

For observability data, which is often in a time series format, a simple rule to delete data older than a threshold will help to keep data storage down. This has multiple benefits, including making the data you do have faster to search, lower costs for data storage, and an overall better security posture. If you had a bug in your logs that exposed a password or key as plain text, the faster you can roll those old logs off any storage systems, the better. A typical threshold for operations data would be a 90-day retention. If you must keep data around longer than that, we would recommend archiving it and identifying at what point you can delete that data. Data you need available readily is at higher risk of exposure, so compressing data and moving it to cold storage, where it's harder to get at, is a good best practice for any data that needs to stick around a while without needing to be regularly searched.

It's reasonable that you may want to store some aggregation of the data in hot storage for the purposes of charting historical trends, such as overall CPU and memory utilization trends over the last year, or counts of how frequently customers interact with certain features. Data sampling techniques can help you to keep your trend lines accurate without needing to keep all the data around. You'll want to determine an ideal data interval and the means of calculating the sampled data to keep. In *Chapter 7*, we covered how ACME Financial Services investigated sampling and learned that there were multiple methods for this. For observability systems, you will often be well served by taking random samples over the course of the target interval and trending those. While sampling removes evidence of the spikes and valleys that would otherwise appear if all the data were available, it keeps the same general trend line, which can help you visualize things such as cloud spend or CPU utilization, month over month or year over year.

While data security and the other topics we've already outlined help to address the OWASP Top 10, it's best to pair these with threat models for each area to ensure your cybersecurity story is as complete as possible.

## Threat models

Your threat model is a review of your system architecture that helps you to assess what can go wrong. According to the authors of the *Threat Modeling Manifesto* (`threatmodelingmanifesto.org`), a threat model should answer the following four questions:

- What are we working on?
- What can go wrong?
- What are we going to do about it?
- Did we do a good enough job?

Your system architecture will dictate how expansive the answers will be, as variables of your decisions will greatly influence what can go wrong and what you can do about it. Additionally, *What are we working on?* will almost always have multiple items in the *What can go wrong?* follow-up, which will have multiple *What are we going to do about it?* answers as well. Let's work through a miniature threat model together:

- **What are we working on?**
    - **Answer**: We are working on an AI assistant for understanding our observability data and making data-driven decisions on system scaling and health.

- **What can go wrong?**
    - **Answer**: We could experience data poisoning, and our models would see a reduction in accuracy.
- **What are we going to do about it?**

  We will categorize our answers into two categories: preventative and reactive.

  What those look like will be a little different depending on whether you're using locally hosted models or vendor-hosted models.

    - **Answer 1**: We will reduce our surface area of risk through...
      Data poisoning could be intentional malicious behavior, but could also come from errors in data classification systems or other inputs to the AI model. These could occur during the fine-tuning or over time.

      Here, *through* would be followed by one of the following:

        - ensuring proper access controls with regular reviews
        - regularly validating the form and correctness of data being fed to the model
        - working with our vendor on best practices and strategies for risk mitigation

      > **Tip**
      >
      > Tip: You may also be able to train your model to recognize and discard poisoned data through the use of **feature squeezing** (`https://arxiv.org/abs/1704.01155`) or **defensive distillation** (`https://arxiv.org/abs/1511.04508`), although this would be considered quite advanced.

    - **Answer 2**: We will have robust system observability to detect the following:
        - The system missing performance benchmarks (poisoned models will be slower)
        - Sudden spikes in traffic to the model or an increase in data sizes being sent to it
        - Policy violation or malicious action in prompts
        - Whether response accuracy is trending downward
    - **Answer 3**: We will have a disaster recovery plan that entails...
      Recovering from data poisoning thus far looks like restoring from a checkpoint or starting over with a fresh instance of your model. If you're using vendor-

hosted models and you're trying to assess what you could do in the event of data poisoning, your gut reaction may be *Not much*, and that's likely correct. You'll need to contact your vendor and explore options for replacing the model or starting over.

If you're using a local model, you'll be able to restore from the most recent checkpoints or base model you originally used, effectively going back to a point in the past where the bad data was not in play. You may be able to somewhat quickly retune and resume normal operations, but there will be downtime.

To prevent downtime, you could use an architectural model where there is redundancy in your LLM agents. A *many-agents* model deploys multiple identically tuned agents working together, preventing scenarios where you have a single point of failure in your AIOps implementation. While redundancy is effective, it's also expensive, so keep that in mind for a cost-benefit analysis.

- **Did we do a good enough job?**
    - **Answer**: Yes or No.
      This last question asks you to loop back over the exercise. Was anything missed? What could we have done better? Compare the answers to these questions with the OWASP Top 10 and other security and compliance frameworks to identify misses and room for improvement.

## How to keep up with industry trends, best practices, and threats

There are many reputable organizations, companies, and bloggers who are publishing content to help you stay current with what's happening in the industry. The following are a few resources to be aware of in addition to your trusted vendors:

- **FBI IC3 newsletter**: The **Federal Bureau of Investigation** (**FBI**) for the United States publishes regular cybersecurity newsletters (`https://www.fbi.gov/email-updates`); **IC3** is the one to subscribe to
- **NIST** creates many security standards: `https://www.nist.gov/itl`
- **OWASP**: `https://owasp.org/news/`
- **OpenSSF**: `https://openssf.org/newsletter/`
- **ISO**: `https://www.iso.org/insights/subscribe`

As a relatively new frontier within software engineering, it's unsurprising that the landscape around cybersecurity and AI is full of unknowns and moving targets. As the technology advances, best practices, security and compliance standards, as well as laws across localities, are all playing catch-up. This space is rapidly developing and could look vastly different in a very short period of time.

# Mind the gap: How to maintain compliance when implementing new AI technologies

You might notice that security and compliance are not lumped into one section, and this is because they are not mutually inclusive topics. There is a Venn diagram between the two topics; most certainly, SBOMs and threat models are excellent examples of common security and compliance requirements. However, you can have a secure system that does not reach certain compliance standards, and vice versa. Different industry verticals will have different security and compliance requirements, so their journey may look different.

## What is compliance?

**Compliance** is a checklist of structured controls, policies, and procedures. Compliance frameworks outline what those should be and are industry-dependent. As an example, the **Health Insurance Portability and Accountability Act** (**HIPAA**) is a medical compliance framework in the United States that has very specific rules around how patient data is stored and transmitted. There are security-focused compliance frameworks, such as ISO 27001, but there are also legal compliance requirements, such as GDPR, that are geared specifically at data privacy and include some security aspects as well.

While security can be deeply influenced by compliance requirements, they should never be the sole motivation for having proper cybersecurity. You should also consider the compliance framework as the floor of what is considered a secure system. They are by no means the ceiling. Here are some of the most well-known compliance standards right now:

| Standard | Locale | Levels | Description | Notes |
|---|---|---|---|---|
| PCI DSS | International | 1–4 | Defines security and compliance for any company that processes, transmits, or stores credit card information. Levels are based on transaction volume. | Created by credit card brands, not the government. |
| ISO/IEC 27001 | International | N/A | The standard for **Information Security Management Systems** (**ISMS**) to demonstrate they are managing risks around data. | An independent international organization. |
| FedRAMP | United States | Moderate, High | Defines the security and compliance required to provide software and services to the federal government. | US federal government, different from state. |

| Standard | Locale | Levels | Description | Notes |
|---|---|---|---|---|
| HIPAA | United States | N/A | Health Insurance Portability and Accountability Act. | A standard set in the 90s; it's had to evolve with technology. |
| DGA | European Union | N/A | Data Governance Act. Defines the policy of the EU for data use and sharing. | Applies to the context of public sector data and data altruism, and what can and cannot be shared. Fills gaps in the GDPR. |
| GDPR | European Union | N/A | General Data Protection Regulation: how personal data can and cannot be used. | This was a historic move and radically changed data handling globally. |
| EU AI ACT | European Union | Applies to a variety of systems, but not all | A sweeping piece of legislation that codifies into law standards of ethics and other regulatory requirements. | Applies not just to systems *in* the EU, but also to systems accessible *from* the EU. |

*Table 9.3: Common compliance standards*

Although they may look similar on the surface due to some shared focus areas, each of these standards has nuance and requires care to achieve the relevant certification of their governing bodies. Notably, ISO has various certifications for which it oversees the compliance standards.

These don't just include cybersecurity, but many are still relevant to software engineers, such as the ISO 26262, which is the standard for automotive software.

In LLM-based AI, there are a few areas where you could find yourself running into compliance or regulatory risks that didn't exist in previous generations of machine learning. The EU AI Act is a perfect example of this. It's very broad and covers a variety of AI use cases. They provide a nice exploratory tool to help you understand the new laws, which is worth a look regardless of locale: `https://artificialintelligenceact.eu/ai-act-explorer/`.

## Compliance risk 1: Data sources unknown

The amount of data that has gone into training LLMs is more than can easily be conceived. Unfortunately, this came with several notable examples of models being trained on data that was not obtained legally. That hasn't had any impact on consumers of LLMs yet (`https://www.npr.org/2025/09/05/g-s1-87367/anthropic-authors-settlement-pirated-chatbot-training-material`), but it may present compliance concerns in the future should laws change.

## Risk 2: Skills and MCP servers may not pass muster

While it is immediately tempting to leverage the skills and MCP server marketplaces, these plugins for your AI model may not have been designed with the same legal and regulatory compliance. Unless a skill or MCP server is totally secured from connecting to exterior sources or limited to only well-known datasets, there's always a risk of compliance violation.

## Risk 3: Data loss

Data loss is never great, but it doesn't always result in a compliance nightmare. However, some industries need to retain records of the prompts and responses given to end users. For example, think about a financial advisory AI app that gives you recommendations on how to invest your savings. Those prompts and responses would need to be able to be stored and auditable. This would allow you to demonstrate that you're abiding by various regulatory mandates such as anti-money laundering, consumer protection laws, and United States **Securities and Exchange Commission** (**SEC**) rules. If you're only relying on the LLM context window to keep this information, you've already lost.

### Risk 4: Bias in the AI

The only downside to data sampling and sanitization is that if that data is used for model training or tuning, it can help introduce bias. This bias could lead to mistakes from the AI agent. Bias can occur from tuning data and from within the current context. If the end user has some bias, the AI will likely be swayed by that as well. This is known as **availability bias**. In other words, the availability of data makes the assumptions seem statistically more likely. That data existing, or the absence of any data to balance it out, can then reinforce the user bias. Being mindful of bias during training and tuning phases for your model will be key to ensuring that it's as impartial as possible. Just because we jokingly say, "*It's always DNS*," doesn't mean we want the AI agent leaping to that conclusion in real scenarios. From a compliance standpoint, a bias in training could cause an AI agent to take more destructive actions than necessary, allowing it to become the reason for data loss or a credentials leak. Using model accuracy evaluation tools can also help capture and surface bias.

#### Mitigations

Observability is part and parcel of compliance. If you've been following the recommendations we've been making throughout the book, then you already know you can capture all those prompts and responses and then extract and store them efficiently.

Policy, policy, policy. Your company policies, both written and technical, should enforce the compliance standards to which your organization is subjected. You can make your AI aware of policy through the use of instruction files, inclusion in prompts, and training. Use balanced data during training to help ensure the safety of operations and keep bias to a minimum.

And finally, despite our hopes that this book will help you be widely successful in your AIOps implementation, don't forget about the humans. Human approvers may be required for compliance, either legal or policy, and this still remains a best practice for now.

## Summary

In summary, AI for observability and operations is a very promising area of the technical landscape. There are problems that are not easily solved and involve large quantities of data. This is the exact type of problem LLM-based AI was intended to solve, without everyone needing to be a machine learning or data science expert.

But, as with any new technology, there are still some rough edges. It's important to be aware of those and smooth them out during your implementation.

As we head into our final chapter, we'll look at ACME Financial Services and how they're putting all of these learnings to use.

# Further reading

The following resources are recommended for further reading:

- Tokens: help.openai.com/en/articles/4936856-what-are-tokens-and-how-to-count-them
- Context engineering: https://www.anthropic.com/engineering/effective-context-engineering-for-ai-agents
- On fine-tuning:
    - https://www.redhat.com/en/topics/ai/what-is-peft
    - https://docs.cloud.google.com/vertex-ai/generative-ai/docs/models/tuning-checkpoints
- On security and compliance incidents mentioned:
    - https://snyk.io/blog/toxicskills-malicious-ai-agent-skills-clawhub/
    - https://securitylabs.datadoghq.com/articles/shai-hulud-2.0-npm-worm/
- SBOM comparison: https://scribesecurity.com/blog/spdx-vs-cyclonedx-sbom-formats-compared/
- Defending against data poisoning:
    - https://arxiv.org/pdf/1511.04508
    - https://arxiv.org/pdf/2503.09302
- Data security posture management: https://www.paloaltonetworks.com/cyberpedia/dspm-data-ai-compliance
- FBI AIOps whitepaper: https://www.ic3.gov/CSA/2025/251215.pdf

# 10

# ACME Financial Services: How Will the AI Future Shape Our Company?

As we bring ACME Financial Services' journey to an end and set you off on your own path, we will examine where we started and where we've ended up, and peer into our crystal ball to help you anticipate what may come next. In this chapter, we will be covering the following topics:

- What does building trust in AI look like?
- What it means to be on the bleeding edge of AI before countries enforce regulations
- The importance of securing the platform
- Where your organization may differ from ours

## Technical requirements

For this chapter, there are no technical requirements.

## Our story thus far

Before diving into the new directions that our fictitious company, ACME Financial Services, might go, let's review the incredible journey the company has already undertaken. ACME Financial Services, after having completed their cloud migration, discovered that their observability practices were not sufficient or even adequate for their new cloud-native architectures. They had a slew of problems to solve and formed an observability working group to look into solutions. The initial proposal for tooling and training was accepted and implemented. After the implementation, they realized that the improvements they had made fell short of what was needed for the company to succeed. Costs didn't drop as much as they expected, and senior leadership was not happy.

With their jobs being on the line and an unhappy senior leadership pushing for lower costs, the observability working group reconvened with the goal of finding ways to reduce operational costs, taking the following steps:

1. Determining what was driving the operational costs
2. Consulting their vendors on strategies to reduce those costs
3. Having discussions with the consumers of the observability tools

Along the way, they discovered new ways that the tooling could be used across the company to reduce costs and positively impact multiple areas.

The result was a plan to implement sampling, as well as moving from policy-based data standards to programmatically enforced data standards, which they hoped would lead to immediate improvements. The outcome of this would be the increased utility of metrics and decreased costs of running the observability tooling.

With the low-hanging fruit identified, they sought more ways to drive improvements and return on investment. When they talked with the SREs and application developers who were using the observability tools, they got divergent feedback. The observability working group also discovered that they had originally looked at the observability problem through too small a lens, which caused them to miss many opportunities for company-wide improvements and maximizing tool utility.

It had become obvious that it was too difficult to coordinate the implementation of common data across all the teams in the company. They would need a centralized control that would be in charge of enforcing common observability standards.

The observability working group created another proposal for senior leadership that detailed their findings and recommendations. Their proposal included an **Internal Developer Platform** (**IDP**) with capabilities augmented by the agentic AI capabilities of their observability vendor, along with details about the IDP and platform team. They pitched a platform that enabled a new and scalable concept called **self-service**, a new utility for the observability tooling, including the new concept of **business process observability**, and plans for cost management.

After a difficult series of conversations with senior leadership and several years of work to implement the proposal, the original goals of the project were met and even exceeded. New business intelligence, such as feature interaction metrics, created the framework for data-driven product decisions. Company processes and procedures were reshaped in ways that the working group hadn't foreseen, but ACME Financial Services came out of it much more efficient and seeing lower overall costs.

# Evolving trust in the observability platform

It took ACME Financial Services many years of effort to update the company's observability practices and reshape the company around a new way of operating. Putting all the pieces in place was just the beginning as that is what allowed the company to evolve within the new paradigm. It was one thing to enable the use of a new tool and to provide data that was previously unavailable, but quite another for the tools and data to become part of workflows. Once workflows incorporated the new methods, it was yet another task for teams to start trusting the feedback that the observability platform provided. It was not a quick process and one that could not be rushed. ACME Financial Services cares deeply about its reputation with customers, and trying to force the company to trust the observability platform was a difficult task. Before any goals or mandates could be established, there would need to be a critical mass of teams within the company that had modified their practices and showed tangible benefits. These teams would be examples for others as the whole company transitioned their workflows. Only once those examples and success stories existed could more stringent plans be created.

This is not to say that senior leadership and the observability working group took a step back once everything was in place. They aggressively pushed for consumption of the data and use of the observability platform, while also stressing that teams would need to evolve their practices. Senior leadership also pushed for OKRs to track company adoption of the observability platform, with the goal of having 100% of the teams across the whole company using it. They also created a KPI to track the accuracy of the suggestions made via the platform's AI agent, and set an initial goal that the suggestions provided by the platform would be correct 80% of the time. Their definition of accuracy was a suggestion from the observability platform that was accepted without modification. This was a very ambitious goal, and everyone knew that such drastic changes take time and motivation, so those leading the effort tried to motivate the teams and allow them to determine the timeframe.

## The SREs' path to trust

It isn't surprising that the SRE teams were the first to incorporate the tooling and the first to really trust the suggestions from the tool. They were already very familiar with the type of data produced by the observability platform, as well as already being heavily data-driven. In order for the SREs to do their work, they had to rely on third-party-produced data and observability tools. The SRE teams also introduced the observability working group to the concept of self-service and recommended several ways to use ACME Observability more effectively. Extending their workflows to incorporate suggestions from ACME Financial Services did not require significant changes for the SRE teams.

However, even with the SRE teams rapidly adjusting to the new workflows, they did not trust the suggestions they were given blindly. They were always aware that any mistake they made could cause an incident, so they were very cautious about big changes by nature. They heavily scrutinized every suggestion provided before approving it and allowing it to be accepted. Whenever possible, they required changes be made in non-production environments first and evaluated them. A series of metrics had been created to track KPIs on the observability platform's correctness, but the SREs felt that that was too broad for their comfort level. They needed something that would only track the correctness of the products they used. The company-wide metrics had provided a blueprint for how to do this, so they created metrics based on the company-wide ones but that were focused on their products. Then, they closely monitored the metrics around the correctness of the suggestions that the observability platform provided. When changes needed to be made to a suggestion by the observability platform, they ensured that the tool knew about the changes and provided tweaks to help it in the future.

Eventually, the recommendations from the tool started to regularly be 100% accurate and didn't need any tweaks or modifications from the SREs. Being cautious by nature, the SRE teams did not rush to automate acceptance of the observability platform suggestions. Instead, they continued to monitor their correctness metric until they became confident that the tool exhibited a sustained period of 100% correct suggestions. Once that milestone was reached, the SRE teams started to allow the tool suggestions to be implemented without review and approval by the SREs themselves.

This was not the end of their trust journey, though. Allowing the suggestions from ACME Observability to merge without review just created a new avenue for the SREs to monitor the actions of the tool. The SREs created alerts to inform them whenever a change was incorporated from the tool without their approval, and then created a process to review those changes. If changes were made outside of normal business hours, then they were reviewed early the next business day. As their trust in the tool's actions continued to grow, they slowly reduced the frequency of their reviews. It went from every change to a daily review, to every other day, to every week, and so on. Eventually, the reviews became so infrequent as to almost not happen at all.

## The developers' path to trust

Unlike the SREs, the application developers were much slower to adopt the new observability platform. Engineers had a reputation for adopting new tools rather quickly when it made their lives better, but in this instance, they didn't have a strong foundation in observability data, which meant they had a difficult time understanding how it would benefit them. They were also being asked to incorporate a new paradigm, observability-driven development, into their design process, and they needed to understand what that meant in order to make the requested changes.

Similar to the SREs, the application developers intended to start by heavily scrutinizing the suggestions that came from the observability platform. This ended up being a little chaotic at first, as some developers scrutinized the changes while others blindly accepted them without understanding anything that was being done. Once an application team addressed that inconsistency and got everyone to scrutinize the suggestions, they started to make progress. The application developers reviewed suggestions from the observability platform for correctness, as well as to understand the root cause that triggered the suggestion. The application developers knew that they were going to need to incorporate observability-driven development into their workflow, so they used the tool suggestions as a place to start learning about what kind of data is needed and what kind of problems can be identified.

Once a suggestion from the observability platform was accepted, it was heavily tested in development and preproduction environments before being deployed into production. This meant creating testing scenarios that could create the issue that was being fixed and observing that the change did in fact fix the problem. As the suggestions from the observability platform continued to help alleviate production issues, the application developers started to trust them more and also started to gain an understanding of how to design their applications to be observed. This knowledge was critical for the application developers to successfully implement observability-driven development.

With a basic understanding of the kinds of data that can prove useful to the observability platform, the application developers began to change their design process to make it easier to observe and understand the inner workings of their applications. At first, this was a slow process, which is usual when implementing a new concept. As their experience grew and they incorporated more observable designs, the quality and type of suggestions received by the observability platform also improved. This increased the application developers' confidence in their new processes and the suggestions being provided. Making easily observable application designs quickly became a self-reinforcing process change.

## A trust framework was born

As various teams within ACME Financial Services charted a path to trusting the recommendations from the observability platform, the observability working group recognized similar patterns. They used those patterns to come up with a framework that teams across the company could use to standardize growing trust in the platform's suggestions. They broke the process into three phases: an experimentation phase, a trust phase, and a verification phase. The framework was designed to be iterative, meaning that it could be used multiple times to steadily build or improve trust as circumstances change. More aggressive targets, or new and improved systems in the observability platform, could be reasons to go through the process again.

### The experimentation and dry-run phase

In this phase, the team gets used to interacting with the AI tool, in this case, the observability platform and its agentic capabilities, and learns what things it does well and where it needs help. They can use tools such as DeepEval to help test and evaluate the results of their agentic platform.

Also in this phase, benchmarks start to develop. They use natural language processing scoring techniques to evaluate the correctness of the recommendations from the platform. To evaluate the observability platform, the company recommends using ROUGE or BERT. Each team that uses the observability platform will determine an appropriate score from the scoring system that indicates their satisfaction with the suggestions. This will be the threshold that indicates the solution is ready for use in production and against which future performance will be measured.

Finally, they decide on a low-risk, high-value task to solve with an MVP and tune the responses from the AI for that task. This should include consideration of what the team wants to do, how they want to do it, and what access level is required by the AI.

By the end of this phase, the team should be receiving responses that meet the determined score from the natural language processing scoring system. This indicates that the task is ready to move into production, but not yet ready to trust and automate.

### The trust phase

In this phase, the team builds trust in the suggestions returned by the AI for the determined task. They should be continually monitoring the responses from AI for accuracy and reliability. They scrutinize any responses that do not meet the defined score threshold and decide whether the suggestion is in fact correct or whether the AI knowledge or prompt needs to be tweaked. They continue testing with production data for as long as is necessary to trust that the AI can automatically apply the suggestions without human interaction.

Once the team trusts the output from the AI, they should take on the task of automating the application of the suggestions. By the end of this phase, no one should be involved in reviewing or approving suggestions from the AI for the defined task.

### The verify phase

In this phase, human involvement for the specified task should start decreasing. Suggestions from the AI are being accepted and applied without human intervention, so human actions revolve around monitoring and verifying the actions performed by the AI.

A key difference between the trust phase and the verify phase is that in the trust phase, each suggestion is evaluated as it comes in, whereas in the verify phase, suggestions are evaluated after they have been applied, as part of a regularly scheduled review. Observability tools take over the task of monitoring whether the AI behaves as expected.

The frequency of the scheduled reviews would depend on the number of suggestions over a period and the criticality of the task being performed. The team should pick a cadence that they find acceptable and start there. As trust in the suggestions is reinforced through the review process agreeing with the implemented suggestions from the AI, the time between reviews can increase.

By the end of this phase, there should be little to no verification review processes required for changes related to the specific task. The team is then ready to choose a new task and perform the process again from the beginning.

## How trust changed the company

It was one thing to tell teams in ACME Financial Services to do something, but quite another for them to embrace it. In order to achieve the maximum benefit from ACME Observability, the observability working group knew that teams would need to trust the suggestions provided and eventually turn over responsibility for some things to the tool. Once the teams allowed the tooling to be responsible for tasks in its domain, they would have more time to work on more productive work for the company.

### How SREs were impacted by trusting the tool

Once the SREs reached a point where they trusted the suggestions provided by ACME Observability and allowed them to be implemented without review, their work started to change rather drastically. All cluster and application scaling was handled by the observability platform. Incidents from usage spikes all but completely disappeared. Incidents caused by an application deployment were automatically addressed by rolling back to a previous version.

Incidents as a whole dropped drastically. This benefited the SREs in two key ways:

- The SREs didn't have to spend as much time performing **Root Cause Analyses** (**RCAs**). Even with ACME Observability helping automate the RCA process, it was still time-consuming for an SRE to put the data into a report and present it to leadership along with what was done to prevent the issue from happening again.
- With more of their time freed up, the SREs were able to focus on other tasks they needed to perform. The implementation time for large efforts such as network modernization and migration dropped as the SREs were able to devote more time without interruption. This meant the SREs could improve and strengthen ACME Financial Services' infrastructure much faster, such as adopting new best practices and implementing better redundancy.

Perhaps contrary to what some might have expected, the total number of SREs needed within ACME Financial Services didn't decrease. Large and old companies such as this have a long history of legacy and outdated infrastructure implementations that need to be improved, but the SREs rarely had time to tackle them unless a situation became critical. Even worse, many of those legacy implementations were more costly or inefficient and had to be accepted as the cost of doing business. Many of them were so thorny, in fact, that no one wanted to touch them even though they performed some critical function within the company. The people who had originally created them had long since left the company, and the effort to understand and modernize them was so large that the SREs just didn't have the time. It put ACME Financial Services in a somewhat vulnerable position because it was far from certain that those systems could be recreated if something failed or a change prevented them from operating. This risk was not well understood by any of the decision-makers. Now, those legacy implementations can be improved and ACME Financial Services has strengthened its resilience while also reducing operating costs.

## How developers were impacted by trusting the tool

As the application developers gained trust in the suggestions provided by ACME Observability, they began to be proactive instead of reactive. Instead of waiting for the tool to suggest changes for things such as improving performance, handling an error case, or reducing network congestion, the application developers started querying the tool for suggestions. Since the observability data provided by their applications had improved, the tool was able to understand what was occurring inside an application and provide useful suggestions to solve problems before they occurred.

The quality of the applications improved measurably. They became more performant, more resilient, and more secure. The observability tool was able to not only suggest changes based on how the application was used but also automatically mitigate security vulnerabilities that had been found in dependent packages. Updating dependencies to mitigate vulnerabilities was always a time-consuming task that the application developers completely offloaded to the observability platform.

With fewer bugs and performance issues, the application developers were able to concentrate on creating value for the company. They were able to implement new features much faster because they didn't have to spend significant portions of their time diagnosing and determining fixes for production issues or working through dependency updates. They were also able to work on long-desired application redesigns to bring their applications in line with the company's various standards, such as authentication and trust, visual design, and log formatting. This resulted in a more uniform look and feel and consistent function for the company's customers.

# Business process observability bears fruit

Implementing business process observability provided insight into the workings of the company's applications and their interactions that the company never had before. They found many failures in application interactions that led to less than expected resiliency, redundant actions, and bottlenecks. Some insights that they gained after implementing business process observability included the following:

- Opening a new account involved multiple applications across several business areas. Each performed its own authorization verification, and if any part of the process failed or determined that authorization was not granted, then an error bubbled up and left the process in an unknown state. Reattempting the creation wasn't guaranteed to succeed.
- Applications didn't share a trust model. Each application would verify authentication and authorization independently, which created a bottleneck and resiliency concern in their authentication system. This undermined the applications' design to ensure resiliency through scaling their Pods.
- They found many examples of a request ping-ponging across applications, for example, A->B->C->A->B->D, because an application later in the request pipeline needed data from an application earlier in the pipeline in order to make a decision.

With these kinds of insights, ACME Financial Services was able to improve their process flow across most of their business operations. They ensured that no point in a process was a bottleneck or limited the resiliency of their applications.

Incident response became much more efficient. Instead of bringing everyone into a call to diagnose a problem, the incident response teams now knows exactly which applications are involved in a process. This allows efficient troubleshooting, as well as avoiding burnout among application developers for issues that are not attributable to their application.

# The importance of securing the observability platform

ACME Financial Services were enjoying the multiple benefits that the new observability platform provided. The observability platform had become so integral to the way the company operated that it joined a small set of technologies deemed critical to the success of the company. The fact that the observability platform can act on its own and has access to large amounts of company data also added to the need to protect it with the strictest access controls and other security mechanisms. They also had to make sure that the observability platform doesn't violate any of the myriad regulations that govern areas of the company. Since the observability platform acts upon large amounts of data, they have to constantly verify that business or country regulations around strict access or storage of that data are being met. That's in addition to the increased danger of having so much data available in one location. Since the observability platform connects to so many systems, it has the potential to leak more data than any previous system they have used. ACME Financial Services is no stranger to securing sensitive data systems, and they have restricted access to the observability platform in line with their most sensitive systems.

The company's more traditional data systems were secured using accepted procedures, but the observability platform required additional thought and restrictions because of where the data could be consumed. In most of their traditional systems, data was stored and then access to that data was controlled such that no data could leave the company's network. ACME Observability, like many of the newer observability tools, provides optional functionality by connecting to the internet. This kind of functionality makes it very hard to control where the company data is consumed, and that makes it incredibly dangerous. The observability working group had to ensure that no data could leave the company's network, which meant all data had to be stored and accessed only from within the company. That also meant that they could not enable any functionality in ACME Observability that uses internet resources. Luckily, most of that functionality was available to be installed locally, with the trade-off being increased storage and compute needs for the tool and manual version upgrades. This was an acceptable trade-off for ACME Financial Services and one they were familiar with, so they had plenty of procedures to ensure the latest and most secure versions were being run.

## Who can access the data

In addition to access and security controls for the systems, ACME Financial Services also had to manage what data authorized people are allowed to see. One application team's data should not be accessible by another application team. A financial advisor should not be able to see client data for someone they are not advising. These kinds of controls are standard in ACME Financial Services, but the new observability platform added another layer to the problem.

The company has always attempted to follow good security practices. Even with access to source code repositories rigorously controlled, the company has strict policies that state that sensitive data should not be stored in any source code repository. They treat supporting data from a production system just like secrets or encryption keys. Since the observability platform opens change requests in source code repositories, they had to be concerned with what data the tool might attach to justify its suggestion. They made sure to configure ACME Observability to provide links to itself rather than embed supporting data.

## Managing the system

ACME Financial Services had come to trust the actions performed by their new observability platform, but that also created a larger burden around managing the platform itself. Since the company had come to rely upon actions taken by the observability platform, it meant that things such as version upgrades were incredibly tense and cautious affairs.

ACME Financial Services had ended up with a fairly common architecture:

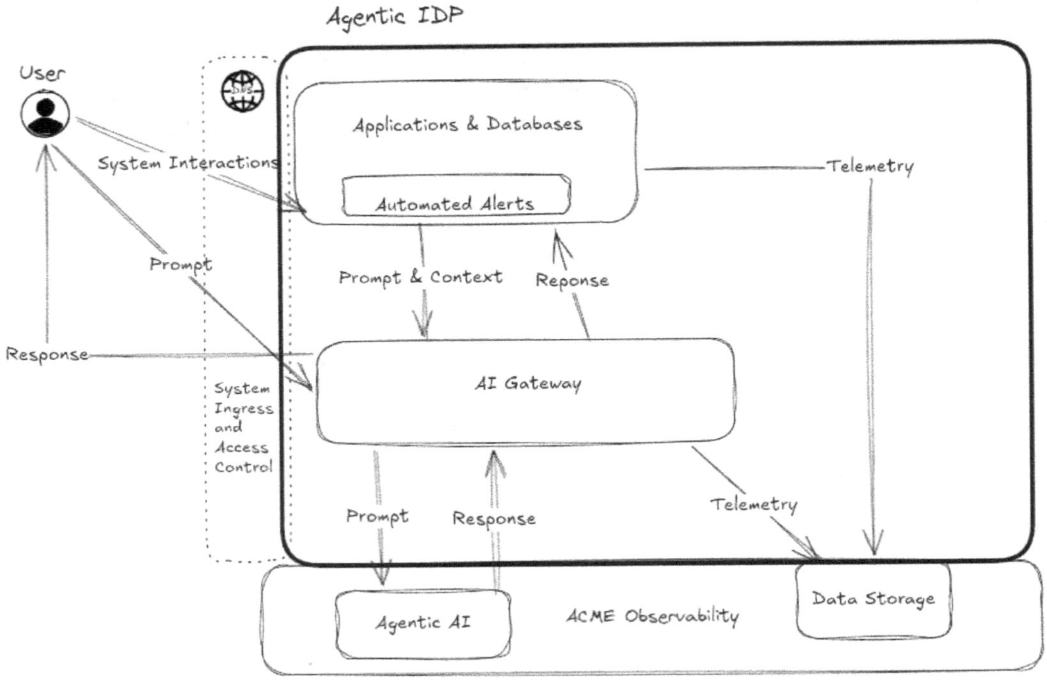


*Figure 10.1: ACME Financial Services' AIOps integration architecture*

This also meant that they had the same concerns with managing the system as many other companies. A change to any component could have serious impacts on the functionality of the system.

Any upgrade to the observability platform is undertaken with great care using a slow and methodical process. Because the platform automates some functionality in response to automated alerting, it means that any change caused by an upgrade could have serious ramifications. It isn't enough to just look for functionality differences or to read over changelogs. ACME Financial Services decided to incur the costs of running two versions of the platform in order to perform upgrades. The current version of the platform will run and act as it had been. A new complete stack with upgraded components will then run alongside the current platform version, with access to all the same data and systems as the current platform but it will not be allowed to make changes. The decisions and metrics of the new platform version will be monitored and compared against the decisions and metrics of the current platform version.

If there is a deviation, then it will be scrutinized based on the type of deviation. If it produces the same outcome but uses different reasoning to get there, then the reasoning is inspected to verify that it is legitimate and reasonable. If the outcome is different, then that produces a very involved analysis. Is the old outcome or the new outcome better? What data is used to make the decision? Does the vendor have an explanation for why the newer version produces a different result?

They will run both versions of the tools until there is confidence in the new version, then switch over and allow it to actually do the work. They will keep the old system running a while longer and continue to compare results until they are satisfied that the new version is running properly. Only once they are completely confident in the new version will they tear down the old version of the platform.

They also had to create a comprehensive set of actions and reasons for the decisions taken by the observability platform. This was necessary to provide confidence in the decisions the tool is making, but more importantly, it was required for regulatory compliance. The ability to automate actions related to regulatory compliance would not be possible without the necessary supporting documentation that the company could use during a regulatory investigation.

### Watch the drift

The new observability platform comes with a new area of concern. Since the observability platform has become so integral to business operations, the company has to be concerned with any outcome drift. Even with the tooling being isolated to just data within ACME Financial Services, the observability platform could still consume data that could cause its effectiveness to decline. They use dashboards and metrics to track the effectiveness of the decisions being made by the observability platform. The detailed evaluation of decisions used for audits is also conducted as part of the process to look for any drift in the platform's actions.

## The continual efforts to stay current

Despite all the changes that have been implemented and the success that has come with them, ACME Financial Services can never allow themself to relax. They have always had to stay current with changes in laws and regulations across the multiple regulated markets where they provide services, but now they have to keep track of a whole lot more.

## Monitoring industry trends

At the start of their journey, ACME Financial Services hadn't kept up with the changes in observability practices and tooling, which led to them being in an unmanageable position once they migrated to the cloud. They now know that they need to continually monitor changes in observability practices, but they also have to keep track of security trends around observability tooling. The new observability platform provides benefits across the company, but it would also be potentially catastrophic if that platform were compromised because it has access to so much data and so many systems used by ACME Financial Services.

One of the most basic security guidelines the company has started to track is NIST guidelines. They have made sure to stay up to date on the evolving recommendations and concerns for securing their systems, workloads, and data stores. The FBI also publishes papers and alerts around cybercrime and security considerations, which need to be evaluated. Both NIST and the FBI even have focus areas for AI, which is a core part of the observability platform that the company has implemented.

Of course, they have to monitor industry changes in observability as well. They have stayed in contact with the vendors of their observability tools and receive regular updates on changes in the products, as well as where the vendors see things changing in the future. The company also monitors project trends and discussions in open source projects such as OpenFeature and OTel. It is an awful lot to keep track of, but not keeping on top of the rapid changes would mean even more work later.

## Expansion increases the effort

ACME Financial Services originally only served customers in the US, but with the increased efficiency enabled by the observability platform, they have expanded to additional countries. This comes with increased and varying regulatory compliance. The regulations in the US are complicated enough and regularly changing, but those regulations only cover the US. Europe has a different set of regulations, and some of those require data to stay within Europe. In some countries, there are multiple regulatory bodies to monitor for changes in order to stay compliant.

Maintaining compliance with that many regulations and tracking regulatory changes is daunting work. It would have been very costly and slowed new feature development drastically if ACME Financial Services hadn't included regulatory compliance in their plans for the new observability platform. The amount of work to track regulatory changes hasn't decreased, but the cost of regulatory compliance has become manageable because the observability platform is able to help developers and architects understand when violations would occur.

## The cost of early adoption

Because of the timing of the problems at ACME Financial Services, the company has found itself unexpectedly on the cutting edge of AI's impact on observability tools and practices. The industry is far enough along that tools and new practices exist, but not so far along that anything is known as the best or most cost-effective way to solve their problems. This alone means the company has had to accept a larger degree of risk and accept that drastic changes might be required should the industry shift in a new direction. But there is an even bigger concern: governments.

All over the world, governments have been talking about regulating AI, and that is a core part of the new observability platform. ACME Financial Services has had to monitor the discussions and provide input whenever doing so would help the business use cases. A draconian or overly restrictive regulation could jeopardize all the work they have already done. This isn't exactly unfamiliar territory because they have already needed to track regulations across their various businesses, but this is the first time they have been able to be involved in the discussions around regulations. Usually, regulations change and the company has to react, so providing feedback is not a position ACME Financial Services tends to find itself in. The company has committed to helping shape regulations governing AI that would allow it to continue to benefit from AI-powered observability tools.

## Always monitoring the cost

ACME Financial Services has achieved such a level of success with the observability platform that a new kind of cost concern has become paramount. At the beginning of the project, they worried about the cost of running the platform and being able to show the benefit from that expenditure. They now have metrics to show how the platform is positively affecting costs across the entire company, but that doesn't mean that the cost of running the platform is irrelevant.

As the observability platform becomes more popular, the number of requests to the platform increases. As the requests increase, so do the processing resources required to perform the requests and respond in a timely fashion. With the platform enabled to implement decisions on its own, it isn't even necessarily company employees who are adding to the load on the platform. The platform could actually end up straining itself with queries.

The cost for the resources to run the platform is to be constrained and monitored. The observability working group will meet regularly to look over costs, types of queries, the source of queries, and other cost-related data points and evaluate how the platform is performing. Are the response times staying reasonable or increasing? Are the queries a good use of the platform? If they are not, the working group will contact the originators and ask them to stop using the platform in a specific way.

Sometimes they will be able to optimize the cost by making queries more effective or tuning the platform to better handle situations. Sometimes they will have to accept that more resources are needed and scaling the platform is the correct solution. It is a never-ending process to ensure that the costs of the platform do not spiral out of control.

## Incorporating changes into roadmaps

Changes based on the various areas being tracked for changes have had to work their way into company roadmaps. This isn't a foreign process because they have had to do it for regulatory changes in the US, but the number of changes has increased and, at times, caused the re-evaluation of priorities within some areas of the company.

Regulatory changes tend to come with a deadline for implementation. This is a process ACME Financial Services is already well acquainted with; however, the number of changes required increases with the expanded countries where they operate. With more changes and sometimes conflicting deadlines, hard discussions have had to occur to ensure the company implements changes for regulatory compliance by a host of deadlines.

They have also had to consider improvements and changes in security best practices or changes to observability practices. This is a less familiar area for the company, and they have had to learn how to manage planning these improvements while also allowing for new feature development and regulatory compliance changes.

Application roadmap discussions have expanded from mostly new features, enhancements, and bug fixes to include planning around a larger number of changes for regulatory compliance. Platform roadmaps have had to expand to include more changes for regulatory compliance, as well as including more frequent security improvements and application version updates. With the volume of changes now required, it is impossible to prevent reducing the velocity of new feature rollouts, but having discussions that are informed by upcoming changes to regulations and best practices helps reduce the impact. Even with this reduced velocity, they are still delivering functionality faster than they did at any time in the company's history. The changes brought about by the observability platform have provided more capacity with the same workforce.

The company has experienced some growing pains, but eventually, they have been able to settle into a process that has allowed them to implement regulatory changes with enough time to verify compliance before significant penalties could be assessed, and to improve their software offerings as the primary objective, allowing application and security upgrades to have a longer horizon. They have discovered that this is a natural fit to manage timelines since application upgrades and security enhancements need to move more slowly because of their larger impact across the whole company.

## So, what's next?

ACME Financial Services has been on a long and expansive improvement odyssey. What started out as a need to update their observability practices after completing their cloud migration has ended up reshaping the company in ways no one foresaw at the start. Their journey has enabled the company to transition from very manual processes that consumed large amounts of company time and productivity to streamlined automated processes and, in some cases, complete hands-off operation. That is quite the cultural shift, especially in areas of the business that are heavily regulated and therefore very nervous about change. It's fair to ask where they should go next. What areas could be improved with their new observability practices? As the observability industry continues to evolve, there is little doubt that there will be new areas that can be improved.

Already on the horizon, there is work being done to improve security and threat detection using observability tools. This would be especially interesting to ACME Financial Services. Some of the markets they serve are very strict about interactions with embargoed or hostile countries, and being able to proactively detect firewall misconfigurations or other exploits that allow this kind of traffic would be an immense help in their regulatory compliance. That's on top of basic improvements such as detecting security misconfigurations based on traffic patterns or application behavior.

The observability working group's job is never really done. They will need to regularly evaluate the effectiveness of the observability platform and ask a usual set of questions. Are teams relying on it too much, or are they maximizing the platform's benefits for the team? Does a benefit justify the potential cost or resource increase for the observability platform? Is there anything new in the observability community that would make the platform better?

However, the observability working group knows that regardless of where the industry goes, ACME Financial Services has done the kind of work that will enable them to adopt and benefit from new directions and processes around observability.

## Summary

The journey of our fictitious company is one designed to resonate with you, the reader, and we hope it has achieved that goal. The work done by our imagined observability team is work being done by operations experts industry-wide. We interviewed engineers and executive leaders who all told similar stories of cloud transformations, exploding costs, and the struggle to make something of the AI technological wave. By centering AI in an operational solution, it moves from a solution in search of a problem to a solution to one of the hardest IT problems at hand. We've created this simple checklist to help you break down your AIOps project approach:

- Define an outcome you seek to achieve through your AI implementation (OKR).
    - Start with one. You don't need more.
- Evaluate tools and vendors to choose the technology stack you know you need now, with exit criteria for what would lead to migration.
    - Use cost-benefit analysis frameworks to aid this decision-making process
- Rank your AIOps use cases from the easiest implementation to the most difficult.
- Use the crawl, walk, run approach to implement your use cases. Iterate to success.
- Apply the **Software Development Life Cycle** (**SDLC**): design, build, test, repeat.
    - Center security and observability at every stage
- Measure your outcomes.
- Define your KPIs.
- Gather DORA DevOps and other performance metrics.

As technologies are advancing, the patterns for analysis, system design, and best practices that we've outlined are intended to last even as some of the specifics may eventually become obsolete. While the code we wrote may be gone in five years, if you can move forward with those patterns and practices in mind, you'll be able to ride this and the next AI wave to success.

# Join us on Discord

For discussions around the book and to connect with your peers, join us on Discord at `packt.link/discordcloud` or scan the QR code below:

# 11

# Unlock Your Exclusive Benefits

Your copy of this book includes the following exclusive benefits:

EPUB PDF

### DRM-Free PDF Version

Download DRM-free PDF and ePub copies of this book.

### 7-Day Packt Library Access

Get 7-day unlimited access to 8,000+ books and videos. No credit card required.

Available for first-time Packt+ trial users only.

### Next-Gen Reader Access

Read this book on Packt Reader with progress sync, dark mode and note-taking.

Follow the guide below to unlock them. The process takes only a few minutes and needs to be completed once.

# Unlock this Book's Free Benefits in three Easy Steps

## Step 1

Keep your purchase invoice ready for *Step 3*. If you have a physical copy, scan it using your phone and save it as a PDF, JPG, or PNG.

For more help on finding your invoice, visit `packtpub.com/en-us/unlock?step=1`.

> Note
>
> **Note**: If you bought this book directly from Packt, no invoice is required. After *Step 2*, you can access your exclusive content right away.

## Step 2

Scan the QR code or go to `packtpub.com/unlock`.

On the page that opens (similar to *Figure 16.1* on desktop), search for this book by name and select the correct edition.

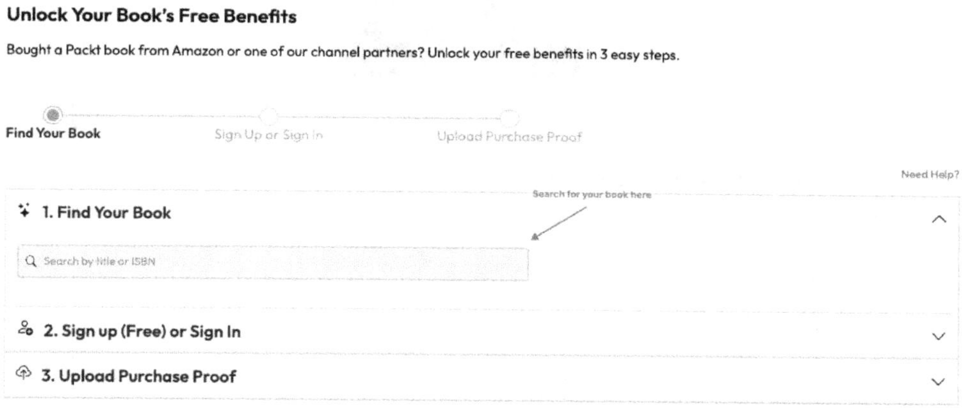


*Figure 16.1: Packt unlock landing page on desktop*

## Step 3

After selecting your book, sign in to your Packt account or create one for free. Then upload your invoice (PDF, PNG, or JPG, up to 10 MB). Follow the on-screen instructions to finish the process.

## Need Help

If you get stuck and need help, visit `packtpub.com/unlock-benefits/help` for a detailed FAQ on how to find your invoices and more. This QR code will take you to the help page.

Note

**Note**: If you are still facing issues, reach out to `customercare@packt.com`.

# Other Books You May Enjoy

If you enjoyed this book, you may be interested in these other books by Packt:

**Platform Engineering for Architects – First Edition**

Max Körbächer, Andreas Grabner, Hilliary Lipsig

ISBN: 978-1-83620-359-9

- Make informed decisions aligned with your organization's platform needs
- Identify missing platform capabilities and manage that technical debt effectively
- Develop critical user journeys to enhance platform functionality
- Define platform purpose, principles, and key performance indicators
- Use data-driven insights to guide product decisions
- Design and implement platform reference and target architectures

**Modern Network Observability – First Edition**

David Flores, Christian Adell, Josh VanDeraa

ISBN: 978-1-83508-106-8

- Collect and normalize data from various sources using Telegraf and Logstash
- Enrich operational data with crucial context from a Source of Truth such as Nautobot
- Visualize data and create insightful dashboards with Grafana
- Automate alerts and responses for your network operations strategy using Prefect
- Understand when to build or buy an observability stack, with tips and best practices
- Explore practical machine learning techniques to enhance observability data value

## Packt is searching for authors like you

If you're interested in becoming an author for Packt, please visit `authors.packt.com` and apply today. We have worked with thousands of developers and tech professionals, just like you, to help them share their insight with the global tech community. You can make a general application, apply for a specific hot topic that we are recruiting an author for, or submit your own idea.

## Share your thoughts

Now you've finished *Observability in the AI-Native Era, First Edition*, we'd love to hear your thoughts! Scan the QR code below to go straight to the Amazon review page for this book and share your feedback or leave a review on the site that you purchased it from.

*https://packt.link/r/1-806-38959-2*

Your review is important to us and the tech community and will help us make sure we're delivering excellent quality content.

# Index

## A

# B



# C

# T

www.ingramcontent.com/pod-product-compliance
Lightning Source LLC
Chambersburg PA
CBHW080846310326
42139CB00004B/31
*9781806389599*